CONFLUENCE OF CULTURES

French Contributions to Indo-Persian Studies

CONFLUENCE OF CULTURES
French Contributions to Indo-Persian Studies

edited by
Françoise 'Nalini' DELVOYE

MANOHAR
CENTRE FOR HUMAN SCIENCES, NEW DELHI
INSTITUT FRANÇAIS DE RECHERCHE EN IRAN, TEHRAN
1995

First published 1994
Reprinted 1995
ISBN 81-7304-092-3

Published by Ajay Kumar Jain, Manohar Publishers & Distributors,
2/6 Ansari Road, Daryaganj, New Delhi – 110 002
Laser typeset by Pradeep Kumar Goel for Aditya Prakashan,
F-14/65, Model Town II, Delhi – 110 009 and
printed at Rajkamal Electric Press, G.T. Karnal Road, Delhi – 110 033

Contents

Foreword

It is my privilege to present before the Indian public this collection of articles on the confluence of the Indian and Persian cultures, mainly in the medieval period of Indian history, but extending even into the colonial and post-colonial periods. These ten essays by French scholars, many of whom have been known to me for a long period of time, cover a vast area, ranging from illustrated manuscripts, metal-work, gardens and architecture, to music and cuisine, and also include the domains of religious writings of the Isma'ilis and so-called Wahhabis in India. In time, they run from the early days of the Sultanate of Delhi under Iltutmish to the twentieth century. In their regional coverage, they include western India and the Deccan, as much as the Indo-Gangetic plain. It is commendable that French scholars have been able to bring together such a wide-ranging set of articles with a common unifying theme of Indo-Persian culture.

Though, for a number of obvious reasons, British interest in India has historically been far greater than that of the French, nevertheless French studies on India in the classical Indological tradition and from the point of view of social anthropology have been strong in the present century. In this process, unfortunately, the French tradition has not been able to devote as great attention to medieval India as might have been hoped. Still, a beginning was made by Garcin de Tassy in the last century, and studies of medieval Indian popular religion and culture have been continued in this century by scholars like Charlotte Vaudeville and more recently her distinguished students such as Françoise Mallison. However, reading these scholars, one is sometimes given the impression that their work would have been even further enriched by exposure to the Indo-Persian cultural context. On the other hand, French scholars of Islam beyond Kabul and Qandahar, that is of the Iranian, Turkish and Arab world, have shown some interest in India but largely as an off-shoot of their main research. It is unfortunate that the writings of Louis Massignon, or more recently Charles-Henri de Fouchécour and Jean Aubin, have not been much read in India. Though India was not their primary focus, they have each in their own way, pointed out the central importance of India for a better understanding of the Islamic world of the medieval period.

This book reflects the strengths of the French tradition of scholarship on the Islamic world, namely a close attention to texts and manuscripts, as well as a combination of textual work and field-work. This is of particular interest to a student of history like myself, who comes from a tradition where these two domains of text and field have largely remained separate. At the same time, the traditional approach of classical philology has some of its own points of weakness from the perspective of a historian, and so it is necessary to pose the texts in the light of historical questions. As a first step towards bringing these works by scholars from a different tradition, which while belonging to the mainstream of Western scholarship, is not that of the familiar Anglo-Saxon world, this book makes a welcome contribution.

I would particularly like to compliment the editor, herself a scholar of cultural history, literature and music, for having brought this difficult task to completion. Hopefully, this will set the trend for future works along the same lines, where Indian and French scholars can work together in collaboration.

MUZAFFAR ALAM

Centre for Historical Studies
Jawaharlal Nehru University
New Delhi

Acknowledgements

I would like to express a deep feeling of gratitude to Sanjay Subrahmanyam, who has been involved - willy-nilly - at all stages of the making of the volume, from judicious and discerning advice, to apposite remarks and pertinent suggestions born out of his own experience of publication and edition. He participated in translating one paper, typing another one, and particularly in editing and proof-reading some of the contributions and the introduction.

I am thankful to Yves Porter for his initiatives in the field of Indo-Persian studies while in India, and for his efforts in coordinating the first and the second symposia. He also kindly intervened with several of the contributors, to facilitate the submission of their texts.

I am grateful to the Institut Français de Recherche en Iran (IFRI), Tehran-Paris, and its former director Bernard Hourcade, for encouraging the publication of the present volume, and for granting me an editing allocation to tide over expenses incurred.

I would like to express my particular thanks to the Centre for Human Sciences (CSH), New Delhi, and its director Olivier Guillaume, for support in co-organising the first symposium at Ivry, and for encouraging and supporting the publication of the present volume, both formally and informally, in a number of ways. The CSH also generously financed the translation of five of the papers in this volume, and provided other facilities while preparing the manuscript for press.

Special thanks are due to Sangita Lavakare (Centre for Human Sciences), for editing and typing one paper and especially for her aid with the computer, as also to my old friends Vinay Bhide and Bernard Bel, for help in IBM-Macintosh conversions.

Many thanks are in order to Rashmi Patni who translated four papers from French into English, in a short space of time, in spite of technical difficulties in the case of some texts and problems of communication between Delhi and Jaipur.

I am also grateful to Shalini Saran, my neighbour and a professional photographer of Islamic architecture, who judiciously selected the cover picture from her own photographs, after going through the typsecript of the volume.

Mention should also be made of Ramesh Jain, the Director of Manohar, who showed monumental patience during the months between the initial stages and the completion of the work.

Finally, a special word of thanks for Muzaffar Alam, who kindly consented to write the foreword to this volume.

NALINI DELVOYE

New Delhi
April 1994

List of Contributors

Michel BOIVIN is an historian who has specialised in the history of ideas and Islamic studies. Lecturer at the University of Savoie (Chambéry), he was awarded a Ph.D. by the Sorbonne in 1993 for his doctoral dissertation on the renewal of Ismaili Shī[c]ism in the contemporary period. He is also the author of various publications on reformism, modernism and Shī[c]ism in the present day Indo-Iranian world.

Françoise 'Nalini' DELVOYE has a Ph.D. (1976) and a D.Litt. (1991) in Indian studies from Sorbonne University. An English version of the D.Litt. thesis, *Tānsen et la tradition des chants dhrupad en langue braj du XVIe siècle à nos jours*, is in preparation for publication. Author of a number of articles, she is presently continuing work on the socio-cultural history of medieval India - especially the aristocratic patronage to music as documented by Indo-Persian and vernacular sources. She is the co-author (with Chander Shekhar) of *Directory of Scholars and Institutions in the Field of Indo-Persian Studies in India*, New Delhi: Manohar, 1994.

Khandu DEOKAR was trained in draughtsmanship at the I.T.I. in Lonavla, and has participated in the preparation of the exhibition entitled "Banaras, an Urban Space", as part of the *Année de la France en Inde* (1989). He also collaborated in the production of the exhibition catalogue (Paris: Créaphis, 1989). He is attached to the Chanderi urban study project of the Collège de France, directed by Professor Gérard Fussman, and the Gingee project of the Ecole Française d'Extrême-Orient, directed by Dr. Jean Deloche.

Marc GABORIEAU graduated in philosophy and in Islamic studies, and holds a Ph.D. and a D.Litt. from Paris. He has done fieldwork in Nepal and Northern India on Muslim communities and published two books on Nepali Muslims (*Minorités musulmanes dans le royaume hindou du Népal*, Paris: Klincksieck, 1977; *Ni Brahmanes, ni Ancêtres: colporteurs musulmans du Népal*, Paris: Société d'ethnologie, 1993) and on Tibetan Muslims (*Récit d'un voyageur musulman au Tibet*, Paris: Klincksieck, 1977). He is currently conducting research on early 19th century Islamic reform movements in South Asia. He is senior research fellow (Directeur de recherche) at the CNRS and teaches historical anthropology of South Asian Muslims as professor (Directeur d'études) at the Ecole des Hautes Etudes en Sciences Sociales in Paris.

Assadullah Souren MELIKIAN-CHIRVANI, trained in classical Arabic and Persian, holds a Ph.D. and a D.Litt. from Paris in the history of Iranian art. He is senior research fellow (Directeur de recherche) at the CNRS, to which he has been attached since 1970. Author of a large number of learned papers, he has done extensive research on Iranian Buddhism, and its implications for art- and architectural history, as well as for Persian literature. His more recent research deals with Persian literature as an archaeological field, and the interplay of function, symbolism and the origin of artefacts. He is the author of *Islamic Metalwork from the Iranian World, 8th-18th centuries*, London: Victoria and Albert Museum, 1982, amongst many other works.

Yves PORTER is extensively trained in Persian, but also in several other oriental languages (Pashto, Turkish, Arabic and Urdu). He obtained his Ph.D. in Iranian studies in 1988. He has published one book (*Peinture et Arts du Livre*, Paris-Tehran: Institut Français de Recherche en Iran (IFRI)-Louvain: Peeters, 1992, to appear in English as *Painters, Paintings and Books. Arts and Technology in Indo-Persian Literature, 12th-19th Centuries*, New Delhi: Manohar) and more than 20 articles in the fields of art-history and technology. Presently, he teaches Islamic art-history at the *Université de Provence* in Aix en Provence (France).

Francis RICHARD is Head Keeper of Persian Manuscripts in the Oriental Division of the Manuscript Department of the Bibliothèque Nationale in Paris, where he has worked since 1974. Specialist in the fields of Persian literature, codicology and history of the cultural relations between the Indo-Iranian world and the West, he has published numerous papers. He is the author of an exhibition catalogue, *A la Cour du Grand Moghol* (held in 1986, at the Bibliothèque Nationale in Paris), and in 1989 published the first volume of a new *Catalogue des manuscrits persans, I, Ancien Fonds*, of the Persian Manuscripts in the Bibliothèque Nationale. He is now preparing the subsequent volumes for publication.

Delphine ROGER holds a DEA degree from the Ecole des Hautes Etudes en Sciences Sociales (Paris, 1987) for her dissertation concerning historical sources for a study of Muslim cuisine in India. She is currently pursuing research on culinary traditions among the Muslims of Hyderabad, and has authored articles on the subject. She has contributed since 1992 to several fascicules of *L'Histoire du Monde*, Paris: Larousse.

Klaus RÖTZER studied archaeology at Strasbourg and Naples before going on to teach French at Kabul for ten years. Since then, he has taught French in India, at the universities of Pune, Benaras and Hyderabad. He is a specialist on ancient and medieval hydraulic works in the sub-continent, and has published several articles on the subject in learned journals such as the *Bulletin de l'Ecole Française d'Extrême-Orient*. He is currently engaged in research on the fortress-town of Gingee in Tamilnadu, under the aegis of the Ecole Française d'Extrême-Orient.

Živa VESEL has a Ph.D. in Iranian studies, and is a research fellow attached to the CNRS. She has published *Les encyclopédies persanes. Essai de typologie et de classification des sciences*, Paris: Edit. Recherche sur les Civilisations, 1986, and a number of articles on the history of science in medieval Iran, particularly on mineralogy, agriculture and the occult sciences. She has contributed to the *Encyclopédie de l'Islam*, *Encyclopaedia Iranica*, etc.

Thierry ZARCONE holds a Ph.D. in Islamic languages and literatures from Strasbourg University. He is a research fellow of the CNRS (at the Centre for Turkish and Ottoman Studies, Sorbonne Nouvelle University, Paris). His research interests relate to the intellectual history of Turkey and Central Asia. He has contributed various articles to learned journals and authored *Mystiques, philosophes et francs-maçons en Islam. Rizā Tevfīk, penseur ottoman (1868-1949); du soufisme à la confrérie*, Paris: Editions d'Amérique et d'Orient Jean Maisonneuve, 1993. He is co-editor, with M. Gaborieau and A. Popovic, of *Naqshbandis. Historical Developments and Present Situation of a Muslim Mystical Order*, Istanbul: IFEA/Isis Press, 1990.

List of Illustrations and Plans

Yves PORTER
(All photographs by the author)

Francis RICHARD

Assadullah Souren MELIKIAN-CHIRVANI

PLANS: Klaus RÖTZER - Khandu DEOKAR

Note on Transliteration

Although authors were asked to follow the system of transliteration adopted by F. Steingass in his *Comprehensive Persian-English Dictionary*,[1] the contributions to this volume display some discrepancies in their mode of transliteration.[2]

Vowels have been transliterated according to both the conventional Iranian system[3] and Steingass.

The *ez̤āfe* has been denoted by *-e* or *-i*, according to authors' choice.

The Arabic article *-al* or *'l* in some composed words has been written as XXX al-YYY (*e.g.* Nūr al-Dīn) or XXXu'l-YYY (*e.g.* *Ṣirāṭu'l mustaqīm*).

Some consonants have been variously transliterated, though fairly consistently within each papers. Varying diacritical marks have been used for the following:

ث (of *ās̤ār*) has been denoted by *th*, *t͟h* or *s̤*.

خ (of *k͟hān*) has been transliterated both as *kh* and with an horizontal stroke below as *k͟h* (especially in papers using Indian terms to avoid confusion with the aspirated *kh*).

ذ (of *ẕikr*) has either been denoted by *dh*, *d͟h* or *ẕ*.

ش (of *shāh*), like the Sanskrit *ś* (of Śiva) and the Sanskrit *ṣ* (of Viṣṇu) have been written as *sh*, except in some quotations, *i.e.* *š* and *ś*.

ض (of Faẓl) has been denoted by *ż* or *ẓ*.

ط (of *sulṭān*) has been denoted both by *ṭ* and *t̤*, especially in papers using Indian words in which the retroflex *t* is conventionally denoted by *ṭ* (*e.g.* *ghāṭ*), to avoid a confusion between the two consonants.

ظ (of *niẓām*) has been denoted by *ẓ* or *z̤*.

غ (of *g͟hunyat*) has been denoted by *gh* or *g͟h*.

1. See F. Steingass in his *Comprehensive Persian-English Dictionary* (2nd. Indian edn., New Delhi: Oriental Books Reprint Corporation, 1981).

2. See for instance various systems of transliteration used in articles by Peter Hardy, Simon Digby and Yohanan Friedmann, in the volume edited by Marc Gaborieau, *Islam et Société en Asie du Sud, Puruṣārtha*, Vol. 9, Paris: Editions de l'EHESS, 1986, in spite of the editor's reference (p. 19) to the transliteration system "borrowed, with slight modifications", from Barbara D. Metcalf, ed., *Moral Conduct and Authority. The Place of* Adab *in South Asian Islam*, Berkeley: University of California Press, 1984.

3. See C.-H. de Fouchécour, *Eléments de persan*, Paris: Publications Orientalistes de France, 1985, pp. 22-37 and *Abstracta Iranica*, Vol. 14, Tehran / Paris: Institut Français de Recherche en Iran, 1991, pp. XIX-XX. See also A.S. Melikian-Chirvani, *Islamic Metalwork from the Iranian World (8th-18th centuries)*, London: Victoria and Albert Museum, 1982, pp. 10-1.

Most contemporary personal names are not transliterated rigorously but follow the common usage (*e.g.* Aga Khan).

Common place-names follow the usage in the Indian sub-continent (*e.g.* Delhi, Agra, Lucknow, ...). Diacritical marks have been added to place-names which are not so well-known (*e.g.* Bhaironāth, Shivālā, etc.)

Introduction

In this brief introduction, it is not my intention to present an overview of the historical development of Indo-Persian culture and its study in various parts of the world, but rather to bring out the French interest in this field of studies.[1] A more general discussion must await the introduction to a later volume which brings together the papers of an Indo-French seminar on a similar theme held at the Centre for Historical Studies, Jawaharlal Nehru University, in February 1994.

The French Interest for the Iranian World

French interest in Iran and its culture can be traced back to the presence in the Safavid realm of French missionaries from the time of Shāh ^{c}Abbās I (1588-1629). Emissaries were exchanged between Iran and the France of Louis XIII, and one of the early products of this exchange was the translation into French of the *Thousand and One Nights*. With the creation of the French *Compagnie des Indes* in the 1660s, the need to develop a competence in Persian increased for commercial and diplomatic reasons. Jean-Baptiste Colbert (1619-83), the powerful minister of the French king Louis XIV, hence promoted the creation of a school in 1669 to train emissaries and translate diplomatic correspondence from Persian, which was given the title of the *Ecole des Jeunes de Langues*.

More than a century later, after the French Revolution, the institutional basis for the teaching of oriental languages was overhauled in France as part of a wide-ranging reform in educational institutions. In this context, there was created an *Ecole Nationale des Langues Orientales Vivantes* in 1795, the embryo from which the modern *Institut National des Langues et Civilisations Orientales* (INALCO) has eventually developed. The first teacher of Persian there was Langles from 1796 to 1824, and he was followed by others like E.M. Quatremère, remembered among other reasons for his translations into French of sections of ^{c}Abd al-Razzāq Samarqandī's fifteenth-century text *Maṭla^{c} al-Sa^{c}dain wa Majma^{c} al-Baḥrain* (1843) and of Rashid al-Dīn's history of the Mongols, *Jāmi^{c} al-Tawārīkh*. Other texts that were translated in the period included the well-known rendition of Firdausī's *Shāh-nāma*, by Jules Mohl (1838).

1 . My discussion draws to a considerable extent on Bernard Hourcade, "Iranian Studies in France", *Iranian Studies*, 1987, XX, 2-4, pp. 1-51.

From the time of Napoleon III (1852-70), the French interest in archaeology in Iran also grew, with the encouragement of the Qajar ruler Nāṣir al-Dīn (r. 1848-96). Descriptions of sites such as Persepolis, and Takht-e Bostan, were followed by excavations at Susa. French archaeological and geological surveys of Iran helped eventually to locate major petroleum deposits in that country in the 1890s, and partly as a result Nāṣir al-Dīn Shāh granted the French government a monopoly of archaeological excavations in his kingdom in 1894, which they held until it was revoked by Reza Shāh in 1931.

Scientific articles on Iran began to appear at much the same time on a regular basis in French journals like the *Revue du Monde Musulman*, as also in more specialised journals like that supported by the French Archaeological Delegation in Iran, titled *Mémoires de la Mission Archéologique Française en Perse.*

Another major field of interest for French scholars of Iran was Zoroastrian studies, on which the best-known French authority of the nineteenth century was James Darmesteter (1849-94), first attached to the IVth section of the Ecole Pratique des Hautes Etudes, and then professor at the College de France from 1885. Darmesteter is known for his complete translations into English and French of the *Avesta*, of which a partial translation had already been made into Latin in the late eighteenth century by the celebrated traveller and scholar A.H. Anquetil-Duperron (1731-1805). Darmesteter, whose life and work were commemorated recently by seminars in Bombay and Pune (15-22 December 1993), had as successors in the field of ancient Iranian languages such eminent scholars as Antoine Meillet, Emile Benveniste and Gilbert Lazard.

After the Second World War, Iranian studies in France entered a new phase. The field was now given a place at the Sorbonne, with support from the French Ministry of Foreign Affairs; it was also supported within the Centre National de la Recherche Scientifique (CNRS), itself created in the course of the 1940s. At the Sorbonne, Louis Massignon (1883-1962), a great authority on Islamic mysticism, founded the Institute of Iranian Studies, while in 1947, Henry Corbin created a Department of Iranology in Tehran's new French-Iranian Institute in order to work in closer contact with Iranian scholars. An important publication series, the *Bibliothèque Iranienne*, was launched by this Department, and some twenty-two texts in Arabic and Persian on diverse aspects of religion and philosophy were published. This Department was also instrumental in supporting the early works of such scholars as Gilbert Lazard, Marijan Molé and Jean Aubin.

In France, the Institut d'Etudes Iraniennes (IEI) created at the Sorbonne by Louis Massignon, was developed by Gilbert Lazard after his return from Iran in 1951, with the help of scholars such as Molé and de Menasce. The library of this Institute grew into a rich one, by the donation of the private collections of Darmesteter, Massé, Molé and other Iranologists. Later, in 1966, a Chair of Iranian Studies was created at the Sorbonne, and held by Professor Lazard. Since then, the IEI has continued to flourish, in association with the CNRS, and in independent premises.

Since 1970, Iranian studies have continued to expand and acquire new dimensions in France. If on the one hand, classical studies in philosophy, grammar, linguistics and philology have been stressed, the orientation towards the social sciences has not been neglected either. The central organisations in this process include, besides the INALCO, the Sorbonne Nouvelle, and the EPHE, the Institut Français de Recherche en Iran (IFRI), itself created in 1983 by the amalgamation of the Délégation Française en Iran (DAFI) and the Institut Français d'Iranologie de Téhéran (IFIT). Two journals, *Studia Iranica*, founded in 1972, and *Abstracta Iranica* (which has been publishing critical abstracts of research relevant to Iranian studies since 1978), play a significant role in this.

Indo-Persian Studies in France

While the focus on Iran proper thus has a considerable history in France, Indo-Persian studies have not been pursued in such a systematic or continuous fashion. We have seen that the works of Darmesteter were relevant to India as much as to Iran, in view of the Parsi presence in western India, and as a consequence, he visited India in 1886-87 at the behest of the French Ministry of Education. Even earlier, in the eighteenth century, the presence of the French in India in various military and administrative capacities had helped create a basis for Indo-Persian studies in France through the collection of manuscripts.

In point of fact, it is worth noting that a significant proportion (about one-third of the total collection) of the 2,600 manuscripts preserved in the Persian section of the Bibliothèque Nationale in Paris, are of Indian origin. This process of collection had begun gradually in the seventeenth century itself, through the activities of occasional travellers and adventurers. In the eighteenth century, the process of accumulation continued on a much larger scale, on account of such collectors as

Anquetil-Duperron, Jean-Baptiste Gentil and Antoine Polier, as well as missionaries and traders. Some of these manuscripts, especially those of Gentil and Polier, originate from Delhi, while others are of Deccani or Iranian origin.

In the nineteenth century, other additions took place, amongst which special mention must be made of Charles d'Ochoa's acquisitions in 1843-44 at Ahmedabad, of Persian texts from Gujarat and the Deccan. Besides, the mission of Darmesteter to India in the 1880s, which we have mentioned above, further stimulated the acquisition of manuscripts for the Bibliothèque Nationale.

Reference has already been made to the contribution of Quatremère in translating sections of the travel-account of ᶜAbd al-Razzāq Samarqandī, emissary of the Timurid ruler Shāhrukh to Calicut and Vijayanagar. The study of relations between the Iranian world and India in the fifteenth century was revived after a long hiatus by Jean Aubin in the 1950s, through his studies of the chronicler Nīmdihī (in a series of articles titled "Indo-Islamica"), and his analyses of trade relations between the Persian Gulf and India from the eleventh to the sixteenth centuries. The occasional journal *Mare Luso-Indicum*, inaugurated in the early 1970s, brought together a group of scholars who combined an interest in the trade of the Indian Ocean, with a study of Iran, and the Indo-Persian world of Gujarat and the Deccan. Since the 1980s, this journal has been replaced after a hiatus by the bi-lingual *Moyen Orient et Océan Indien / Middle East and Indian Ocean, XVI-XIXth c.*, of which seven volumes have appeared to date.

Parallel to this comparatively new (or newly revived) interest for the Indo-Persian world, interest had also begun to grow on that part of Central Asia which had historically felt Iranian influence either directly or indirectly. Those whose work extended in this direction, included Aubin himself, in his researches on the political history of Timur and the Timurids, as well as researchers like Jean During whose primary focus was on cultural and religious studies, in particular music and Sufic mysticism.

We have noted that in January 1983, the Délégation Archéologique Française en Iran (DAFI) and the Institut Français d'Iranologie de Téhéran (IFIT) had been amalagamated to form the Institut Français de Recherche en Iran (IFRI). However, the Tehran establishment of this Institute was closed down by the Iranian authorities, within a few months of its creation, in November 1983 and reopened only in 1992. The focus of the Institute thus shifted in part to other neighbouring areas such as India and Turkey, and a research fellowship (with a post of *allocataire de recherche*) was inaugurated in 1986 in India, attached initially to the Mission Archéologique Française en Inde (MAFI), and then after August 1989, to the Centre de Sciences Humaines (CSH), New Delhi. Between 1986 and 1989, this post was held by Yves Porter, who was thus the first French scholar to launch Indo-Persian studies from India, while combining textual research and field-work for his doctorate on the Persian Art of the Book in India. The French version of this work has been published, and its English translation is to appear soon.

Porter was succeeded between 1989 and 1991 by Françoise 'Nalini' Delvoye, who compiled an inventory on Persian manuscript holdings in Indian libraries and collections concerning music, while at the same time completing her D.Litt. thesis on Tānsen and the tradition of *dhrupad* songs in northern India. Since 1992, the same post has been held by Eric Phalippou, whose research largely concerns the comparative anthropology of the Parsi and the Irani communities in India.

Today, one can count a substantial number of French scholars with an interest in Indo-Persian studies, even if this is not the primary field of research of many of those listed below.[2] Amongst those whose work is largely focused on political, economic and social history, and comparative history, we may number Jean Aubin, Jean Calmard and Anne Kroell. In the field of religious studies, scholars include Marc Gaborieau, Michel Boivin, Eric Phalippou and Thierry Zarcone, the latter primarily interested in India's Central Asian connection. Amongst art-historians and historians of technology, the names of A.S. Melikian-Chirvani, Chahryar Adle, Yves Porter, Amina Okada, Živa Vesel and Klaus Rötzer suggest themselves; several of them appear as contributors in this volume. In the field of literature, the work of Charles-Henri de Fouchécour is of obvious relevance, though surprisingly no specialist exists of the so-called *sabk-i Hindī* style of Persian poetry. Other aspects of Indo-Persian socio-cultural history are represented by Denis Matringe, Nalini Delvoye and Delphine Roger. Finally, the Head Keeper of Persian manuscripts at the Bibliothèque Nationale, Francis Richard has interests that span art-history, codicology and the history of cultural interchange between Iran and India, and Asia and Europe.

2 . See B. Hourcade, et al., *Annuaire des Etudes Iraniennes en France*, Téhéran-Paris, Institut Français de Recherche en Iran, 1989. [*Abstracta Iranica*, Volume hors collection]

Round-tables and Seminars on Indo-Persian Culture: An Indo-French Venture

In view of this growing interest of French scholars for Indo-Persian studies, a joint Indo-French Seminar on "The Evolution of Medieval Indian Culture: the Indo-Persian Context", was planned in collaboration with Jawaharlal Nehru University, and was to be held in New Delhi in early 1991. However, unforeseen events intervened, and the seminar had eventually to be postponed to February 1994. Since the French scholars who were invited to participate had already prepared their papers, the Centre for Human Sciences (CSH), New Delhi and the Institut Français de Recherche en Iran (IFRI), Paris-Tehran, with the collaboration of the Institut d'Etudes Iraniennes (IEI), Paris, decided to organise a symposium entitled "Aspects de la culture indo-persane" in Ivry on 13-14 January 1992, under the direction of Yves Porter and the present editor. The publication of the twelve papers presented there in French, was then considered in an English translation. However, due to various reasons, only nine contributors could submit the final versions of their papers.

A second symposium with a larger international participation (with one British, one Italian and two Indian participants) was organised the following year in Paris, on 5 April 1993 by the Centre d'Etudes de l'Inde et de l'Asie du Sud (CEIAS), as part of the "Inter-disciplinary Research Programme on the Peripheral Islamic World", headed by Marc Gaborieau. Among the papers presented there by French scholars, only one (M. Boivin) could be got ready within the stringent deadline to be included in the present volume.

Presentation of Contributions

The contributions to this volume which emerged then from the two symposia of 1992 and 1993 have been classified broadly in chronological order. A more meaningful subject-wise presentation had to be eschewed since some important fields of research - such as Indo-Persian literature - were poorly or not at all represented here, and the other papers did not lend themselves to any obvious classification. Five papers were originally sent to the editor in English (these are the papers of A.S. Melikian-Chirvani, T. Zarcone, F. Delvoye, M. Gaborieau, and D. Roger), while the other five have been translated in India (Ž. Vesel, Y. Porter, F. Richard, K. Rötzer-K. Deokar and M. Boivin).

The first of the papers is by **Živa Vesel**, who presents the text entitled *al-Sirr al-Maktūm* ('The Occult Secret'), as one of the earliest testimonies to Indian interest for Arabo-Persian culture. This Arabic treatise on occult sciences was written by the renowned theologian Fakhr al-Dīn Rāzī (b. Rayy, 1149; d. Herat, 1210) and soon translated into Persian for the Sultan of Delhi, Iltutmish (r. 1211-36). Fakhr al-Dīn Rāzī was a prolific author, who wrote mostly in Arabic but also in Persian on a variety of subjects. The author recalls the historical context in which the Persian translation of *al-Sirr al-Maktūm* was commissioned, noting that Rāzī himself went twice to India, a fact which may have promoted the popularity of his work. A detailed presentation of the contents of the work - largely devoted to talismanic and astral magic - refers to a manuscript dated 1587, kept in the Bibliothèque Nationale, Paris. The author discusses its possible affiliation with the Sabean cosmology, and presents later reactions to this compendium of occult knowledge.

The following paper by **Yves Porter** moves to a period when the Sultanate of Delhi, consolidated by Iltutmish, had already fragmented to form a number of regional Sultanates in different parts of India. Amongst these was the Mālwa Sultanate founded by the Khaljīs in Central India, and the author makes an original attempt tc collate epigraphical and architectural evidences available in Mandu and in a few towns of the Mālwa region, with textual data of the Khaljī period, provided by the *Ma'āṣer-e Maḥmūdshāhī*. Written in 872/1467-68, by ᶜAlī b. Maḥmūd Kermānī, a courtier of Maḥmūd Khaljī (r. 839/1435-873/1469) of Iranian origin, this Persian chronicle throws light on the Khaljī dynasty and particularly on the events of the reign of Maḥmūd Khaljī, including the building activity in his capital Mandu. The description of some of the monuments situated around the main lakes of Mandu mentioned in the *Ma'āṣer-e Maḥmūdshāhī* includes the ramparts and the gateways, the Dilāwar Khān Mosque and the Dowlat-khāna, the Jamaᶜ Masjid, Hushang Shāh's Tomb, the "Golden Palace", known today as the Jahāz Mahal and a *madrasa* known at present as the Ashraf Mahal, which was still incomplete when the author of the *Ma'āṣer* died in 873/1469. An hospital mentioned in the chronicle cannot be located today and the mosque constructed by Malik Moghiṣ, the father of Maḥmūd Khaljī, is not mentioned in the *Ma'āṣer*. Other monuments built by the Sultan in Nālcha, Dipālpur, Chanderi and the tomb of Maḥmūd's grand-father in Dhār are also referred to in the light of the information provided by the chronicle, including vivid accounts of artisans and artists "from India and Khorāsān" who participated in the multi-cultural creativity noticed during Maḥmūd Khaljī's reign.

Most relevant passages are fully translated into English, with references to the edited text. The paper is illustrated by nine black and white photographs and the plan of Nālcha (by Klaus Rötzer).

A century later, the Mughal emperor Humāyūn (r. 1530-43 and 1555-56), represented another distinguished patron of the arts, this time in northern and north-western India. After a biographical sketch of the second Mughal emperor, highlighting some artistic aspects of his reign, **Francis Richard** moves on to discuss Humāyūn's library and the persons employed as librarians and calligraphers there, as well as some famous Iranian painters, who had fascinated the emperor while in Iran and when he settled in Kabul for five years. Besides twelve isolated paintings known for having been made either for Humāyūn or at his court, and the Lalbhai collection manuscript of the *K͟hamsa* of Niẓāmī (c. 1555), another unpublished manuscript of the same work (Smith-Lesouëf 216 of the Bibliothèque Nationale, Paris) is presented in detail by the author. Composed in the *Kitābk͟hāna* of Humāyūn c. 1545, the manuscript is illustrated by ten paintings (reproduced in black and white) - including only one attributed to a renowned painter, Maulānā Darvīsh Muḥammad from Herat - which are described and thoroughly analysed. A close study of the paintings compared with other contemporary illustrated albums, leads Richard to conclude that this manuscript pertains to the Timurid tradition from Herat, and further that it bears a clear influence of the royal Safavid *Kitabk͟hāna* of Tabriz. The author raises the possibility of the involvement in the composition of Mīr Sayyid ᶜAlī, the most famous master of the Tabriz school, and suggests that this manuscript which is slightly older than the *K͟hamsa* of the Lalbhai collection, may well be the oldest known 'Mughal' manuscript.

In the following essay, **Assadullah Souren Melikian-Chirvani** develops an aspect of his earlier pioneering work, *Islamic Metalwork from the Iranian World (8th-18th centuries)*, and studies metalwork as an integral part of the age-old cultural interchange between the Indian subcontinent and the Iranian world, dating back to the Achaemenids. An introduction on the Iranian culture in India, stresses the field of the Persian literature produced in India, especially the "Indian style" of poetry known as *sabk-i Hindī*, patronised by the Mughal emperors and the Deccani rulers. Contemporary to such a literary efflorescence, figural painting, calligraphy and book illumination also were influenced by a "high Iranian style", as was metalwork. The author notes that although "there is as yet no rigorous set of rules that can be applied to determine the attribution of metalwork to Hindustan ... versus Iran ... it is reasonable to posit that an object preserved in present-day India or Pakistan, or known to have come out of India or Pakistan, that happens to have been commissioned by characters with Indian names, or indeed by characters recorded in historical chronicles, stands a fair chance of having been made in some atelier in Hindustan". He adds, "When the decoration displays some features, however minute, that depart from Iranian design, the possibility changes to a high degree of probability".

A highly convincing study of three decorated wine bowls (*bādiya*) executed at the end of the reign of Jahāngīr and during the reign of Shāh Jahān, is supported by the careful examination of a pillar-candlestick (*shamᶜdān*) and some other artefacts of what the author terms "the Iranian Court Style of Hindustan", such as a basin (*lagan*). It is interesting to note that while the objects are based on "the Iranian ornamental vocabulary", the decoration, which includes the calligraphic panels, argues for origins in India. The point appears to be that these objects, while made in India, were deliberately intended to have an "Iranian look".

The essay then goes on to discuss another series of three pictorial wine bowls, which reproduce faithfully a western Iranian model, even if they have uncommon pictorial and calligraphic elements. All the objects studied are reproduced in full and in some cases with details. Equally, the Persian text of all the dedicatory inscriptions, the calligraphic borders which sometimes help identify the owner of the bowl, and all poetic verses in various metres are reproduced with an English translation, and identified where possible.

External influences on Indo-Persian culture form the theme of the following paper as well, in which **Thierry Zarcone** investigates Turkish Sufism in India with particular reference to the Yasawiyya order. Founded in Transoxiana by Ahmad Yasawī, who was born in Turkestan in 1167 and was "influential among the Turkish-speaking tribes of Central Asia", the order appears at some stage to have been subsumed under the Naqshbandiyya. Nevertheless, through various accounts (hagiographies, travelogues, etc.), the author argues that it is highly likely that Yasawī dervishes had entered India by the fourteenth century, even if no organized group identifying itself as Yasawī spread out in India. The author refers to various Yasawī Sufis known in Kashmir, Agra, etc., among whom some Shaykhs appear to have had a dual affiliation, to the original Turkish order - of which some specific pratices were known in India - and with the Naqshbandiyya from Central Asia, who came to be well-established in the subcontinent.

The next paper, by **Françoise 'Nalini' Delvoye**, argues that as an important object of artistic patronage, art-music constitutes a rich field of research in the socio-cultural history of medieval India. The author surveys a wide corpus of Indo-Persian texts documenting both the Indian and Persian musical traditions in medieval India. She questions the standard classification of available textual sources into various literary genres, such as theoretical treatises, historical chronicles and more literary writings in verse and prose, arguing that the information provided by each text is too disparate to be classified according to traditional categories. Through various examples, she demonstrates the problems faced by authors of an Indo-Persian cultural background, while depicting Indian music. References to representative cases highlight some characteristics of Indo-Persian literature on music, such as its practice-oriented technical approach and its remarkable sociological awareness. However, a crucial question remains of the existence of any "Indo-Persian music" in performance.

The paper of **Klaus Rötzer** and **Khandu Deokar** takes us into the epoch known traditionally as the twilight of Mughal rule in India, namely the eighteenth and nineteenth centuries. Amongst the most visible traces of Mughal rule in India are the gardens introduced by the dynasty, beginning with Bābur, the first Mughal emperor, who came to India in 1526. Now, though extant 'Mughal gardens' built by the imperial family and nobility in the late sixteenth and seventeenth centuries have been well studied, gardens built later, on the Mughal model, in predominantly Hindu regions have been neglected. The authors have studied the adaptations and transformations of 'Mughal gardens' built in Benaras and its surroundings, in the second half of the eighteenth and in the nineteenth century, "when Mughal power was no more than a memory".

While engaging in an initial survey of gardens of various styles conceived in the extremely dry climate of Iran and Central Asia, and on the other hand in the Indo-Gangetic plain, the authors define the origins, the forms and the functions of this style of gardens. Their purpose is to develop the contrast between the cultural significance of the garden in Iran and Central Asia on the one hand, and in India on the other.

An exposition of the general characteristics of Mughal gardens meant to be 'lived' in, with planted spaces and architectural structures, and of the Mughal gardens of Hindu princes, leads to the case-study of ten gardens of the second half of the eighteenth century, minutely described with plans, introduced by an historical overview and a presentation of their general characteristics. Most of these gardens are of the Iranian type called *chahār bāgh*, which later on assimilated the rain-fed reservoir (*pokharā*), and even later accomodated some English influence as well.

Also from the early nineteenth century, **Marc Gaborieau**'s paper is a thorough case-study of the so-called 'Wahhabi' literature of the years 1818-57, with a view to illustrating the transition from Persian to Urdu as "the religious and cultural language of the Indian Muslims". Following an historical survey of Indian 'Wahhabism', the author notes the importance of oral expression for the preaching of its missionaries, and the fact that this had necessarily to be done in Urdu, since Persian was no longer a spoken language in India by this time. He also discusses the printing of religious books of vulgarization in various languages, from which it emerges that the most common books were written directly in Urdu, with the earliest being composed in 1822-23 and printed in 1848. However, when it came to those works which were meant to offer a learned doctrinal statement, Persian was still preferred. We see this from the example of the first manifesto of the 'Wahhabi' movement, the *Ṣirāṭu'l-mustaqīm*, which was compiled around 1818 in Persian.

The author hence concludes that in the transition from Persian to Urdu in northern India, the Wahhabis ought not to be seen as the key innovators. Their role however was in accelerating the process by which Urdu emerged as an authoritative language, by using it for proselytisation. The author confirms Garcin de Tassy's observations in this regard. At the same time, the situation was complicated by the competition between Urdu and English as languages of power, especially after 1857.

The following paper by **Michel Boivin** continues the discussion of socio-religious themes, by focusing on Ismaili Shīᶜism in the period from 1885 to 1957. It is noted that the recent history of Ismaili Shīᶜism represents a significant encounter between "an Iranian and an Indian religious tradition", the consequences of which need to be evaluated. Forced to leave Persia the 46th Imām, Ḥasan ᶜAlī Shāh, was welcomed by the Khojas in Bombay where he settled around 1845. His prerogative of being recognised as the spiritual head of the Ismaili community, was however challenged by a minority among the Ismailis. The issue was legally settled by the British (in the 'Aga Khan Case' of 1866), but his grand-son Sulṭān Muḥammad Shāh, the 'Aga Khan' (Imām from 1885 to 1957) nevertheless tried to harmonize the Iranian and the Indian traditions, by the creation of a 'neo-Ismailism'. The study is based on Aga Khan's own writings, mostly published in English and some publications or communications in Urdu for the Ismailis.

The author concludes that by elaborating a view of Islam in which primacy was given to 'Fundamentals', the Aga Khan intended to achieve several objectives, which included the establishment of a common platform within the Ismaili tradition, the construction of a bridge between the Ismaili community as a whole and the rest of the Muslim community, and the elaboration of "a new Muslim ethics" which could help in finding solutions to contemporary challenges.

Finally, and in a lighter vein, **Delphine Roger**'s paper studies the importance of the Persian heritage on Muslim cookery of Hyderabad, the Deccan city founded by Muḥammad Qulī Quṭb Shāh (r. 1580-1612). The author gives a general presentation of the classification and combinations of food-products aimed at a notion of perfect balance. One element of the backdrop is made up of Ayurvedic science of medicine and its classification of all substances in five elements, indissociable with the dietetic system which it promotes. The Greek medicine (*Yūnānī*) is the other "medico-philosophical" system known in India since the tenth-eleventh centuries, through Arabic and Persian translations of treatises and which was particularly well patronised by the Sultans of Golconda at Hyderabad. The *ḥakīm*s or *Yūnānī* doctors are said to excel in combining the four elements of fundamental energies, *i.e.*, heat/cold and dryness/moisture, according to humours and temperaments. This mixed tradition of Ayurveda and *Yūnānī* medicine, linking popular and scholarly discourse is seen to work remarkably well in Hyderabad, where *ḥakīm*s may be seen as "food consultants" and even as cooks. The author illustrates this observation with references to some famous Hyderabadi "medicated foods", such as preserves (*murabbā*) and syrups (*sharbat*) and tempting dishes, such as the rich and spicy *pilaf* rice with meat (*biryānī*). Such diets prescribed "according to seasons, individuals and ages" characterize the "well-being oriented cookery" of Hyderabad which often leads to "culinary extravaganzas".

However, with the new economic and political order that has emerged since the decline of the Nizams and the establishment of the modern state of Andhra Pradesh, this complex relationship between cookery and medicine "related to a royal notion of food" and "based on a vision of the body and of the universe which is not current any more among the Muslims of Hyderabad" is an endangered tradition.

The notes are presented according to the format of each author, except for bibliographical references which have been more or less systematised, both in the notes and the separate bibliography given after each contribution.

Though rather eclectic in its range of coverage, this collection of essays is quite representative of the emerging trends in French studies on Indo-Persian culture. These trends have been further consolidated in the past few years through the academic exchanges between France and India, and most recently by the joint Indo-French conference on Indo-Persian studies held at Jawaharlal Nehru University, which has already been mentioned above. It is to be hoped that further studies, both in the form of collected essays and individual monographs, will continue to emerge, to do justice to this important and hitherto somewhat neglected field of research.

The Persian Translation of Fakhr al-Din Rāzi's *al-Sirr al-Maktūm* ('The Occult Secret') for Iltutmish*

ŽIVA VESEL

Scientific knowledge in Islamic India drew on two traditions. On one hand, its roots lay very largely in the tradition of Arabic science, but on the other hand, the tradition of Indian science, known through translations from Sanskrit, was also drawn upon.[1] From the corpus of Arabic science, Islamic India preferred Iranian authors who wrote in Arabic as well as in Persian. This is the case with the treatise on occult sciences which will be introduced here, and which was written in Arabic by Fakhr al-Din Rāzi; the treatise was known in India through a Persian translation made at the very beginning of the Delhi Sultanate.

The author of the treatise, the Iranian theologian Fakhr al-Din Rāzi, born in Rayy in 1149, and who died in Herat in 1210, is an important figure for the history of ideas in Iran.[2] He is known for his attempts to reconcile theology with philosophy. The most important Ash'arite theologian after Ghazzāli, he is the author of many works in the field, including the longest commentary on the Quran still extant. At the same time, Rāzi was well acquainted with philosophical matters, as he was an assiduous reader of Fārābi and Ibn Sinā; as a consequence, he as well as Naṣir al-Din Ṭusi (d. 1273), took part in a debate on

* The same transliteration has been used for both Persian and Arabic names (long vowels other than ā indicated for Arabic works only).

1. For an overview of these writings, see for instance the catalogue of Persian manuscripts by C.A. Storey, *Persian Literature. A Bio-Bibliographical Survey*: Vol. II, Part 1, London, 1958; Vol. II, Part 2, London, 1971; Vol. II, Part 3, Leiden, 1977; for a summary of translations from and into Sanskrit, practised in India, see M.S. Khan, "Arabic and Persian Source Materials for the History of Science in Medieval India", *Islamic Culture*, 1988, LXII, 2-3, pp. 113-40.

2. For Rāzi's biography, cf. N. Māyel-e Heravi, *Sharh-e hāl va zendagi va monāẓerāt-e Emām Fakhr al-Din Rāzi*, Kabul, 1343; for his work, see S.H. Nasr and W.C. Chittick, *An Annotated Bibliography of Islamic Science*, Tehran, 1975, Vol. I, pp. 362-4 and F. Kholeif, *A Study on Fakhr al-Din al-Rāzi and His Controversies in Transoxiana*, Beirut, 1966, pp. 109-203.

rational interpretation in the work of Ibn Sinā.[3] A complete scholar of his time, Rāzi has left behind about a hundred titles in Arabic and a few works in Persian. His work contains, among other things, a few scientific treatises - mostly on medicine - and a substantial number of treatises on occult sciences dealing respectively with physiognomony, astrology (in Persian), geomancy, chiromancy, the interpretation of dreams (in Persian), and with talismanic magic which he expounded in his *al-Sirr al-Maktūm* ("The Occult Secret"), the text which is dealt with here.

The attribution of the *Sirr* to Rāzi is not open to doubt; however, we do not know the date of its composition, nor to whom it was dedicated or by whom it was commissioned. The *Sirr*, which has not yet been edited, is to be found in a large number of copies in the original Arabic[4] and in a few copies in Persian translation.[5] The Bibliothèque Nationale in Paris has various versions of this text, among which is a copy of the complete Persian translation of the *Sirr*, made for Iltutmish and his son and heir Rokn al-Din Firuzshāh,[6] a few aspects of which will be analysed here.

Let us begin by recalling the historical context in which the translation was commissioned.[7] Cultural contacts between Iran and India, during the Islamic period, had been established with the occupation of

---

3. Rāzi has written a commentary on the *Ishārāt* of Ibn Sinā, and Nāṣir al-Din Ṭusi has in turn written a commentary on this commentary of Rāzi.

4. For a description of original *Sirr* in Arabic, see the catalogue of Brockelmann, Vol. I, p. 669/margin 508.

5. Cf. Storey, *op. cit.*, Vol. II; Part 1, p. 49, N° 87/2.

6. The Bibliothèque Nationale copies are as follows:

1° a copy of the Arabic original - unfortunately lacking a beginning; cf. Baron de Slane, *Catalogue des Manuscrits Arabes* [de la Bibliothèque Nationale], Paris, 1883-95, T. I, N° 2645.

2° A copy of the translation into Persian of the full Arabic text, by an anonymous translator for Iltutmish and his son Rokn al-Din Firuzshāh (f. 2r) dated 1587 (Indian *nastaᶜaliq*) : Cf. Blochet, *Catalogue des Manuscrits Persans* [de la Bibliothèque Nationale], Paris, 1912, Vol. II, p. 142, N° 896-7. (Agha Bozorg Teherāni, *al-Ẕari'a*, p. 170, N° 1132 attributes a Persian rendering of the text to Rāzi himself but there is no trace of it in the catalogues).

3° A selection of passages from the *Sirr* translated by ᶜAbd al-Malik Shirāzi, in 1378-79 under the title *Mokhtasar-e Takvin*, directly from the Arabic original: Cf. Blochet, *Catalogue des Manuscrits Persans*, Paris, 1934, Vol. IV, p. 324, N° 2399.

4° An illustrated folio, showing a talismanic image, belonging to the genre "degrees of the sky". This folio has been detached from a manuscript supposedly of the *Sirr*, preserved in the Raza Library in Rampur, which was executed for Akbar. See F. Richard, "Une page du recueil de talismans et de signes zodiacaux d'Akbar dans la collection Gentil", *Arts Asiatiques*, 1986, XLI, pp. 116-7.

7. See for instance A. Ahmad, *An Intellectual History of Islam in India*, Edinburgh, 1969, and *Idem*, *Studies in Islamic Culture in the Indian Environment*, Oxford, 1964.

Lahore by the Ghaznavids; they continued under the Ghorids and their "slave" generals Aybaq and Qubacha. With the accession of Iltutmish (r. 1211-36),[8] the cities of Multān and Delhi became cultural centres in which scholars and men of letters took up residence. Iltutmish, who, thanks to his prudent policies, protected himself from the Mongol threat, collected at his court many of those who fled the large towns of eastern Iran. Reputed to be both pious and tolerant - despite his destruction of Indian idols and his attempts to exterminate the Isma'ilis - and held in esteem by Sufis, Iltutmish emerged as the protector of the Iranian cultural heritage. He gave shelter at his court, among others, to the historian Jozjāni, the man of letters ᶜOwfi (two refugees from Aybaq's court) and Fakhr-e Modabber, a very interesting author who has left behind a treatise on the "art of war" and a "Mirror for Princes". This then was the context in which the translation of *al-Sirr al-Maktūm* was commissioned by Iltutmish himself, who had heard about that treatise and, wished to read it, as the translator informs us in his preface (*Sirr*, ff. 2v-3r).[9]

It is important to note the following coincidence: Rāzi had spent half of his life in the eastern part of the Iranian world - in Transoxania, Khwarezm, Bamiyan, Ghazna and Herat, and being close to the Ghorid court between 1187 and 1198-99, he accompanied Shihāb al-Din Ghori at least twice to India. Would this fact have facilitated the circulation of Rāzi's works in the region ? From the dates, one notices that the *Sirr* was translated very soon after its composition, no more than twenty-six years after Rāzi's death. There is every reason to believe that the translation was commissioned at the very end of the reign of Iltutmish (1236), when Rokn al-Din Firuzshāh was already in line to succeed his father.

Regarding the contents of the *Sirr al-Maktūm*, Rāzi informs us in his preface (f. 2v) that he has explained therein the doctrines of the Sabeans, showing with the aid of solid arguments which of these doctrines were in contradiction with the Islamic dogma. One learns, at the same folio 2v, that the translator took it on his personal initiative to expurgate some other passages when they were offensive to Islamic beliefs.

What should one understand by Sabeans in this context ? According to Michel Tardieu,[10] this name was used to designate two different

8. M. Habib and K.A. Nizami, *A Comprehensive History of India*, Vol. V: The Delhi Sultanate, Delhi, 1970, pp. 209-37; art. "Iltutmish" in *Encycl. de l'Islam*², etc.

9. In this paper, references to folio numbers are from the manuscript of the full Persian translation, cf. *supra* Note 6 (2°).

groups: on one hand, the Sabeans mentioned in the Quran - whom Tardieu identifies with the Gnostics *stricto sensu* -, and on the other hand, the Sabeans of Ḥarrān (a town in northern Mesopotamia). Among the latter, who were a pagan sect, we have to distinguish two categories. First, the Sabeans of Ḥarrān in the proper sense, who practised a popular religion which was a syncretic combination of Greek astrology (with Babylonian elements) and hermetism. One aspect of their doctrine was the cult of planetary divinities (or spiritualities, *ruḥaniyyāt*). Second, there were the Sabeans of Baghdad or the "Greek" Sabeans: for there had existed in Ḥarrān, parallel to the syncretic religion, a philosophical sect (a Platonic school) headed by Thābet b. Qorra, but which migrated to Baghdad in the 9th century. The contents of the *Sirr al-Maktūm* deal exclusively with the syncretic beliefs of the Sabeans of Ḥarrān (and not with the teachings of the Platonic School) in spite of the fact that Rāzi refers a number of times to Thābet b. Qorra.

The *Sirr al-Maktūm* contains an introduction and six chapters. After quotations from Quranic verses and the Hadith, Rāzi continues his introduction with a description of the celestial and sub-lunar world. He makes it clear that the contents of the work are a form of initiatory material which, according to the ancient sages, was not to be freely divulged. He refers to various authorities, including Aristotle, Abu Maᶜshar Balkhi and Thābet b. Qorra and expounds, finally, the advantages of the science of the Sabeans: the first of the advantages consists in acquiring knowledge of the celestial and sub-lunar world, the second in acquiring certain powers, among other things, to neutralise enemies and to overcome maladies which even physicians cannot cure, because, Rāzi clarifies that whoever possesses this science will overcome maladies since he commands the spirits, while the physician commands only the bodies (f. 3r) - an astonishing remark since there is little discussion of medicine later on.

The First Chapter (ff. 6r-13r) brings together the general principles of Sabean cosmology. The Second Chapter (ff. 13v-78r) deals with technical knowledge regarding the sky (*i.e.* astrology), "indispensable for the practice of the science of the Sabeans"; this chapter establishes lists of signs, correspondences, influences, attributes, etc. concerning planets, signs of the zodiac, the Fixed Stars, the 360 degrees of the sky, the two poles, lunar mansions, etc. The Third Chapter (ff. 78r-88v) describes the fabrication of talismans, according to rules expounded in

---

10. M. Tardieu, "Ṣābiens coraniques et Ṣābiens de Ḥarrān", *Journal Asiatique*, 1986, CCLXXIV, pp. 1-44.

the Second Chapter. The Fourth Chapter (ff. 88v-115r) describes the ritual of astral magic (*daʿvat al-kavākeb*: "prayer to planets"). The Fifth Chapter (ff. 115r-133v) is devoted to the traditional range of talismans, meant to create friendship or hostility between two persons, as well as to obtain riches, fame, protection against wild beasts, etc. The Sixth Chapter (ff. 133v-143r), titled "the properties of substances" (*khavāṣṣ al-ashyā*), contains recipes to make potions - which Rāzi calls "talismans"; the treatise, which in all contains 143 folios, ends with a section on poisons and antidotes.

The main part of the work is devoted to talismanic and astral magic, the working of which is based on the astrological system. The *Sirr al-Maktum* is a veritable compendium of occult knowledge, given the number of sources quoted, some of which are apocryphal : Aristotle, Tankeloshā or Teukros, Abu Ẕātes Bābeli, Hermes, Apollonius of Tyane, Ṭomṭom Hindi, Ibn Wahshiyya, Abu Maʿshar, Aḥmad Sijzi, Thābet b. Qorra, etc. Among these authors, Ṭomṭom Hindi (Ṭomṭom, the Indian) is mentioned by Rāzi on f. 63, in connection with his work on the "Degrees of the Sky". (We should note that Rāzi engages here in real textual criticism, by clarifying that "he found a number of copies of the "Degrees of the Sky", which he compared and which showed some variants, but that he could not find any valid sign, while reading them, which would indicate that any one of these copies was the most reliable"). Opinions differ regarding Ṭomṭom Hindi, whose historicity as a personage is difficult to evaluate.[11] The name might have been the Arabicisation of Dindymus, King of the Brahmins, who is said to have entertained a correspondence with Alexander. It is not known whether he was an Indian or a Greek ascetic, who lived in Taxila. On the other hand, some scholars have thought that the name refers to the Indian astronomer/astrologer Kanaka, who was at the court of Baghdad, under the caliph al-Ma'mun. Still others have identified Ṭomṭom Hindi with Tankeloshā/Teukros, the well-known author of occult works in the Babylonian tradition. Among a number of works attributed to Ṭomṭom Hindi, the one on the "Degrees of the Sky" (360 degrees, thirty per zodiac sign) is confirmed by Ibn Khaldun,[12] but the same sort of work is attributed elsewhere to Tankeloshā. The question of the identity of Ṭomṭom Hindi seems in-

11. See for instance A. Hauber, "Ṭomṭom (Ṭimṭim) = *Dandamiz* = *Dindymus* ?", *Zeitschrift für Deutsche Morgenländischen Gesellschaft*, 1909, Vol. 63, pp. 457-72.

12. Ibn Khaldun, *Discours sur l'Histoire universelle*, Transl. V. Monteil, Paris, 1967-68, Vol. III, p. 1088. See also Ibn Khaldun, *The Muqaddimah*, Transl. F. Rosenthal, New York, 1958, Vol. III, Ch. 6, section 27, p. 156 sq.

soluble for the time being, though it has been the object of extensive scholarly investigation. Whatever the case, this author is regularly mentioned in Islamic occult literature.

Regarding the astral talismanism which forms a central part of the *Sirr al-Maktūm*, Ibn Khaldun gives us an introduction to it, in his *Muqaddima*, written around 1377:[13] "the maker of talismans has recourse to the spiritual influences of astral bodies, to the secret of numbers, to the particular qualities of beings and to the positions of the celestial sphere, which, according to astrologers, influence the world of elements (...). Philosophers state therefore that (...) talismans, are the union of a spirit with a body (...). They mean to say that superior and celestial natures become linked with inferior natures; the former being astral spiritualities. This is why the makers of talismans generally take recourse to astrology". Elsewhere, he clarifies that:[14] "no one doubts the real influence of sorcery" (which means talismanic magic as well here), however, says Ibn Khaldun, "These sciences are prohibited by various religions, because they are dangerous and because they orient the soul towards the astral bodies or other objects, rather than in the direction of God. This is why treatises on magic are extremely rare..."

This opinion is representative of a sort of Muslim orthodoxy, which meant in turn that Rāzi's enterprise was bound to create ripples. According to Ḥaji Khalifa, the *Sirr al-Maktūm* was the target of refutation by Sheykh Zeyn al-Din ibn Sarija b. Moḥammad al-Malati (d. 1386).[15] We may recall that Ghazzāli (d. 1111), who belonged to the same theological school as Rāzi, had already condemned this type of knowledge, by terming it "blameful".[16] Ibn Khaldun who quotes Rāzi in his *Muqaddima* a number of times, and who held him in the greatest esteem, mentions the *Sirr al-Maktūm* as a reference work on magic which had been in current use in eastern Iran. He clarifies that he himself had never managed to find it and adds: "The Imām Fakhr al-Din however, is not considered as a specialist in the field of magical matters, but it may well be the contrary which is true".[17]

How are we to understand this apparent contradiction, by which a renowned theologian writes treatises on the occult sciences ? The case of Rāzi is, however, not a peculiar one, for other religious authors have

13. *Ibid.*, pp. 1097-8.
14. *Ibid.*, p. 1087.
15. Ḥāji Khalifa, *Kashf al- Ẓonun*, ed. G. Fluegel, London, 1842, Vol. III, pp. 586-7.
16. L. Gardet, and M.M. Anawati, *Introduction à la théologie musulmane*, Paris, 1970, pp. 113-21.
17. Ibn Khaldun, *op. cit.*, III, p. 1095.

shown similar interests.[18] From the point of view of medieval erudition, which was by its very nature encyclopaedic, the occult sciences could be the subject of a treatise just like any other "science". Occult sciences occupy a specific place in the classification of knowledge, being generally classified amongst the applied branches of physics (*ṭabiᶜiyyāt*) and mathematics (*riyāẓiyyāt*). As for the beliefs of the Sabeans, the fact that they are dealt with by a theologian is even easier to understand. The sect of the Sabeans of Ḥarrān is often described in Islamic literature, for instance by Ibn al-Nadim,[19] but above all in treatises dealing with "Religions and Sects", a specific genre of scholarly literature. Several authors have left behind treatises of this sort, including Shahrestāni[20] as well as Fakhr al-Din Rāzi;[21] there, one finds mention of various sects (with the Sabeans appearing side by side with Brahmins, philosophers, "materialists" (*dahriyyun*), the Arabs of the pre-Islamic epoch, etc.) which are contrasted to the Religions of the Book. It is thus well within the logic of the culture of the period to be interested in the Sabeans; this fact might have provided Rāzi a first motivation to write the *Sirr al-Maktūm.* A second reason could have been more personal and would explain the large number of occult treatises which he has left us. Rāzi was a scholar in the strongest sense of the term, and was thus particularly anxious to preserve in a written form a rare type of knowledge which was tending to disappear. At the beginning of his chapter on physiognomony, in his Persian encyclopaedia *Jāmeᶜ al-ᶜOlum*[22] he declares : "It is a noble science which is no longer studied in our times, because of its difficult nature", a remark which one does not find in his Arabic treatise on physiognomony.[23] Given that Rāzi wrote about the end of the 12th century or in the early 13th century, and that according to historical documents, the Sabeans of Ḥarrān disappeared at the end of the 11th century, it is not improbable that he wished to preserve their knowledge out of sheer curiosity.

---

18. For the work of Kāshefi and Sheykh Bahā'i, see for instance Živa Vesel, "Le *Lava'eḥ al-Qamar*, a treatise on astrology by Ḥoseyn Vāᶜeẓ Kāšefi", to be published in *Proceedings of the Second European Conference of Iranian Studies* (Bamberg, 30 Sept.-5 Oct. 1991).

19. [Ibn al-Nadim] *The Fihrist of al-Nadim*, Transl. B. Dodge, New York/London, 1970, Vol. II, pp. 745-73.

20. Shahrastani, *Livre des Religions et des Sectes*, Translation, Introduction and Notes by D. Gimaret and G. Monnot, Paris, 1986.

21. See Kholeif's Bibliography, in Note 2 *supra.*

22. F. Rāzi, *Jāmeᶜ al-ᶜOlum*, ed. M. Tasbiḥi, Tehran, 1346, p. 101.

23. Y. Mourad, *La physiognomonie arabe et le Kitāb al-Firāsa de Fakhr al-Din al-Rāzi*, Paris, 1939.

The *Sirr al-maktūm* is thus one of the first texts which Islamic India mined from Arabic sources in the Iranian world. It seems that this work enjoyed some success in the Indian world, for we know that the Persian translation of the *Sirr* made for Iltutmish was later re-copied at least twice: one copy kept at the Bibliothèquè Nationale of Paris, dated 1587, is copied in Indian *nasta^caliq* (it is not known by whom it was commissioned) and another illustrated copy of high quality was made for Akbar, as has been suggested by Francis Richard.[24] Without casting doubt on the popularity of occult literature in princely courts, it seems that the *Sirr al-Maktūm* of Rāzi should also be understood in relation to the wider cultural preoccupations of Islamic society, on account of its references to the Sabean sect. This particular aspect of the work may explain, in part, the interest which sovereigns have had in it over the centuries.

Translated from French by Sanjay Subrahmanyam

REFERENCES

Ahmad, Aziz, *Studies in Islamic Culture in the Indian Environment*, Oxford: Clarendon Press, 1964.

—— *An Intellectual History of Islam in India*, Edinburgh: Edinburgh University Press, 1969. [Islamic Surveys, 7]

Baron de Slane, *Catalogue des Manuscrits Arabes* [de la Bibl. Nationale], Paris: Imprimerie Nationale, 1883-95.

Blochet, F., *Catalogue des Manuscrits Persans* [de la Bibliothèque Nationale], Paris: Imprimerie Nationale, Vol. II, 1912; Vol. IV, 1934.

Brockelmann, C. *Geschichte der arabischen Literatur*, Vol. I, Leiden: E.J. Brill, 1943.

*Encyclopédie de l'Islam*², Six Vols. published, Leiden: E.G. Brill, 1960.

Gardet, Louis and M.M. Anawati, *Introduction à la théologie musulmane*, Paris: J. Vrin, 1970.

Habib, M. and K.A. Nizami, *A Comprehensive History of India*, Vol. V : The Delhi Sultanate, Delhi: The Indian History Congress, 1970.

Hāji Khalifa, *Kashf al-Ẓonun*, ed. G. Fluegel, London: The Oriental Translation Fund, 1842, Vol. III.

Hauber, A., "Ṭomṭom (Ṭimṭim) = *Dandamiz* = *Dindymus* ?", *Zeitschrift*

24. See Note 2 (2° and 4°).

für Deutsche Morgenländischen Gesellschaft, 1909, LXIII, pp. 457-72.

[Ibn al-Nadim] *The Fihrist of al-Nadim*, Transl. B. Dodge, New York/ London: Columbia University Press, 1970, Vol. II.

Ibn Khaldun, *Discours sur l'Histoire universelle*, Transl. V. Monteil, Paris: Sindbad, 1967-68, Vol. III.

—— *The Muqaddimah*, Transl. F. Rosenthal, New York: Bollingen Foundation, 1958, Vol. III.

Khan, M. Saber, "Arabic and Persian Source Materials for the History of Science in Medieval India", *Islamic Culture*, LXII, 2-3, 1988, pp. 113-40.

Kholeif, F., *A Study on Fakhr al-Din al-Rāẕi and His Controversies in Transoxiana*, Beirut: Dar al Machreq, 1966.

Māyel-e Heravi, *Sharh-e hāl va ẕendagi va monāẓerāt-e Emām Fakhr al-Din Rāẕi*, [Kabul], 1343.

Mourad, Y., *La physiognomonie arabe et le Kitāb al-Firāsa de Fakhr al-Din al-Rāẕi*, Paris: P. Geuthner, 1939.

Nasr, S.H. and W.C. Chittick, *An Annotated Bibliography of Islamic Science*, Tehran: Imperial Iranian Academy of Philosophy, 1975, Vol. I.

Rāzi, Fakhr al-Din, *Jāmeᶜ al-ᶜOlum*, ed. M. Tasbiḥi, Tehran: Asadi, 1346.

Richard, Francis, "Une page du recueil de talismans et de signes zodiacaux d'Akbar dans la collection Gentil", *Arts Asiatiques*, 1986, XLI, pp. 116-7.

Shahrastani, *Livre des Religions et des Sectes*, Translation, Introduction and Notes by D. Gimaret and G. Monnot, Paris: Unesco, 1986.

Storey, C.A., *Persian Literature. A Bio-bibliographical Survey* (London, 1927): Vol. II, Part 1, London: Luzac & Co, 1958; Vol. II, Part 2, London: Luzac & Co, 1971; Vol. II, Part 3, H. Science, I. Occult Arts, Leiden: E.J. Brill, 1977.

Tardieu, M., "Ṣābiens coraniques et Ṣābiens de Ḥarrān", *Journal Asiatique*, 1986, CCLXXIV, pp. 1-44.

Teherāni, Agha Bozorg, *al-Ẕari'a*, Tehran: Eslāmiyye, 1387.

Vesel, Živa, "Le *Lava'eḥ al-Qamar*, A Treatise on Astrology by Ḥoseyn Vāᶜeẓ Kāšefi", to be published in *Proceedings of the Second European Conference of Iranian Studies* (Bamberg, 30 Sept.- 5 Oct. 1991). (Forthcoming)

2

Khalji Architecture of Mālwa in the Light of the *Ma'āser-e Maḥmudshāhi**

Yves Porter

The architecture of Mandu, though well known, has never been analysed in the light of the *Ma'āser-e Maḥmudshāhi*, the chronicle of ᶜAli b. Maḥmud Kermāni (872/1467-68), although it is an excellent contemporary source.[1] This chronicle records events concerning the reign of Maḥmud Khalji, including monuments constructed or completed by him. In this article, we propose to study this document, focussing our attention on the interface between information recorded in the text, and the inscriptions and architectural remains which survive from the Khalji period. This study will show, among other things, the activity and the movement of artists and artisans who flocked to the court of Mandu, many of whom, like our author, were of Iranian origin.

The earliest settlement of Mandu goes back to the pre-Muslim period; some architectural remains and inscriptions point to the existence of a town named Mandapa-Durga. Under the Paramāras this town had known a certain emminence which it lost after ᶜAlā' al-din Khalji's invasion in 1305. Until the beginning of the fifteenth century, the history of Mandu appears to be obscure. With the weakening of Tughluq power, and after the sack of Delhi by Tamerlane (1398), Dilāwar Khān Ghori, the governor of Mālwa, proclaimed himself independant in 804/1401. He died five years later and was succeeded by his son Hushang Shāh. In 1436, a faithful servitor of Hushang Shāh did away with the king's descendants, and seized power under the name of Maḥmud Shāh

* This research has been completed with the help of a visit to Mandu in the summer of 1990. This visit was financed by the French Institute of Iranian Research (IFRI), in collaboration with the Centre for Human Sciences (CSH) at Delhi. An earlier visit, in the company of Mr. Klaus Rötzer, had already permitted me to familiarize myself with the monuments of Mālwa. We were warmly welcomed there by the Conservator, Mr. A.K. Soni of the Archaeological Survey of India. My thanks are due to this institution, as well as to the directors of the IFRI and the CSH and Mr. Rötzer for their help and collaboration.

1. ᶜAli b. Maḥmud al-Kermāni, *Ma'āser-e Maḥmudshāhi*, ed. N.H. Ansari, Delhi, 1968. U.N. Day has profusely used this text for his history of Mālwa. See his *Medieval Malwa. A Political and Cultural History, 1401-1562,* Delhi, 1965.

I Khalji, thus establishing a new dynasty which lasted for almost a century. Maḥmud's reign was spent mainly in waging external and internal wars. His reputation travelled beyond frontiers of India and he even received an investiture from the Abbasid Caliph of Cairo.[2] His court attracted numerous intellectuals, artisans and poets, of whom the author of the *Ma'ās̱er*, ᶜAli b. Maḥmud Kermāni, was one.

While he was living in Jaunpur, at the court of the Sharqi Sultans, our author was invited to Mandu by Maḥmud Khalji. In 1465, ᶜAli b. Maḥmud went to meet the king, first at Ranthambhor and then at Azizabad. He was eighty-nine years old at this time. At the behest of Maḥmud, he wrote the chronicle *Ma'ās̱er-e Maḥmudshāhi* which he based, in his own words, on the documents that he had compiled. During the two years that he spent in writing this work, he was also able to record the events that he had witnessed. After furnishing the genealogy of the Khaljis, the author describes the reign of Hushang Shāh and then of Maḥmud upto 872/1467-68. The author was then ninety-one years old. The king died the following year and was succeeded by his son, Ghiyās̱ al-din, whose reign was as peaceful as his father's had been turbulent. As a result of the wealth and talent accumulated during the reign of Maḥmud, Mandu witnessed a veritable artistic floraison during this period.

* * *

The fort of Mandu is situated on a vast plateau bounded by ravines. Three sets of monuments are grouped around the principal lakes. The Royal Enclave is situated around the Munj Talāo and the Kapur Talāo; the complex around Malik Moghis̱' mosque is in the proximity of the Sāgar Talāo; and the so-called Bāz Bahādur palace is located on the sides of the Rewā Kuṇḍ. Most probably, all these lakes were built in the pre-Muslim period. In this article, we will deal first with the fortifications, then with the Royal Enclave, and the monuments grouped around Malik Moghis̱' mosque alongwith some others, dispersed in Mandu and finally, with the monuments in some of the other towns of Mālwa: Nālcha, Dipālpur, Ujjain and Chanderi. We will restrict this study only to those monuments which are described in the text of the *Ma'ās̱er, i.e.*, to those belonging to the period before 1468.

---

2. Day, *op. cit.*, p. 213.

Ramparts and Gateways

The ramparts of Mandu form undeniably one of the most extraordinary fortified complexes in India. Fereshta describes them as "the most extraordinary in the then world".[3] The construction of these ramparts, as of certain gateways (*e.g.* Bhangi and Rāmpol) goes back to the pre-Muslim period. Moreover, it is probable that during the occupation of the Paramāras, it was primarily the area around the Munj Talāo which was meant to be fortified. The Rāmpol Gate, in contrast with the other gates mentioned in the *Ma'āser*, is situated within the fort and was undoubtedly a part of this inner enclosure. The only remaining pier of this gate - now called Tripolia - is located between the Jāma^c Masjid and the Ashrafi Mahal.

After the invasion of the Muslims and the establishment of the Ghori dynasty, Dilāwar Khān and his son Hushang Shāh restored and extended these fortifications. In fact, Hushang Shāh shift his capital from Dhār to Mandu. It therefore became necessary for him to give the capital the defences which would render it impregnable. On his death bed, Hushang Shāh entreated his son Ghazani Khān to complete the building work begun by him. This included the large mosque, the *madrasa* and the walls.

The gates mentioned in the text are the Delhi Gate, the Tārāpur Gate, the Jājnagar Gate, as well as the Shāhpol and the Rāmpol Gates.[4] The Delhi Gate situated in the north and the Tārāpur Gate in the south are the most monumental as well as the most important from the strategic point of view. The Delhi Gate is also called *Borj-e sharaf*;[5] like most of garrison gates it could also accomodate guards under its vaults. On entering the fort, towards the right, there is a small mosque with a square courtyard which is undoubtedly contemporary to the one built by Dilāwar Khān.

The Tārāpur Gate, reputed for its impregnability, placed as it was at the top of a rock over three hundred metres high, was never taken but treacherously. The gate consists of an external archway facing a flight of stairs, which is protected by high walls and enclosed on the other side by another gate. An inscription attributes its foundation to Dilāwar Khān.[6] A third gate was added here by Akbar, as indicated in another incription.

---

3. D.R. Patil, *Mandu*, Archeological Survey of India, 1982, p. 9.
4. Another gate of the same name not mentioned in the text exists in the north of the fort, on the outer wall. The Rāmpol Gate mentioned in the text is indeed inside the fort.
5 . *Ma'āser*, *op. cit.*, p. 28.
6. Patil, *op. cit.*, p. 23, gives 1406-07 as the date whereas Dilāwar Khān dies in 1405.

The Jājnagar Gate, "to the east of Shādiābād",[7] is undoubtedly the one that is now called Jahāngirpur. This is the most oriental of the gates of Mandu. It is through this gate that in 1408 Hushang Shāh entered Mandu.[8]

Dilāwar Khān Mosque and Dowlat-khāna

The mosque of Dilāwar Khān is, without doubt, the most ancient among the monuments of the Muslim period in Mandu. It seems natural that it is around this important edifice that the official buildings, the palace and the *madrasa* are situated. Until the completion of the new mosque in 1441, it is this which was the *Jāma^c Masjid* of Mandu, a fact that is confirmed by an incident reported in the *Ma'āser*: in 839/1435, at the beginning of the reign of Maḥmud Khalji, before the king had been able to consolidate his newly acquired power, the ex-officers of Hushang Shāh made an attempt to penetrate into the palace (*dowlat-khāna*) by scaling the walls of the Jāmaᶜ Masjid.[9] This mosque attached to the palace could be none other than the one built by Dilāwar Khān around 1405.

A *madrasa* also appears in proximity of the mosque. Our chronicler informs us that in 837/1434 at the death of Hushang Shāh, "his corpse was placed in the *madrasa* and his son Ghazani Khān entered into the *dowlat-khāna*".[10]

It is again in the same *dowlat-khāna* that the "coup d'état" by the future Maḥmud took place. It was here that he poisoned the king Ghazani Khān, son of Hushang, seizing power in place of Masᶜud Khān, son of the former, thus establishing the Khalji dynasty. This palace is also called *kushk-e dowlat*.[11]

Thus to all appearances, the walls which touch those of the *qibla* in Dilāwar's mosque belong to the first royal palace of Mandu.

Jāmaᶜ Masjid

The present Jāmaᶜ Masjid owes its foundation to Hushang Shāh, even though it was completed only under the reign of Maḥmud. It is certainly the most beautiful monument of Mandu. From 1441 onwards it replaced Dilāwar Khān's mosque as the Jāmaᶜ Masjid.

7. *Ma'āser, op. cit.*, p. 18.
8. *Ibid.*
9. *Ibid.*, p. 29.
10. *Ibid.*, p. 26.
11. *Ibid.*, p. 28.

"At this time, he ordered the completion of the Jāma[c] Masjid situated near the Rāmpol Gate which had been begun under the order of Hushang Shāh. In the year 841/1438-39, master builders began the work. In very little time, two hundred and thirty cupolas [resting on] three hundred and eighty stone columns were erected. The form given to the *maqsura* dome was comparable to the orb of the sky. A large *miḥrāb* and a superb *minbar* were also constructed. The brilliant purity of its dais bespoke the purity of the divine croyance and the solidity of the pillars demonstrated the force of the sovereign's faith."[12]

Hushang Shāh's Tomb

"Skilled architects traced the plans of the building on the *qibla* side of the mosque and in the centre [of this place], a large domed building was constructed (...) in little time."[13]

The tomb of Hushang Shāh has been admired since by numerous visitors. Fereshta mentions it[14] and the architects Loṭf-allāh Mohandes, son of Ostād Aḥmad (Shāh Jahān's architect), Khwāja Jādu Rāy, Ostād Shiv Rām and Ostād Ḥāmed have left an inscription here dated 1070/1659.

The *Ma'āṯer* also mentions that "the king decided to construct a building meant as a rest house for travellers behind the mosque of Shādiābād, at the site called Khuldābād ...".[15] This is the portico comprising three galleries supported by rows of pillars which is situated on the western side of the courtyard in the tomb of Hushang Shāh.

The 'Golden Palace'

"At the beginning of the month of Rabi' al-avval of the year 844/1441, the king ordered the construction of the Golden Palace and from the depths of the lake called Munj Talāo he had high columns and arches of stone erected (...) Above the arches, a flat roof was laid. Artists called by the king from India and Khorāsān, constructed the palace (...) This building of Shādiābād is such that it was nicknamed *Jennat al-Hend* and compared to a second paradise (...)".[16]

---

12. *Ibid.*, p. 40: Description of the construction of the Jāma[c] Masjid and the *Rowze-ye moqaddase*. Fereshta (*Tārikh-i Firishta*, English Transl., Vol. IV, p. 123) says: "In the year 843 (A.D. 1439), he [Solṭān Maḥmud] commenced the repairs of the palace of the late Sooltan Hooshung [Solṭān Hushang] and the musjid built in commemoration of that monarch, near the Rampoora gate. This splendid edifice has two hundred and thirty minarets [sic] and three hundred and sixty arches". See also the description of this monument in P. Brown, *Indian Architecture*, pp. 61-2 and in Jahāngir, *Tūzuk-i Jahāngiri*, English Transl. A. Rogers, Repr., New Delhi, 1989, Vol. I, p. 365.
13. *Ma'āṯer*, *op. cit.*, p. 41: Tomb of Hushang Shāh.
14. Fereshta, *op. cit*, Vol. IV, p. 114.
15. *Ma'āṯer*, *op. cit.*, p. 61.
16. *Ibid.*, p. 58: Construction of the Golden Palace.

The "Golden Palace" is also named in the text as the place where Maḥmud stayed on his return from compaigns.[17]

Undoubtedly the building which would correspond best with this description is the Jahāz Mahal, specially if we indeed imagine it "with a flat roof" as mentioned in the text. Actually, the pavilions of the terrace are datable from the reign of Ghiyāṯ al-din. As for the monumental staircase, it forms part of the transformations made by Jahāngir to the building and its garden.[18] It is difficult nowadays to imagine this palace as 'golden', as a large part of its facade is no longer covered with coloured glazed tiles.

According to certains authors, some of the architectural forms executed in Mandu are Hindu motifs "deliberately incorporated in the architecture".[19] An example of this is the labyrinth of canals in serpentine form which adorns the terrace of Jahāz Mahal. This architectural motif recurs in the Nīlkanṭh pavilion belonging to the Moghul period. It is, however, interesting to note that this serpentine canal can also be seen in the hospital-mosque of Divrije, in Turkey, which dates back to the Seljukian period.[20] Similarly, certain Persian miniatures also represent canals having this form.[21] Lotus shaped ponds are another example of motifs presumed to be 'Hindu' in origin. Not far from the Jahāz Mahal, the Jal Mahal has a large pond in the shape of a lotus in front; several ponds possessing this form have been discovered in Lashkari Bāzār. A recent sales catalogue of a London antique shop also displays

17. *Ibid.*, pp. 76 and 102

18. Jahāngir arrived in Mandu on 23 Esfand/6 March 1617. He had sent the architect ᶜAbd-al Karim ahead of him in order to repair the old buildings and to reconstruct some of them. 3,00,00 rupees or 2,000 Persian tomans were spent on this. On the 28th Esfand, ᶜAbdul Karim was paid for the (re-?)construction of the monuments of Mandu and received the title of Maᶜmur Khān (Jahāngir, *op. cit.*, Vol. I, p. 364). This same Maᶜmur Khān was sent, a little later, to Lahore to complete the construction of the palace there (*Ibid.*, pp. 375-6). Several monuments of Mandu are attributed to Jahāngir, including the Nāhar-jharokhā or the Hāthi-pol. On 20 Mehr 1026/12 October 1617, Prince Khorram, the future Shāh Jahān was welcomed by his father in a *jharokhā* at Mandu (*Ibid.*, pp. 393-4; see also p. 399); perhaps it refers to the Nāhar-jharokhā ? It is probably during this period that repairs and additions were made notably in the 'Jahāz Mahal'. In fact, Jahāngir tells us that his wife Nur Jahān resided in a palace surrounded by lakes, probably the 'Jahāz Mahal'. Some grand parties were given here. (*Ibid.*, pp. 385 and 397).

19. See E. Moynihan, *Paradise as a Garden, in Persia and Mughal India* (1979), London, 1982, p. 94.

20. See T. Burkhardt, *L'art de l'Islam,* Paris, 1985, p. 272, photo R. Michaud.

21. See for example a *Khamsa* of Neẓāmi, conserved at the Topkapi Museum (H.762/K.412), copied at Tabriz in 886/1481, fol. 196 (Bahrām at the house of the Princess of the white pavilion); reproduced in I. Stchoukine, *Les peintures des manuscrits de la Khamse de Nezāmi au Topkapi Sarayi Müzesi*, Paris, 1977, pl. XLVII.

a fountain of the Ghaznavid period with polylobed contours.[22] There is thus no reason to see in these forms examples of Hindu motifs transposed 'surreptitiously' into Muslim architecture.

Ashrafi Mahal

The monument now known by the name of Ashrafi Mahal is, in fact, a *madrasa* begun probably by Hushang Shāh[23] and continued by Maḥmud.

> "In the year 845/1442, when the king had completed the task of subjugating the country (...) he ordered the construction of a *madrasa* which was called *Bām-e behesht* and the minaret known by the name of *ᶜalam-e eslām* (The Standard of Islam). Engineers traced the plans opposite the Jāmaᶜ Masjid, near the Rāmpol Gate. Artisans and artists from Khorāsān and Hindustān assembled in the capital and in little time set to work. They did not spare any ornamentation. The four walls were adorned with designs in coloured stone - red cornelian, green jade, blue onyx, yellow *sang-e maryam*, white alabaster, black marble and still others. Persian artisans made inscriptions of great beauty on the doors, on the walls and on the ceiling in *s̱uls̱* and *moḥaqqaq* characters with glazed tiles (*kāshi-kāri*). They deployed more science in the lines of the arabesques than the engineers were capable of conceiving. They also made designs of polychrome glazed tiles on the upper level of the dome.
>
> To the left and the right, a *khāneqāh* and a *madrasa* were constructed where savants and illustrious men assembled every day and where students of theology pursued their research (...) On the left, there is the *khāneqāh* where travellers receive the benefits of charity. On its northern extremity a minaret rises high beyond the reach of birds (...) At the back, on the eastern side, a garden was built. It is now already some twenty and odd years that the artists have been working at the construction and the embellishment of these buildings, but the work is not yet over."[24]

The author of the *Ma'ās̱er* concluded his book in 872/1467-68, and did not live to see the completion of this monument. Maḥmud himself died a year later (873/1469). It is probable that the monument was later turned into a tomb and completed by Ghiyās̱ al-din. However, no such

---

22. See Spink & Son, *Indian and Islamic Works of Art*, Londres, 1992, p. 6.
23. *Ma'ās̱er*, *op. cit.*, p. 23.
24. *Ibid.*, pp. 45-6: Construction of the *madrasa Bām-e behesht*. Although there is no doubt that the monument in question is the 'minaret' *Standard of Islam*, the famous 'Tower of Victory' constructed by Maḥmud on his return from Chittor, in 846/1443 is not mentioned by this name by our author. Fereshta, *op. cit.*, Vol. IV, pp. 126-7 signals: "...he built a beautiful *pillar* [sic] seven stories high, in front of a college, which he founded opposite the musjid of Sooltan Hooshung".

intention is communicated anywhere in our text. Three tombs aligned on a north-south axis occupy the centre of a mortuary hall, whose dome has collapsed. Strangely, but obviously for reasons of symmetry, the entrance is situated on the western side, facing the entry of the mosque. Therefore the monument does not possess a *miḥrāb*. The tomb in the middle is indoubtedly that of Maḥmud; the one towards the north belongs to Ghiyās̱ al-din; in the south we can make out the emplacement of a tomb though it has disappeared. It was probably the tomb of Nāṣer al-din destroyed by Jahāngir.[25] Akbar had earlier got this monument repaired, as is testified by an inscription in the eastern niche. Dated Muḥarram 1014/May-June 1605, this inscription indicates that the restoration was effected by a certain Moḥammad Tāher b. Solṭān ᶜAli Sabzevāri.[26]

The 'Tower of Victory' called in the text '*the standard of Islam*', is now almost entirely destroyed. Only the base and the initial portion of the staircase remain. Jahāngir visited this monument and had it restored. He says about this edifice: "It has seven storeys, and in each storey there are four chambers (*suffa*) containing four windows. The height of this tower (*minār*) is 54 1/2 cubits, and its circumference 50 yards (*gaz*). There are 171 steps from the ground to the seventh storey. In going and returning I scattered 1400 rupees."[27]

Construction of the Hospital

> "In the year 846/1443, the king ordered the construction (or restoration) of the hospital (...). Artists from diverse origins were employed for this work and they built a pharmacy. Experienced pharmacists were sent to the four corners of the inhabited world to look for remedies indispensable to both Hindu and Muslim physicians (...); a *ḥammām* was also constructed (...)[28] The best physicians were looked for, among whom Mowlānā Fażl-allāh Maḥfuẓ was one (...)."[29]

No indication concerning the localisation of this hospital is available.

---

25. Jahāngir, *op. cit.*, Vol. I, p. 365. As we indicate a little later (See Note 32), it is probable that Malik Moghis̱ was also buried in this monument.

26. Abu al-Fażl mentions an "octagonal" tower and the tombs of the Khalji Kings, *Ā'in-e Akbari*, English Transl., *The Ā'in-i Akbarī by Abu l-Fazl Allami* (1927-49),Three Vols., Vol. II, Transl. H.S. Jarrett, Repr., Delhi, 1989, p. 208.

27. Jahāngir, *op. cit.*, Vol. I, pp. 381-2.

28. One of the *ḥammāms* which can still be seen at Mandu is in the *dowlat-khāne*, in the Royal Enclosure. Another, unquestionably from the Mughal period, is situated on the banks of the Lal Bangla tank.

29. *Ma'ās̱er*, *op. cit.*, p. 64. Fereshta, *op. cit.*, Vol. IV, p. 129, gives 849/1445 as the date of the construction of the hospital and indicates that Mowlānā Fażl-allāh, director of the hospital, was the personal physician of Maḥmud.

1. Mandu, Delhi Gate

2. Mandu, Masjid of Dilāwar Khān

7. Mandu, Ashrafi Mahal. The so-called Tower of Victory

8. Mandu, Masjid of Malik Moghis

6. Mandu, Ashrafi Mahal

5. Mandu, Jāma[c] Masjid

Mosque of Malik Moghis̲

Curiously, the *Ma'ās̲er* does not mention this mosque although it was constructed by the father of Maḥmud Khalji. The toponym Moghis̲pur is cited once in the text.[30] However, it is not possible to ascertain whether it refers to this part of Mandu.

The mosque of Malik Moghis̲ was constructed near the Sāgar lake in 835/1432, as indicated by an inscription above the principal entry. The majestic size and antiquity of this monument make it a serious rival of the Dilāwar mosque. It is probable that this mosque formed the centre of Khalji headquarters even before Maḥmud seized power in 1435. A caravanserail dated 1437 faces the mosque. Adjoining the mosque are the ruins of a large building. Perhaps these belong to the *Dār al-Shafā* or a *madrasa*. Not far from the mosque are situated numerous tombs. It should be noted that there is no reference in the *Ma'ās̲er* to the tomb of Malik Moghis̲, although it mentions the one built for his father, Malik ᶜAli Shir at Dhār.[31] According to the author of the note on Malik Moghis̲ in the *Encyclopedia of Islam*, this personage is burried in the tomb of the Khaljis.[32]

It is probable that under Hushang Shāh, the Khalji clan lived together at a distance from the Ghori royal family. It is also likely that a large part of Hushang Shāh's army lived at this site. In fact, this area is situated close to the Sāgar lake, at a safe distance from the Royal Enclave. Its central position in the fort allows for rapid movement towards the fortifications, to defend the gates in case of attack. It is certain that during the period when the *Ma'ās̲er* was being written, the geographical separation between the Ghoris and the Khaljis no longer existed.

Jahāngir mentions the Sāgar lake and the monuments as well as an *idgāh* situated between the lake and the Nīlkanṭh pavilion.[33]

Other Towns of Mālwa: Nālcha

In the *Ma'ās̲er-e Maḥmudshāhi* we find the description of a palace with gardens constructed by Maḥmud Khalji around a huge tank at Nālcha, about ten kilometres from Mandu:

"The king ordered the construction of the Jahān-namā palace which is

30. *Ibid.*, p. 25.
31. *Ibid.*, p. 58.
32. See Abdus Subhan, art. 'Malik Mug̲h̲ith̲', in *Encyclopédie de l'Islam*², Vol. VI, p. 256.
33. Jahāngir, *op. cit.*, Vol. I, pp. 371, 384 and 386. This *idgāh* still exists; it is situated at a height, between the Rewā Kuṇḍ and Nīlkanṭh.

> a marvel among the palaces of the world. Truly, the garden and the palace of Jahān-namā, [along with] the tank and the dome at Nālcha are architectural feats and wonders. In the year 846/1442, he ordered the construction of a garden at Nālcha, at a distance of three *koruh* from Shādiābād (Mandu). Trees were planted along the sides of each canal and, along the edges of each parterre, flowers were sown. In the centre of the garden, a palace named Jahān-namā was constructed. On the side of the garden, at the foot of the palace, a pond of alabaster was built, which was reinforced at the edges by master stone cutters (*sang-bast*). In the middle of the tank a building with a dome was constructed. From the stone edges of this tank, a bridge across the water was built leading upto this building, and from the two arms of the bridge, a marble passage measuring the height of a man was constructed."[34]

As a matter of fact, the tank at Nālcha is much anterior to Maḥmud Khalji. It is a huge reservoir from the Paramāra period (11th-12th centuries), with sides measuring about 365 metres and bounded by basalt *ghāṭ*s. The eastern and western sides of the tank are built on dams about 60 metres wide. On its western side, the tank is linked to an initial reservoir, now dry, by a partially subterranean canal which divides itself into a *trishūl* (symbol of Shiva) and opens into the tank in the form of three carved apertures. At the place where the canal joins the tank, the remains of a Hindu temple can be seen. On the eastern side, below the barrage, is another reservoir with *ghāṭ*s on the southern side and a pillar holding a miniature temple dedicated to Nāga - protector of the place. It is thus a pre-Islamic site of occupation that was restituted and completed by Maḥmud Khalji.

In fact, it appears that from the Ghori period this site was occupied, in particular by Najm al-din Qalandar Ghauṡ-e Dahr who died in 1432. This member of the *qalandar* brotherhood settled down by the tank during the reign of Hushang Shāh.[35] Well preserved till today, his tomb is situated on the eastern side of the tank.

A palace complex occupying about half the southern side of the tank includes some buildings which can be attributed to the period of Maḥmud, notably a large domed pavilion and a group of four small pavilions arranged around a square pond. The bridge and the island described in the text still exist but without the least trace of the marble on the bridge. As for the domed pavilion, only the base survives. The small mosque made of inexpensive material on the northern side of the

---

34. *Ma'āṡer*, *op. cit.*, p. 48: Construction of the palace of *Jahān-namā*, the *Delgoshāh* garden and the lake of Nālcha.

35. See Day, *op. cit.*, p. 66. See also A.M. Schimmel, *Islam in the Indian Subcontinent*, Leiden, 1980, pp. 39-40.

tank belongs certainly to a slightly later period.

In 871/1467, Maḥmud preceded Sheykh Nur al-din at Nālcha and received him on the banks of the "*ḥowż-e khāṣ*"; "here he founded the *madrasa Dār al-Ḥadis̱*".[36] Fereshta and Jahāngir also mention the tank at Nālcha which fell on the route from Dhār to Mandu.[37]

Dipālpur

Seventy kilometres to the north of Mandu, the Dipālpur lake is also a work of the pre-Muslim period. A domed pavilion (*gonbad*) and a *chautara* were erected here by Maḥmud:

> Among the inventions of the sovereign there is one domed pavilion which he got constructed in the centre of the lake at Dipālpur. What is astonishing is that from the bottom of this lake, which appears more like an immense sea, he raised a building and a platform (*chautara*) strongly reinforced with mortar and stone and very similar to the lighthouse in Alexandria; on its side, a domed pavilion was erected. This palace which has no parallel in the world was completed in 846/1443."[38]

Jahāngir halted by the side of this lake which he calls "Debālpur Bheriyā", but he makes no mention of any building.[39]

Dhār

The only monument of Dhār mentionned in the *Ma'āṯer* is the tomb of the grandfather of Maḥmud, Malik ᶜAli Shir:

> "Towards the middle of the year 854/1450-51, the King ordered the restoration (or construction) of the tomb of Malik ᶜAli Shir, as well as of a *madrasa* and a *khāneqāh* (...). At Jennatābād Dhār, the architects completed a monument. Hermits assembled in this tomb; this tomb was also a *khāneqāh*, where travellers halted (...); it was also a meeting place for savants."[40]

However, this tomb does not appear to have been identified. According to a popular belief, the tomb opposite that of Kamāl al-din Mālawi, disciple of Neẓām al-din Chishti is the tomb of Maḥmud himself. If this belief seems absurd since the tomb of Maḥmud in Mandu is well known, it would be reasonable, on the contrary, to identify this tomb as that of Malik ᶜAli Shir. In any case, an inscription placed above

36. *Ma'āṯer*, *op. cit.*, p. 118.

37. Briefly mentioned by Fereshta (*op. cit.*, Vol. IV, p. 125), who gives 845/1441 as the date of these works; he also mentions the construction of mosques at Nālcha. See also Jahāngir, *op. cit.*, Vol. I, p. 361.

38. *Ma'āṯer*, *op. cit.*, pp. 48-9: The *chautara*, the dome and the tank of Dipālpur.

39. Jahāngir, *op. cit.*, Vol. I, pp. 359-60.

40. *Ma'āṯer*, *op. cit.*, p. 58: Restoration - or construction - of the tomb of Malik ᶜAli Shir.

the entry of the tomb of Kamāl al-din, dated 861/1456, indicates that this monument was restored by Maḥmud.[41]

Ujjain

"Among the marvellous inventions of this sovereign (...) there is the Nur Palace. This is situated in the town of Ujjain, which is one of the mainstays of the State of Mālwa. In the ancient times it was the capital of the rājahs of India and the residence of Rājah Bekramājit. It is here that the King ordered the construction of a palace on a hilltop (...)

They constructed four marble vaults
Which rested on nine stone vaults.

They gave to the ceiling the form of a sublime dome erected without columns following the rules of wisdom. On the four pillars (sides) of its sublime ceiling, they constructed four more domes. Each courtyard (*pishgāh*) was fit for a king and each yard (*ṣaḥn*) was a paradise illuminating the spirit. All around (the palace) large rose beds were planted.

It is not surprising that light distanced itself from paradise.
When the construction of the Nur Palace was begun by royal order.
It was completed in the year eight hundred and fifty four (1450),
By royal order, which makes the enemy flee and caresses the friend."[42]

This palace of Ujjain is mentioned again on the occasions when Maḥmud passed this place on way to Chittor, in 858/1454 and then in 871/1467.[43]

Chanderi: Kushk Mahal

"When the monsoon was approaching (...), the King directed himself towards Chanderi and decided to settle down in its neighbourhood. After a few days, the enlightened mind (the King), ordered the construction of a palace in the gracious town of Fatḥābād. In reality, this palace founded by him is more beautiful than Dār al-Sorur (the City of Joy).[44] Excellent engineers with incomparable genius beautified and adorned it. In imitation of the seven levels of the sky, seven storeys were constructed. Painters and decorators represented all kinds of marvellous figures. It is indeed an unusual period when architects (take immense pains ?) in finishing buildings. They are still engaged in the construction of this building."[45]

---

41. See J. Burton-Page, art. 'Dhār', monuments, in *Encyclopédie de l'Islam*^{2}, Vol. II, p. 226.
42. *Ma'āser*, *op. cit.*, p. 59: Construction of the Nur Palace at Ujjain.
43. *Ibid.*, pp. 81, 82, 121.
44. Does it amount to a play of words ? *Shādiābād* also signifies "the city of joy".
45. *Ma'āser*, *op. cit.*, p. 61: Construction of the palace of Fathābād. Fereshta (*op. cit.*, Vol. IV, p. 128) mentions the construction of this building.

S.A. Rahim indicates four inscriptions found in the Kushk Mahal of Chanderi. One of them is dated 895/1489.[46] According to the author of the *Ma'āṣer*, although the building was begun in 1445, it had still not been completed at the time when he was writing (1467-68). There is, however, an interval of twenty years between the date of this inscription and the text of ᶜAli b. Maḥmud Kermāni. Of the four inscriptions three are mason marks and cite the name of one Malik Mallu Solṭāni. They are not dated. The fourth, dated 1489, is a graffiti. It is quite probable that this monument was never completed.

Conclusion

ᶜAli b. Maḥmud Kermāni offers us, with his work, a lively account of Maḥmud Khalji's reign. Beyond the description of events, one is invited to witness the process leading to the formation and the consolidation of the Khalji dynasty. The text of the *Ma'āṣer* is full of references to artisans, *sheykh*s, and physicians hailing, like our author, "from India and Khorāsān" who came to contribute to the fulfilment of royal ambitions. Some others, less fortunate, came as part of war booty, as is the case of the painter Mowlānā Moghis̱ al-din Naqqāsh or the jeweller Mowlānā Moḥammad Almās Tarrāsh.[47] These men from diverse origins who gathered at Mandu succeeded in producing artistic creations with a distinctively original flavour by blending different styles and influences. This was to be particularly well illustrated during the reign of Ghiyās̱ al-din. During this period, the architecture shows the use of glazed tiles of Iranian influence framed in local creations, and the arts of the book as well reflect the blend of local and Iranian styles.

Translated from French by Rashmi Patni

REFERENCES

Abu al-Faẓl Allami, *Ā'in-e Akbari*; English Transl., *The Ā'īn-i Akbarī by Abu l-Fazl Allami* (1927-49), Three Vols., Vol. II, Transl. H.S. Jarrett, Repr., Delhi: Low Price Publications, 1989.

Abdus Subhan, art. 'Malik Mughi̲th̲', in *Encyclopédie de l'Islam*[2],

46. *Epigraphica Indica*, Arabic and Persian Supplement (1965), Delhi, 1987, pp. 19-22.

47. *Ma'āṣer*, *op. cit.*, p. 97.

Leiden: E.J. Brill, Vol. VI, p. 256.

ᶜAli b. Maḥmud al-Kermāni, *Ma'āser-e Maḥmudshāhi*, ed. Nurulḥasan Anṣāri, Delhi: Jamal Printing Press, 1968.

Brown, Percy, *Indian Architecture (Islamic Period)*, Bombay: Taraporevala, 1956.

Burkhardt, Titus, *L'art de l'Islam*, Paris: Sindbad, 1985.

Burton-Page, J., art. 'Dhār', monuments, in *Encyclopédie de l'Islam²*, Leiden: E.J. Brill, Vol. II, p. 226.

Day, Upendra Nath, *Medieval Malwa: A Political & Cultural History, 1401-1562*, Delhi: Munshi Ram Manohar Lal, 1965.

Encyclopédie de l'Islam (*EI²*), Six Vols. published, Leiden: E.J. Brill, 1960-.

Epigraphica Indica, Arabic and Persian Supplement (1965), Delhi: Archeological Survey of India, 1987.

Fereshta, Moḥammad Qāsem, *Tārikh-i Firishta*, English Transl. John Briggs, *History of the Rise of the Mahommedan Power in India, Till the Year A.D. 1612*, (1829), Four Vols., Repr., Delhi: Atlantic Publishers & Distributors, 1989. (Vol. IV)

Jahāngir, *Tūzuk-i Jahāngiri or Memoirs of Jahāngir* (1909-14), English Transl. A. Rogers, ed. H. Beveridge, Repr., Two Vols. in One, New Delhi: Low Price Publications, 1989.

Moynihan, Elizabeth B., *Paradise as a Garden in Persia and Mughal India* (1979), Paperback edn., London: Scolar Press, 1982.

Patil, D.R., *Mandu*, New Delhi: Archeological Survey of India, 1982.

Schimmel, Annemarie, *Islam in the Indian Subcontinent*, Leiden: E.J. Brill, 1980.

Spink & Son, *Indian and Islamic Works of Art*, London: Spink, 1992.

Stchoukine, Ivan, *Les peintures des manuscrits de la Khamse de Nezāmi au Topkapi Sarayi Müzesi*, Paris: Geuthner, 1977.

3

An Unpublished Manuscript from the Atelier of the Emperor Humāyūn, the Khamsa Smith-Lesouëf 216 of the Bibliothèque Nationale

FRANCIS RICHARD

It is well known that the life of Humāyūn, son of the founder of the Mughal Empire, was turbulent, alternating between successes and setbacks. Nāṣir al-Dīn Muḥammad Humāyūn was born in 1508, at Kabul, and succeeded his father to the throne of Agra in 1530.[1] In 1543, he was forced to leave India, after suffering a total rout in the military campaign against Shēr Khān Sūr. His three step brothers, ᶜAskarī, Hīndal and especially Kāmrān, who had received Kabul as a fief from Humāyūn, were sometimes his allies; they were more often his opponents, having serious and sometimes violent differences of opinion with Humāyūn. Driven away from his Indian empire, Humāyūn was forced to spend the year 1544 in Iran, first at Herat and then at Qazvin. Here, for sometime, Humāyūn enjoyed the hospitality of Shāh Ṭahmāsb, who also offered him the assistance of some troops. Thereafter, Humāyūn proceeded to Tabriz, and, after a brief stay, he went to Kandahar in 1545, and then on to Kabul, which he finally won back from Kāmrān. Kabul was the favourite city of his father, Bābur, who had resided there, and who had desired to be buried there. Historians are of the opinion that Humāyūn's short exile of a few months in Iran, where he was profoundly impressed by the *scriptoria* and the Safavid royal ateliers, had a decisive influence on the growth of Mughal art, especially painting. After spending a few years waging wars around Kabul, he finally undertook the reconquest of India in 1554, reoccupying the throne of Delhi in 1555. However, shortly thereafter, in January 1556, he died of an accident on the terrace of the library in the Delhi palace. His tomb in Delhi is an imposing symbol of the re-established Mughal power.

1. Some elements for Humāyūn's biography can be found in S. Digby's article "Humāyūn", *Encyclopédie de l'Islam*, Vol. III, 49-50, 2nd edn., 1962, pp. 595-7.

A poet in Persian,[2] and a lover of books like his Timurid ancestors, Humāyūn is said to have transported his library with him in trunks loaded on camels. It is said[3] that the books found by Bābur at the time of the siege of Milwat in 1526, were distributed by him, after examination, between Humāyūn and Kāmrān. However, it is very difficult to form an exact idea of the size of Humāyūn's library today. Though it is certain that Humāyūn inherited a large part of the library of Bābur and of his Timurid ancestors, very few volumes are in fact easily identifiable now as having actually belonged to Humāyūn. We are aware of the magnificent Timurid *Shāh-nāma*, with paintings copied for Muḥammad Jukī, which had belonged to Bābur, then to Humāyūn, and was subsequently handed down to Akbar and his successors, and bears their respective stamps. Humāyūn's stamp[4] had a circular form, and carried the device *Humāyūn b. Muḥammad Bābur Padishāh al-Ghāzī*. One knows also of a *Timur-nāma* calligraphed by Sulṭān ᶜAlī Mashhadī, and illustrated by Bihzād, which belonged to Humāyūn's library, and which probably disappeared from it during its pillage by Gujarati soldiers in 1536.[5] However, it is far from established that all the Timurid manuscripts which figured in the libraries of the later Mughals were already in Humāyūn's library. Since much of the collection was subsequently scattered, a detailed research in this area still remains to be done.[6]

Humāyūn was a distinguished patron of the arts throughout his reign. Amongst his panegyrists was Navīdī of Neyshabur (d. 973/1565), a poet who was also in his service. It appears that when Humāyūn left Iran, the poet Shauqī Tabrizī accompanied him to Kabul, where he died in 954/

2. D.N. Marshall, *Mughals in India, I. Manuscripts*, London, 1967, N° 179, p. 54 and N° 654, p. 189; ᶜA. Khayyāmpūr, *Farhang-i Sukhanvarān*, Tabriz, 1340 AH, p. 633; Ḥ. Ḥasan, *Researches in Persian Literature*, Hyderabad, 1958.

3. Sh. Abdul Aziz, *The Imperial Library of the Mughuls*, Delhi, Repr., 1974, pp. 56-7.

4. Manuscript of the Royal Asiatic Society of London, described and reproduced by J.V.S. Wilkinson and L. Binyon, *The Shāh-nāmah of Firdausī*, London, 1931.

5. C. Huart, *Les Calligraphes et les Miniaturistes de l'Orient musulman*, Paris, 1908, p. 222 (to be compared with the *Akbar-nāma*, Transl. H. Beveridge, Vol. I, Calcutta, 1907, pp. 309-10). Today, it is generally believed that this manuscript is the same as the *Ẓafar-nāma*, which was added to Akbar's library some years later. Moreover, according to the account in the *Akbar-nāma* (*ibid*., p. 571), some royal books stored in trunks were lost by Humāyūn during the battle of Qibtchaq in 1550 and were recovered some months later in a good state, at the conclusion of another battle against Kāmrān and his troops.

6. Regarding this subject, see the catalogue of M. Brand and G.D. Lowry, *Akbar's India. Art from the Mughal City of Victory*, New York, 1985, where it has been discussed on several occasions. Cf. also J.P. Losty, *The Art of the Book in India*, London, 1982, pp. 74-85. The *Dīvān* of Ḥāfiẓ, N° 151 of the Bankipur Library bears annotations by Humāyūn himself with the date of 962/1555.

1547. The Indian *tadhkirāt* may also provide names of some poets who composed verses for Humāyūn. It is possible and interesting to prepare a list of works dedicated to Humāyūn, including those which were composed at his command. Such a list would also reveal a number of historical and scientific books[7] and even if this list were somewhat modest, it would help us to have a better understanding of Humāyūn's personality and his passion for astronomy (or astrology), and love of science and literature. Not only had he collected a number of men of letters in his court, but he, like all the Timurids, also had a librarian (*kitābdār*) in his service, whose duty was to preserve the manuscripts, and have them copied. According to the *Akbar-nāma*, Humāyūn's first *kitābdār*, Darvīsh ᶜAlī was fatally wounded at Ujjain in 1536; the *Humāyūn-nāma* mentions that Mullā Surkh had been his *kitābdār* until his betrayal in 1541; according to *Akbar-nāma*, during Humāyūn's exile, it was Mullā Balāl who was the faithful librarian of the emperor, and finally, perhaps Niẓām or his son Bahādur had also served as his librarian.[8]

We do not have much information about the calligraphers of this

---

7. As an example, (Comp. F. Keshavarz, *A Descriptive and Analytical Catalogue of Persian Manuscripts in the Library of the Wellcome Institute*, London, 1986, pp. 56, 264, etc.) Yūsuf b. M. Ṭabīb Khurāsānī Yūsufī, poet and physician who died around 950/1543, dedicated the medical treatise *Riyāẓ al-Adviyah* to Humāyūn in 1539, with the signature "Ḥakīm Yūsufī *munshī* of Humāyūn" the *Badāᶜī al-Inshā*. One may also cite a treatise on the subject of precious stones dedicated to Humāyūn in 1529, before his accession, by Muḥ. b. Ashraf Rustamdārī (C.A. Storey, *Persian Literature. A Bio-bibliographical Survey*, Vol. II, 2, London, 1971, p. 453), a commentary on the Logic of Jurjānī dedicated to Humāyūn by Abū'l-Baqā Ḥusaynī (Aḥmad Munzavī, *A Comprehensive Catalogue of Persian Manuscripts in Pakistan*, Vol. II, Islamabad, 1984, p. 929, N° 1575), a Persian translation of the Sanskrit *Hitopadeśa* done for him by Muftī al-Mulk (Munzavī, *op. cit.*, IV, 1984, pp. 2187-8, N° 3955 and VI, 1987, pp. 977-9), or the encyclopedia entitled *Javāhir al-ᶜUlūm-i Humāyūnī*, c. 1555, compiled by M. Fāẓil b. ᶜAlī Miskīnī Qāẓī Samarqandī (Storey, *op. cit.*, Vol. II, 2, 1971, pp. 350-9). A treatise on music, the *Davāzdah Maqām* of Ḥaydar Tuniyānī, was dedicated to Humāyūn (Marshall, *op. cit.*, N° 578, p. 171), as also the *Siyar al-ᶜĀrifīn*, the biographies of *Chishtī* sufis written by Jamālī Kanbō Dihlavī (*Ibid.*, N° 790 (1), p. 226) and the commentary on the treatise on astronomy of Qūshjī by Muṣliḥ al-Dīn Lārī (*Ibid.*, N° 1339, p. 360), who became the *ṣadr* of the emperor.

One should finally mention the historians who were in the service of Humāyūn, especially Mihtar Jauhar and Bāyazīd Bayāt, the latter having left the service of Kāmrān to serve under Humāyūn in 1545 at Kabul at the time of the seizure of the city (Storey, *op. cit.*, Vol. I, Part II, 2, London, 1933, pp. 536-40). Another historian, Ghiyāth al-Dīn Muḥammad Jāmī (Marshall, *op. cit.*, p. 152, N° 495) was also a historiographer in Humāyūn's service. Ibrāhīm b. Jarīr (Storey-Bregel', *Persidskaïa Literatura*, Vol. I, Moscow, 1972, p. 403) wrote a *Tārīkh-i Humāyūnī* around 1549-50. Of course, mention must also be made of the famous Khwānd-Amīr who after having been in the service of Bābur served Humāyūn until his death in the year 942/1535-36.

8. Abdul Aziz, *op. cit.*, p. 59; Abū l-Fadhl, *Akbar-Nāma*, Transl. H. Beveridge, *op. cit.*, Vol. I, pp. 318 and 452.

period. Humāyūn had two important persons working under him to draft official Persian documents of the empire. These persons later also worked under Akbar, and one of them, *Mīr Munshī* Muḥammad Asghar Ashraf Khān (d. 973/1565 or 983/1575-76) was an accomplished poet and a calligrapher in different styles of writing, especially in the Nastaᶜlīq style.[9] The other, called Mīr Qāsim b. Mīr Manṣūr, came from Iran after Humāyūn's exile; he was a *munshī* skilled in writing in the Taᶜlīq style.[10] We have not been able to find any mention of calligraphers employed by Humāyūn to copy manuscripts.

It is beyond doubt that Humāyūn had acquired a taste for painting fairly early in his life and that he already had artists in his service before his exile from India. But no work belonging to this period is known with certainty. While in Iran, Humāyūn was fascinated by the royal ateliers of Tabriz and had met reputed Iranian artists. Soon after, when he settled down in or around Kabul, during the period 1550-55, he rapidly conceived the project to produce a monumental *Ḥamza-nāma* or *Dāstān-i Amīr Ḥamza*,[11] comprising of large paintings on cloth. This project was ultimately completed by Akbar.

One of Humāyūn's first actions, after he regained control over Kandahar and then Kabul, was to take advantage of the state of the mecenate of Shāh Ṭahmāsb, who had considerably reduced the activity of his royal ateliers (*kitābkhāna*), and to invite two of the Shāh's artists to his court.[12] It was thus that the two famous painters ᶜAbd al-Ṣamad Shīrīn Qalam Shīrāzī, who was also a good calligrapher,[13] and Mīr

9. Abdul Aziz, *op. cit.*, p. 21; M. Mohiuddin, *The Chancellery and Persian Epistolography under the Mughals, from Bābur to Shāh Jahān, 1526-1658...* , Calcutta, 1971, pp. 32-3; M. Bayānī, *Ahvāl va Āthār-i Khwushnivisān*, Vol. I, Tehran, 2nd edn., s.d. [1363/1984-85], N° 109, p. 68.

10. Qāẓī Aḥmad Qumī, *Gulistān-i Hunar*, ed. A.S. Khwānsārī, 2nd edn., Tehran, s.d., pp. 45-9.

11. L. Binyon, J.V.S. Wilkinson and B. Gray, *Persian Miniature Painting, including a Critical and Descriptive Catalogue of the Miniatures exhibited at Burlington House*, London, 1933, pp. 119-21.

12. Bāyazīd Biyāt [= Bayāt], *Tadhkira-i-Humāyūn wa Akbar*, ed. M.H. Ḥosain, Calcutta, 1941, pp. 65-9, refers to the arrival of various artists in Kabul. In the introduction to his edition of *Gulistān-i Hunar* (*op. cit.*, p. XLI), Aḥmad Suhaylī Khwānsārī lists ten artisans apparently invited by Humāyūn to the court of Ṭahmāsb, though he does not mention his sources: besides the ones named below, he refers to Maulānā Fārsī, Qāsim *mudhahhib* and Ustād Yūnus *zarrgar*.

13. For a study on ᶜAbd al-Ṣamad, see *The Houghton Shahnameh, introduced and described by Martin Bernard Dickson and Stuart Cary Welch*, Vol. I, Cambridge (Mass.), 1981, pp. 192-200; Bayānī, *op. cit.*, Vol. II, N° 546, pp. 401-2, devotes an entry to him. The *Akbar-nāma* says that Humāyūn had made his acquaintance in Tabriz. A more detailed and recent article has been devoted to him by P. Soucek, "ᶜAbd al-Ṣamad Šīrāzī", *Encyclopaedia Iranica*, Vol. I, 2, New York, 1982, pp. 162-7.

Sayyid ᶜAlī b. Mīr Manṣūr Muṣavvir,[14] known also as a poet under the pseudonym Judā'ī, arrived in Kabul in November 1549, together with the binder Fakhr. Both these artists followed Humāyūn to India in 1554.[15] These two artists had produced several paintings for the great royal *Shāh-nāma* and for the *Khamsa* of Shāh Ṭahmāsb. They practiced their art at the court of Kabul alongwith other artists, namely, Mīr Muṣavvir, who had come from Tabriz at the same time as his son Mīr Sayyid ᶜAlī, and with Maulānā Darvīsh Muḥammad [16], and Maulānā Yūsuf [17], both of whom were natives of Herat. Dūst-Muḥammad, or "Mullā Dūst" of Herat, who was obliged to leave the atelier of Tabriz because of the restrictions imposed by Shāh Ṭahmāsb, worked at first under Kāmrān and then, from 1550, under Humāyūn, whom he accompanied in 1554.[18] It is not known whether Maulānā Darvīsh Muḥammad and Maulānā Yūsuf accompanied Humāyūn to India, and there is no mention of these artists after the departure of the emperor in 1554.

Several authors have made an attempt to compile lists of the paintings done for Humāyūn or at his court.[19] Many of these have been

---

14. *The Houghton Shahnameh...*, Vol. I, pp. 178-91, contains a chapter on Mīr Sayyid ᶜAlī. Several paintings of the *Khamsa*, made for Shāh Ṭahmāsb and produced at Tabriz around 1540 have been attributed to this artist. In his analysis of the works of Mīr Sayyid ᶜAlī, in a recent article, "The Worldly Vision of Mīr Sayyid ᶜAlī" (in *Persian Masters. Five Centuries of Painting*, Bombay, 1990, pp. 85-98), A. Welch defines their specific features and shows the extreme care and attention that has been devoted in these paintings to details and objects.

15. In the catalogue *Miniatures de l'Inde impériale, les peintres de la cour d'Akbar (1556-1605)*, Paris, 1989, A. Okada illustrates well (pp. 43, 57, 60 and Nº 1 and 25) the importance of the role of Mīr Sayyid ᶜAlī and ᶜAbd al-Ṣamad in the creation and consolidation of the imperial atelier of painting of Akbar. Mīr Sayyid ᶜAlī probably left India in 1572 where as ᶜAbd al-Ṣamad was made governor of Multan in 1585.

16. "Maulānā Darvīsh Muḥammad, who is my master is a pupil of Shāh Muẓaffar; he has no equal fineness of brush, nay he has even surpassed Shāh Muẓaffar: but he is not so symmetrical or expert or refined, and he is apt to make very crude strokes (...)", T.W. Arnold, "Mīrzā Muḥammad Ḥaydar Dughlāt, on the Herat School of Painters" in Binyon, Wilkinson and Gray, *Persian Miniature Painting*, *op. cit.*, 1933, Appendix II, p. 191; W.M. Thackston, *A Century of Princes. Sources on Timurid History and Art*, Cambridge (Mass.), 1989, p. 362 (new translation; compare also the interpretation by I. Stchoukine, *Les peintures des manuscrits Tīmūrides*, Paris, 1954, p. 20 and 27).

17. Mullā Yūsuf, native of Herat, was the student of Bihzād but was a better illuminator than painter (Arnold, *loc. cit.*; Thackston, *loc. cit.*). So far, we have not been able to identify any work either by him or by Maulānā Darvīsh Muḥammad.

18. *The Houghton Shahnameh...*, Vol. I, p. 119. For the biography of Dūst-Muḥammad and his homonym, see also C. Adle, "Autopsia in Absentia, sur la date de l'introduction et de la constitution de l'Album de Bahrām Mirzā par Dūst-Mohammad, 951/1544", *Studia Iranica*, 1990, XIX, 2, pp. 219-56. More recently, C. Adle, "Les artistes nommés Dūst Moḥammad au XVIᵉ siècle", *Studia Iranica*, 1993, XXII, 2, added a lot of important and new remarks.

19. Notably Brand and Lowry, *op. cit.*, p. 23.

either published or presented. A brief enumeration is as follows:

— 'The Princes of the House of Timur assembled around Humāyūn', painting on cloth done by ᶜAbd al-Ṣamad at Kabul around 1550, preserved at the British Museum.[20]

— 'Young music-player with a young painter (Akbar as a child) in a landscape where Majnūn appears', painted by ᶜAbd al-Ṣamad in 958/1551, which is preserved in Tehran in the Gulshan Album at the Gulistan Museum.[21]

— 'Akbar presenting a miniature to his father'; done by the above mentioned artist around 1550-55 and figuring in the same Album.[22]

— 'Horseman and the squire', another painting done in 1557 by the same artist and included in the Gulshan Album of which perhaps other paintings could also be attributed to him.

— 'Young man and musician', anonymous, preserved at the St. Louis Art Museum.

— 'Young man writing', by Mīr Sayyid ᶜAlī, c. 1550-55.[23]

— 'The court of Humāyūn, with Humāyūn, Hīndal and Kāmrān in a landscape with stones', c. 1550-55, attributed to Dūst Muḥammad, and preserved in Berlin.[24]

— 'Two faces', anonymous, c. 1550-55 at the Fitzwilliam Museum.

— 'Prince hunting', c. 1550-60 from the same collection.

— Portrait of 'Shāh Abū l-Maᶜālī', by Dūst-Muḥammad, c. 1556-60.[25]

— 'Couple of musicians', c. 1550, preserved in a private collection.[26]

— 'Humāyūn in a mountain clearing', an eighteenth century copy of a painting done in c. 1553, which could be attributed to Mīr Sayyid ᶜAlī and is kept at the British Museum.[27]

In most of these paintings, Humāyūn, his young son and some of their close relatives wear the *kulāh-i Humāyūnī*, a particular headgear which Humāyūn must have adopted for himself and his entourage at the time of the capture of Kabul, or maybe before, during his stay at the

---

20. S.C. Welch, *India, Art and Culture, 1300-1900*, New York, Metropolitan Museum, 1985, N° 84, p. 142.
21. Binyon, *et al.*, *op. cit.*, N° 232.
22. *Ibid.*, N° 230.
23. Brand and Lowry, *op. cit.*, N° 6, p. 137.
24. S.C. Welch, *India...*, *op. cit.*, N° 85, pp. 144-5.
25. Brand and Lowry, *op. cit.*, N° 81, p. 157; A. Welch and S.C. Welch, *Arts of the Islamic Book. The Collection of Prince Sadruddin Aga Khan*, London-Ithaca, 1982, N° 49; Exhibition on the *Trésors de l'Islam*, Geneva, 1985, N° 118.
26. S.C. Welch, *India...*, *op. cit.*, N° 86, pp. 146-7.
27. N.M. Titley, *Persian Miniature Painting and its Influence on the Art of Turkey and India - The British Library Collections*, London, 1983, Fig. 65, pp. 88-9.

court of Tabriz, and which remained in fashion till the early years of Akbar's reign. This tall hat with a square base, folded up on the edges, and partially covered by knots made from the turban scarf, seems somewhat an adaptation of a local headgear.

Apart from these few isolated paintings, the only known manuscript is a *Khamsa* of Niẓāmī which is dated c. 1555.[28] It is preserved in the Lalbhai collection and contains several paintings, some of which are attributed to Mīr Muṣavvir.

* * *

Yet another manuscript, unpublished and unlisted uptil now, could be added to this list. This manuscript is preserved at the Bibliothèque Nationale in Paris under the shelf-mark of Smith-Lesouëf 216, and belongs to the rich collection of the bibliophile Auguste Lesouëf (1829-1906), which was bequeathed to the State by his sister, Mrs. Smith, in 1913. Probably acquired from a bookshop, its present binding of green goatskin, decorated with a gold stamp can be traced to Iran in the nineteenth century. As for its earlier itinerary, on f. 95 one finds a note signed by an owner, in which the name has been scratched out, but the date Urūmī (Urmiya) of 27 Shavvāl 1176/May 11, 1763 can still be read. A certain number of stamps of earlier owners also survive, but they are hardly explicit and generally illegible[29] and do not throw much light on the earlier history of this volume. Moreover the absence of the last few pages deprives us of the colophon which may have been there. Also, the restoration of the first page, which is covered by a piece of paper, has concealed such information as might have been available there.

The manuscript Smith-Lesouëf 216 is a *Khamsa* of Niẓāmī consisting of 293 folios. It is copied in a beautiful Nastaᶜlīq script of 25 lines per page, arranged in 4 columns.[30] The text comprises respectively the

---

28. P. Chandra, *The Tuti-Nama of the Cleveland Museum of Art*, Graz, 1976.

29. On top of f. 97, can be read the name of Mīrzā Ḥusayn; a stamp in the name of Muḥammad figures on f. 1; another bearing the words *Yā Muḥammad* figures on f. 40, 197 and 293; a stamp with *[...] al-Faraj* of 1077 AH (/1666-67) on f. 119v; a stamp with *Ḥasan [...]* of 1141 AH (/1728-29) on f. 12; a stamp *M. [...] Luṭf-ullāh* of [...]17 AH on f. 23, 25-5v and 179; a stamp with *Muḥammad Mubīn* of 1182 AH (/1768-69) on f. 114; a stamp *ᶜAbd-ullāh* on f. 267 and another with the date 1192 AH (/1778) on f. 283; some illegible stamps are to be found on on f. 65, 92 and 93. None of these stamps appear to be of a dignitary of the Mughal court.

30. The dimensions of the manuscript are 170 x 250 mm and the written surface measures 115 x 195. The titles are calligraphed in Naskhī, alternately in blue and red, and sometimes they have been omitted.

Makhzan al-Asrār, on f. 1v-26; the *Khusraw va Shirin*, f. 26v-95; the *Laylā va Majnūn*, f. 95v-142; the *Haft Paykar*, f. 142v-92v; whereas the *Iskandar-nāma* is divided according to the custom, in *Sharaf-nāma* (f. 193v-262) and *Iqbāl-nāma* (f. 262v-92v), in this case with an incomplete end.

The manuscript which has unfortunately been greatly damaged by humidity, contains a large number of restorations, many of which are old. It has also been collated and numerous verses, absent in the copy, have been inserted in the margins at a later date, in a different handwriting. Many of the restorations were probably done in the nineteenth century, when the manuscript was bound.

The manuscript is copied on oriental paper, with widely spaced laid lines, running sometimes vertically, and sometimes horizontally. But European paper, with watermarks representing a hand,[31] has been used for the folios 51-64, 66-69, 250-51 and 288-93. However, f. 293, is a white sheet of another type of European paper, added to the manuscript. This hand watermark paper is from Genoa - numerous specimens dating between c. 1510-50 testify to its extensive use at that time. This paper appears to have been exported in large quantities to the Hispanic world. Since the use of European paper was extremely rare in Iran in the sixteenth century, it may be conjectured that paper brought either from the Portuguese establishments in India, or from Ormuz, was used for this *Khamsa*. Whatever its origin, this paper, being datable, allows us to advance c. 1545-55 as the outer limit for dating this copy of our manuscript.

As for the quires which constitute the volume, they were originally quaternions. Some of the apparent irregularities may be ascribed to the condition of the manuscript. The order of the leaves was also disturbed during binding and it should be re-established in the following manner: f. 1-177, 182-83, 180-81, 178-79 and 184-293. We also find a gap of two leaves between f. 287 and 288, two leaves between f. 289 and 290, and the three final leaves after f. 292, which are missing.

The folios 2v to 292v of the manuscript Smith-Lesouëf 216 are decorated with frames consisting of a blue line and a gold band, whereas the columns of the text are separated by two gold bands. On f. 1v (222 x 132 mm) and 2 (214 x 125 mm), two illuminated pages enclose, within clouds on a golden background, the first 22 *bayt* of the

31. C.-M. Briquet, *Les Filigranes. Dictionnaire historique des marques du papier dès leur apparition vers 1282 jusqu'en 1600*, ed. A. Stevenson, Amsterdam, 1968, types N° 10 731 with the mark A.P. (visible here for example on f. 289) and type N° 10 736 with the mark B.F. (visible on f. 51 sq.).

text. The names of the text and the author were given in cartouches. The decor of these pages, which are unfortunately heavily damaged [cf. folio 2, Pl. I] reminds us of the initial pages of the manuscripts of Herat or Tabriz. The five bands of illuminated frontispieces of f. 26v, [cf. Pl. II] 35v, 142v, 193v and 262v are in floral decoration in arabesque style on a blue background. A golden cartouche on each frontispiece bears, in white letters, the titles of the different poems, preceded by the word *kitāb*. Each of these frontispieces is distinctive, despite a basic similarity in the decorative lay out. We are tempted to compare this manuscript with the manuscripts of the first quarter of the sixteenth century.

Of the ten paintings which illustrate the manuscript, some (f. 288 to 292) are mutilated, and others (f. 4, 38, 73v, 169 and 183) are damaged. Their brief description is as follows:

1. F. 4 (137 x 118 mm) 'The ascent (*mi*[c]*rāj*) of Muḥammad, mounted on Burāq, guided by Jibrā'il (Gabriel) and escorted by the angels'. The faces are covered by golden painting. [Pl. III]
2. F. 38 (113 x 113) 'K͟husraw, on horseback, passes by the spring where Shīrīn having alighted from her horse, is bathing, and he sees her for the first time'. [Pl. IV]
3. F. 65v (165 x 136) 'The architect Farhād is holding the exhausted horse of Shīrīn and Shīrīn herself on his shoulders, and is leading them towards the canal which he has dug in the mountain'. Shīrīn's hairstyle has a different form compared to other feminine hairstyles in the manuscript. [Pl. V]
4. F. 73v (128 x 114) 'Shīrīn in the balcony of her palace, engaged in an argument (*munāẕira*) with K͟husraw who is seated on a throne in the garden'. A text in Persian placed on the facade of the building by the painter reads *dar īn ravāq nivishta-and bīẕar ki juẕ-i nikūhī-i ahl-i karam nak͟hwāhad mānd* ('in this portico, it is inscribed that nothing will remain except the good deeds of generous men'). [Pl. VI]
5. F. 112 (114 x 95) 'Nawfal, seated on his throne and surrounded by some officers, is angry and prepares himself to combat the tribe of Layla'. Nawfal and one of his officers are wearing the *kulāh-i Humāyūnī*. [Pl. VII]
6. F. 169 (208 x 115) 'On Monday, the king Bahrām Gūr, dressed in a green coat, gets ready to attend the feast in the pavilion with a green dome; servants bring him food and musicians are playing in his presence'. In fact, the painting has a green dome on top, but the rest of it represents a verdant garden. Bahrām is represented here with the features of a young adolescent, and is wear-

ing the *kulāh-i Humāyūnī* which distinguishes him from those who surround him. [P1. VIII]

7. F. 183 (212 x 114) 'On Thursday, Bahrām is seated under a sandalwood coloured dome; a waiter offers him some drink; other servitors are standing'. Here Bahrām is represented in a more conventional manner and wears a crown. [Pl. IX]
8. F. 238 (117 x 105) 'During the war against the Rūs, Iskandar who is shown with the wherewithal of a warrior on horseback, has just caught, with his lasso, the head of an enemy who falls down from the horse'. The manner of painting the horses evocate the folio 65v representation of Shīrīn's mount. [Pl. X]
9. F. 288 (120 x 114) 'Iskandar is shown standing on the bow of a ship holding an astrolabe in his hand. As advised by the sage, he is getting constructed a marble dome in order to continue on his route towards the country of Khāqān'. The left side of the painting where the dome was represented has disappeared, because the margin of the page which was torn has been replaced. [Pl. XI]
10. F. 292 (116 x 60) 'A personage with his chest bare is shown leading three men who are carrying the coffin of Iskandar, on which is kept his turban'. Behind the funeral procession, some kind of balls and bands appear hanging on dead branches.[32] [Pl. XII]

* * *

The manuscript Smith-Lesouëf 216, undoubtedly composed and illustrated in the *Kitābkhāna* of Humāyūn, is of considerable interest. The paintings have been executed with great care. The study of the more damaged ones is, however, a difficult task. Due to the large variety of characters contained in each illustration, it is also not easy to determine whether the volume has been painted entirely by a single artist, or by several artists.

On f. 4, a vertical inscription below the representation of Miʿrāj gives us the name of the artist: *Kār-i Maulānā Darvīsh Muḥammad* (work of Maulānā Darvīsh Muḥammad). We have found no other signature or attribution in the manuscript. There is no reason also to ques-

32. According to an old Iranian custom, while accompanying a funeral procession, one carried poles which had small blades attached at the top. In northern Afghanistan, the custom of attaching small bands of cloth on top of poles continues till today.

I. Manuscript Smith-Lesouëf 216, folio 2. Photo Bibliothèque Nationale, Paris.

tion this attribution of at least one of the paintings to an artist,[33] whose presence in Kabul in 958/1551 is mentioned by Bāyazīd Bayāt. However, since he no longer mentions this name in the list of persons who accompanied Humāyūn in 1554, probably because he was dead at that time and it is possible to date the manuscript Smith-Lesouëf 216 from Kabul around the years 958-61/1551-54.

Moreover, the painting of ᶜAbd al-Ṣamad in the Gulshan Album, which represents his young student Akbar, aged nine years, painting in the presence of a young musician,[34] is dated from the *Nawrūz* of the year 958/1551. This painting should be compared with that on f. 169 of our *Khamsa*, in which the artist has painted the portrait of the young prince and heir apparent Akbar instead of showing Bahrām Gūr in his green pavilion, undoubtedly to please Humāyūn who had commissioned the work. In this painting, Akbar's age appears to be the same as in the painting of ᶜAbd al-Ṣamad.

Similarly, on f. 112, the painting which was supposed to show Nawfal, becomes the portrait of Humāyūn, surrounded by some members of his court. Even though his features have been somewhat altered, one recognizes clearly in Nawfal, with a pointed beard, the emperor Humāyūn, as he has been represented in his official portraits.[35] One can see that the painter, who is undoubtedly Maulānā Darvīsh Muḥammad, has paid homage to the probable addressee of the manuscript in this manner.

It would be extremely interesting to try and establish a relationship between the manuscript Smith-Lesouëf 216, and some manuscripts, which one can relate to a princely *scriptorium* established at Kabul in the second half of the fifteenth century and the first half of the sixteenth century. The existence of such an atelier at Kabul, under the patronage of Ulugh Bēgh II and of Kāmrān b. Bābur, Humāyūn's step-brother,

---

33. Compare with notes 12 and 16 *supra*.

34. Binyon, *et al.*, *op. cit.*, N° 232 and Pl. CV B; in the album *Iran, Persian Miniatures, Imperial Library*, Paris, 1956, where the scene is republished (Pl. XXIV), B. Gray and A. Godard are of the view that it is certainly a portrait of the young Akbar aged nine years. See also Brand and Lowry, *op. cit.*, p. 23. One can also compare it with the painting of ᶜAbd al-Ṣamad, "The Presentation of a Miniature by Akbar to his father, the Emperor Humāyūn", in the same Gulshan Album where the young Akbar is also represented (Binyon *et al.*, *op. cit.*, N° 230, pp. 147-8 and Pl. CIV B.).

35. Cf. the painting on cotton from the British Museum and other works which have already been cited. Two good examples of these official portraits, copied and integrated in Mughal albums, are N° 332 and 333 of *An Annotated and Illustrated Checklist of the Vever Collection* by G.D. Lowry and M.C. Beach, Washington, 1985.

who proclaimed himself *Shāh* in 1543,[36] has been confirmed by C. Adle in his recent and well documented studies. He has pointed out that the *Yūsuf va Zulaykhā* of Jāmī, ornamented with six paintings, which was discovered in the former Kevorkian collection,[37] was copied for Kāmrān by the calligrapher ᶜAbd-ullāh Shīrāzī, unquestionably at Kabul, around 1522-43.

An attentive examination of the paintings of the Smith-Lesouëf 216, with their remarkably fine linework and richness of palette, would be necessary in order to define their place among the paintings of the different schools of the Iranian world of that time. One thing which strikes the attention immediately is that, with the exception of two persons on f. 112, and one other person on f. 169, all the masculine characters wear turbans without feathers. The form of this turban is reminiscent of the headgear seen in the paintings of Bukhara, in the neighbouring Sunni kingdom of the Shaybanides, in the years 1530-50. The feminine hair styles are, with one exception (f. 65v), akin to those seen in the paintings in the manuscripts of Tabriz, in the years 1530-40;[38] as is the case with regard to f. 73v.

The ship in the shape of a bow, ornamented with a horse's head, as seen on f. 288, could easily remind one, by its form, of the ships represented in Herat towards the end of the fifteenth century. This could also be said of the architecture of the palace seen on f. 73v, or of the horses and the war equipment of the participants of the battle on f. 238. However, one should note that one could also compare them to the works produced in Tabriz thirty or forty years later, which follow the same models. The painting showing the meeting of Khusraw with Shīrīn, on f. 38 is undoubtedly related, in our opinion, to the painting of Tabriz. On the other hand, that of Farhād and Shīrīn on f. 65v is in a style very different from the one we find in a representation of the same scene in a manuscript of Manchester, which was probably done around 1530 at Tabriz,[39] and which, according to S.C. Welch, could be

36. C. Adle, "Entre Timurides, Mogols et Safavides. Notes sur un *Chāhnāmé* de l'Atelier-Bibliothèque Royal d'Ologh Beg II à Caboul (873-907/1469-1502)", which is on pp. 136-47 of the sale catalogue *Art Islamique et Orientalisme*, Paris, Hôtel Drouot (June 15, 1990), where this article has appeared as an annexe to the description of N° 183.

37. *Sotheby's Catalogue*, London, April 23, 1979, N° 156. A colour plate accompanying the notice shows that the paintings are very different from those of the manuscript Smith-Leṣouëf 216 and belong rather to the Bukhara School.

38. For example, those of a Niẓāmī of Manchester which S.C. Welch attributes to ᶜAbd al-Ṣamad (B.W. Robinson, *Persian Paintings in the John Rylands Library. A Descriptive Catalogue*, London, 1980, pp. 148-51).

39. F. 37v of Ryland's Persian 6 (Robinson, *op. cit.*, N° 551 and Pl. p. 24).

a work by Mīr Sayyid ᶜAlī in his youth. In any case, the work in the manuscript Smith-Lesouëf 216 has been executed with great care, and appears to be of a superior quality.

The influence of the painting of Tabriz on the *Khamsa* of the Bibliothèque Nationale is evident, and one detail confirms it. In the painting on f. 169, the cartouches have hemistiches of Persian verses in red letters on the border of a brown carpet, where a young prince Bahrām Gūr (Akbar) is seated.[40] Though substantially faded and almost illegible these verses could be compared to those of Ḥāfiẓ, which are inscribed in red in similar cartouches of an identical carpet, seen in a painting of the Gulshan Album ('A shaykh teaching two disciples near a spring').[41] We have other examples of Persian distichs, copied in the same manner; in red letters on the borders of a carpet, in one of the paintings attributed to Mīrzā ᶜAlī in the *Khamsa* of Shāh Ṭahmāsb ('Barbad playing before Khusraw');[42] also in one of the carpets of the 'Camp of nomads', a work preserved at the Fogg Art Museum of Harvard which is attributed to Mīr Sayyid ᶜAlī, and is undoubtedly related to the *Khamsa* of 1540;[43] as well as in the 'School scene' attributed to the same Mīr Sayyid ᶜAlī and dated Tabriz, c. 1540, from the old Vever collection.[44] But we find a comparable carpet with Persian verses written in red in cartouches in the painting of the 'Seated Prince' by Mīr Sayyid ᶜAlī dated Kabul, 1550-55.[45]

Should one conclude then that Mīr Sayyid ᶜAlī was involved in the illustration of the manuscript of Smith-Lesouëf 216 ? Or shall we say simply that Maulānā Darvīsh Muḥammad got inspired by a decorative element which had been used by the master from Tabriz working in Humāyūn's *Kitābkhāna* and who will be later the head of his atelier ? Even if the analysis of other details could lead us to draw more paral-

---

40. Carpets of this type framed by a border with cartouches containing Persian *bayt* written in the Nastaᶜlīq style identical to the carpets seen in these paintings, were produced in large numbers at Tabriz towards the middle of the sixteenth century. For examples see A.U. Pope and P. Ackerman, *Survey of Persian Art*, Vol. XI, London, 1938-39, Pl. 1144-7, 1152-3 and 1156-62.

41. Unsigned painting from the 1540s, reproduced on the cover and on an unnumbered Pl. before p. 357 in the Catalogue of B. Atabāy, *Fihrist-i Muraqqaᶜāt-i Kitābkhāna-i salṭanatī*, Tehran, 1353/1974-75 (but not described, it would appear, in entry N° 1663 devoted to the Gulshan Album).

42. F. 77v of the *Khamsa* (S.C. Welch, *Royal Persian Manuscripts*, London, 1976, Pl. 26).

43. *The Houghton Shahnameh...*, *op. cit.*, Vol. I, Fig. 238.

44. Glenn D. Lowry, *A Jeweler's Eye*, Washington, 1986, N° 59.

45. Work already cited *supra*. Comp. *The Houghton Shahnameh...*, Vol. I, Fig. N° 247, p. 190.

lels of this type, the answer to these questions remains unsatisfactory because, so far, no other work of Maulānā Darvīsh Muḥammad, is known with any degree of certitude.

Even while awaiting a more rigorous study, leading to the rediscovery of other works from the same atelier, one can already conclude that Smith-Lesouëf 216 is a manuscript which is true to the Timurid tradition from Herat, and which is substantially influenced by the royal Safavid *Kitābkhāna* of Tabriz. Thus the influences on the Mughal ateliers of India are already visible, integrating in the tradition received from the Timurids, contributions from Iran, Bukhara, India and Europe. On the other hand, if the *Khamsa* of Paris of *circa* 1545, may be attribuable to different artists amongst them Maulānā Darvīsh Muḥammad, is confirmed to be slightly older than the *Khamsa* in the collection of Lalbhai of Ahmedabad, then it might well be the oldest known 'Mughal' manuscript.

Translated from French by Rashmi Patni

REFERENCES

Abdul Aziz, Sh., *The Imperial Library of the Mughuls*, Repr., Delhi: Idarah-i Adabiyat-i Delhi, 1974. (I.A.D., 25)

Abū l-Fadhl b. Mubārak ᶜAllāmī, *Akbar-nāma*, English Transl. H. Beveridge, Vol. I, Calcutta: Asiatic Society of Bengal (Bibliotheca Indica), 1907.

Adle, Chahryar, "Autopsia in Absentia, sur la date de l'introduction et de la constitution de l'Album de Bahrām Mirzā par Dūst-Mohammad, 951/1544", *Studia Iranica*, 1990, XIX, 2, pp. 219-56.

— "Entre Timurides, Mogols et Safavides. Notes sur un *Chāhnāmé* de l'Atelier-Bibliothèque Royal d'Ologh Beg II à Caboul (873-907/1469-1502)", *Art Islamique et Orientalisme*, Paris, Hôtel Drouot (June 15, 1990), pp. 136-47. (Sale Catalogue)

— "Les artistes nommés Dūst Moḥammad au XVIᵉ siècle", *Studia Iranica*, 1993, XXII, 2. (In Press)

Arnold, T., "Mīrzā Muhammad Haydar Dughlāt, on the Herāt School of Painters" in Binyon, Wilkinson, Gray, *Persian Miniature Painting, including a Critical and Descriptive Catalogue of the Miniatures exhibited at Burlington House, January-March 1931*, London: Oxford University Press, 1933, Appendix II.

Atābāy, Badrī, *Fihrist-i Muraqqaᶜāt-i Kitābkhāna-i salṭanatī*, Tehran, Zībā, 1353/1974-75.

Bayānī, Mahdī, *Aḥvāl va Āṯhār-i Khwushnivisān*, Vols. I-IV, Tehran: Intishārāt-i ᶜIlmī, 2nd edn., s.d. [1363/1984-85].

Bāyazīd Bayāt, *Tadhkira-i-Humāyūn wa Akbar of Bāyazid Biyāt*, ed. M. Hidayat Hosain, Calcutta: Asiatic Society of Bengal (Bibliotheca Indica), 1941.

Binyon, Laurence, James, V.S. Wilkinson & Basil Gray, *Persian Miniature Painting, including a Critical and Descriptive Catalogue of the Miniatures exhibited at Burlington House, January-March 1931*, London: Oxford University Press, 1933.

Brand, Michael & Glenn D. Lowry, *Akbar's India. Art from the Mughal City of Victory*, New York: The Asia Society Galleries, 1985. (Exhibition Catalogue)

Briquet, Charles-Moïse, *Les Filigranes. Dictionnaire historique des marques du papier dès leur apparition vers 1282 jusqu'en 1600*, ed. A. Stevenson, Amsterdam: The Paper Publications Society, 1968.

Chandra, Pramod, *The Tuti-Nama of the Cleveland Museum of Art*, Graz: University of Graz, 1976.

Digby, S., "Humāyūn", *Encyclopédie de l'Islam*², Vol. III, 49-50, Leiden: E.J. Brill, 1962, pp. 595-7.

Encyclopaedia Iranica, ed. Ehsan Yarshater, London-Boston-Henley, 1982-; Vol. I, 2, New York: Routledge and Kegan Paul, 1982.

*Encyclopédie de l'Islam*², Leiden: E.J. Brill, 1960-.

Gray, Basil & André Godard, *Iran, Persian Miniatures, Imperial Library*, Paris: UNESCO, 1956.

Hasan, Hādī, *Researches in Persian Literature*, Hyderabad: Government Press, 1958.

Huart, Clément, *Les Calligraphes et les Miniaturistes de l'Orient musulman*, Paris: E. Leroux, 1908.

Keshavarz, Fatemeh, *A Descriptive and Analytical Catalogue of Persian Manuscripts in the Library of the Wellcome Institute*, London: Wellcome Institute, 1986.

Khayyāmpūr, ᶜAbdul-Rasūl, *Farhang-i Sukhanvarān*, Tabriz: Chāp-i Azarbayjān, 1340 AH.

Losty, Jeremiah P., *The Art of the Book in India*, London: The British Library, 1982. (Exhibition Catalogue)

Lowry, Glenn D., *A Jeweler's Eye*, Washington: Arthur A. Sackler Gallery, 1986. (Exhibition Catalogue)

— & Milo C. Beach, *An Annotated and Illustrated Checklist of the Vever Collection*, Washington: Sackler Gallery - University of

Washington, 1985.

Marshall, D.N., *Mughals in India. I. Manuscripts*, London-Bombay: Asia Publishing House, 1967.

Mohiuddin, Momin, *The Chancellery and Persian Epistolography under the Mughals, from Bābur to Shāh Jahān, 1526-1658. A Study on Inshā, Dār al-Inshā and Munshis, based on Original Documents*, Calcutta: Iran Society, 1971.

Munzavī, Aḥmad, *A Comprehensive Catalogue of Persian Manuscripts in Pakistan*, Vol. II, Islamabad: Iran-Pakistan Institute, 1984.

Okada, Amina, *Miniatures de l'Inde impériale, les peintres de la cour d'Akbar (1556-1605)*, Paris: Editions de la Réunion des Musées Nationaux, 1989. (Musée Guimet, Exhibition Catalogue)

Pope, Arthur U. & Philis Ackerman, *Survey of Persian Art*, Vol. XI, London-New York: Oxford University Press, 1938-39.

Qāẓī Aḥmad Qumī, *Gulistān-i Ḥunar*, ed., Aḥmad Suhaylī Khwānsārī, Tehran: Manuchehrī, 2nd edn., s.d. [1981]

Robinson, Basil W., *Persian Paintings in the John Rylands Library. A Descriptive Catalogue*, London: Sotheby - Parke - Bernet, 1980.

Sotheby's, London, Sale Catalogue of Islamic Paintings (April 23, 1979).

Soucek, P., "ᶜAbd al-Ṣamad Šīrāzī", *Encyclopaedia Iranica*, Vol. I, 2, New York: Routledge and Kegan Paul, 1982, pp. 162-7.

Stchoukine, Ivan, *Les peintures des manuscrits Tīmūrides*, Paris: Geuthner, 1954. (Institut Français d'Archéologie de Beyrouth, Bibliothèque Archéologique et Historique, 60)

Storey, Charles A., *Persian Literature. A Bio-bibliographical Survey*, London: Luzac & Co, 1935-.

— & Yuri E. Bregel', *Persidskaïa Literatura, bio-biograficeskiï Obzor*, Vols. I-III, Moscow, "Nauka", 1972.

Thackston, Whelers M., *A Century of Princes. Sources on Timurid History and Art*, Cambridge (Mass.): Agha Khan Programme for Islamic Architecture, 1989.

The Houghton Shahnameh, introduced and described by Martin Bernard Dickson and Stuart Cary Welch, Vols. I-II, Cambridge (Mass.): Harvard University Press, 1981.

Titley, Norah M., *Persian Miniature Painting and its Influence on the Art of Turkey and India - The British Library Collections*, London: British Library, 1983.

Trésors de l'Islam, Geneva: Musée d'Art et d'Histoire, 1985. (Exhibition Catalogue)

Welch, Anthony, "The Worldly Vision of Mir Sayyid 'Ali", *Persian Masters. Five Centuries of Painting*, ed. Sheila R. Canby, Bombay: Marg Publications, 1990, pp. 85-98.

— & Stuart Cary Welch, *Arts of the Islamic Book. The Collection of Prince Sadruddin Aga Khan*, London-Ithaca: Cornell University Press - Asia Society, 1982.

Welch, Stuart C., *Royal Persian Manuscripts*, London: Thames & Hudson, 1976.

— *India, Art and Culture, 1300-1900* (1985), New York: Metropolitan Museum - Ahmedabad, Mapin Publishing Pvt., Repr., 1988. (Exhibition Catalogue)

Wilkinson, James V.S. & Laurence Binyon, *The Shāh-nāmah of Firdausī*, London: The India Society, 1931.

The Iranian Style in North Hindustan Metalwork

ASSADULLAH SOUREN MELIKIAN-CHIRVANI

Cultural interchange between the Indian subcontinent and the Iranian world is as old as history in both these vast areas comprising many present-day countries. It started under the Achaemenids when Iran became the model for the first documented kingdom founded by the Maurya dynasty and when a palace was erected at Pataliputra on a Persepolitan plan.[1] It continued in Buddhist times,[2] with far-reaching consequences on the iconography of architecture and the visual arts, as I have indicated elsewhere. When Islam entered the subcontinent following a complex pattern, barely studied as yet, it was essentially in the garb of Iranian culture.

From the beginning, there was a process, best illustrated by metalwork, of import, local imitation and absorption into the powerful indigenous tradition.[3] It happened many times, in vastly different parts of the subcontinent, taking forms that we are only beginning to grasp, as isolated objects turn up here and there.

Its latest avatar took place under the Moghul dynasty which, like others before, traced its origins to clansmen of Turkish stock. These found themselves in a milieu already permeated with Iranian culture where Persian was the one language of literature and polished usage in Islamic circles since the days of Amīr Khosrow. They surrounded themselves with hundreds of Persian literati and artists who went to and from between Iran and Hindustan as it was called by Persian speakers. The impact on Iran itself was enormous. A major school of poetry developed in a style known as "the Indian style", [*sabk-e Hendī*] because it was evolved by the expatriate poets at Islamic

1. Percy Brown, *Indian Architecture (Buddhist and Hindu Periods)*, Bombay, 1965, p. 5.

2. See the writer's paper on the origins of the architectural *stūpa* in Eastern Iranian lands from where it travelled as far south as Ajanta: "Recherches sur l'architecture de l'Iran Bouddhique I. Essai sur les origines et le symbolisme du stūpa iranien", *Le Monde Iranien et l'Islam*, Vol. III, Paris, 1975, pp. 1-61.

3. A.S. Melikian-Chirvani, "Islamic Metalwork as a Source on Cultural History", *Arts and the Islamic World*, London, Winter 1982-83, I, 1, pp. 36-44. See "The making of Islamic culture in India: the evidence of metalwork", pp. 41-4.

courts.[4] Persian lexicography took a new impetus in Hindustan with the famous "Jahangirian Dictionary" [*Farhang-e Jahāngīrī*] written by Mīr Jamāl ad-Dīn Ḥoseyn Injū Shīrāzī after Akbar formally commissionned him to do so at a court reception in Kashmir in Ẕīqaᶜde 1005 / 16 June - 15 July 1597.[5] The learned prince completed it twelve years later, in 1017, the fourth year of Jahāngīr to whom he dedicated the work.[6] The movement spread throughout India. It included the Deccan where an elusive man of letters calling himself Moḥammad Ḥoseyn with the nom-de-plume Borhān Khalaf Tabrīzī, who lived in Golconda, completed in 1062 / 14 December 1651 - 1 December 1652 a dictionary known as the *Borhān-e Qāṭeᶜ*, the most exhaustive ever until then.[7] Borhān Tabrīzi, the author, dedicated his work to the ruler, ᶜAbdullāh Quṭb Shāh. With the parallel development of works offering poetry selections and biographical entries, and of historical chronicles of every kind, the volume of Persian literary activity in Hindustan exceeded anything seen anywhere at any time before - Iran included.

The appearance of what could be called a high Iranian style in the Islamic arts of the subcontinent coincided with this climax of Persian literary production. It apparently touched figural painting at an earlier stage and was limited - few Moghul miniatures really 'resemble' Iranian miniatures. Leaving aside the case of direct copies, confusion is rarely possible and certainly never in the 11/17th century. But one powerful school of calligraphy continued to strive to work in pure Iranian style, mostly in the *Nastaᶜlīq* script.[8] The same was true of a whole movement in book illumination [*taẕhīb*] as I hope to show elsewhere.[9]

---

4. A proper historical study of the massive emigration of Persian literati to Hindustan in the 10/16th and 11/17th century has yet to be written. Their work is best analyzed in the introductory monographs in recent printed editions of the Safavid-period *dīvāns* such as, for example, the *Dīvān-e Abū Ṭāleb-e Kalūm-e Hamadānī*, ed. Moḥammad Qahremān, Mashhad (*Enteshārāt-e Āstān-e Qods-e Raẕavī*), 1369/1990 with a highly informative survey of poetical trends in Hindustan, particularly under Shāh Jahān, in the first 56 pages.

5. Mīr Jamāl ad-Dīn Ḥoseyn b. Fakhr od-Dīn Ḥasan Injū Shīrāzī, *Farhang-e Jahāngīrī*, ed. Raḥīm ᶜAfīfī, Mashhad-Tehran, 1371/1972 - 1374/1975 (Three Vols.). See editor's preface, Vol. I, page six, and pp. 3-4 of Injū Shīrāzī's own preface [*dībāche*].

6. *Ibid*, editor's preface page eight. Injū Shīrāzī's preface [*dībāche*], Vol. I, p. 11.

7. *Borhān-e Qāṭeᶜ*, ed. Moḥammad ᶜAbbāsī, Tehran, 1344/1965; see editor's preface pp. 58-61, particularly pp. 60-1.

8. Conveyed in its extreme form by pages copying the style of "Mīr ᶜAlī". See S.C. Welch, A. Schimmel, M.L. Swietochowski and W.M. Thackston, *The Emperor's Album*, New York, 1987, N° 95, pp. 274-7.

9. See example of illumination [*taẕhīb*] in the Iranian style, *ibid*. Pl. 3 and 2 (the opening double page to Jahāngīr's "album", as the *moraqqaᶜ* is referred to). While nearly all details in the formal ornament are borrowed from the Iranian vocabulary, they are associated in ways that repeatedly depart from Iranian usage. Note the secondary lobing in the five-lobed arches on the outer frame, which will be found further in this paper in the decoration of Muḥammad Ṣādiq's bowl.

Considered in this perspective, the identification of a Hindustani school of metalwork closely following the Iranian model is no surprise. Its wares have failed to attract much attention so far.[10] This is largely because few pieces have found their way into museum collections, and these are scattered across the world from India and Pakistan to Europe and North America. There is as yet no rigorous set of rules that can be applied to determine the attribution of metalwork to Hindustan versus Iran. But it is reasonable to posit that an object preserved in present-day India or Pakistan, or known to have come out of India or Pakistan, that happens to have been commissioned by characters with Indian names, or indeed by characters recorded in historical chronicles, stands a fair chance of having been made in some atelier in Hindustan. When the decoration displays some features, however minute, that depart from Iranian design, the possibility changes to a high degree of probability.

1. *The Metalwares of a Court Milieu*

Such appears to be the case with a small group of wine bowls of the type known as *bādiya*, with a deep well rising from a low ring foot, and a slighty everted lip.

The earliest among them is a small *bādiya* of a size hitherto unrecorded in Iranian metalwork.[11] No significance can be read into this observation at this stage, if only because the numbers of published pieces is statistically minimal. It is decorated with formal motifs of Eslīmī type, or arabesque to use the old-fashioned western term, arranged in two interlacing and connecting patterns (Figs. 1, 2). As is usual on Iranian bowls of the *bādiya* type with repeat patterns, the

10. On a first attempt at dealing with the schools of Hindustan, see Melikian-Chirvani, *Islamic Metalwork from the Iranian World (8-18th centuries)*, London, 1982, pp. 348-55. On the evidence of pieces with related calligraphy (from the quadruple viewpoint of content, internal arrangement of the sections of words, layout on the object, and epigraphical characteristics of the types of calligraphy, in particular Muḥaqqaq as here), I now realize that the vase N° 164, illustrated p. 349, belongs not to north-western Hindustan but to the Golconda-Haydarabad school in the Bahmanid Sultanate on which I am currently gathering material.

11. Worked from a (cast ?) sheet of copper hammered on a stake; the foot disc worked separately hammered to give it tapering sides and hot soldered to the ringfoot. Tinned, engraved, inlaid with black composition. Diameter of opening: 12.8 cm. Diameter of foot: 5.05-5.1 cm. Height: 7.2-7.5 cm. Published: Christie's *Islamic Manuscripts, Miniatures and Works of Art*, London, 10 October 1989, lot 441, p. 97, illustrated. The catalogue comments: "It is difficult to say whether this bowl was made in Persia for a Kashmiri client, or in Kashmir itself. At this period there was little to distinguish between the two." This statement, it will be seen, is unfounded. The name was read in part only. The problematic element "Faghū", which can be seen in the published photograph, was left out. The poem was left unread.

everted lip carries a border of calligraphy broken up in five elongated panels which are linked with each other by quatrefoils. The panels enclose a poem written in *Nasta^clīq* calligraphy of a very high standard and the name of the patron.

A date in small digits appears over it, 1023 / 11 February 1614-30 January 1615. I have not had time to search through *dīvāns* to identify the author whose literary style points to a period roughly contemporary with the bowl. The verses, probably taken from an ode [*ghazal*] are on the *khafif* metre:

ساقیا پایهٔ شراب بیار یکدو ساغر شراب ناب بیار
داروی درد عشق یعنی می کوست درمان شیخ و شاب بیار

Cupbearer bring us the substance of wine
  Bring us one or two cups filled with wine[12]
The drug for the pain of love, that is, wine,
  Where is it ? Bring us the remedy of master and disciple

صاحبه خواجه یوسف فغو کشمیری ۱۰۲۳

Owned by Kh^wāja Yūsuf Faghū Kashmīrī 1023 / 11 February 1614-30 January 1615.

The name "Faghū", if that is the correct reading and transliteration, does not appear to have been recorded so far. The *nesbat*, "Kashmīrī", broadly points to some connection with Kashmir, which may have been close or distant. Kashmir may very well have been no more than the owner's ancestral country, regardless of his birthplace or residence. Until his name is traced to a source, not much can be built on it. However, it is an unlikely name in 11/17th century Iran and, as such, makes a provenance from Hindustan plausible.

This attribution finds some support in the presence of a decorative feature not usually found in Iranian metalwork. A scrolling motif rising out of nowhere and ending nowhere is introduced amidst the two interlacing and interconnecting patterns. Another feature for which I find no

12. The rendering of *pāya*, clearly written, is tentatively submitted. Borhān, *loc. cit*, p. 238, records as one of its rarer meanings *forū rīkhtan yārān-rā*, "pouring out for the boon companions". That is apparently the meaning here, unless we understand *pāya* in its literal sense of "foundation", used to refer to some "stand" - such as a low table ? - on which the cups might be laid out.

parallel in metalwork from Safavid Iran is the succession of low escutcheons in the form of trilobate arches with a broad squat cusped arch in the middle that rise from the foot ring.

Taken in conjunction, the two decorative features that depart from Iranian design as we know it, the names unlikely to have been those of an Iranian in Iran and the Kashmiri connection of sorts, point to a probable Hindustani provenance.

Next in time comes up an unpublished *bādiya* which was bought in Delhi and turned up on the German art market with a label ascribing it to "Eastern Iran" (Fig. 3).[13] The copper object was retinned in this century, after World War II, and reinlaid with black composition.

While the shape faithfully reproduces the Iranian model, the design shows several distinctive features. The general layout follows the Iranian formula. A repeat pattern runs on the main part of the body. It is isolated by a moulding from the border on the everted lip in which elongated panels with five-lobed extremities instead of three lobes are linked by intervening octafoils. All panels but one enclose rows of formalized blossoms. The seventh panel encloses a short inscription in a fine *Nastaᶜlīq* script from a professional hand. It names the patron and gives the date written, as before, in tiny digits over the name:

صاحبه خواجه محمد صادق ١٠٢٦

> Owned by Khʷāja Muḥammad Ṣādiq 1026 / 9 January - 28 December 1617.

This is surely the Khʷāja Muḥammad Ṣādiq who succeeded Khʷāja ᶜAbd ur-Raḥīm when the latter died shortly after the Nowrūz, *i.e.* March 21 of the year of Shāh Jahān's accession to the throne. Muḥammad Ṣāliḥ Kanbū, in the *Shāh Jahān-Nāma*[14] tells us that Khʷāja Muḥammad Ṣādiq, having received an imperial robe [*khalᶜat*], a studded belt for a dagger and 30,000 *rūpiya*, was dispatched to his appointment. A man such as this would, indeed, have been likely to own vessels in the Iranian court style cultivated in the emperor's entourage.

Various features in what is otherwise a Persianizing pattern on a purely Iranian model, place this *bādiya* outside mainstream Iranian

13. Technique as described in note 11. The object was tinned afresh in this century, and reinlaid with black composition. Diameter of opening: 23.6-24 cm. Diameter of ringfoot: 8.7-8.8 cm. Height: 14.1-14.5 cm. Inside, one double filet is finely incised 0.5 cm below the shaped rim.

14. Muḥammad Ṣālih Kanbū, *Shāh Jahān-Nāma*, ed. Waḥīd Qurayshī, Lahore, 2nd edn., 1967 (Three Vols.), Vol. II, p. 262. A later inscription written in cursive script inside, near the lip, reads "Master [*sarkār*] Saᶜid Allāh Khān".

design as applied in the art of Iran. Most obvious are the broad five-lobed escutcheons coming down on the sides like pendents, each of the five lobes being in turn lobed. The fussiness has a baroque touch and the motif displays a lack of proportion that is fundamentally alien to Iranian design. Another oddity, by Iranian standards, is the way in which the trilobate cusped finials prolonging these five-lobed escutcheons almost run into the undulating festoon below.

Lesser details suggest that the ornament, while drawing entirely on the Iranian decorative vocabulary, was not conceived in an Iranian atelier. Such is the succession of bi-lobed half-palmettes inside the festoon. The half-palmette is quite Iranian. What is not, is its use in one single scrolling band inside a festoon. Just as unusual is the break of continuity from one side to the next of the cusped arches of the festoon. Another blatant break with Iranian usage lies in the succession of escutcheons with formalized blossoms on the everted lip. The motifs, pointed downwards, would be used in another context. In this emplacement, one would expect motifs horizontally oriented, such as scrolls, or calligraphy all around.

A third *bādiya* appeared at auction in London where it was again described as Safavid, a dynastic characterization implying an Iranian provenance (Fig. 4).[15] Like the previous two *bādiya* it is decorated with a repeat pattern on the body and a calligraphic border on the everted lip. While it looks very Iranian at first glance, a closer look reveals a series of features that do not occur in metalwork from Iran.

The calligraphic border is divided into five panels, as is the case with the border on the bowl commissioned by Khʷāja Yūsuf Faghū Kashmīrī in 1023 / 11 February 1614-30 January 1615. It should be noted at this stage that while a few Iranian vessels decorated with five panels of calligraphy are known,[16] the number has yet to be recorded on a *bādiya*. What is more, the panels are isolated by octafoils, the dividing device commonly used in Hindustan. Finally, some of the formal blossoms terminating the volutes within the five calligraphic panels are typically Hindustani with their long sinuous lobes, as over the words *qadaḥī por sharāb kon.*

Several differences with the Iranian way of using the motifs borrowed by the Hindustani designer from the Iranian repertoire can be detected in the repeat pattern. The fleur-de-lys motifs enclosed between

15. Seen at Christie's South Kensington, *Oriental Ceramics and Works of Art*, 22 April 1993. Part of lot 223.

16. Melikian-Chirvani, *Islamic Metalwork* (see note 10), N° 123, pp. 287-8.

two half-palmettes linking at the top have no parallel in Iran.[17] The narrow border of blossoms engraved on the inner face of the everted lip is likewise unparalled in Iranian metalwork.

Inside, on the bottom, is a large rosette engraved and inlaid with black composition. The idea of such a rosette inside a *bādiye* is, again, unmatched in Iranian metalwork.[18] The detail itself is purely Hindustani at that period (Fig. 5). The six almond-shaped lobes of the rosette, while of Iranian origin, go back to much earlier Iranian design. They are ensconced in the midst of six trilobate blossoms which also have a distinctly Hindustani touch.

In short, while based entirely on the Iranian ornamental vocabulary, the decoration, including the calligraphic panels, betrays its Hindustani origin. That it was intended to have an "Iranian look" is not in doubt.

The dedication inscription is worded in accordance with the usage of Iranian literati in Safavid times. The respectful mode of address *Khʷāja* points, as in the case of Yūsuf Faghū Kashmīrī and Muḥammad Ṣādiq, to a man of eminence in literary circles or in the sphere of government, and quite possibly both, as often happened at the Moghul court:

صاحبه خواجه یوسف بج

Owned by *Khʷāja* Yūsuf Bajj.

The selection of verses is interesting. These are the first two lines from a famous ode [*ghazal*] by Ḥāfeẓ which is in the *Możāreᶜ* metre:

صبح است ساقیا قدحی پر شراب کن
دور فلک درنگ ندارد شتاب کن
زان پیشتر که عالم فانی شود خراب
مارا ز جام بادهٔ گلگون خراب کن

'Tis morning, o cupbearer, fill our cup with wine
The rotation of heaven tarries not, make haste
Before the mortal world turns into a ruin
Make us a ruin from the bowl filled with rose colored wine[19]

---

17. This remark is made bearing in mind that no systematic analysis of the ornamental repertoire of metalwork has yet been attempted.

18. Such rosettes are normally reserved in Iran for *ṭabaqs* and *lagans* (*Islamic Metalwork*, Pl. 132A, p. 302).

19. *Dīvān-e Mowlānā Shams od-Dīn Moḥammad Ḥāfeẓ-e Shīrāzī*, ed. Yahiyā Qarīb, Tehran, 2nd edn., 1356/1977, p. 358.

Did these verses have a particular resonance in Hindustan ? They occur on a *bādiya* made in 1026 / 9 January - 28 December 1617 for one Khʷāja Muḥammad Bājīv (or Bāṣū ?) Kashmīrī.[20] Here too, slight details in the decoration, thoroughly Iranian in its detail, betray the Hindustani origin - the octafoils breaking up the epigraphical border, the rather oddly disproportionate arches with a high point and a low cusp, the arcade incised on the foot. Acquired in the subcontinent for the Victoria and Albert Museum by Caspar Purdon Clarke, reportedly in Kashmir, the *bādiya* dated 1026/1617 belongs in the same group as the undated object published here (Fig. 4). The latter was probably executed around that time.

A very consistent group of Persianizing and sometimes quasi Iranian looking bowls of the *bādiya* type thus appears to have been executed in years ranging from the end of the reign of Jahāngīr to the reign of Shāh Jahān, in an area that is likely to have been close to the seat of Moghul power.

Such an assumption derives some support from a highly important pillar-candlestick preserved in a private collection (Figs. 6, 7).[21] The tapering shaft rising from a splayed base reproduces the common Safavid model from which it differs in one respect: the spreading base is not flush with the upper edge of a ring-like pedestal, but rises below the edge of the ring-like pedestal. The latter thus marks off a dished area. There is nothing to prove that such a device was never used in Safavid Iran, but none has yet been recorded on a pillar-candlestick.

The decoration, closely looked at, displays a few details that are not found in Safavid Iran. The top part, as in most Safavid candlesticks of the early 11/17th century, is divided into three horizontal borders by simulated mouldings, the central border being reserved for a succession of calligraphic cartouches. These are separated by the octafoils preferred by Hindustan designers. The borders above and under the calligraphy encloses festoons of polylobed escutcheons. The idea finds a parallel on an Iranian candlestick in the Victoria and Albert Museum.[22] But the escutcheons here are five-lobed not trilobate as they invariably are in Iran.

---

20. Melikian-Chirvani, *Islamic Metalwork*, N° 165, pp. 350-1. Illustrated Pl. 165, p. 35.

21. Multiple alloy of golden hue cast, engraved and inlaid with black composition. Height: 24.9 cm. Diameter of opening: 7.9 cm. Diameter of base: 15.23. Illustrated [Hotel Drouot] Ader Picard Tajan, *Tableaux Orientalistes*, Paris, 19-20 November 1990. Part of lot 331. Text and date unread. Reproduced p. 159.

22. Melikian-Chirvani, *Islamic Metalwork*, N° 141, pp. 314-5. Reproduced p. 141. The lower band on the "capital" encloses interlacing scrolls instead of raised escutcheons, but the pattern is matched on the spreading foot.

Such small details might be brushed aside if it were not for the name of the owner who commissioned it. It appears on the top part or capital of the pillar. The calligraphic border is broken up into three panels which include the two hemistichs of a distich followed by the owner's name. The verses are taken from a Ma<u>s</u>navī or romance in the *Motaqāreb* metre that I have not been able to trace to its literary source:

مرا مانده دلرا چرا سوختی　　دلم را بداغ جفا سوختی

Why did you burn me, the disconsolate one ?
Why did you scar my heart with the brand of your cruel tyranny?

The name is introduced by the set Arabic formula "His servant" [*ᶜabduhu*] conveying mystical dedication to God which can be equally used by patrons or by artists signing their work. There is no doubt here that the formula refers to the patron:

عبده حیدرالحسینی ١٠٢٧

His servant Ḥeydar al-Ḥuseynī 1027 / 29 December 1617-18 December 1618.

This name is presumably that of *Mīrzā Ḥeydar valad-i Mīrzā Muẓaffar-i Ṣafavī*, "Prince Ḥeydar son of Prince Muẓaffar the Safavid", the great-great-grandson of Shāh Ismaᶜīl, who lived at the court of Shāh Jahān, as we hear from Muḥammad Ṣāliḥ Kanbū in the *Shāh Jahān-Nāma*.[23] Ḥeydar, as the son of Mīrzā Muẓaffar, was the brother of Mīrzā Muẓaffar's daughter, whom Jahāngīr requested to become his spouse. Solemn engagement ceremonies were held in the fifth year of his reign, in Rajab 1019 / 19 September - 18 October 1610. As the emperor's brother-in-law, Ḥeydar's position was high indeed. However, he must have been unassuming. Later in the *Shāh Jahān-Nāma* he is described as having a position of only one thousand footmen and two hundred horsemen under his command. He may have been a retiring man of religious inclinations, which would agree with the way in which he is identified on the candlestick he commissioned. On the candlestick, his name is simply followed by the qualifier "Ḥuseynī". This was regularly used by the descendants of Sheykh Ṣafī who in their protocol

23. *Shāh Jahān-Nāma, loc. cit.* (see note 14), Vol. I, p. 29 and Vol. II, p. 321 where the name of "Prince Ḥeydar the Safavid" [*Mīrzā Ḥeydar-i Ṣafavī*] crops up in Zī'l-Qaᶜda 1052 / 21 January - 19 February 1643. In Vol. I, pp. 39-40, after telling us that Jahāngīr asked for the hand of the daughter of Moẓaffar-e Ḥosayn Mīrzā, the historian gives his genealogy: "This prince of an exalted race is the issue of Sulṭān Ḥusayn Mīrzā son of Bahrām [Mīrzā], son of Shāh Ismaᶜīl."

VI. Folio 73v: 'Shīrīn engaged in an argument with Khusraw'.
Photo Bibliothèque Nationale, Paris.

V. Folio 65v: 'The architect Farhād holding Shīrīn on his shoulders'. Photo Bibliothèque Nationale, Paris.

IV. Folio 38: 'Khusraw, on horseback, passes Shīrī[illegible]'. Photo Bibliothèque Nationale, Paris.

III. Folio 4: 'The ascent (*mi*[c]*rāj*) of Muḥammad'. Photo Bibliothèque Nationale, Paris.

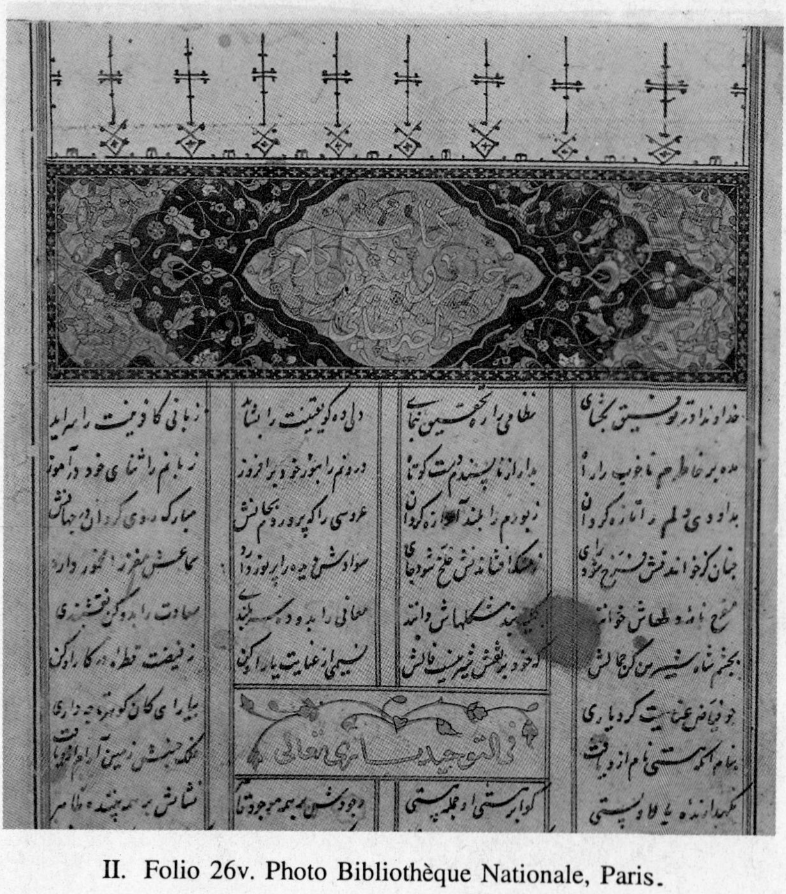

II. Folio 26v. Photo Bibliothèque Nationale, Paris.

invariably give precedence to their status as *sayyeds* over their royal titles - hence, no doubt, the omission of *Mīrzā* in the narrow space allowed by the cartouche. That the direct descendant of Shāh Isma^cīl should have commissioned a candlestick [*sham^cdān*] of traditional Safavid type is no great surprise. Nor is the fact that the Persian verses selected were very much those one would have found on a Safavid candlestick. Two more distichs are enclosed in the central calligraphic border, half-way up the shaft and in the calligraphic border running on the splayed base where it continues slightly to the left, in keeping with Safavid metalwork calligraphic layout. They are taken from a famous passage in Sa^cdī's "Garden of Scents" [*Būstān*] in the *Motaqāreb* metre:

شبی یاد دارم که چشمم نخفت
شنیدم که پروانه با شمع گفت
که من عاشقم گر بسوزم رواست
ترا گریه و سوز باری چراست

One night I remember my eyes would not go to sleep
I heard the butterfly telling the candle:
I am a [mystical] lover, if I burn 'tis right
[But] you, why should you weep and endure this burning ?[24]

Not all objects were heavily decorated. Indeed, some were barely so. One of the more remarkable products of what may henceforth be termed the Iranian Court Style of Hindustan is a basin [*lagan*] normally associated with a matching ewer for pouring out water [*āftābe*; Eastern Persian and Hindustani pronunciation: *āftāba*] (Figs. 8, 9). This one if of a type well known in Safavid Iran, which combines two modules: that of the squat, large-size bowl with rounded sides topped by a short vertical rim, and the basic shape of the usual water basin [*lagan*], with circular flat bottom and outcurving walls.

When it appeared in an art show in Riyadh, it was published as "Saudi Arabian".[25] Later, when its owner consigned it to Sotheby's for sale it was described as "Safavid" and, therefore, by implication, as

---

24. *Kulliyāt*, ed. Moḥammad ^cAlī Forūghī, Tehran, 1343/1964, p. 119; *Būstān-e Sa^cdī*, ed. Gholāmḥoseyn Yūsefī, Tehran, 1359/1980, p. 114, ll. 1964-5 (end of Chapter III).

25. *The Unity of Islamic Art*. An Exhibition of Islamic Art at the Islamic Art Gallery, The King Faisal Center for Research and Islamic Studies, Riyadh, 1405/1985. Illustrated in color p. 122. Caption p. 123.

Iranian.[26] The label, while far more plausible, was nonetheless inaccurate.

The name of the patron who commissioned it is engraved in champlevé on the vertical slightly concave surface of the rim. Ensconced in the middle of a continuous scroll carrying half-palmettes, it is written in a cursive script of the *Naskhī* type. The choice of *Naskhī* rather than *Nasta^clīq* would in itself be rather unusual for an Iranian designer (Fig. 10). The formula reads:

صاحبه ملا احمد

Owned by Mullā Aḥmad.

I have not yet traced this "Mullā Aḥmad" for sure. Could this be the Mollā Aḥmad-e Ṭabasī mentioned by Monajjem in the *Tārīkh-e ᶜAbbāsī* ? An "eminent man", he mas murdered in (or some time after) Rajab 998 / 6 May - 4 June 1590.[27] If so, it would point to some link between Mollā Aḥmad and Hindustan.

A later inscription was written in four lines in a cursive script from a non-professional hand (Fig. 11). It was engraved firmly if clumsily. I tentatively submit the following reading:

١ از تائيد اجزال حوالها حسيني اينچنين

٢ عبداله خان اوزبک ازتحويل

٣ حريم بكند عمل يلي النثار[؟]

٤ بخلف

1. In support of the generous donation of the Ḥuseynī deeds thus does
2. ᶜAbdilāh [= ᶜAbdullāh] Khān Ūzbak make

---

26. Sotheby's *Islamic Works of Art, Carpets and Textiles*, London, 16 April 1986, lot 188, illustrated p. 83. Entry headed "A Safavid Brass Basin, circa 1600." Diameter of opening: 30.2 cm.

27. Mollā Jalāl ad-Dīn Monajjem, *Tārīkh-e ᶜAbbāsī*, ed. Seyfollāh Vaḥid Niyā, Tehran, 1366/1987, p. 88. Farīd Bhakkārī, *Ẕakhīrat ul-Khawānīn*, ed. Syed Moinul Haq, Karachi, 1961-74 (Three Vols.); Vol. II, p. 10 mentions among the high-ranking *amīrs* a Mollā ᶜAlī-e Aḥmad-e Muhr-kan, a famous artist who engraved seals: could he be a son of the former ? And could ᶜAlī-e Aḥmad have designed early on in his career the basin ? All this goes no further than mere conjecture. At least one other Mollā Aḥmad is mentionned by Malik Shāh Ḥoseyn Sīstānī, *Ehiyā ol-Molūk*, ed. Manūchehr Sotūde, Tehran, 1344/1966, pp. 346 and 364 - the latter in 1005 / 25 August 1596 - 13 August 1597. The date would fit the probable period of the object. The status of the man, in the employ of the prince of Sistan, would also fit the piece but, again, there is no evidence that he went to Hindustan.

3. this remittance to the shrine a deed with enduring benefits [?]
4. for posterity

While much remains uncertain in the suggested reading, *ejzāl-e ḥavāleha* ("generous donation of the deeds") seems fairly clear. So does, most importantly, the name ᶜAbdullāh Khān Ūzbak. Jahāngīr says that on 22 Muḥarram 1015/30 May 1606, he elevated him to a position which placed 2500 footmen and 1500 horsemen under his command.[28] Farīd Bhakkārī notes that he was "one of the great amīrs. He had five thousand horsemen under his command. Mālwa and "Mātdū" were in his fief. When the imperial army appeared, he was seized with panic [*vāhīma*] and fled with ᶜAlī Mūhan to Gujarāt where he led a rebellious life [*baghī varzīd*]."[29]

The remittance of an object belonging to him to a shrine [*harīm*] implies that it was highly valued. If the "ᶜAbdilāh Khān Ūzbak" whose name was engraved on the walls of the *lagan* is, as I am inclined to believe, the ᶜAbdullāh Khān Ūzbak who rebelled against Akbar's armies, rather than the ruler of Tūrān carrying the same name, it dates the piece to some time late in Akbar's reign, probably in the last decade of the 16th century as seems stylistically probable. A rosette is engraved inside, on the bottom (Fig. 9). With its almond-shaped lobes, it is alien to the then contemporary repertoire of Iran, but fits with the archaistic survivals of Iranian ornament in Hindustan at that time. Determining the place of manufacture of such a piece is not easy. It is quite remarkable for its heavy, beautiful casting in a multiple alloy which is, perhaps, one shade more yellow than the deeper golden hue of Safavid cast vessels. The restraint in the decoration is remarkable. Perhaps this reflects the more austere tastes of a man with a religious turn of mind - if "Mullā" was indeed related to his actual status.

2. *The Pictorial Wine Bowls*

It is against this background of vessels in the Iranian taste produced for the literati and holders of high office in the Moghul court that a famous bowl in the Prince of Wales Museum, long thought to be

28. *Jahāngīr-Nāma*, ed. Muḥammad Hāshem, Tehran, 1359/1980, p. 42.

29. Bhakkārī, *loc. cit.*, Vol. I, pp. 209-10. Kvāja Niẓām od-Din Aḥmad, *Tabaqāt-i Akbarī*, ed. B. De, Calcutta, 1913-31, (Three Vols.), Vol. II, reviewing p. 425 ff. "the names of high ranking amīrs who found service in the exalted house" of Akbar. He succinctly notes p. 430, under "ᶜAbdullāh Khān Ūzbak" that "he was one of the exalted *amīrs*. Seized by panic, he left the government of Mālwa, went to Gujarāt, and having entered the ranks of the rebels, passed away." No date is given.

unique, must be reconsidered (Fig. 12).[30] The bowl once again reproduces very faithfully a western Iranian model, the footed wine bowl rising from a narrow foot, with low sides breaking off at a steeper angle at the transition of the broadly curving lower part of the walls, and a calligraphic border running at the top.

The layout of the calligraphic bands is uncommon and would appear to have been used only for bowls of a very high standard, particularly regarding the calligraphy itself. The closest Iranian equivalent is a later bowl in the Museum für Angewandte Kunst in Vienna, dated Zhū'l-Ḥijja 1076 / 4 June - 3 July 1666. There, in the upper border, elongated panels enclosed in slender cartouches with lobed extremities alternate with quatrefoils whose lobes are tangent to theirs. The difference is that on the Viennese bowl very narrow bands of interlacing scrolls run above and below the succession of calligraphic cartouches.

Below the simulated moulding separating the upper from the lower area, a succession of calligraphic cartouches are isolated from one another by trilobate escutcheons oriented upwards. Very slender curving filets come out of these to close off the panels. Towards the bottom, a second succession of similar panels enclosing calligraphy appears on both. They unquestionably draw on the same tradition.[31] Whether this was first established in Iran, as is likely, or in Hindustan as the relatively late date of the Vienna bowl might imply, is a question that cannot be answered for the time being.

The main area on the sides of the Prince of Wales Museum bowl is covered with figural scenes engraved with great skill. Handled in a style attempting to be thoroughly Iranian, they are almost entirely successful in this respect. Two hunting scenes succeed each other in a frièze that runs continuously around the bowl. The only separation between the two is provided by trees at opposite ends that could belong to either the one or the other. In one tableau, the hunter is a horseman wearing the costume of the later Shāh ᶜAbbās I period including the

30. Technique as described in note 11. Prince of Wales Museum, Bombay, Inventory N° 56.61. Tinning much worn leaving brownish red copper surface apparent. Diameter of opening 34-34.7 cm. Diameter of foot 12.15-12.2 cm. Height 15.4-16.5 cm. First published, P. Chandra, "Two Early Mughal Metal Cups", *Bulletin of the Prince of Wales Museum*, 1955-57, 5, pp. 57-60. Last published, Welch, *India: Art and Culture, 1300-1900*, New York, 1985, N° 119, pp. 190-1. The text compresses in somewhat distorted form the entry I sent to the Museum. It was reprocessed by the Museum without prior consultation with me while the book was already in printing stage.

31. W. Hein in *Kunst des Islam im Schloss Halbturn* (exhibition organized by the Museum für Angewandte Kunst, 28 May - 26 October 1977), Vienna, 1977, Pl. 128, p. 85. In the entry, p. 76, the date is inadvertently converted to 1665.

highly distinctive fur cap, the sash tightly fastened around the tunic and breeches falling just below the knees (Fig. 13). This is the attire that can be seen, for example, in a miniature dated 1041/1631.[32] The subject matter is the highly traditional hunt. The horseman in full gallop has just caught a wild ass [*gūr-e khar*] in the noose of his lasso [*kamand*], while a stag runs on a parallel course. Behind him, a mountain goat [*boz-e kūhī*] and a gazelle [*āhū*] run away in the opposite direction. This is the king as the triumphant hunter, possibly seen as "the second "Bahrām Gūr", an eulogistic title that refers to the feats of *Bahrām-e Gūr*, "Bahrām-of-the-Wild-Asses", celebrated in the *Shāh-Nāme* for his prowess when hunting wild asses.[33]

One detail here betrays the Hindustani handling: the face with the eyes slightly apart. It is remotely influenced by European figural art, and quite unlike the archetypal faces found in similar pictorial bowls from Iran.[34]

The other tableau provides a sequel to the Royal Hunt, Iranian style (Fig. 14). An elephant trots on, carrying a howdah in which a lion, possibly doped, peacefully waits. A hunt valet wearing a felt hat of sorts with a western touch to it leans on the rim of the lion cage, happily unconcerned about his forearm, within snapping reach of the lion. A hunt scout in Hindustani garb runs ahead of the elephant, in turn preceded by a horseman dressed in Safavid fashion and brandishing the pole of a banner [*derafsh*]. Leading the whole procession, a Hindustani horseman in full gallop rests his scimitar and waves his round shield at the Safavid horseman behind him. Is this a lion hunt organized for a royal guest from Safavid Iran ? Until a historical source yields a better clue, the assumption may be retained.

Most remarkable is the succession of the first twelve distichs from the *Sāqī-nāme* ["Cupbearer's Book"] by Ḥāfeẓ, precisely as they appear in the printed edition given by Yahyā Qarīb:

---

32. Arthur Upham Pope, ed. *A Survey of Persian Art*, Twelve Vols., Tokyo, New York, 2nd edn., 1965, Vol. IX, Pl. 917B shows such an attire in a miniature dated, according to the *Survey*, 1041 AH.

33. The celebration of the king as the royal hunter is as old as Persian poetry and goes far beyond Islam to pre-Achaemenid times. In the highly literate court milieu of Iran and Hindustan, specific links with this or that hunt, whether sung by Ferdowsī, Neẓāmī or others, need not be sought. All would be vividly present to the mind, part and parcel of themes absorbed as hundreds or thousands of verses were known by heart. Images such as these would be intended to conjure up various poetical passages.

34. Compare Melikian-Chirvani, *Islamic Metalwork*, N° 152, pp. 332-3. Illustrated Pl. 152, p. 333.

بیا ساقی آن می که حال آورد
کرامت فزاید کمال آورد
بمن ده که بس بیدل افتاده‌ام
وزین هر دو بیحاصل افتاده‌ام
بیا ساقی آن آب آتش خواص
بمن ده مگر یابم از غم خلاص
فریدون صفت کاویانی علم
برافرازم از پشتی جام جم
بیا ساقی آن ارغوانی قدح
که دل زو طرب یابد و جان فرح
بمن ده که از غم خلاصم دهد
نشان ره بزم خاصم دهد
بیا ساقی آن کیمیای فتوح
که با گنج قارون دهد عمر نوح
بده تا برویت گشاید باز
در کامرانی و عمر دراز
بیا ساقی آن آتش تابناک
که زردشت میجویدش زیر خاک
بمن ده که در کیش رندان مست
چه آتش پرست و چه دنیا پرست
بیا ساقی آن جام جم ده مرا
تعلل مکن دم بدم ده مرا
چه خوش گفت جمشید با تاج و گنج
که یک جو نیرزد سرای سپنج

Come, O Cupbearer, that wine which brings about a spiritual state
  Which increases God's grace, which brings perfection,
Give it to me for I have become downhearted
  And of these two I have become deprived
Come, O Cupbearer, that liquid which has the properties of fire
  Give it to me, perchance I shall find release from Self
In the manner of Fereydūn, the Kāviyānī banner
  I shall raise with the help of the bowl of Jamshīd
Come, O Cupbearer, that carmine red cup
  Through which the heart finds entertainment and the soul mirth
Give it to me that it may release me from grieving
  That it may show me the way to the Banquet of the Elect
Come, O Cupbearer, that elixir of victory
  That gives, with the treasure of Croesus, the life of Noah
Give it to me, that they may open in front of you
  The gate of fulfillment and long life
Come, O Cupbearer, that ardent fire
  That Zoroaster seeks in buried dens
Give it to me for in the religion of those who are intoxicated and liberated
  What is the difference between the fire-worshipper and the world worshipper ?
Come, O Cupbearer, that Jamshidian cup, give it to me
  Do not find excuses, give it to me every minute
For Jamshīd, with his crown and his treasure, said, how well,
  That this transient abode is not worth one grain of barley[35]

The poem would seem to have been chosen partly to echo the pictorial scenes. In the second tableau, the Iranian horseman galloping ahead of a Hindustani court attendant holds a banner. The words *Kāviyānī ᶜalam*, the "Kāviyānī banner", occur slightly to the Iranian horseman's right in the calligraphic band (Fig. 15). They usher in his appearance and identify him as the banner bearer. The line which specifies that he carries it "like Fereydūn" implicitly hails the horseman as "the Second Fereydūn". The eulogistic title which refers to the king of the ancient Keyanid dynasty of Iran, according to Islamic historiography and the *Shāh-Nāme*, signifies world kingship in the titulature of Iranian royalty. By virtue of the visual symmetry, this title is equally addressed to the Hindustani horseman whose footman has stuck a ban-

35. Ḥāfeẓ (see note 19), pp. 499-500.

ner on a mound at the extremity of the tableau.

The poem, further designates the bowl as the "Bowl of Jamshīd", another king of Keyanid dynasty in the *Shāh-Nāme* to whom the entire creation is revealed as he peers into his bowl. This is yet again a symbol of world kingship. Finally, the poem expresses the wish that the bowl may show to him who holds it "the way to the Banquet of the Elect."

All this leads one to wonder whether the bowl was not meant to convey in three-dimensional form yet another version of the imaginary encounter of Shāh ᶜAbbās I of Iran and Jahāngīr as illustrated in two famous miniatures now in the Freer Gallery of Art.[36] One of these shows the two rulers embracing each other as they stand on the terrestrial globe, and the other represents them seated side by side on an elevated platform or *takht*. A poem is calligraphed in a band of four panels at the top and another band at the bottom. It has remained unpublished in the original until now (*Motaqāreb* metre):

چو شاه جهانگیر و عباس شاه
دو شاه جوانبخت ظل اله
بشادی گرفته بکف جام جم
بدولت نشینند پهلوی هم
جهان گردد آباد از عدلشان
بباشند آسوده خلق جهان
چو یار و برادر بهم در خورند
الهی بدولت ز هم بر خورند

As Shāh Jahāngīr and ᶜAbbās Shāh
Two shāhs whose good fortune is in its prime, who are God's shadow [on earth]
Joyfully taking Jamshīd's cup in hand
Sit side by side { by good fortune / in [world] government }
The world is made prosperous by their equity
The people of the world find tranquillity

36. M.C. Beach, *The Imperial Image. Painting for the Mughal Court*, Washington DC, 1981, respectively: 1) 176 Illus. p. 31; colour Pl. p. 74 (and cover); entry pp. 169-70 and 2) 17c colour Pl. p. 78, entry pp. 170-1.

Like friend and brother, they are worthy of each other

O God { by good fortune / in government } they enjoy each other ['s company]

Pedestrian as they may be, these Persian verses have some merit in the historian's eyes. They spell out the theme of the two rulers sharing Jamshīd's cup, thus jointly ruling the world. Jahāngīr apparently entertained this idea of an entente cordiale between Safavid Iran and Moghul Hindustan at the very time when the hubris of both rulers pushed the two kingdoms into violent confrontation over the control of Eastern Iranian lands, in present-day Afghanistan.

The themes of the Jamshidian bowl shared by two rulers of Iran (Fig. 14) and Hindustan (Fig. 16), depicted in the guise of royal hunters is struck in much the same fashion on the Prince of Wales bowl. Their idyllic encounter is yet again illustrated and, as the poem tells us in the words of Ḥāfeẓ, the bowl shows them "the way to the Banquet of the Elect" - a banquet of the kind painted in the Freer Gallery of Art miniature.

Unless it is all mere coincidence, this would place the bowl at the same time as the miniature which, Milo Beach suggested, must have been done around 1618 AD.[37] This fits with all the characteristics of the piece and, not least, with the costumes of the later Shāh ᶜAbbās period, which rule out any dating prior to ca. 1615-1620.

A Persian inscription engraved just over the foot after the completion of the object records its mortmain donation [*vaqf*] to a shrine by one Ṣafiya Bēgum.[38] This too has remained so far unpublished in the original:

وقف حضرت ابا عبدالله الحسين عليه السلام نمود اين جام صفيه بيگم.
هر كه طمعكند بلعنت خدا و نفرين رسول گرفتار شود سنه ٩٩١

Ṣafiya Bēgum made a mortmain donation of this bowl to His Majesty Abā ᶜAbdullāh al-Ḥusayn. Peace be upon him. May who ever covets it be damned by the Lord and cursed by the Prophet. In the year 991 / 25 January 1583 - 13 January 1584.

37. *Ibid.*, p. 170.

38. The Turkish title, used in Hindustan, more rarely in Iran, suggests a Moghul princess.

Obviously, the date as it stands now is apocryphal. The reason for this may become clearer when Ṣafiya Bēgum is eventually identified. No such name appears in printed Safavid chronicles nor have I found it in the Hindustani sources accessible to me. There is a strong possibility that the original date actually read "111", *i.e.*, "111 after 1000" as the formula goes, which would place the donation between 29 June 1699 and 17 June 1700. On closer inspection, the first two digits would seem to have had the two half circles of the digit "9" added later.

If the Prince of Wales Museum bowl commemorates a wished-for royal hunting party given by Jahāngīr in honour of Shāh ᶜAbbās I and must, as such, be considered exceptional, it was by no means created in isolation.

At least two other pieces of comparable size fall into the same category of pictorial wine bowls. One is at present in a North American collection.[39] Its shape follows the previous model except for the foot. A low spreading base, slightly convex, is cut off by a broad, thick rib in turn topped by a low waisted ring (Fig. 17). The layout of the decoration and calligraphy is very similar. The upper border of calligraphic panels is arranged in precisely the same order. Panels framed by slender filets with trilobate extremities alternate with quatrefoils to which they are tangent. As on Jahāngīr's memorial bowl, the panels enclose an invocation calling God's graces upon the Fourteen Immune Ones [*Chahārda Maᶜṣūm*], *i.e.* the Prophet Muḥammad, Fāṭima, the Twelve Imāms, written in a good *thuluth/sulus* script. The quatrefoils likewise enclose the *Nadi ᶜAlī*, repeated three times. In the thirteenth quatrefoil, the Koranic verse LXI, 13, from the Chapter of the Battle Lines [= *Sūrat as-Ṣaff*] is calligraphed in the same *Nastaᶜlīq* script (Fig. 18):

نصر من الله و فتح قريب

Triumph comes from God and victory is nearing.

I know of no such occurence on any other wine bowl of this type. The fourteen quatrefoil encloses the name of an owner also in *Nastaᶜliq*, but clearly from a different hand (note the eye of the *ṣād*; the much thicker and shorter long slanting ligatures as in the group H-B-H in *ṣāḥibuhu* and, tellingly, the absence of slender volutes carrying formalized blos-

39. M. Dunn, *Antiques, Works of Art*, Claverack, 1992, reproduced in colour. Described as "Mughal" and dated in the first quarter of the 17th century. "Inscriptions" (no further specification) inaccurately characterized as "from both sects", meaning Sunni and Shiite.

soms replaced by more broadly spaced curves with two minute lobes, but no blossoms). This indicates that the bowl was acquired with one quatrefoil left blank. The first owner required an artist to engrave her name, presumably in the same workshop, shortly after the completion of the object. This "Raẓa" [for Raẓiya ?] Khānum" has yet to be identified.

Below, a border of fourteen panels alternating with quatrefoils enclosing formal ornament reproduce in the same fine *Nasta^clīq* script a famous ode by Ḥāfeẓ, in the *Ramal* metre. I hope to discuss elsewhere the interesting variants it includes:

در همه دیر مغان نیست چُه من شیدائی
خرقه جائی گرو باده و دفتر جائی
دل که آئینهٔ شاهیست غباری دارد
از خدا میطلبد صحبت روشنرائی
کرده‌ام توبه بدست صنم باده فروش
که دگر می نخورم بی رخ بزم آرائی
جویها بسته ام از دیده بدوران که مگر
بکنارم [کذا] به‌نشانند سهی بالائی
شرح این قصه مگر شمع برآرد بزبان
ورنه پروانه ندارد بسخن پروائی
این سرودم چه خوش آمد که سحرگه میگفت
بر در میکدهٔ با دف و می ترسائی
گر مسلمانی همینست که حافظ دارد
آه اگر از پی امروز بود فردائی

In the entire Zoroastrian hermitage there is none love-stricken like me
I from the house of those in robes, pledged to wine, and attached to his register
The heart that is the imperial mirror has a film of dust
It begs God for enlightened companionship

I expressed my repentance to the wine-selling idol:
Henceforth I would not drink wine away from the face that adorns the Banquet
From my eyes to the hem of my robe I shed streams of tears perhaps
They will seat near me one, lithe and slender,
Perhaps the candle will bring to its lips a comment upon this tale
Otherwise, the butterfly has no fear from the spoken word
How delighted I was by this song that a Christian
At dawn recited with flute and tambourine on the threshold of the tavern:
If to be a Muslim is that which Ḥāfeẓ displays
O that today may be followed by a tomorrow[40]

Two sets of key words in the poem give a hint at the reasons for its selection. One is the "Zoroastrian hermitage" [*deyr-e Moghān*] with the esoteric undertones attached to the ancient royal custom of secret wine libations celebrated by the inner circle [*khavāṣṣ*] on solemn occasions, in particular the Nowrūz.[41] The other key words are "the imperial mirror" [*ā'ine-ye shāhenshāhī*] referring to the red surface of the lumi-

40. Qarīb, *loc. cit.*, p. 401. The numerous variants in the bowl's text are not found elsewhere. In particular, the bowl has *be dowrān* "to the rotation" [of the wine bowl]" or "to our time" where Qarīb has "*be dāman*"; *Sayyed* Abo'l Qāsem Anjavī [*i.e.* Injū'ī], *Dīvān-e Khʷāje Ḥāfeẓ-e Shīrāzī*, Tehran, 2nd edn., 1346/1967, p. 248 has *be-dāman*, followed by *Sayyed* Moḥammad Reẓā Jalālī Nā'inī and Naẕir Aḥmad, *Dīvān-e Khʷāje Shams od-Dīn Moḥammad Ḥāfeẓ-e Shīrāzī*, Tehran, 3rd edn., 2535 sh./1976, p. 646. In line 4, all printed editions have *mī ṭalabam* ("I beg the Lord, etc.") instead of *mītalabad* "begs the Lord, etc." (but this version is recorded by Qarīb in one manuscript). In line 5, all have *ṣanamī*, "an idol", instead of *ṣanam*, "the idol" (but this version is recorded in three manuscripts by Qarīb and adopted in some other printed editions: Khānlarī, Afshār). In line 8, *bekenāram* clearly written, is metrically wrong. Qarīb, Anjavī Shīrāzī, and Jalālī Nā'inī and Aḥmad all have *dar kināram. Bar kenāram* is also found. In line 9, all three have *serr-e in nokte*, "the esoteric meaning of this anecdote", but the bowl version is *sharḥ-e in qeṣṣe*, "the commentary of this story"; Qarîb mentions this version in one manuscript and Anjavī Shīrāzī notes that Pazhmān Bakhtiyārī opts for it in his edition of Ḥāfeẓ. In line 11, *īn sorūdam*, "this song" differs from Qarīb (*in ḥadiṣam*, "this account", p. 402), Anjavī Shīrāzī (same, p. 248) and Jalālī Nā'inī and Naẕir Aḥmad (same, p. 647). In line 13, the bowl has *hamīnast* (lit. "is that very [thing] that, etc.) where the printed editions all read *az īnast* "is of the kind that". This points to a poem remembered by heart by someone who misremembered at least one word [*sorūdam*]. He tripped over the metre in line 8, which rules out an Iranian with a traditional literary background.

41. Melikian-Chirvani, "The Wine-Bull and the Magian Master", in *Recurrent Patterns in Iranian Religions from Mazdaism to Sufism / Studia Iranica*, Paris, 1992, Cahier 11, pp. 101-34, 3 Plates. See also by the same writer "From the Royal Boat to the Beggar's Bowl", *Islamic Art*, New York, 1990-91, IV, pp. 3-111.

nous wine reflecting the Beloved One's face thus revealed to the drinker as he bends over it.[42] The metaphor describes the search for God. Only His reflection - knowledge of Him through intermediary links - is seen by man when led to it along the path of initiation of which wine libations symbolize the essence.

This would fit rather well with all that we know of Jahāngīr's inclinations, including his fascination with Ḥāfeẓ. He quotes the Persian poet's famous distich about the light of wine right at the beginning of the *Jahāngīr-Nāma* ("Cupbearer illuminate our bowl with the light of wine - Musician, say that the world has complied with our desire") in the preface, when he recounts the Nowrūz celebrations in the first year of his reign.[43]

Unfortunately, admiration for Ḥāfeẓ was too universal among Persian readers at the time, as it is today, to be of much use as evidence to connect the bowl with Jahāngīr. Some link with the imperial house (perhaps as an intended gift for a princess, which could account for the feminine patron) is the most that can be inferred at this stage from the selection of the verses.

The visual motifs, with their royal slant, are consistent with such a link. The first tableau deals with the literary theme of Khosrow watching the sculptor Farhād hammering away at a mountain side which is reduced here to a rocky mound.[44] Further left, two royal hunts are illustrated. In one, a prince aims his bow at two wild asses [*gūr-e khar*]. Further left, a royal horseman in full gallop confronts an enormous lion about to jump under the eyes of a young prince standing near by and "biting the finger of amazement", as the Persian phrase goes, literally rendered by the designer. Are these to be seen as allusions to Bahrām Gūr and the wild asses, Bahrām Gūr hunting lion - or other similar royal episodes ?[45] This is highly probable but equally impossible to demonstrate.

---

42. On this theme spelled out in precise terms, on a wine bowl in a poem by Helali composed for that very bowl at the Herat court in 916/1510-11, see Melikian-Chirvani, *Islamic Metalwork*, pp. 279-81.

43. *Jahāngīr-Nāma*, *loc. cit.*, p. 29.

44. The theme is first dealt with by Neẓāmī's model in *Khosrow va Shīrīn*, ed. Ḥasan Vaḥīd Dastgerdī, Tehran, 1313/1934. See particularly p. 237: "With his pick-axe Shīrīn's portrait [*ṣūrat*] on this stone - he carved in low relief [*bar zad*] as [beautiful as] Mānī had done the images of the Arzhang". Many poets followed his model. Amīr Khosrow and Hātefī were widely read. There is no evidence that this image conforms to one version rather than the other. They probably added up as a source of inspiration.

45. The problem is the same. See Neẓāmī *Haft Peykar*, ed. Ḥasan Vaḥīd Dastgerdī, Tehran, Repr., n.d. Bahrām Gūr hunting wild asses, particularly p. 69: "Its [the king's horse's] hoof had dug the grave of a hundred wild asses", etc.

Two scenes might yield more precise clues when traced to the historical sources relating the incidents that they appear to illustrate. In the first one, two men (irate huntsmen ?) dressed in the later Shāh ᶜAbbās period fashion are engaged in a scuffle, using their firearms - one long musket, and a much shorter pistol - like cudgels to strike each other.[46] In the second scene, two elephants with royal trappings carrying young princes have their trunks locked in battle. On the right hand elephant, the two princes wear Safavid court robes and turbans. On the left hand elephant, a prince is seated cross-legged in rather precarious balance as the animal is goaded by his driver, ankus in hand.

The horses, the elephants and the lion are very finely handled, the humans a little less so. Some of the trees are superb. The use of shading in the form of finely incised strokes for the mane of the lion, the underbelly of two horses and the leaves of some trees or the detail of the rocky mound hewn by Farhād leave little doubt that the pattern was drawn by a *naqqāsh* [painter-designer].

A remarkable miniature, to which very little attention has been given, indeed proves that the most famous painter-designers [*naqqāshān*] were involved in designing metalwork. It surfaced in a commercial show at Colnaghi's, London, in 1979.[47] In the main field, two pigeons and a single dovecote above them are done without any attempt at the trompe l'oeil effect usual in Moghul miniatures, suggesting that the artist may have been working in a workshop where Iranian influence overwhelmingly prevailed, although the utterly original composition is pure Hindustani vintage. The painter-designer's signature is written in fine Hindustani *Nastaᶜlīq*. It runs in a single panel of calligraphy which forms part of a border of similar panels filled with formal scrolls pointing to the early 11/17th century, within Jahāngīr's reign. The signature reads:

عمل منصور نقاش

Made by Manṣūr, painter-designer.

It appears on an object done as a perfect working model, lovely as it may be. Shaped like a domed cover with a slight cusp, it is topped by a finial typical of Moghul art, half-way between the Timurid-period

46. Hunting with rifles was a princely pastime, much loved among others by Daniyāl who had a favorite rifle that he had named "one [shot] and a dead body", going so far as to coin a distich and have it engraved on his rifle. See *Jahāngir-Nāma*, p. 21.

47. T. Falk and S. Digby, *Paintings from Mughal India*, London, 1979, Cat. Nº 22, pp. 48-9.

finial and the lotus-bud of India. The piece is sparsely decorated on a golden ground (which is probably to be understood as the fine golden multiple alloy) with three silvery lobed rosettes [*shamsa*] in the otherwise plain band immediately above the border of three panels. Whether of silver (inlaid ? overlaid ?) or simply tinned, with a resultingly more subdued sheen, is impossible to say. Although the ornament is sparse, the designer has carefully indicated non-ornamental details that are seen in actual metalwork. Such are the two simulated mouldings between filets framing the panels with the signature and the formal scrolls at the base, or the moulding separating the border with the rosette from the upper section. The carefully rendered zigzag between two simulated mouldings at the top, and the pointed simulated ribs coming down from the finial are typical too. All this demonstrates that the famous Manṣūr, admired by Jahāngīr,[48] also designed metalwork. Other cases will no doubt be identified.

Different artists may have collaborated in designing the scenes on the pictorial wine bowls which could explain certain discrepancies, particularly in the bowl in North America.

A third bowl leaving the other two well behind has recently been acquired by a private collector who chose to remain anonymous (Fig. 20).[49] It has been silvered by electrolysis and retains the thin silver film presumably intended to make up for the original tinning that was rubbed off, as shown by the surface of the copper body coming through here and there.

The bowl reproduces precisely the same models as the other two except for nuances in the profile of the foot which comes closer to the Prince of Wales Museum piece, with its double incurving line allowing a salient edge halfway up.

The decorative programme looks more Iranian at first glance. As on Safavid bowls, the invocation to the *Chahārda Ma^cṣūm* is written in a single continuous border. The *Nasta^clīq* calligraphy is in a thoroughly

---

48. In the *Jahāngīr-Nāma*, p. 318, Jahāngīr recounts the commission he gave to "*Ustād* [the master] Manṣūr-e *naqqāsh* who is addressed as the proud rarity of our time [*Nādir ul-ᶜAsr*] to paint a couple of *shaenghār-e shāhī* birds with black spots sent by the ruler of Iran". The anecdote underlines Jahāngīr's passion for hawking birds. A miniature of two birds in Jahāngīr's *moraqqaᶜ* (see the *Emperor's Album*, color Plate 45), carries an inscription ascribing it to Manṣūr. I do not believe the inscription to be from Manṣūr's hand. The calligraphy is mediocre, unlike that in the Colnaghi miniature (which, ironically and without any apparent reason, was rejected as not by the master by some Western scholars). He can be seen to have been an accomplished calligrapher from his drawings.

49. Unpublished. Technique as in Note 11; silvered in the late 19th century. Diameter of opening: 32.5-33.2 cm. Diameter of foot: 10.85-10.9 cm. Height: 14.2 cm.

Iranian ductus, possibly from an Iranian hand. The one feature shared with the two other bowls is the quatrefoil of identical design and proportion separating the beginning and end of the calligraphic border. Instead of the two borders enclosing panels of Persian verses which are missing here altogether, the main field is framed by borders of inlerlacing scrolls. Right at the bottom, a festoon of incised interlacing arcades again underlines the apparent intention to stick more closely to the Iranian decorative programme.

But the detail of the ornament and the pictorial scenes leave no doubt as to the Hindustani nature of the design. The arcade at the bottom, with its interlacing trilobate arches that have no outer cusp or point, are unlike any such arcade in Safavid metalwork from Iran. The spandrels are filled in twos with formal blossoms pointed downwards alternating with cross-hatching. No such arrangement has been recorded in Iranian metalwork, nor have the trilobate cusped escutcheons enclosing fleur-de-lys that serve as pendents hanging from the arches. The pictorial frieze in the main field is more typically Hindustani in character than are those on the other two bowls. A landscape with animals, birds, and flowers runs on without a break.

The idiosyncratic details it shares with the North American bowl show beyond doubt that the two pieces were made at about the same time, drawing on the same repertoire. These details include the treatment of rocky promontories with clusters of three to four vertical curves suggestive of tufts of vegetation, the two identical animals emerging behind the rocks at the top and looking back in identical fashion, and a grouping of European castle towers with conical roofs, to mention but the most obvious.

Clinching evidence of the common background to the two pieces will be found in the wording of the invocation calling God's graces upon the *Chahārda Maᶜṣūm*. The concluding invocation uses the same qualifiers in the same succession when naming the twelfth Imām:

صل على الحجة القائم الدائم الخلف الصالح المنتظر المظفر المهدي
صاحب الزمان

> May God's grace descend upon the proof, permanent, enduring, the successor, pure in God's mind, awaited, triumphant, the Guide, the Master of Time.

It is shorter by one word, *hādī*, "leader", which is missing right at the end before "the Master of Time".

The patron who commissioned it (his name is written in *Nasta^c^līq*, from the same hand as in the invocation, with the same extremely fine ground of volutes carrying formal blossoms) has yet to be traced to a source.

صاحبه کاظم بندهٔ آل محمد

Owned by Kāẓim, servant of Muḥammad's house.

Two later owners had their names very carefully engraved below two diametrically opposite arches in the escutcheon-like space determined by the interlacing. The first one, neatly crossed out with vertical lines, is not easily made out. It may read "Khudādād". The other, perfectly clear, in good *Nasta^c^līq* of the late 11/17th century or early 18th century, says:

صاحبه [کذا] حاجی خانم

Owned by Ḥājī Khānum

The bowl must by then have been in Iran where the Turkish title "Khānum" was common, in contrast to Hindustan. One may speculate that it might have left Delhi at the time of Nāder Shāh's incursion.

It would, indeed, have been seen as a royal treasure well worth carrying away with the loot. In its mastery, particularly perceptible in the handling of the animals, it outstrips even the Prince of Wales Museum bowl. It draws more extensively on the Hindustani repertoire, particularly in the marvellous motif of the tall incurving stalk carrying lotus-like blossoms.

This may well have been created in the entourage of Manṣūr.

At that point the Persianizing style was no longer derivative. It had become absorbed into the art of Hindustan, rethought in its own terms to create masterpieces worthy of the centuries-old tradition of the subcontinent.

REFERENCES

I. Primary Sources in Persian

Abū Ṭāleb, *Dīvān-e Abū Ṭāleb-e Kalīm-e Hamadānī*, ed. Moḥammad Qahremān, Mashhad (*Enteshārāt-e Āstān-e Qods-e Raẓavī*), 1369/1990.

Borhān-e Tabrīzī, *Borhān-e Qāṭe^c^*, ed. Moḥammad ^c^Abbāsī, Tehran, 1344/1965.

Farīd Bhakkārī, *Zakhīrat ul-Khawānīn*, ed. Syed Moinul Haq, Karachi, 1961-1974 (Three Vols.).

Jahāngīr, *Jahāngir-Nāma*, ed. Muḥammad Hāshem, Tehran, 1359/ 1980.

Ḥāfeẓ, *Dīvān-e Khʷāje Ḥāfeẓ-e Shīrāzī*, ed. Sayyed Abo'l Qāsem Anjavī [*i.e.* Injū'ī], Tehran, 2nd edn., 1346/1967.

— *Dīvān-e Khʷāje Shams od-Dīn Moḥammad Ḥāfeẓ-e Shīrāzī*, eds. Mohammad Reẓā Jalālī Nā'inī and Naẕīr Aḥmad, Tehran, 3rd edn., 2535 sh./1976.

— *Dīvān-e Mowlānā Shams od-Dīn Moḥammad Ḥāfeẓ-e Shīrāzī*, ed. Yahiyā Qarīb, Tehran, 2nd edn., 1356/1977.

Malik Shāh Ḥoseyn Sīstānī, *Eḥiyā ol-Molūk*, ed. Manūchehr Sotūde, Tehran, 1344/1966.

Mīr Jamāl ad-Dīn Ḥoseyn b. Fakhr ad-Dīn Ḥasan Injū Shīrāzī *Farhang-e Jahāngīrī*, ed. Raḥīm ᶜAfīfī, Mashhad-Tehran, 1371/1972-1374/ 1975. (Three Vols.)

Mollā Jalāl ad-Dīn Monajjem, *Tārīkh-e ᶜAbbāsī*, ed. Seyfollāh Vaḥīd Niyā, Tehran, 1366/1987.

Muḥammad Ṣāliḥ Kanbū, *Shāh Jahān-Nāma*, ed. Waḥīd Qurayshī, Lahore, 2nd edn., 1967. (Three Vols.)

Neẓāmī, *Haft Peykar*, ed. Ḥasan Vaḥīd Dastgerdī, Tehran, Repr., n.d.

— *Khosrow va Shīrīn*, ed. Ḥasan Vaḥīd Dastgerdī, Tehran, 1313/1934.

Saᶜdī, *Būstān-e Saᶜdī*, ed. Gholāmḥoseyn Yūsefī, Tehran, 1359/1980.

— *Kolliyāt*, ed. Moḥammad ᶜAlī Forūghī, Tehran, 1343/1964.

II. Secondary References

Beach, Milo C., *The Imperial Image. Painting for the Mughal Court*, Washington DC, Freer Gallery of Art, Smithsonian Institution, 1981.

Brown, Percy *Indian Architecture* (1942-43), Two Vols., Vol. I., *Buddhist and Hindu Periods*, Bombay, Taraporevala, Repr. 1965.

Chandra, Pramod, "Two Early Mughal Metal Cups", *Bulletin of the Prince of Wales Museum*, 5 (1955-57), pp. 57-60.

Christie's, *Islamic Manuscripts, Miniatures and Works of Art*, London, 10 0ctober 1989.

— *Oriental Ceramics and Works of Art*, London, 22 April 1993.

Falk, Toby and Simon Digby, *Paintings from Mughal India*, London, Colnaghi, 1979.

Hain, Wilhelm, in *Kunst des Islam im Schloss Halbturn* (Exhibition organized by the Museum für Angewandte Kunst, 28 May-26 October 1977), Vienna, 1977.

Melikian-Chirvani, Assadullah Souren, "Recherches sur l'architecture de l'Iran Bouddhique I. Essai sur les origines et le symbolisme du stūpa iranien", *Le Monde Iranien et l'Islam*, Vol. III, Paris, 1975, Société d'Histoire de l'Orient, published by Droz of Geneva.

— *Islamic Metalwork from the Iranian World (8-18th centuries)*, London, 1982 (Victoria & Albert Museum, published by HMSO)

— "Islamic Metalwork as a Source on Cultural History", *Arts and the Islamic World*, I, 1, London, Winter 1982-83.

— "From the Royal Boat to the Beggar's Bowl", *Islamic Art*, IV, New York, Bruschettini Foundation, 1990-91.

— "The Wine-Bull and the Magian Master", in *Recurrent Patterns in Iranian Religions from Mazdaism to Sufism / Studia Iranica Cahier*, 11, Paris, 1992.

Pope, Arthur Upham, ed. *A Survey of Persian Art* (1938-58), Tokyo, New York, 2nd edn., 1965 (Twelve Vols.), Vol. IX.

Sotheby's, *Islamic Works of Art, Carpets and Textiles*, London, 16 April 1986.

The Unity of Islamic Art. An Exhibition of Islamic Art at the Islamic Art Gallery. The King Faisal Center for Research and Islamic Studies, Riyadh, 1405/1985.

Welch, Stuart Cary, *India. Art and Culture, 1300-1900* (1985), New York, Metropolitan Museum - Ahmedabad, Mapin Publishing Pvt., Repr., 1988. (Exhibition Catalogue)

Welch, S.C., Annemarie Schimmel, Marie L. Swietochowski and Wheeler M. Thackston, *The Emperor's Album*, New York, 1987.

Turkish Sufism in India: The Case of the Yasawiyya*

THIERRY ZARCONE

The Inward Dimension of the Naqshbandiyya in India

In a study devoted to the religious and cultural history of the lodges of Central Asian dervishes in Istanbul, I noticed that one of the lodges studied was founded by a Turk... from India.[1] This dervish had emigrated from India to Mecca, Europe and finally to the Ottoman Empire. Numerous sources tell us that Uzbek dervishes often left Transoxiana for the West to perform the *ḥajj* and used to stop for some time in Istanbul and in other cities situated on the road to Mecca. The Meccan itinerary southwards via India had also gained favour with dervishes from Transoxiana. It was this consideration which led me to investigate the question of Turkish Sufism in India. Of course, it is well known that the Naqshbandiyya, Kubrawiyya, and Firdusiyya orders had been introduced into India from Central Asia. Nevertheless, these orders, apart from the Naqshbandiyya whose peculiarities we shall discuss later in this paper, did not have a genuine Turkish seal. More interesting for our purpose, I am convinced, is the case of the Yasawiyya order - because of its original Turkish origin.

It is somewhat surprising that the study of Turkish Sufism in India has hitherto been neglected and that only rarely have Yasawiyya activities appeared in scholars' books. This can be seen from the two volumes of S.A.A. Rizvi's work on the history of Sufism in India which provide us with considerable information regarding Muslim mysticism in the subcontinent. In this monumental work, no chapter and not even a paragraph is dedicated to the Yasawiyya. Mention is made only of a certain Yasawī Shaykh who fights against 'infidels' in Bengal.[2] Furthermore, no attention has been paid to the ambiguous role played by the Naqshbandiyya. As it will be shown later, two different dimensions

* A Turkish translation of this article has been published under the title "Hindistan'da Türk Tasavvufu/ Yeseviyye Örnegi" in the Journal *Dergah* (Istanbul), April 1993, N° 38, pp. 19-20.

1. T. Zarcone, "Histoire et croyances des derviches turkestanais et indiens à Istanbul", *Anatolia Moderna*, Paris, 1990, 2, pp. 387-444.

2. S.A.A. Rizvi, *A History of Sufism in India*, Two Vols., New Delhi, 1986.

of this order evolved in India; the best example is given by Aḥmad Sirhindi's orthodox expression of the aforesaid order contrasting with that of Palangposht, in which Qalandarī and Yasawī influences are obvious. Concerning this topic, we have at our disposal quite a lot of relevant documentation, both in Persian and Turkic languages, in the form of manuscripts and lithographs.

The understanding of the following needs some explanation concerning the Sufi milieux in Transoxiana. The most prestigious leader of Turkic Islamic mysticism was Aḥmad Yasawī, eponym of the Yasawī order, who was born in Sayrām, in Turkestan, in 1167 AD. He studied first in Yasi, then in Bukhara, one of the major cultural centres of the Islamic world of his time. He entered the mystical way under the spiritual guidance of Shaykh Arslān and Yūsuf Hamadānī, one of the Khwāja of Turkestan. Because of his Turkish extraction, he was influential among the Turkish-speaking tribes of Central Asia who had preserved under the outer cloak of Islam many of the old pre-Islamic customs.[3] Aḥmad Yasawī named four successors. One of them, Sulaymān Ḥakīm Atā (died in 1183 AD), was the most famous among the Turks. Nevertheless, most representative of Central Asian Sufism because of the unrivalled fame he gained, was Bahā' al-Dīn Naqshband, follower of Yūsuf Hamadānī - like Aḥmad Yasawī - and of Halīl Atā, Khalīfa of Sulaymān Ḥakīm Atā.[4] It is thus clear that the Naqshbandiyya traces its descent as much from the *silsila* of the Khwājagān as that of the Yasawiyya. The rise and the spread of the Naqshbandiyya caused the Yasawī order to decline, but, from closer observation, it emerges from evidence that the 'way' of Aḥmad Yasawī did not altogether disappear, in spite of being overwhelmed by the new order. It can be easily seen from my earlier work on Istanbul dervish lodges that, from the fifteenth century and up to the beginning of the

3. On Aḥmad Yasawī and his cult in Central Asia, see F. Iz, *E.I.*², Vol. I, p. 308; V. Gordlevskiy, "Hodja Ahmed Yesewi", *Festchrift Georg Jakob*, Leipzig, 1952, pp. 57-67; F. Köprülü, *Türk edebiyatïnda ilk mutasavvïflar* (The First Mystics in Turkish Literature), Ankara, 1966; S.M. Demidov, *Turkmenskiy Ovliady*, Ashhabad, 1976; S.M. Demidov, *Sufismus in Turkmenien, Evolution und Relikte*, (1st edn., Astrakhan, 1977), Hamburg, 1988, pp. 42-5; L.Iu. Man'kovskaia, "Towards the Study of Forms in Central Asian Architecture at the End of the Fourteenth Century: the Mausoleum of Khavja Ahmad Yasavī", *Iran*, 1985, XXIII, pp. 109-27. Concerning the spreading of the Yasawiyya in Anatolia, see I. Melikoff, "Les origines du soufisme anatolien", *Turcica*, 1988, XX, pp. 7-18 and A.Y. Ocak, "Un cheik yesevī et babaī dans la première moitié du XIIIe siècle en Anatolie: Emīrci Sultān", *Turcica*, 1980, XII, pp. 114-24.

4. On the major Khalīfa of the Yasawiyya, see Köprülü, *Türk edebiyatïnda ilk mutasavvïflar*, *op. cit.*, pp. 74-82 and K.G. Zaleman, "Legenda pro Hakim-Ata", *Bulletin of the Imperial Academy of Sciences of St. Petersburg*, Sept. 1898, T. IX, N° 2.

twentieth century, certain Sufis from Turkestan and India, who used to call themselves Naqshbandī, were in fact as attached to Yasawī practices as to those of the Naqshbandī. It would seem logical that, in some cases, we should find the same occurrence in India.

A good example is given by Simon Digby's study on the history of a Naqshbandī lodge established in the Deccan in the late seventeenth and early eighteenth centuries. Regarding the clientèle of this *dargāh*, Digby writes that the dervishes, like the two founders of the lodge, - Bābā Palangposht and Bābā Musāfir - were "immigrants into the Indian subcontinent from the North-West, Tūrānis or Central Asians, with a few assimilated and equally immigrant Afghans and Kashmiris".[5] Belonging to the lodge too were soldiers of the Mughal army of annexation in the Deccan. What is relevant for our topic is Digby's criticism of Yohanan Friedmann - author of a study on Aḥmad Sirhindi's Naqshbandiyya - who "attributes an overwhelming contemporary revivifying influence on Naqshbandiyya and other Sufi movements in seventeenth century India to Shaykh Ahmad Sirhindi...".[6] Digby maintains that there is not even a single mention of Ahmad Sirhindi's influence over Bābā Palangposht's *dargāh*, which he depicts as a "Turanian cultural outpost in the Deccan".[7] Nor does he talk of any Yasawī influence. Nevertheless, from the detailed picture he gives of the Sufi customs cultivated among the lodge members, we understand that their beliefs appear to be a fusion of Qalandariyya and what I prefer to call Yasawiyya-Naqshbandiyya instead of just Naqshbandiyya.[8] Then, what is common to Bābā Palangposht's *dargāh* in the Deccan and to the Uzbek or so-called Indian *tekke* in Istanbul is that the Yasawiyya is still alive under the cloak of the Bahā' al-Dīn Naqshband's order. This is one of the reasons for which, in my earlier work, I focused on the characteristics of this threefold compound 'Yasawiyya-Qalandariyya-Naqshbandiyya' - which I present as a keystone for the understanding of the inner dimension of Turkic Sufism in Central Asia and in the Turkic diaspora. It is now obvious that an analysis of the Yasawiyya in India leads us to emphazise the inward dimension of the Naqshbandiyya in the subcontinent. It comes as no surprise to us that

5. S. Digby, "The Naqshbandīs in the Deccan in the Late Seventeenth and Early Eighteenth Century A.D.: Bābā Palangposh, Bābā Musāfir and their Adherents", in M. Gaborieau, A. Popovic and T. Zarcone, eds., *Naqshbandis: Historical Developments and Present Situation of a Muslim Mystical Order*, Istanbul, 1990, p. 167.

6. *Ibid.*, p. 170.

7. *Ibid.*, pp. 168, 170.

8. Digby remarks that "qalandārī custom of celibacy has been preserved" in that *dargāh*; cf. Digby, *id.*, p. 206.

major material regarding the Indian Yasawī is in fact provided by Persian sources dealing particularly with Naqshbandī subjects, generally with Shaykh biographies.

As a conclusion to my earlier work on the dervishes from Turkestan and India in Istanbul, I had shown that, in some cases, the *nisba* 'Hindī' used by so-called Indian dervishes reveals that these dervishes had in fact been Turks from Central Asia established first in India before reaching the Ottoman Empire. They represented there, as it has been shown for India, a mixing of the Yasawiyya, Qalandariyya and Naqshbandiyya, although the lodges to which they belonged were reputed to be Naqshbandī and sometimes Qādirī.[9] The same situation existed also in the Arab lands where several *Takiyyat al-Hunud* (lodge of the Indians) were founded, in Egypt, in Palestine, etc. There is one in Cairo, partly destroyed, whose minaret which still exists today is locally called *Takiyyat al-Hunud wa 'l-Bakīstan.*[10] Another lodge interestingly called *Takiyyat Bayrām Bābā* was built in Aleppo (in Syria), at the end of the fifteenth century. The founder claimed that he belonged to the Qalandariyya and was a follower of both Aḥmad Yasawī and Bahā' al-Dīn Naqshband.[11]

At times, one might get the impression that the Yasawiyya is a branch of the Chishti order, as may be understood from the index of Hermann Ethé's *Catalogue of Persian Manuscripts in the Library of the India Office*. He states that "Ahmad Yasawi (Khwājah or Sulṭan) called Atā, (was) the founder of the Yasawi branch-family of the Chishti order...".[12] However erroneous this definition may be, it reveals to us that, in some cases, the Yasawiyya could have been integrated by a pure Indian order. Still, Indian *taẕkirat* (biographies) provide us with an unambiguous biography of Aḥmad Yasawī as, for example, that of Dārā Shikuh's *Ṣafinat al-awliyā*. In this book, the

9. Zarcone, "Histoire et croyances des derviches turkestanais et indiens à Istanbul", pp. 184-94.

10. See D. Behrens-Abouseif, *The Minarets of Cairo*, Cairo, 1985, p. 69 and ᶜAlī Bāshā Mubārak, *Al-Khiṭaṭ al-tawfiqiyya al-jadīda li-Miṣr al-Qāhira wa mudunihā wa bilādihā al-qadīma wa' l-shahīra*, Cairo, 1982, Vol. II, p. 284. Concerning the 'Indian lodges' in Arabic lands, see my forthcoming paper "Couvents ouzbek et indiens et Kalenderhāne dans les provinces arabes de l'Empire ottoman".

11. Cf. Kāmil al-Ghazzī, *Kitāb Nahr al-dhahab fi Tārīkh Ḥalab*, Halab, n.d., Vol. II, pp. 408-9; Muḥammad Rāghib al-Ṭabbākh, *Aᶜlām al-nubalā' bi-tārīkh Ḥalab al-shahbā'* (1923), Damascus, 1988, Vol. VII, pp. 388-9; H. Gaube, *Arabische Inschriften aus Syrien*, Beirut, Wiesbaden, 1978, p. 57.

12. H. Ethé, *Catalogue of Persian Manuscripts in the Library of the India Office*, Oxford, 1903. His interpretation seems to have been inspired by the reading of some manuscripts among which is M. Bulaq's *Maṯlūb al-Ṭālibīn* (Ms. N° 653).

founder of the Yasawiyya is clearly pictured as a Turkish follower of Yūsuf Hamadānī and as representing the first link of the Atā dervish branch continued by Manṣūr Atā, Sa'id Atā, Sulaymān Ḥakim Atā etc.[13]

Another difficulty in dealing with the question of 'Turkish Sufism' in India is that of the "Turk" ethonym. In Henry George Keene's book, *The Turks in India*, published in 1879, we read that "the word Turk must be understood as meaning a Mussalman Tartar who has become partly Aryanised in features and habits...".[14] Nevertheless, the blurring of ethnic distinction between central Asian Turks and Persian speaking Tājīk among the immigrants from Central Asia has been customary. This is clearly shown in Simon Digby's work on the Naqshbandī of the Deccan. The Qalandar dervishes whose lives he analysed "were recent immigrants from Transoxiana and belonging to the settled or 'Tajik' population even though they were commonly called 'Mughals' or 'Turks' in the Indian ethnic classification of the time".[15]

Naqshbandī-Yasawī Dervishes in India

We now turn to a discussion of the material on Yasawī Sufism. Several sources tell us that the Yasawiyya spread reached its highest point in the sixteenth century. We learn for instance from a Turkish traveller's account of Seydī Alī Reis, that Yasawī Sufis were present everywhere in the Islamic world, Sind, Panjab, Afghanistan, Mawarannahr, Khorasan, Azerbayjan.[16] It can therefore be assumed that Yasawī dervishes had entered India, Anatolia and Syria as far back as the fourteenth century. There are some other dervishes about whose order we are unaware, although it is obvious that they were attached to Qalandarī practices - celibacy for example - and had established them-

13. Cf. Dārā Shikuh, *Ṣafinat al-Awliyā*, Kanpur, 1318/1900. The *Khazinat al-Aṣfiyā'* of M. Gulām-Sarwar Lahorī (Kanpur, 1914) provides us too with biographies of Aḥmad Yasawī (pp. 531-2) and of the major representatives of the Yasawiyya: Khwāja Ḥakīm Atā (p. 534), Khwāja ᶜAbd al-Malīk, Khwāja Manṣūr (p. 535), Khwāja Tāj Atā (p. 535), Khwāja Sa'īd Atā (pp. 535-6), Khwāja Zangi Atā (p. 536-8), Khwāja Sayyid Atā (p. 560).

14. H.G. Keene, *The Turks in India*, London, 1879, p. 8.

15. Digby, "The Naqshbandīs in the Deccan", p. 169. See also S.B.P. Nigam, "Organisation of Turkish Nobility in India. 1206-1398", *Islamic Culture*, 1965, XXXIX, 4, pp. 271-83. Concerning the 'Turk' in Indian literature, see A. Schimmel, "Turk and Hindu: a poetical image and its application to historical fact", in S. Vryonis, ed., *Islam and Cultural Change in the Middle Ages. Fourth Giorgio Levi Della Vida Biennial Conference*, Wiesbaden, 1975, pp. 107-26.

16. Köprülü, *Türk edebiyatında ilk mütasavvıflar*, p. 63.

selves in the subcontinent. This is the case of both Shaykh Muḥammad Turk who came from Turkestan and settled in Narnaul and of Shāh Khidhr, the two having reached India in the beginning of the thirteenth century.[17] The introduction of the Yasawiyya in India could yet be dated, according to the material we have at our disposal, from the time of the Mongol invasion of Central Asia which caused many Muslims to flee in the direction of lands beyond the Indus as they did to Anatolia. The valley of Kashmir because of its position was Islamized directly from Central Asia and Khorasan and not through the South. During the fourteenth century, Persians and Persianized Turks began to enter this area and exercised considerable influence on the social and cultural life of the inhabitants of the Valley. As Muhammad Ishaq Khan has noted, Sufi saints played an important role in bringing about an Iranian orientation of the Kashmiri's culture.[18] Moreover, the Islamisation of the Valley is traditionaly attributed to a Sufi dervish whose name is Bulbul Shāh.[19] In a book of dervish biographies, written by ᶜAlī Shir Nawāyī in oriental Turkish (Chaghatay), it is stated that a Yasawī dervish named Khwāja Bahā' al-Dīn, a grandson of Ismāᶜīl Atā (the latter died in 1302),[20] escaped from Central Asia by force and settled in Kashmir. There, he gained fame and made many disciples among the inhabitants of the Valley.[21]

17. On Muḥammad Turk Narnuli, see ᶜAbd al-Ḥaqq Dihlawī, *Akhbār al-Akhyār fi asrār il-Abrār*, Bombay, 1280/1864, pp. 50-1 and I.H. Siddiqui, "The Early Chishti Dargahs", in C.W. Troll, ed., *Muslim Shrines in India*, Delhi, 1989, pp. 2-3. On Shāh Khidhr, see ᶜAbd al-Haqq Dihlawī, *op. cit*., pp. 52-3; Digby, "Qalandars and Related Groups: Elements of Social Deviance in the Religious Life of the Dehlī Sultanate of the Thirteenth and Fourteenth Centuries", in Y. Friedmann, ed., *Islam in Asia*, Jerusalem, 1984, pp. 84-5, and Zarcone, "Histoire et croyances des derviches turkestanais et indiens à Istanbul", pp. 181-2.

18. See M.I. Khan, "Persian Influences in Kashmir in the Sultanate Period (1320-1586)", *Islamic Culture*, 1977, LI, 1, pp. 1-10 and A. Ahmad, "Conversions to Islam in the Valley of Kashmir", *Central Asiatic Journal*, 1979, Vol. XXIII, pp. 3-18

19. Cf. Ahmad, "Conversions to Islam in the Valley of Kashmir", p. 8. See also P.N.K. Bamzai, *Kashmir and Central Asia*, New Delhi, 1980, pp. 211-21.

20. Ismā'il Atā was the major Khalīfa of Sayyid Atā, himself second Khalīfa of Ḥakīm Atā who was Khalīfa of Aḥmad Yasawī; see Köprülü, *Türk edebiyatïnda ilk mütasavvïflar*, p. 378; D. De Weese, "Atā'īya Order", *Encyclopaedia Iranica*, Vol. II, 8, pp. 904-5.

21. Alī Shīr Nevāyī, *Nesāyimü 'l-Mahabbe min Shemāyimi 'l-Fütüvve*, text edited in transcription by Kemal Eraslan, Doctoral Thesis, Istanbul, 1979. The paragraph concerning Khwāja Bahā' al-Dīn is the following: "Ismāᶜīl Atāga nebīredür. Bu khānvādede alardïn ᶜalīhimmetraq ve muᶜazamraq ötmeydür. Dāyim qush salmaqqa ve av avlamaqqa tabl ü ᶜalem bile ishtigāl körgüzüler irmish. Zamān pādshāhï alarga ilnin irādet ü hücūmïdïn yaman iltip mülkdin ikhrāc buyurupturlar. Kishmīrga barïp ol khalq alarga mürid bolgandurlar" (p. 385). See the commentaries of Fuat Köprülü on the biographies of the Yasawī dervishes contained in this book in "Orta-Asya türk dervishligi hakkïnda notlar" (Notes regarding Turkish dervishes from Central Asia), *Türkiyat Mecmuasï*, 1965, XIV, pp. 259-62.

There is no indication whether Khwāja Bahā' al-Dīn belonged to the Naqshbandiyya or not; however, it is asserted that a Yasawī-led Sufi movement evolved in this area.

On the other hand, we learn from a Turkish source that a certain Shaykh Sharīf Muḥammad al-Hindī, established in Agra, both a follower of Ḥājjī Bektash, a Turkish mystic,[22] and of Aḥmad Yasawī, was in the service of the Mughal ruler Humāyūn who favoured him with the title of *ṣadr-i āṣaf*, or private counsellor. We know that immigrants from Central Asia held high offices in the Mughal state, particularly in the late seventeenth and early eighteenth centuries, but it is quite surprising to find a Yasawī dervish filling this office. After the conquest of North India by Sher Shāh, in the middle of the sixteenth century, Muḥammad al-Hindī followed the Emperor to Iran. There, Humāyūn called for Shāh Tahmāsp's help. After a warm welcome to Humāyūn, the Shāh finally tried to force them to adopt the Shiᶜa creed. Muḥammad al-Hindī chose to flee Iran and reached Istanbul; later he settled in Romania.[23]

In the beginning of the sixteenth century, when the Yasawiyya spread westwards and southwards, there was in Central Asia a competitive atmosphere among the followers of the three major Sufi orders of this area: the Yasawiyya, the Naqshbandiyya and the Kubrawiyya. The Yasawiyya was not absorbed only by the Naqshbandiyya though such was usually the case, but by the Kubrawiyya as well. The best example is that of ᶜAbd al-Wahhāb Khwāja, a pupil of Barzishābādī, founder of the Zahabiyya branch of the Kubrawiyya, though ᶜAbd al-Wahhāb Khwāja came from a family of Yasawī Shaykhs whose *silsila* went back to Ṣadr Atā, a *khalīfa* of the great Yasawī Zangī Atā (died 656/ 1258 A.D.). This ᶜAbd al-Wahhāb Khwāja left Transoxiana for India during the reign of Shāhjahān.[24]

In this last example, which is that of a dervish known to belong to a Yasawī family, the association Yasawiyya-Naqshbandiyya - of which

---

22. There is no indication whether he came directly from Turkestan or from Anatolia. The second hypothesis could be more accurate because of Muḥammad al-Hindī's alleged Bektashi appartenance and of his flight from Iran to the Ottoman empire. On the Bektashi order, see J.K. Birge, *The Bektashi Order of Dervishes*, London, 1965.

23. Cf. Nev'īzāde ᶜAtā'ī, *Hadāikü 'l-Hakāik fi Tekmileti 'l-Shakāik* (1634-35), in *Shakā'ik-i Nu'māniyye ve Zeyilleri*, Vol. I, Istanbul, Repr., 1989, p. 191. For further details on the flight of Humāyūn to Iran, see M.R. Kazimi, "Humayun in Iran", *Islamic Culture*, 1969, XLIII, 1, pp. 5-11.

24. Cf. De Weese, "The Eclipse of the Kubravīyah in Central Asia", *Iranian Studies*, 1988, XI, 1-2, pp. 45-83 and Rizvi, *A History of Sufism in India*, Vol. II, pp. 124-5.

mention has been made previously - is salient because of the dervish's name. He was called Khwāja Ḥāfiẓ Aḥmad Yasawī Naqshbandī (died 1116/1704 AD). Here we have a case of no definite limits between the two mystical affiliations. The Shaykh is a representative in fact of both the last stage of the Yasawiyya and of the rising Naqshbandiyya from Central Asia. Nevertheless, Khwāja Ḥāfiẓ incarnates more the Naqshbandiyya in the eyes of Indian hagiographers than the Yasawiyya.[25] The conflation of both orders emerges in the *Khazinat al-Aṣfiyā'* where the biographical notices of Yasawī saints are found in the book's sub-division dealing with the Naqshbandī Shaykhs.[26] According to the *Khazinat al-Aṣfiyā'*, Khwāja Ḥāfiẓ Aḥmad Yasawī Naqshbandī travelled as far as the Hijaz, Jerusalem, Mecca and Medina, Damascus, Iraq, Rumelia, and Russia. He went then to Kashmir and adopted the Valley as a retirement-place in order to escape from society and to perform the *khalwat*. There, he used to attend meetings at Shaykh Agāh Mulā Shāh's famous lodge and gained two prominent disciples, Khwāja Niẓām al-Dīn ben Mu'in al-Dīn and afterwards Khwāja Nūr al-Dīn Muḥammad Āftāb.[27] Mulā Shāh's lodge was well-known in the Kashmir Valley, the founder himself (died in 1072/1661), having been the *murshid* (spiritual master) of Prince Dārā Shikuh. Khwāja Niẓām al-Dīn ibn Mu'in al-Dīn seems to have been a zealous propagandist of the Naqshbandiyya in Kashmir.

However detailed and informative the biographies of Yasawī Shaykhs mentioned above may be, nothing assures us that any organized Yasawī group spread out in India. It might be argued only that the Yasawiyya was still alive inside some branches of the Naqshbandiyya established in India. In addition to these, a description may be found in an Indian manual of practical Sufism, of an exercise usually experienced among Yasawī dervishes: the *dhikr* of the saw

25. It is also the opinion of Köprülü, in *Türk edebiyatinda ilk mütasavviflar*, p. 64.

26. *Khazinat al-Aṣfiyā'* is divided into seven chapters. Among them four are devoted to Sufi orders: Qādiriyya, Chishtiyya, Naqshbandiyya and Suhrawardiyya; cf. C.A. Storey, *Persian Literature. A Bio-bibliographical Survey*, Vol. II, London, 1943, pp. 1043-4. In another case, the title of the seventeenth chapter of the *Majmua-ye Awliyā* of ᶜAli Akbar Ḥoseyn Ardastani (India Office N° 645) is "Shaykh of the Naqshbandī order and Turkish Shaykh"; cf. Ethé, *op. cit.* In addition to these, Rizvi writes: "The Naqshbandiyya sūfī Khwāja Ahmad Yasawī (d. 514/1120)", in his *Socio-Intellectual History of the Isnā ᶜAsharī Shi'is in India*, Delhi, 1986, Vol. I, p. 190.

27. Cf. M. Gulam-Sarwar Lahori, *Khazinat al-Aṣfiyā'*, *op. cit.*, pp. 656-7. On Shaykh Agāh Molā Shāh, see Rizvi, *A History of Sufism in India*, Vol. II, pp. 115 sq. and M.A. de Kremer, "Mollā-Shāh et le spiritualisme oriental", *Journal Asiatique*, 1869, 6th Series, T. XIII, pp. 105-59. On Khwāja Niẓām al-Dīn ben Mu'in al-Dīn, see Rizvi, *A History of Sufism in India*, Vol. II, p. 184.

(*dhikr-e arra*) named on account of the rasping sound it produces.[28] This is another indication that Indian Sufism was not unaware of Turkish Yasawī mysticism.

REFERENCES

ᶜAbd al-Ḥaqq Dihlawī, *Akhbār al-Akhyār fi asrār il-Abrār*, M. Hashimi, Bombay, 1280/1864.

Ahmad, Aziz, "Conversions to Islam in the Valley of Kashmir", *Central Asiatic Journal*, 1979, Vol. XXIII, pp. 3-18.

ᶜAlī Bāshā Mubārak, *Al-Khiṭat al-tawfiqiyya al-jadīda li-Miṣr al-Qāhira wa muduniha wa bilādihā al-qadīma wa' l-shahīra*, Twenty Vols, Cairo: al-Hay'at ul-Miṣriyyat ul-ᶜāmmat li'l-kitāb, 1982.

Alī Shīr Nevāyī, *Nesāyimü 'l-Mahabbe min Shemāyimi 'l-Fütüvve*, ed. Kemal Eraslan, Doctoral Thesis, Istanbul: Istanbul Üniversitesi Edebiyat Fakültesi Yayïnlarï, N° 2654, 1979.

Bamzai, P.N.K., *Kashmir and Central Asia*, New Delhi: Light and Life Publishers, 1980.

Behrens-Abouseif, Doris, *The Minarets of Cairo*, Cairo: The American University in Cairo, 1985.

Birge, John Kingsley, *The Bektashi Order of Dervishes*, London: Luzac and Co, 1965.

Dārā Shikuh, *Safinat al-Awliyā*, Kanpur, 1318/1900.

De Weese, Devin, "Atā'īya Order", *Encyclopaedia Iranica*, New York and London: E. Yarshater, 1988, Vol. II, 8, pp. 904-5.

— "The Eclipse of the Kubravīyah in Central Asia", *Iranian Studies*, 1988, XI, 1-2, pp. 45-83.

Demidov, S.M., *Turkmenskiy Ovliady*, Ashhabad, 1976.

Demidov, S.M., *Sufismus in Turkmenien, Evolution und Relikte*, (1st edn. Astrakhan, 1977), Hamburg: Reinhold Schletzer Verlag, 1988, pp. 42-5. (Turkmenenforschung band 11)

Digby, Simon, "Qalandars and Related Groups. Elements of Social Deviance in the Religious Life of the Dehlī Sultanate of the Thirteenth and Fourteenth Centuries", in *Islam in Asia*, ed. Yohanan Friedmann, Jerusalem: The Hebrew University of Jerusalem, The Magnes Press, 1984, pp. 60-108.

28. Cf. H. Imdād Allāh, *Ẓiyā' al-Qulub*, Delhi, 1244/1824, p. 15. See my analysis of this book in Zarcone, "Histoire et croyances des derviches turkestanais et indiens à Istanbul", p. 191. On the dhikr of the saw, see J. Fletcher, "The Naqshbandiyya and the Dhikr-i Arra", *Journal of Turkish Studies*, 1977, I, pp. 113-9.

— "The Naqshbandīs in the Deccan in the Late Seventeenth and Early Eighteenth Century AD: Bābā Palangposh, Bābā Musāfir and their Adherents", in *Naqshbandis. Historical Developments and Present Situation of a Muslim Mystical Order*, eds. M. Gaborieau, A. Popovic and T. Zarcone, Istanbul: IFEA/Isis Press, 1990, pp. 167-207.

Ethé, Hermann, *Catalogue of Persian Manuscripts in the Library of the India Office*, Oxford: printed for the India Office by Horace Hart, Printer to the University, 1903.

Fletcher, Joseph, "The Naqshbandiyya and the Dhikr-i Arra", *Journal of Turkish Studies*, 1977, I, pp. 113-9.

Gaube, Heinz, *Arabische Inschriften aus Syrien*, Beirut, Wiesbaden: Kommission bei Franz Steiner Verlag, 1978.

Gordlevskiy, V., "Hodja Ahmed Yesewi", *Festchrift Georg Jakob*, Leipzig: 1952, pp. 57-67.

Gulām-Sarwar Lahorī, M., *Khazinat al-Aṣfiyā'*, Kanpur, 1914.

Imdād Allāh, Ḥajjī, *Ẓiyā' al-Qulub*, Delhi: Mujaba'i Press, 1244/1824.

Iz, F., "Ahmad Yasawī", *Encyclopédie de l'Islam*[2], Vol. I, 2nd edn., Leiden: E.J. Brill, 1975, p. 308. (Abbr. *E.I.*[2])

Kāmil al-Ghazzī, *Kitāb Naḥr al-dhahab fi Tārīkh Ḥalab*, Three Vols, Halab: al-Maṭbaᶜa al-Mārūniyya, n.d.

Kazimi, Masoom Reza, "Humayun in Iran", *Islamic Culture*, 1969, XLIII, 1, pp. 5-11.

Keene, Henry George, *The Turks in India*, London, 1879.

Khan, Mohammad Ishaq, "Persian Influences in Kashmir in the Sultanate Period (1320-1586)", *Islamic Culture*, 1977, LI, 1, pp. 1-10.

Köprülü, Fuat, "Orta-Asya türk dervishligi hakkïnda notlar" (Notes regarding Turkish dervishes from Central Asia), *Türkiyat Mecmuasï*, 1965, XIV, pp. 259-62.

— *Türk edebiyatïnda ilk mutasavvïflar* (The First Mystics in Turkish Literature), Ankara: Ankara Üniversitesi Basimevi, 1966.

Kremer, M.A. de, "Mollā-Shāh et le spiritualisme oriental", *Journal Asiatique*, 1869, 6th Series, T. XIII, pp. 105-59.

Man'kovskaia, L. Iu., "Towards the Study of Forms in Central Asian Architecture at the End of the Fourteenth Century: the Mausoleum of Khavja Ahmad Yasavī", *Iran*, 1985, XXIII, pp. 109-27.

Melikoff, Irène, "Les origines du soufisme anatolien", *Turcica*, 1988, XX, pp. 7-18.

Muḥammad Rāghib al-Ṭabbākh, *Aᶜlām al-nubalā' bi-tārīkh Ḥalab al-shahbā'* (1923), Seven Vols, Damascus: Maṭbaᶜa al-Sabah, 1988.

Nev'īzāde ᶜAtā'ī, *Hadāikü 'l-Hakāik fi Tekmileti 'l-Shakāik* (1634-35), in *Shakā'ik-i Nu'māniyye ve Zeyilleri*, Vol. II, Istanbul: Çagrï Yayïnlarï, Repr., 1989.

Nigam, S.B.P., "Organisation of Turkish Nobility in India. 1206-1398", *Islamic Culture*, 1965, XXXIX, 4, pp. 271-83.

Ocak, Ahmet Yashar, "Un cheik yesevī et babaī dans la première moitié du XIIIe siècle en Anatolie: Emīrci Sultān", *Turcica*, 1980, XII, pp. 114-24.

Rizvi, Sayyid Athar Abbas, *A History of Sufism in India*, Two Vols., New Delhi: Munshiram Manoharlal Publishers, 1986.

— *Socio-Intellectual History of the Isnā ᶜAsharī Shī'is in India*, Two Vols., Delhi: Munshiram Manoharlal, 1986.

Schimmel, Annemarie, "Turk and Hindu: A Poetical Image and its Application to Historical Fact", in *Islam and Cultural Change in the Middle Ages. Fourth Giorgio Levi Della Vida Biennial Conference*, ed. Speros Vryonis, Wiesbaden: Otto Harrassovitz, 1975, pp. 107-26.

Siddiqui, Iqtidar Husain, "The Early Chishti Dargahs", in *Muslim Shrines in India*, ed. Christian W. Troll, Delhi: Oxford University Press, 1989, pp. 1-23.

Storey, C.A., *Persian Literature. A Bio-bibliographical Survey* (1927), Four Vols., London: Luzac & Co., Vol. II, 1943.

Zaleman, K.G., *Legenda pro Hakim-Ata*, Bulletin of the Imperial Academy of Sciences of St. Petersburg, Sept. 1898, T. IX, 2.

Zarcone, Thierry, "Histoire et croyances des derviches turkestanais et indiens à Istanbul", *Anatolia Moderna*, Paris: IFEA-Ed J. Maisonneuve, 1990, 2, pp. 387-444.

— "Couvents ouzbèques et indiens et Kalenderhāne dans les provinces arabes de l'Empire ottoman" (Forthcoming).

Indo-Persian Literature on Art-Music: Some Historical and Technical Aspects

FRANÇOISE 'NALINI' DELVOYE

Medieval Indo-Persian literature represents an important source of information on both Persian and Indian art-music. Written in Persian by authors of Iranian and Indian origin - a fact which may explain the variety of the information provided - it constitutes a rich form of documentation on music, from a historical and a technical perspective (on both its theoretical and practical aspects), often combined with a remarkable sociological awareness. Both Persian and Indian art-music are often referred to, with occasional mentions to folk or popular forms of singing and musical instruments.

Music: Mūsīqī, samā^{c}, ghinā', surod...

The Arabo-Persian terms for music differ according to various authors even at a given time. The word *mūsīqī* of Greek origin is a rather generic term. The word *ghinā'*, which in the Arabic context designates secular music and musical practice in general, is also found in Indo-Persian writings on music, in a rather wide meaning.[1] *Samā^{c}* which in its original Arabic meaning signifies "hearing", hence "the thing heard", hence "music and listening to it", specifically refers to sacred and religious music.[2] *Samā^{c}* is found in Indo-Persian texts in the Sufi context, either when the licitness of music is discussed or in writings on the rules of conduct (*adab*) for listening to music, or in more

1. See for instance the *Uṣūl-i ghinā* (1178/1764-65) of Rāy Cand Aḥmadābādī for Rāy Dāl Cand Ṣāḥib, in the *Catalogue Raisonné of the Buhar Collection,* Vol. 1, *Catalogue of Persian Manuscripts in Buhar Collection* (1921), Calcutta, rev. edn., 1982, N° 236. The 18th century manuscript, ff. 1b-14a, is described as a short tract on "the different tunes and melodies of music".

2. See J. During, *Musique et extase. L'audition mystique dans la tradition soufie,* Paris, 1988, *passim* and pp. 269-72. Nevertheless, in a text like the *Ghunyat al-Munya* (1374-75), *samā^{c}-i Pārsī* seems to designate Persian (art)-music, probably court-music, about which the anonymous author wrote an early treatise - apparently lost to-day - and to which he refers in his text on Indian music (*surod-i hindvī*), see *infra*, Note 23.

descriptive accounts of Sufi musical assemblies, in hagiographical (*tazkira*) and "discourse-based" (*malfūzāt*) literature.[3] In the Indo-Persian context, the term *surod* seems to cover a wide range of music: vocal and instrumental and also dance, which makes it a rather close equivalent of the word *saṅgīta* in Sanskrit.

Generic terms for "musicians" are *muṭribān*, *arbāb-i ṭarab*, *arbāb-i nasāt*, *ahl-i ṭarab*, *ashāb-i ṭarab*, *khuniyāgārān*, etc. Vocalists are often called *surod-goy*, *surod-khwānī*, *goyanda*, *ṣāḥib-i alḥān*, *naghma-sarāyān*, *sarāyanda*, *khwānda*, *qawwāl*, etc. and the generic term for instrumentalist is *sāzanda*; the names of specific instrument-players are generally composed of the name of the instrument followed by *-ī* (*e.g.* *cangī*), *-cī* (*e.g.* *tanbūrcī*) or *-navāz* (*e.g.* *tanbūra-navāz*) and sometimes *-zan* (*e.g.* *daf-zan*) for a lady-player.

Indo-Islamic Aristocratic Patronage to Music [4]

Medieval Arabic and Persian literature indicates the importance of music in the prerequisite knowledge (*ādāb*) imparted to respected rulers, hence aristocratic patronage to musicians was observed in Iran and India as well.[5]

---

3. See B. Lawrence, "The Early Chishti Approach to Samāᶜ", *Islamic Society and Culture*, eds. M. Israeli and N.K. Wagle, New Delhi, 1983, pp. 69-93. For further bibliographical references, see also the review article of *Sufi Music of India and Pakistan. Sound, Context and Meaning in Qawwali* by R.B. Qureshi (Cambridge, 1986) by O. Khalidi, "Qawwali and Mahfil-i Samaᶜ", *Muslim Shrines in India. Their Character, History and Significance*, ed. C.W. Troll, Delhi, 1989, pp. 257-61.

4. On Indo-Islamic aristocratic patronage to music, see S.N.H. Rizvi, "Music in Muslim India", *Islamic Culture*, Jul. 1931, Vol. XV, N° 3, pp. 331-40 and "Observations on 'Music in Muslim India'", by H.G. Farmer, note by the editor, *Islamic Culture*, 1943, Vol. XVII, N° 4, p. 444; see also A. Halim, "Music and the Musicians of the Court of Shāh Jahān", *Islamic Culture*, Oct. 1945, Vol. XIX, N° 4, pp. 354-60 and by the same author, "Muslim Contribution to the Development of North Indian Music", *The Muslim Year Book of India*, Bombay, 1948-49, pp. 107-21, "History of the Growth and Development of North-Indian Music during Sayyid-Lodi Period", *Journal of the Asiatic Society of Pakistan*, Dacca, 1956, Vol. I, N° 1, pp. 46-64, and "Muslim Rulers as Great Patrons of Music", *Essays in History of Indo-Pak Music*, Dacca, 1962, pp. 17-9; D. Bhanu, "Promotion of Music by the Turco-Afghans Rulers of India", *Islamic Culture*, Jan. 1955, Vol. XIX, N° 1, pp. 9-31; D.M. Neuman, *The Life of Music in North India. The Organization of an Artistic Tradition*, Detroit, 1980, Indian edn., New Delhi, 1980, Paperback edn., Chicago and London, 1990, *passim*; Neuman, "Patronage and Performance of Indian Music", *The Powers of Art. Patronage in Indian Culture*, ed. B.S. Miller, Delhi, 1992, Chapter 16, pp. 247-58.

5. See for instance in the context of Khurasan, *Kitāb Naṣīhat Nāma maᶜarūf be Qābūs Nāma*, tālīf Amīr ᶜAnṣar Almaᶜālī Kaikā'ūs bin Iskandar bin Qābūs bin Washamgīr, ed. R. Levy, Hertford, 1951 and the English Transl. by R. Levy, *A Mirror for Princes. The Qābūs Nāma by Kai Kā'ūs ibn Iskandar, Prince of Gurgān*, London, 1951; Chapter XXXVI on "Being a Musician", Text, pp. 111-3; Transl., pp. 186-90; other references to music, Text, pp. 40, 43, etc.; Transl., pp. 62, 67, etc.

From the Sultanate period onwards, many Indo-Islamic rulers encouraged music and dance, of both Persian and Indian origin, with a view to promote the interaction between Persian and Indian culture. This is well-documented by descriptions of music patronised by Muslim rulers and nobles in Arabic documents, such as the *Reḥla* (1357) of Ibn Baṭṭūṭā who travelled in India in 1333-46,[6] and early Indo-Persian chronicles, such as the *Tārīkh-i Fīrūzshāhī* (1356-57) of Ẓīā ud-dīn Baranī.[7]

The genuine curiosity of many Indo-Persian authors - whether commissioned or not - is revealed in the originality and occasionally the exclusivity of the documentation provided by their writings on the musical history of India, of both Indian and Persian origin. The power of observation and the eye for detail manifest in this literature came up to the expectation of Muslim rulers. Their concern to familiarise their courtiers with the techniques and the aesthetics of Indian art-music, the subtleties of which eluded the nobility educated in a Persian culture, inspired the composition of texts on music written in Persian, with guide-lines about the basic concepts.

Well-known Indo-Persian chronicles have been studied as a standard source on medieval Indian history, mostly political and economic, and occasionally in its socio-cultural aspects. They contain precious information on music, which has often been neglected by historians who were not socio-culturally oriented or who were unfamiliar with musical or musicological subjects. So far, only a few musicologists or music-historians have used Indo-Persian sources, though a growing interest has been shown by some eminent scholars of music, who do not have access to this field of documentation mostly for linguistic reasons.[8]

This paper intends to present a corpus of Indo-Persian literature relevant to music, with a bibliographical orientation for further reading.

6. See *The Reḥla of Ibn Baṭṭūṭa* (India, Maldive Islands and Ceylon) (1953), Translation and Commentary, ed. M. Husain, Baroda, 2nd repr. edn., 1976, pp. 9-10, 28-9, 63-4, etc. See also Introduction, pp. l-li and the illustration facing p. 56.

7. See Ẓīā ud-dīn Baranī, *Tārīkh-i Fīrūzshāhī*, ed. S.A. Khān, Calcutta, 1862; repr., Osnabrück, Biblio Verlag, 1981. I am indebted to S. Sarmadee for highlighting the following passages in his forthcoming *Nūr Ratnākar. A Bio-Bibliographical Survey* (*and techno-historical study, of all available important writings in Arabic, Persian, Sanskrit and other allied languages on the subject of song, dance and drama*), Two Vols., Calcutta (Vol. I, pp. 603-23 of the typescript; for references to music in the chronicle, pp. 34, 46, 67-8, 112-3, 129-30, etc.).

8. See Sarmadee, *Nūr-Ratnākar*, *op. cit.*. See also N.P. Ahmad, *Hindustani Music. A Study of its Development in 17th and 18th centuries*, New-Delhi, 1984. See also the present author's bibliography.

A description of the kind of information provided by a wide variety of texts will be followed by an exposition of some problems raised while attempting to classify both the sources and their contents relevant to music - mostly court-music, excluding here religious music (*samāᶜ*), fanfare and military music. I will not discuss the controversial subject of the licitness and the moral position of music in Islam, though references found in religious writings and hagiographical accounts about Muslim musicians - especially Muslim court-musicians - provide biographical information and indicate implicitly the social status of musicians in various Islamic contexts.[9]

The paper will also discuss the difficulties faced by Indo-Persian authors in presenting an alien system of music to an unfamiliar though sympathetic, appreciative and even responsive audience. Both the Indian and the Persian systems consider music as a science and a branch of knowledge (*ᶜilm-i mūsīqī* and *gāndharva-veda* or *gāndharva-śāstra*). Though both are modal music, they reveal a number of features rather alien to each other.[10] Nevertheless I will not analyse the technical concepts of both systems, which would require a more musicological approach and a systematic study of a number of examples to be first placed in their socio-historical contexts. Representative illustrations will bring out some of the most striking features of Indo-Persian literature on music and its unique contribution to the history of art-music and its royal and aristocratic patronage in medieval India.

I will attempt to present this type of literature and discuss some questions raised while exploiting it as a source of documentation supplementary to more traditional and conventional musicological texts written in Sanskrit.[11]

Indo-Persian Texts Related to Music

Most of the examples selected were gathered while searching for documents on Dhrupad, the poetico-musical genre favoured by both Hindu and Muslim rulers from the sixteenth century and of Tānsen, foremost court-musician of Mughal Emperor Akbar (r. 1556-1605), who ex-

---

9. See for instance M.L. Roychaudhuri, "Music in Islām", *Journal of the Asiatic Society*, 1957, Letters Vol. XXIII, Nº 2, pp. 44-103; O. Wright, *The Modal System of Arab and Persian Music, A.D. 1250-1300*, London, 1978, Introduction, pp. 1-19, especially pp. 11-2, 15-8 and the bibliography, pp. 293-6; J. During, *op. cit.*, Annexe II, "Le statut de la musique dans l'islam", pp. 217-47, notes, pp. 256-7 and the bibliography, pp. 259-72.

10. See H.S. Powers, "Mode", *The New Grove: Dictionary of Music and Musicians*, London/New York, 1980, Vol. XII, pp. 376-450, especially Section V, 2, pp. 422-36.

11. See E. te Nijenhuis, *Musicological Literature*, Wiesbaden, 1977.

celled as a poet-composer and a performer of Dhrupad.[12] Other works which were not used in that particular context or were not yet known to me, have been discussed in papers which have been published meanwhile, or which are forthcoming, and will be also referred to. I will lay stress on some less conventional literary sources, which are not classified as "musical texts" in subject-wise library catalogues, and which have hence escaped the attention of most specialists of music history.[13]

Libraries Holding Indo-Persian Manuscripts Relevant to Music

Very few Indo-Persian texts related to music have been edited and published, and hence, manuscript copies are the main source of documentation for scholars. Available in private and public libraries in the Indian sub-continent and in Iranian, European or North American collections, they have not yet been catalogued. as a particular category of text, as has been done for similar Arabic works in *The Theory of Music in Arabic Writings (c. 900-1900). Descriptive Catalogue of Manuscripts in Libraries of Europe and the U.S.A.*, by Amnon Shiloah (1979).[14]

Among Indian libraries holding Indo-Persian manuscripts relevant to music, the most important are the Asiatic Society of Bengal and the Indian Museum in Calcutta, the Khuda Bakhsh Oriental Public Library in Patna, the Salar Jung Museum and Library and the Andhra Pradesh Government Oriental Manuscript Library and Research Institute in Hyderabad, the Government Oriental Manuscripts Library in the University of Madras, the National Museum and the Dr. Zakir Husain Library (Jamia Millia Islamia) in New Delhi, the Library of the University of Bombay, the Arabic and Persian Research Institute in Tonk, the Maulana Azad Library in Aligarh Muslim University, the Rampur Raza

12. See F. Delvoye, *Tānsen et la tradition des chants dhrupad en langue braj, du XVIe siècle à nos jours*, D. Litt. Thesis, Paris, Sorbonne Nouvelle Univ., 1990 (Unpublished). See the Summary in English, "Tānsen and the Tradition of Dhrupad Songs in the Braj Language, from the 16th Century to the Present Day", *Dhrupad Annual 1993*, pp. 37-44 and "Les chants *dhrupad* en langue braj des poètes-musiciens de l'Inde Moghole", *Littératures médiévales de l'Inde du Nord. Contributions de Charlotte Vaudeville et de ses élèves*, ed. F. Mallison, Paris, 1991, pp. 139-85. See also Delvoye, "The Verbal Content of Dhrupad Songs from the Earliest Collections: III. Dhrupad Songs attributed to Tānsen in Court-musicians Repertoires", *Dhrupad Annual 1994*, pp. 1-12.

13. For the texts on music or relevant to music which I could see personally or note down from hand-lists or catalogues, see Delvoye, *Inventaire des textes Indo-persans sur la musique savante de l'Inde*, in collaboration with S. Sarmadee, New Delhi, 1991, pp. 1-51. (Unpublished)

14. See A. Shiloah, *The Theory of Music in Arabic Writings (c. 900-1900). Descriptive Catalogue of Manuscripts in Libraries of Europe and the U.S.A.*, Munich, 1979.

Library in Rampur, etc.[15] There are also other important manuscripts collections in libraries in Alwar, Ahmedabad, Sitamau, etc.[16] Some Indian libraries having Persian manuscripts have only hand-written catalogues to be consulted locally.

In Europe, the most important collections of Indo-Persian manuscripts on music are in the India Office Library and Records in London, which holds the British Library collection as well, and the Library of the Royal Asiatic Society of Great Britain and Ireland in London, the Bodleian Library in Oxford, the Library of King's College in Cambridge, the Chester Beatty Library in Dublin, the Bibliothèque Nationale in Paris, and others, such as the Universiteits Bibliotheek in Leiden, the Königlichen Bibliothek in Berlin, etc., some of them having unique copies of Indo-Persian texts. European collections have been described in printed catalogues and bibliographical surveys.[17]

Catalogues and Hand-lists of Indo-Persian Manuscripts

Indo-Persian texts which appear under "Music", in subject-wise catalogues, represent only a part of the Indo-Persian texts relevant to music, as will be noted later. For other texts, the convergence of information collected from secondary sources and a close reading of the contents of Indo-Persian texts described in catalogues of manuscripts and bibliographical surveys led me to a first selection of and investigation into original and, more rarely, edited copies. Such a search for texts by trial and error implies an intuitive approach and led to many discoveries and disappointments as well. The actual access to manuscripts in specialised libraries in India is often difficult, mostly because of cumbersome administrative rules.[18]

Catalogues may also be misleading, when their authors or compilers do not understand well the exact content of the texts which they describe. A few examples of misunderstandings have been selected among familiar texts mentioned in manuscript catalogues, such as the *Rāg Darpan* of Navāb Saïf K͟hān 'Faqīrullāh', the *Seh Naṣr* of Mullā

15. For details see Delvoye and Chandra Shekhar, *Directory of Scholars and Institutions in the Field of Indo-Persian Studies*, New Delhi, 1994, pp. 79-98.

16. See for instance A.H. Nizami, *Catalogue of Persian Manuscripts and Records in the Shri Raghuvir Library, Sitamau*, Delhi, 1993.

17. See the Catalogues of Indo-Persian manuscripts by H. Ethé, C. Rieu, E. Sachau and H. Ethé, E. Blochet, F. Richard, etc. and the bibliographical surveys of C.A. Storey, D.N. Marshall given in the References.

18. The offer to get photocopies of manuscripts requires patience and at times does not materialize; often some rapid readings with a view to selecting passages worth being reproduced for a more thorough analysis or for collation with other recensions, happened to be unproductive, when the ordered photocopies were never made !

Nūr al-dīn Muḥammad Ẓuhūrī and the *Kitāb-i Nauras* of Ibrāhīm ᶜĀdil Shāh II as also the *Hazār Dhurpad* or *Sahasras.*[19]

Various Literary Genres

From passing remarks to fairly detailed descriptions, music is referred to in many Indo-Persian texts belonging to various literary genres (such as musicological texts, historical chronicles, poetry and ornate prose, memoirs and other personal writings, etc.). A preliminary inventory of Indo-Persian sources relevant to music available in Indian libraries, showed a wide diversity of documentation and raised the problem of classification of texts and data.[20] An exposition of some of the more representative texts could be done genre by genre, according to the criteria of literary historians. Actually, some important texts recognised as belonging to one particular literary genre may provide diverse information on historical, theoretical and practical aspects of music; hence the classification by literary genre is not a valid one. A regional study could also have been contemplated, such as the Indo-Persian texts documenting the history of music in Gujarat or Deccan in the medieval period.[21]

---

19. See the notice of the *Rāg Darpan* of Navāb Saïf Khān 'Faqīrullāh', in the typed list of manuscripts on music of the Salar Jung Museum and Library, Hyderabad (Manuscript Mus. 3/4291, p. 21): "A treatise on Indian music compiled in 1076/1666, by Faqīrullāh, for Mān Singh of Gwāliyār. It is based on some Sanskrit works." and the notice of the *Seh Naṣr* of Mullā Nūr al-dīn Muḥammad Ẓuhūrī, "intended to be a sort of an introduction to Now Ras - A work on Indian Music by Ibrahim ᶜAdil Shah of Bejapur who was a patron of the author", in *A Descriptive Catalogue of the Islamic Manuscripts in the Government Oriental Manuscripts Library, Madras*, Madras University, 1939, N° D. 75 (d), p. 218. The *Kitāb-i Nauras* is however a collection of lyrics in the Dhrupad genre (See Nazir Ahmad, *Kitab-i-Nauras by Ibrahim Adil Shah II*, Introduction, Notes and Textual Editing, New Delhi, 1956 and Delvoye, "The Verbal Content of Dhrupad Songs from the Earliest Collections: II. The *Kitāb-i Nauras* of Ibrāhīm ᶜĀdil Shāh II, Sulṭān of Bijapur (r. 1580-1627) and its Persian Preface by Mullā Nūr al-Dīn Muḥammad 'Ẓuhūrī' - I", *Dhrupad Annual 1991*, pp. 38-54 and Part II, *Dhrupad Annual 1993*, pp. 1-23. Another example is the notice on the *Hazār Dhurpad* and *Sahasras* in the bibliographical survey of Marshall, *op. cit.*, N° 313, p. 101, in which the texts are distinguished as different: "*Hazār dhurpad-e-nāyak Bakhshava*: A work on Indian music and musicians containing a collection, made by order of the Emperor Shāh Jahān, of the compositions of Bakhshava..." and as a separate entry "*Sahas ras*: Translated into Hindustāni from Sanskrit presumably and dedicated to Shāh Jahān, this appears to be a work on Indian music."

20. See Delvoye, *Inventaire...*, *op. cit.*

21. See for instance Delvoye, "Indo-Persian Texts on the Artistic Patronage of the Sultans of Gujarat (14th-16th c.)", paper presented at the Indo-French Seminar on "The Evolution of Medieval Indian Culture: The Indo-Persian Context", organised by the Centre for Human Sciences and the Centre for Historical Studies (Jawaharlal Nehru Univ.), New Delhi, 14-16 Feb. 1994 (Forthcoming). See also Delvoye, "The Verbal Content of Dhrupad Songs from the Earliest Collections: II. The *Kitāb-i Nauras* of Ibrāhīm ᶜĀdil Shāh II,..., *op. cit.* Parts I and II.

1. *Musica Speculativa: Indo-Persian Musicological Texts*

Indo-Persian musicological texts attract our attention first, since they are specifically described in subject-wise published catalogues and hand-written lists of Persian manuscripts preserved in public and private collections in India and abroad. They are classified under the headings "Music", "Philosophy" and more often "Miscellaneous".[22]

Indo-Persian Treatises on Indian Music

Original texts written in Persian or more often translations with commentary - occasionally summarised - into Persian of theoretical treatises in Sanskrit or, more rarely, in vernacular languages, constitute the main part of this type of texts, whether commissioned or not.

Two Early Indo-Persian Treatises on Indian Music

Two early Indo-Persian texts often mentioned, based on Sanskrit works on music which they duly name, include partial or complete translations into Persian of those treatises (some of which are not available today), with first-hand observations about vocal and instrumental practice and musical life in provincial Muslim courts.

22. Among important collections of Indo-Persian manuscripts in India with hand-lists catalogues, see for instance the Persian manuscripts on music of the Andhra Pradesh Government Oriental Manuscripts Library and Research Institute (henceforth A.P.G.O.M.L.& R.I.), in Hyderabad, which holds 8915 Persian manuscripts and 6337 Arabic manuscripts. Manuscripts in all languages mixed (Arabic, Persian, Urdū, Hindustānī, Sindhī, etc.) are described in hand-written catalogues, classified subject-wise. Ten texts specifically on music written in Persian, are mentioned alphabetically in Volume II of the hand-list, under the heading "Falsafa", pp. 79-88. The Sālār Jung Museum and Library, Hyderabad, published nine volumes of the subect-wise *A Catalogue of the Persian Manuscripts in the Salar Jung Museum & Library*, compiled by Muhammad Ashraf (1965, 1966, 1967, 1969, 1975, 1980, 1983, 1988). Manuscripts specifically "on music" kept in the Oriental Manuscripts Section of the Sālār Jung Museum and Library, are listed in an unpublished hand-written catalogue, n.d. (c. 1965-66 as per Rahmat Ali Khan's estimation), as a part of *A Concise Descriptive Catalogue of Persian Manuscripts in Sālār Jung Museum and Library*, Vol. XI: X. The Sciences, Mental, Moral and Physical (Contd.). 9. Arts, Agriculture, Technology, Music, Games, etc. In the Government Oriental Manuscripts Library (henceforth G.O.M.L.), located inside the University of Madras, the notices of manuscripts specifically on music are scattered in the four volumes of *A Descriptive Catalogue of the Islamic Manuscripts in the Government Oriental Manuscripts Library, Madras*, Madras, 1939, 1950, 1954, 1961. Another important collection is preserved in the Rampur Raza Library. The subject-wise catalogues of Persian manuscripts prepared by Imtiāz ᶜAlī ᶜArshī have not yet been published and have to be consulted in the library only. Twenty-six manuscripts are classified under "music" (*mūsīqī*), with some information about the authors if known, the number of folios, the date whenever available, etc. So far, none of these texts could be seen by me, due to the difficult access to manuscripts, for which, till recently, an authorization obtained from the District Magistrate was required; the permission has been recently granted to some American and French scholars.

As an early example commissioned by a noble interested in both Persian and Indian music, who intended to educate the nobility close to him which was not familiar with Indian music, the Ghunyat al-Munya, (1374-75), by an anonymous author, is worth mentioning. Its preface clearly indicates the intention of Malik Shams al-dīn Ibrāhīm Ḥasan Abū Rajā, then Governor of Gujarat, who ordered the text to be composed and of which a single illustrated manuscript is available today. It represents an early didactic treatise, dealing with the theory (*ᶜilm*), the practice (*ᶜamal*) and the etiquette (*ādāb*) of Indian art-music and dance.[23] The author mentioned the names of seven earlier Sanskrit works on music, which he studied with a critical approach, since the music practised in his time was already different. In his preface, he explicitly indicates that he is "interpreting" the facts in a realistic manner. He provides a precious appreciation of the music performed in his time and various comments about the relevance of theoretical concepts described in Sanskrit texts.[24] Another valuable feature of this early text, is the accompanying drawings of twenty musical instruments described in the second chapter of the first part.

Even more representative of Indo-Persian writings on music, the *Lahjāt-i Sikandar Shāhī* composed by one Ḥammad, better known as Yahiā al-Kābulī, protected by Miān Bahwa (or Bhūwa), the prime minister of Sulṭān Sikandar Lodī (r. 1489-1517) represents another remarkable example of the Sultanate period.[25] It contains a translation

---

23. See the Manuscript N° 1863, India Office Library, London, described in Ethé, *op. cit.*, Vol. I, Notice N° 2008, pp. 1116-7 and in C.A. Storey, *Persian Literature, A Bio-Bibliographical Survey*, Vol. II, Part 3, G. Arts and Crafts, Leiden, 1977, Notice N° 701, pp. 411-2. A rotograph copy of this manuscript is available at the Seminar Library, Aligarh Muslim University (N° 180). See also the edition of this manuscript with an introduction in English by S. Sarmadee, *Ghunyat-ul-Munya. The Earliest Known Persian Work on Indian Music*, Bombay, 1978. The preface covers fols. 1a-3a of the manuscript, see edn. cit., pp. 3-4. The seven Sanskrit texts used by the author are listed on fol. 2b-3a, see edn. cit., p. 4.

24. *Ibid*, fol. 2b, see edn. cit., p. 3.

25. See Storey, *op. cit.* Notice N° 705, p. 414. See the incomplete manuscript N° P 780/5126 L, not dated (probably 16th c.) kept at the Tagore Library, Lucknow University (207b fols.), described in Nazir Ahmed, "The Lahjat-i-Sikandar Shahi, A Unique Book on Indian Music of the Time of Sikandar Lodi (1489-1517)", *Islamic Culture*, July 1954, Vol. XXVIII, N° 3, pp. 410-17. A rotograph copy of this manuscript is available at the Seminar Library, Aligarh Muslim University (N° 235). Another manuscript not dated, complete but extremely damaged is kept at the G.O.M.L., Madras. It is described in *A Descriptive Catalogue..., op. cit.*, Vol. I, Notice N° D. 518, pp. 531-2 and contains 168 pages. A not dated and apparently recent copy of this text, contains 176 pages and is described in the same catalogue, Notice N° D. 519, p. 532. See the critical edition in preparation by S. Sarmadee. See also S.B.F. Husaini, *A Critical Study of Indo-Persian Literature, during Sayyid and Lodi Period (1414-1526)*, New Delhi, 1988, pp. 227-47; M.Z. Huda, "Sultān Sikandar Lūdī - A Poet and Patron of Letters", *Journal of the Asiatic Society of Pakistan* (Dacca), 1969, Vol. XIV, N° 3, pp. 289-304.

with comments of Śārṅgadeva's *Saṅgīta-ratnākara* (early thirteenth century), which is the most famous theoretical text in Sanskrit, often commented upon by Indian musicologists and still a reference for students of music.[26] Yahiā al-Kābulī follows the structure of the *Saṅgīta-ratnākara* in seven chapters and mentions six other Sanskrit texts which he had drawn upon.

Indo-Persian texts on music are not mere translations, as can be seen by studying, for example, seventeenth century works such as the *Tarjuma-i Kitāb-i Pārijātak* (1665-66) of Mīrzā Raushan Ẓamīr, the first Persian translation and commentary of the *Saṅgīta Pārijāta* of Paṇḍit Ahobāla.[27] The translator was, in his own words, a "born-slave" of Emperor Aurangzeb. He was a treasurer (*bakhshī*) and a court-chronicler (*waqā'i*ᶜ*-nigār*) in Surat where he died, as well as a good poet in Braj.[28] The *Rāg Darshan* was translated by Khūshḥāl Khān b. Karīm Khān - supposedly a descendant of Tānsen - and also known as a poet, using 'Anūp' as his *takhallus*, while attached to the court of Muḥammad Shāh of Delhi.[29] After the death of the Mughal emperor, he went over to Hyderabad where he was patronised by different nobles. The *Shams al-Aṣwāt* (1697-98) by Khūshḥāl Khān's son Ras Baras Khān, is a "translation and adaptation" of the Sanskrit *Saṅgīta Darpaṇa* of Paṇḍit Damodara.[30]

---

26. See *Saṅgīta Ratnākara of Śārṅgadeva*, Sanskrit Text and English Translation with Comments and Notes, Vol. I (Chapter I, Treatment of Svara), English Translation by R.K. Shringy, under the Supervision of P.L. Sharma, Delhi/Varanasi, 1978; Vol. II (Chapters II-IV), by R.K. Shringy, under the Supervision of P.L. Sharma, New Delhi, 1989. See also Delvoye, "The Influence of *Saṅgīta-ratnākara* on Indo-Persian Texts on Music", presented at the Seminar on "Śārṅgadeva's *Saṅgita-ratnākara*", organised by the Sangeet Natak Akademi, Varanasi, 22-26 Feb. 1994.

27. See Marshall, *op. cit.*, N° 1922, p. 499. The manuscripts of the India Office Library, London, are described in Ethé, *op. cit.*, Vol. I, N° 2009-10, p. 1117; see also the British Museum manuscript now preserved in the India Office Library, described in Rieu, *op. cit.*, Vol. II, Egerton 793, pp. 489a-b and Vol. III, p. 1088b. Another manuscript is available at the A.P.G.O.M.L.& R.I., Hyderabad; Hand-list "Falsafa", N° 418, p. 85. This text was again translated by Paṇḍit Dīnanāth in 1724, son of Bāsudeo. It would appear to have been part of the library of the emperor Muḥammad Shāh, see Nijenhuis, *op. cit.*, pp. 28-9 and note 152, p. 28.

28. See Sarmadee, *Nūr-ratnākar*, Vol. II, notice on Mīrzā Raushan Ẓamīr (Personal Communication, 1985).

29. See Marshall, *op. cit.*, N° 918, p. 260, *Rāg Darshan* in addition to the notice of the *Rāg rāgini-e-rūz u shab*. A manuscript is preserved in the G.O.M.L., Madras, *A Descriptive Catalogue..., op. cit.*, Vol. I, N° D. 515, p. 530-1 and its restored copy, A Descriptive Catalogue..., op. cit., Vol. IV, N° D. 1024, p. 1206. Another copy is available at the A.P.G.O.M.L.& R.I., Hyderabad; see the Hand-list, under "Falsafa", N° 393, p. 85.

30. See Ethé, *op. cit.*, Vol. I, N° 2022, pp. 1122-3. See also a manuscript in the Salar Jung Museum and Library, Hyderabad, Mus. 9/4294, p. 23 of the unpublished typed list of manuscripts.

Regarding the accuracy of such translations, opinions diverge. In the celebrated essay "On the Musical Modes of the Hindoos", originally written in 1784 and enlarged later on, Sir William Jones names some Persian texts on Indian music, such as *A Present from India* (*Tuḥfat al-Hind*) of Mīrzā K͟hān, which he often quotes.[31] While mentioning the *Saṅgita Darpaṇa* as one authority translated into Persian and used by Mīrzā K͟hān, William Jones adds: "But my experience justifies me in pronouncing that the *Moghols* have no idea of accurate translation, and give that name to a mixture of gloss and text with a flimsy paraphrase of them both; they are wholly unable, yet always pretend, to write *Sanscrit* words in *Arabic* letters; that a man, who knows the *Hindoos* only from *Persian* books, does not know the Hindoos; and that an *European*, who follows the muddy rivulets of *Mussalman* writers on *India*, instead of drinking from the pure fountain of *Hindoo* learning, will be in perpetual danger of misleading himself and others. From the just severity of this censure I except neither Abūlfazl, not his brother Faiz'i, nor Mohsani Fānī not Mirza Khān himself; and I speak of all four after an attentive perusal of their works".[32]

William Jones's remarks actually highlight a particular feature of Indo-Persian writings on music, which may be seen by some people as a "plus point". While "translating" Sanskrit theoretical works on music, Indo-Persian authors often add interesting comments about some musical aspects which had become obsolete or which they even disapproved of. This shows their preference often for the performance of music more than its theory (*lakṣa* over *lakṣaṇa* / *ᶜamal* over *ᶜilm*). They frequently refer to contemporary music practised around them, especially by court-musicians, using interesting technical terms, which often are not to be found in Sanskrit texts. It is worth mentioning that in most Indo-Persian texts referring to Indian music, technical terms in Sanskrit, Prakrit and various vernacular languages are often spelled letter by letter, and even bear diacritical marks. That terminology belongs to the musicians' parlance of today as well, though it may refer to different concepts, hence it has to be studied and assessed with great care, before any technical comparison or even equation is undertaken.

However, as numerous examples show, even if Indo-Persian authors borrow the traditional structure of Sanskrit theoretical treatises,

---

31. See W. Jones, "On the Musical Modes of the Hindus" (1784), *Asiatick Researches*, 1792, N° 3, pp. 55-87; repr. in S.M. Tagore, *Hindu Music from Various Authors* (1875), 3rd edn., Varanasi, 1965, pp. 125-60.

32. *Ibid*., p. 136.

they almost systematically add up-to-date information about music and judicious remarks and even pertinent criticisms.[33] The drive of Muslim rulers to get important works in Arabic or in Sanskrit translated into Persian was part of their cultural policy to familiarize the Persian-speaking nobility in the Islamic classics from Arabic lands as well as with Indian writings in the field of history, medicine, sciences, religion and mysticism, belles-lettres and art.[34]

Many of their authors were patronised by Indo-Islamic rulers, whose aim by doing so, was to familiarise their courtiers with the art-music of India. Besides patronising court-musicians, they also commissioned the writing of treatises on Indian music, with both a theoretical and a practical approach leading to a better understanding of Indian music. To make precise technical information more accessible to readers, biographical accounts of erstwhile and contemporary musicians are provided. They are often sketchy and stereotyped but still interesting, for example, in the case of exceptional musicians such as the celebrated Tānsen and Nāyak Bakhshū, and a few other court-musicians who were given the title 'Nāyak' and who have been mentioned by Abū'l Faẓl, Navāb Saïf Khān 'Faqīrullāh', Mīrzā Khān or ᶜInāyat Khān Rāsikh.[35] Outstanding patrons of the past are often discussed which provides original information about rulers whose artistic patronage has not always remained celebrated.[36] Obviously, earlier texts normally present a greater guarantee of authenticity than later documents, as a more direct source on musical practices.

References to Sanskrit theoretical texts on music which had been sooner or later translated into Persian, or which had been used by Indo-

33. See Delvoye, "The Influence of *Saṅgīta-ratnākara* on Indo-Persian Texts on Music" *op. cit.*

34. For examples of translations or renderings from Arabic into Persian during the Sultanate period, see I.H. Siddiqui, *Perso-Arabic Sources of Information on the Life and Conditions in the Sultanate of Delhi*, New Delhi, 1992, pp. 44-52.

35. See the *Rāg Darpan* (1666) composed by Navāb Saïf Khān 'Faqīrullāh', an eminent noble of the court of Aurangzeb, eds. N.H. Anṣārī and S. Shukla, "Rāga Darpana" and "Ṣaut al Nāqaus" by Muḥammad ᶜOṣman Qais, *Persian Research Journal Special Number*, Dept. of Persian, Univ. of Delhi, 1981; *Rāg Darpan*, pp. 11-86; *Ṣaut al-Nāqaus*, 2nd part, pp. 1-24. See also the *Risāla-i ẕikr-i mughanniyān-i Hindūstān* (undated) of ᶜInāyat Khān Rāsikh, (b. 1114/1701), a compilation of biographical notices on the most important musicians of India (Nāyak Bacū, Nāyak Gopāl, Amīr Khusrau, Nāyak Bakhsū, Tānsen, Laᶜl Khān, Khus-ḥāl and Bisram, etc.), based on the *Pādshāh Nāma* of ᶜAbd al-Ḥamīd Lāhaurī and the *Mir'at-i Sikandarī* of Sikandar b. Manjhu; edition of the manuscript N° 1734-35 of the Khuda Bakhsh Library, in Patna, by Sayyid ᶜAlī Haider, Patna, 1961.

36. See Delvoye, "Indo-Persian Texts on the Artistic Patronage of the Sultans of Gujarat (14th-16th c.)", *op. cit.*

Persian writers, are occasionally mentioned in Indo-Persian chronicles such as the *Muntakhab al-tawārikh* of Mullā ᶜAbd al-Qādir al-Badā'ūnī. In his account of Sultān Fīroz Shāh Tughlaq (r. 1351-88),[37] al-Badā'ūnī mentions the "one thousand three hundred books of the Brahmans of olden time" kept in the famous temple of Jwālamukhī (having a permanent burning flame).[38] Sultān Fīroz Shāh "ordered some of his translators to translate some of those books into Persian", presumably from Sanskrit.[39] Al-Badā'ūnī - whose dislike for music is well-known - personally saw "some other books which were translated in the name of Sultān Fīrūz [sic], some of them on the Science of "*Pingal*" that is to say on Music, and the kinds of *Akhāra* which they call *Pātur bāzī*, and some other subjects. I found most of them to be profitless, and their paucity of interest is for the most part due to the triviality of their subject matter, and the difficulty of explaining it, as is evident."[40]

Indo-Persian Sources on Persian Music

Among texts which I have inventoried, I have listed some manuscripts clearly identified as "classic" Persian texts, and later documents on Persian music composed in India, which would require a further textual study to assess their originality. The third category includes texts divided into two separate sections on Persian and Indian music.

An interesting example of a text on Persian music written in early fifteenth century and known in India is worth mentioning here. The great theoretician of Irano-Arabo-Turkish musical science and composer ᶜAbd al-Qādir b. Gheybī al-Ḥāfiẓ al-Marāghī (b. Azerbayjan, mid-14th c., d. Herat, 1435), who created an authoritative classification pattern of music, in twelve *maqām*, six *āvāz* and twenty-four *shoᶜbe*, wrote the famous treatise *Jāmiᶜ al-alḥān* and a kind of abridged version of it, the *Maqāsid al-alḥān*.[41] The illustrated copy of the *Maqāsid al-*

37. See ᶜAbd al-Qādir al-Badā'ūnī, *Muntakhab al-tawārikh*, Persian edn. in Three Vols. by Kabīr al-dīn Aḥmad, Aḥmad ᶜAli and W.N. Lees, Calcutta, 1864-69. See also the English Transl. in Three Vols. by G. Ranking (vol. I), W.H. Lowe (vol. II) and T.W. Haig (vol. III), Calcutta, 1884-1925, Repr., Delhi, 1978; Text, Vol. I, pp. 241-57; Transl., Vol. I, pp. 321-41.

38. See al-Badā'ūnī, *op. cit.*, Text, Vol. I, p. 249; Transl., Vol. I, p. 331-2.

39. *Ibid.*

40. *Ibid.*

41. See ᶜAbd al-Qādir b. Gheybī al-Ḥāfiẓ al-Marāghī, *Maqāsid al-alḥān*, ed. Tāqī Binesh, Tehran, 1977-1986 and by the same author, *Jāmiᶜ al-alḥān*, ed. and comment. T. Binesh, Tehran, 1367. See the references to manuscripts preserved in different libraries in Storey, *op. cit.*, N° 702, p. 413.

alḥān preserved in the Bodleian Library in Oxford, was transcribed in Akbarābād (i.e. Agra), in 1077/1666, from a manuscript dated 842/ 1439.[42] A complete illustrated copy of the *Mukhtasar dar mūsīqī* of ᶜAbd al-Qādir al-Marāghī, dedicated to Shāh Rukh, is available in the Government Oriental Manuscripts Library, in the University of Madras.[43]

Another text of interest in relation to this famous Persian author, is the *Risāla-i Mūsīqī* of Muḥammad ᶜAlī, not dated (19th c.) kept in the Khuda Bakhsh Oriental Public Library. The author himself says that he wrote this tract at the request of a nobleman named Mahdī. Later on he says that the present tract is a selection from the treatise of ᶜAbd ul-Qādir", who is presumably the same ᶜAbd al-Qādir al-Marāghī. The text consists only in six *bāb*: on *avāz*, on *maqāmāt*, on *shoᶜba*, on *gūsha*, on *tarāna* and on *uṣūl-i ẓarb*.[44] The fact that manuscripts of these works are available in Indian libraries, indicates their importance for authors on Persian or Indo-Persian music.

A systematic inventory of Indo-Persian writings of the seventeenth and eighteenth centuries on Persian music - as it was known or actually performed in India - may reveal some texts, which are no longer available or seen as relevant in Iran, (since very few works have survived from the Safavid period, in the seventeenth century), but which may still been known in Central Asia. One such treatise is the *Baḥjat al-rūh*, an apocryphal work attributed to Ṣafī al-dīn-i Urmavī (b. Azerbayjan; d. Baghdad, 1294), probably composed in the early seventeenth century, which is one of the last to describe the situation of Iranian music

---

42. See Sachau-Ethé, *op. cit.*, N° 1844, pp. 1061-3. Another copy is preserved in the Aṣafīyah collection (Vol. II, p. 1224, N° 320) in the G.O.M.L.& R.I., Hyderabad. On the works of ᶜAbd al-Qādir al-Marāghī, see also Shiloah, *op. cit.*, pp. 168-75.

43. See the manuscript N° D. 520 in the *A Descriptive Catalogue...*, *op. cit.*, p. 532: "Pages, 109. Lines on a page, 31. Language, Persian, Condition injured. Mode of writing, Nastaliq. Appearance, old. Subject, music. Extent, complete, Author, Abdul Qadir Maraghi. The book otherwise called Kitabuladwar was compiled for King Shahrukh and is full of diagrams and also of pictures of musical instruments. Dated the last day of Muharram 41 A.H. (sic). Scribe not mentioned. Beginning... and end..." My reading of the date mentioned on the last folio is 191. The incipit and the second part of the explicit of the *Mukhtasar dar mūsīqī* are actually similar to those of the manuscript *Maqāsid al-alḥān* of the Bodleian Library (Sachau-Ethé, *op. cit.*, N° 1844, pp. 1061-4; see also Shiloah, *op. cit.*, N° 109, pp. 172-3).

44. See *Catalogue of the Arabic and Persian Manuscripts in the Khuda Bakhsh Oriental Public Library at (Bankipur) Patna*, Vol. XXXII, (Persian Manuscripts), Mixed Contents, Patna, 2nd impr., 1980. *Supplement to the Catalogue of the Persian Manuscripts in the Oriental Public Library at Bankipore*, Vol. II, prepared by M.A Muqtadir, Patna, 1933, Vol. XXXII, Manuscript N° 2241, p. 154-5, *Risālah-i Mūsiqī* of Muḥammad ᶜAlı, fols. 35b-39a.

of the period.[45] It draws some elements from Arabic and Persian "classic" treatises, especially on the classification of *maqāms*, but is more a popularizing than a scientific work. An interesting contribution of the *Baḥjat al-rūh* is its attempt at noting down songs (*taṣnīf*), with their transcription and precise information on their metre and modulations.[46] This reminds us of the Indian collections of lyrics composed in vernacular languages and belonging to court-musicians' repertoires, with their prefaces in Persian, such as the *Hazār Dhurpad* or *Sahasras*.[47]

One may also study in both systems, the link between the theory of modes and the classification of intervals with the actual musical performance, which in later examples often indicate a "fashion" of making inventories. A thorough musicological study of such texts is beyond the scope of this introductory paper, which intends to limit itself largely to assessing the field and raise some points of interest for further research.

It is rather intriguing to notice some later texts, produced around the Mughal court or even in provincial places, far away from the main centres of Persian or Indo-Persian culture. An interesting example is the *Tuḥfat al-naghmat* of Muḥammad Ruhullāh b. Shāh Wajhullāh, compiled for the Nawāb of Arcot, Nawāb Muḥammad ᶜAlī Wālājāh (r. 1749-95), of which a manuscript is preserved at the Government Oriental Manuscripts Library (University of Madras).[48] The text is divided into two sections: the first deals with Persian music and the second with Indian music. The *Tūzuk-i Wālājāhi*, by Munshī Burhān Khān Hāndī (d. 1240/1824) who began his work in 1195/1781 is also an interesting chronicle about the Wālājāhs' artistic patronage, with reference to music.[49]

---

45. See J. During, *La musique traditionnelle de l'Azerbayjān et la science des muqams*, Baden-Baden & Bouxwiller, 1988, pp. 157-60. See also the edition of the *Risāle-ye mūsīqī, Bahjat al-rūh* by H.L. Rabino de Borgomalo, Tehran, 1346/1967.

46. During, *La musique traditionnelle de l'Azerbayjān...*, *op. cit.*, note 7, p. 170.

47. See *supra* Note 19.

48. See the manuscript N° D. 514, described in *A Descriptive Catalogue...*, *op. cit.*, Vol. I, pp. 529-30 (Pages, 34. Lines on a page, 11. Condition, injured; Nastaliq, no date but "appearance old"). See also the restored copy: Persian Manuscript N° D. 774, (*A Descriptive Catalogue...*, *op. cit.*, Vol. III, pp. 916-7; Pages, 22. Lines, 20 in a page; it is bound along with the Manuscript N° D 773", *Tuḥfat al-Shuᶜara*, pp. 200; a biography of poets (of Deccan) by Mīrzā Afẓal of Aurangabad; a restored copy of Manuscript N° D. 439).

49. See the Manuscript N° D 304 of the *Tūzuk-i Wālājāhī* of Munshī Burhān Khān Hāndī, in the G.O.M.L., Madras, edited with notes by T. Chandrasekharan, Madras, 1957; another manuscript, with no variations, said to have been written in 1232 AH, during the life time of the author belongs to the Muslim Library, Madras. See also the English Transl. by S.M.H. Nainar, (Two Vols.), Madras, 1934 and 1939. See also S. Bayly, *Saints, Goddesses and Kings. Muslims and Christians in South Indian Society, 1700-1900*, Cambridge, 1989; Indian edn, 1992, Part I, Chapter 4, especially pp. 164-75.

Were late Indo-Persian texts which refer to Persian music performed in India - and which I have not yet textually studied - describing a kind of music which was still alive or were they merely repeating some earlier treatises produced in Persia or in India ? A closer study of such texts may be of interest for musicologists and musicians specialised in Persian or Iranian music, as much as Persian treatises produced in Central Asia.[50]

Risāla-i mūsiqī, Treatises on Music: Persian, Indian or Indo-Persian Music ?

In many catalogues of Indo-Persian manuscripts, vague notices on numerous *Risāla-i mūsiqī* do not help the reader much, unless he has access to the original manuscript, which in some cases is almost impossible.[51]

One such example is found in the case of two manuscripts on music mentioned in the *Descriptive Catalogue of Arabic and Persian Manuscripts* (Part I) of the Gujarāt Vidyā Sabhā, in Ahmedabad, as a part of a mixed volume, with six texts in Persian estimated c. 1775. The first *Risāla-i-Musiqi* (sic) of an unknown author, is described in the section "Additional Particulars": "Work: The title means 'the Treatise on Music'. There are in the MS. a preface, twelve chapters (*maqām*) and a conclusion. The first is on the importance of music; in the second its meaning is explained; and thereafter topics like the origin and nature of various tunes and harmonic cadences have been treated."[52] The second text, *Risāla-i-Akhir dar Musiqi*, is described as follows: "The Treatise comprises a preface and eleven chapters. The authors explains therein twelve fixed musical modes and supports the theory that the ear is superior to the eye. Then he describes six sounds; harmonic ca-

50. See for instance a recent edition of the *Qānūn-i ᶜilmī va ᶜamali-i mūsiqī* of Zeyn al-ᶜAbedīn Maḥmūd Ḥuseynī, of the 15th century, with the facsimile of the unique Persian-Tajik manuscript and its transliteration in Cyrillic: Preparation, research, manuscript's facsimile and notes by A. Rajabov; Supplemented with the [partial] translation into Russian by A.A. Semenov [(1940), in facsimile]; Preparation and preface by K.S. Aini, Dushanbe, 1987. According to J. During, in his review of the book (*Abstracta Iranica*, 1989, Vol. 12, Entry N° 1071, p. 279), it is a compilation of the *Jāmiᶜ al-alḥān* and of its summary *Maqāsid al-alḥān* of ᶜAbd al-Qādir Marāghī (better known in Central Asia, under the name of ᶜAbd al-Qādir Guyande).

51. Many such treatises are mentioned (without description of their contents) in the section "*Mūsiqi*" of the hand-list of Persian manuscripts kept in the Rampur Raza Library; see *supra* note 22.

52. See the *Descriptive Catalogue of Arabic & Persian Manuscripts*, [Gujarāt Vidyā Sabhā Collection and Apārāo Bholānāth Collection], Part I, compil. and ed. C.R. Naik, Ahmedabad, 1964, N° 122, (f), p. 140.

dences, modulated sweet voice, musical tunes and tones and the effects thereof."[53] Through the sketchy catalogue notice, it appears that both these texts deal with Persian music.

Another such *Risāla-i mūsiqī* (sic) is described in the *Concise Descriptive Catalogue of the Persian Manuscripts in the Collection of the Asiatic Society of Bengal*, in Calcutta, under the sub-section "Translation from Sanskrit" of Chapter IX, "Varia".[54] The notice reads: "A Persian translation of a Hindu treatise on music. The exact title and the names of the author and of the translator are not mentioned. The present copy is incomplete at the end. There is no preface or doxology, and the book opens abruptly with: *bayān-e haqīqat-i nād ki buniyād-i sar ast, badānki nād bi-maᶜnī shod yaᶜnī āvāz ast,* etc..., followed by some details about the fifty-six folios of the manuscript, copied in the beginning of the nineteenth century, etc.[55]

Many *Risāla-i mūsiqī* (of Navāb Saïf Khān 'Faqīrullāh', of Ḥakīm Ḥasan b. Ibrāhīm al-Maudūdī al-Ḥusainī al-Ḥasanī al Cistī, of Jānā Begum, of Muḥammad ᶜAlī and many other anonymous) or two *Risāla dar mūsiqī* (of Ghulām Muḥammad Valīdpūrī and of Qa'im Khān) or a *Risāla-i akhir dar mūsiqī* (anonymous) and a *Risāla dar ᶜilm-i mūsiqī* (anonymous) or a *Risāla-i ᶜilm-i mūsiqī* (of Nāṣir Muḥammad 'Zanj' Ḥammad), etc. by anonymous, known or unknown authors are found in catalogues with not enough details to make out if they are treatises on Persian or Indian music, or on both, until a textual study of each of them is systematically done.[56]

Music in Encyclopaedic Works

Some treatises are actually part of wider encyclopaedia, works on general history and geography from the creation of the world down to the period of writing or compilations of biographical notices, collections of tales and anecdotes, etc., in which music often constitutes a section.[57] Two examples of the seventeenth century can be mentioned:

---

53. *Ibid*, (g), pp. 140-1.

54. See W. Ivanow, *Concise Descriptive Catalogue of the Persian Manuscripts in the Collection of the Asiatic Society of Bengal*, in Calcutta, First Supplement, Calcutta, 1927, N° 918, p. 115.

55. *Ibid.*

56. For details and references, see Delvoye, *Inventaire, op. cit.*, pp. 24-9.

57. See for example the *Mirāt-i Aftābnuma*, by Nawāb ᶜAbd-al-Raḥmān Shāhnawāz Khān Hāshimī Banbānī of Dehlī, 1218/1803, from the creation of the world, down to the thirtieth year of Shāh ᶜAlam's reign, 1202 / 1787). See two manuscripts in the Bodleian Library, Oxford, Sachau-Ethé, *op. cit.*, N° 120 and N° 121 and also in the British Museum, London, described in Rieu, *op. cit.*, N°s 131b, 132b, 133a, etc).

Mullā Tarzī's *Maᶜdan al-Jawāhir* is a collection of moral tales and anecdotes composed in 1616 and dedicated to Emperor Jahāngīr. It contains one chapter on music (*dar bayān-i haqiqat-i surod wa samāᶜ*), of which two manuscripts are preserved.[58] The *Tuḥfat al-Hind* of Mīrzā Khān (1675), another well-known Indo-Persian text has been already referred to as one of the main Persian authorities used by William Jones. The important chapter (V) on music in this huge encyclopaedia on Indian culture, language, literature, etc., deals separately with Indian and Persian music. Numerous manuscripts are available as well as a recent edition by N.H. Anṣārī.[59]

2. *Indo-Persian Historical Chronicles*

Contemporary documents or later retrospective histories, whether commissioned or not, and court-chronicles, along with memoirs and other contemporary writings of a more personal character, relate musical events or document socio-cultural and more rarely technical and aesthetic aspects of Persian and Indian music.

Historical texts of the Sultanate period and the famous Akbarid chronicles in Persian constitute another type of Indo-Persian writing documenting the history of music. Since my work has concentrated largely on the Mughal period, the focus of my research on historical sources has been more on the sixteenth-eighteenth century period. The documentation collected more recently on the Sultanate period and earlier regional cultural history has not yet been thoroughly exploited in that perspective; hence my selection of texts has been done mostly among the Mughal chronicles, for which I will only refer to some published and forthcoming papers, especially on Akbar. Different aspects of Akbar's relationship with music: as a music-composer, a musician and a keen listener but also as a patron of theoreticians of music and musicians, with the remarkable example of Tānsen, (in Akbar's court from 1562 till his death in 1589) are described in Indo-

58. See Ethé, *op. cit.*, Vol. I, N° 793, pp. 522-3, Chapter XIX, fols. 187a-90a and Sachau-Ethé, *op. cit.*, N° 464, pp. 432-3, Chapter XV, fols 124b-7b.

59. See Mīrzā Khān, *Tuḥfat al-Hind* in Marshall, *op. cit.*, N° 1068, pp. 295-6 and Ethé, *op. cit.*, Vol. I, N° 2011-3, pp. 1117-9. See also in the Bibliothèque Nationale, Paris, a manuscript of the first half of the 18th century (Suppl. Persan N° 387) described in Blochet, *op. cit.*, N° 235, p. 190. An unpublished notice by F. Richard has been kindly communicated to me, to be published in the Vol. II of F. Richard, *Catalogue des Manuscrits Persans de la Bibliothèque Nationale*, *op. cit.* See also the Persian edition by N.H. Anṣārī, Vol. I, Tehran, 1968; Vol. II, 2 Parts, Delhi, *Persian Research Journal*, Department of Persian, Univ. of Delhi, 1983. See M. Ziauddin, *Mirza Khan's Grammar of the Braj Bhakha*, Calcutta, 1935 (on music: pp. 23-8) and also N.P. Ahmad, *op. cit.*, pp. 34-55.

Persian sources, mostly contemporary chronicles, such as the fourth book of the *Ā'īn-i Akbarī*, being the third volume of the *Akbar Nāma* of Abū'l Faẓl, other passages of the *Akbar Nāma* and of the *Muntakhab al-tawārīkh* of Mullā ᶜAbd al-Qādir al-Badā'ūnī, and retrospective chronicles (such as the *Pādshāh Nāma* of ᶜAbd al-Ḥamīd Lāhaurī, 1627-47).

I have presented these sources and analysed the information they provide on Akbar as a patron of music elsewhere, hence I will only mention my conclusion.[60] A detailed survey of Indo-Persian, vernacular and iconographical sources documenting the reign of Akbar has led me to raise a number of questions about the interaction of court-musicians of diverse geographical origin, trained in various musical systems, with different aesthetic values, which, in the case of vocal music, applies to the poetic aspect as well as to the melodic aspect. Available documents indicate the coexistence of both systems, but though the curiosity and the taste for experimentation of Akbar are well-known in other fields such as architecture and painting, it is as yet too early to arrive at any conclusion about the existence of a third trend, *i.e.* an Indo-Persian form of music performed in the court of Akbar and other Mughal emperors.

As an example of a chronicle referring to music and musical patronage in regional history, I will mention among important chronicles of Akbar's time, the *Ṭabaqāt-i Akbarī* of Khwāja Niẓām al-dīn Aḥmad (d. 1594). It is an interesting source with some accounts on music in various kingdoms. To give an illustration, in the section on the Sulṭāns of Kashmir, Khwāja Niẓām al-dīn Aḥmad mentions the artistic patronage of Sulṭān Zain al-ᶜAbiddīn (r. 1420-70), as follows:

> "...owing to his munificence, many performers of vocal and instrumental music came from various places to Kashmīr. Among them was Mullā ᶜŪdī, who was one of the poor pupils of Khwājah ᶜAbd-ul-qādir [al-Marāghī?] and came from Khurāsān. He played on the *ᶜŪd* ... in such a way that it was a source of great pleasure to the Sultān; and he was exalted with various favours.... There had also been men in Kashmīr who sang one tune in twelve different modes or variations. [An obvious reference to Persian music.]
>
> At certain times, when the Sultān wished to be gay and cheer-

60. See Delvoye, "The Image of Akbar as a Patron of Music in Indo-Persian and Vernacular Sources", Seminar on "Akbar and His Age", Aligarh Muslim University, (Oct. 1992), Forthcoming in *Medieval India*, ed. I. Habib, Vol. II, Delhi, 1994.

> ful, he ordered that *Rubābs* and *Bīns* and other musical instruments should be made of gold and adorned with gems. There was a very intelligent man of the name of Sahūm, who composed verses in the dialect of Kashmir, and in the sciences and literature of India was the leader of the age.... and he wrote a book called *Mānik* in the science of music, and dedicated it to the Sultān; and owing to this received many favours. The Sultān was himself acquainted with Persian, Indian, Tibetan and other languages; and many books in the Arabic and Persian languages were translated by his orders into the *Hindvī* language; and the *Mahābhārat* which is a most famous book, and the book called *Rājatarangini*, which is the name of a history of the *Bādshāhs* of Kashmīr, were translated into Persian by his order....
>
> When Dūngar Sēn [*i.e.* Dungarendra Singh, r. 1425-59] in particular, the Rāja of Gwāliar, came to know the Sultān's great love for the science of music and singing, he sent two or three valuable treatises on these sciences...".[61]

Such remarks on Sulṭān Zain al-ᶜAbiddīn who commissioned translations and exchanged theoretical texts on music with Gwalior kings in particular, provide interesting information on cross-cultural history. In a similar way the artistic patronage in Gujarat and Malwa or other regions of India, can also be studied from chronicles and literary sources.[62]

3. *Indo-Persian Literary and Anecdotal Writings, Referring to Art-music in India*

While surveying Indo-Persian sources relevant to music, I equally noticed a few literary works - poetry in various metric patterns and prose and ornate prose writings - providing anecdotal and technical information, descriptions of musical scenes, or references to musicians (historical or fictitious) or metaphors of a musical inspiration.

Poetical Works

Among early literary works documenting art-music and its patron-

61. See Khwāja Niẓām al-dīn Aḥmad, *Ṭabaqāt-i Akbarī*, Persian edn. bv B. De, in Three Vols., Calcutta, 1913-35; English Transl. by B. De, rev. and ed. by B. Prasad, for the 3rd Vol., Calcutta, 1927-39; Vol. III, Part II, Section IX, account 8, pp. 652-72, on music, pp. 657-60.

62. For a bibliographical orientation on the socio-cultural history of medieval Gujarat, see Delvoye, "Indo-Persian Texts on the Artistic Patronage of the Sultans of Gujarat, 14th-16th c.", *op. cit.*

age, the *Dīvān* (collection of poetical works) of the Persian poet-scholar Masᶜūd Saᶜd Salmān (born in Lahore, c. AD 1050) offers a good example.[63] A close study of the historic contribution of early Persian poetry shows in the case of three thirteenth century Persian Divāns of poets, that "the *qasida* as well as other medieval literary works await a historical scrutiny by the students of history and culture."[64]

In many later Indo-Persian writings on music, Amīr Khusrau (1253-1325), represents the first great musician - one may even suggest musicologist - of the Indo-Islamic tradition. Known as a prolific court-poet (in Persian and Hindwī), he was also a music-composer and an expert in music theory.[65] Some of the poetical and prose works ascribed to Amīr Khusrau - the authenticity of which is still a matter of controversy - are being studied for the information they provide on musical forms, musicians and dancers performing in the "musical assembly" of the princely court (*shāhī majlis*) and in the religious set up of Sufi *khānqāhs* (*majlis-i samāᶜ*).[66] The socio-cultural history of musical patronage under thirteenth-fourteenth century Sulṭāns is well documented from such literary works in Persian, which show the way to other writings.

Works in Prose and Ornate Prose

A rare example of Indo-Persian fiction work contributing to the

63. See Masᶜūd Saᶜd Salmān, *Divān*, ed. R. Yāsimī, Tehran, n.d., quoted in A. Schimmel, *Islamic Literatures of India*, Wiesbaden, 1973, p. 11.

64. See Siddiqui, *Perso-Arabic Sources, op. cit.*, quotation, p. 73; see also Chapter 3, pp. 53-77.

65. For further bibliographical references, see M. Habib, *Life and Works of Hazrat Amir Khusrau of Delhi*, Aligarh, 1928; M.W. Mirza, *The Life and Works of Amir Khusrau* (1935), Delhi, repr., 1974; *Life, Times and Works of Amir Khusrau Dehlavi*, ed., Z. Ansari, New Delhi, 1975; "Khusrau Nāma", *Persian Research Journal*, Special Number, ed. S.M. Ahmad, Delhi, Department of Persian, University of Delhi, 1988 (in Persian). On Amīr Khusrau and music, see Sarmadee, "Musical Genius of Amir Khusrau", *Amir Khusrau, Memorial Volume,* New Delhi, 1975, pp. 33-61; by the same author, "About Music and Amir Khusrau's own Writings on Music", *Life, Times and Works of Amir Khusrau Dehlavi,* published Hasnuddin Ahmad, New Delhi, 1975, pp. 241-64 and "Ghazal aur Sarud-i Ghazal", *Khusrau Shinasi*, ed., Z. Ansari, New Delhi, 1975; S.Q. Fatimi, "Amir Khusrau's Contribution to the Indus-Muslim Music", Islamabad, Oct. 1975, pp. 3-39. See also Chander Shekhar, "Tauṣīf-i ālāt-i mūsīqī dar āṣār-i Amīr Khusrau Dehlevī", *Persian Research Journal,* Department of Persian, University of Delhi, 1988, pp. 148-65 (in Persian).

66. Among texts attributed to Amīr Khusrau referring to music, see *Iᶜjāz-i Khusrawi*, Lithograph, Lucknow, 1876-77, *Risāla* II, *Khaṭṭ* 9, *ḥarf* iii, pp. 275-91. There is a translation programme for the *Iᶜjāz-i Khusrawi* by a board of scholars, sponsored by the Amir Khusrau Society of America (AKSA), the Smithsonian Institution and the Sahitya Akademi, under the direction of Prof. Nazir Ahmad, Aligarh.

history of the Sulṭāns of the Tughluq Period is the *Basātin ul-Uns* (1325-26), by Muḥammad Ṣadr ᶜAlā (bin) Aḥmad Ḥasan Dabir ᶜAbdusi, entitled Tāj (ul-Mulk) and known as Ikhtisān (ud-Dehlawī).[67] The text written in prose includes *qasida* (panegyrics) and is known for its ornate style, its floridity and its rhetoricism; it provides valuable information about court-music and especially on musical instruments.[68] The poetical and prose work of the poet Mullā Nūr al-dīn Ẓuhūrī, who was born in Persia and who became one of the most celebrated medieval Persian poets in the Sultanate courts of Ahmadnagar and Bijapur, in the Deccan (early seventeenth century) should be given a place of importance in the Indo-Persian literature referring to Indian music.[69] One of his *masnavis* composed (c. 1591) for the Sulṭān of Ahmadnagar, Burhān Niẓām Shāh, includes a portion on music (*surod*) and musicians (*muṭrib*) in which Ẓuhūrī describes various musical instruments of his time, also appearing in contemporary miniature paintings.[70] Another work in ornate prose, the *Seh Naṣr* or "The Three Essays" constitutes the preface (*dibāca*) of the famous collection of *dhrupad* songs attributed to Sulṭān Ibrāhim ᶜĀdil Shāh II of Bijapur, who was one of his royal patrons.[71] Besides their literary value, these texts written in praise of the Sulṭān provide valuable documents on the history of court-music in medieval Deccan.

Such prefaces in Persian to collections of lyrics composed in vernacular languages could constitute another category. Though having in common their literary form, as works in prose and ornate prose, they document the history of music in such a diversified manner, that they

67. See Siddiqui, *Perso-Arabic Sources, op. cit.*, Chapter 5, pp. 90-101; description of manuscripts, Note 2, p. 98. See also S.H. Askari, "Historical value of *Basatin-ul-Uns*, A Rare Literary Work of the Early 14th Century", *The Journal of the Bihar Research Society*, Jan.-Dec. 1962, XLVIII, Parts I-IV, pp. 1-29; description of other available manuscripts, p. 3.

68. On music in the *Basātin ul-Uns*, see Askari, *op. cit.*, pp. 19-29.

69. See Delvoye, "The Verbal Content of Dhrupad Songs from the Earliest Collections: II. The *Kitāb-i Nauras* of Ibrāhīm ᶜĀdil Shāh II...", *op. cit.*, Parts I and II.

70. *Ibid.*, (1993), pp. 10-1, 14 and the plate facing p. 18. See also M. Zebrowski, *Deccani Painting*, London, 1983; Indian edn., New Delhi, 1983, pp. 67-121.

71. Among the early collections of *dhrupads*, the *Kitāb-i Nauras*, "The Book of the Nine Flavours or Sentiments", is a remarkable example of a *rāg*-wise anthology of fifty-nine songs akin to *dhrupad* and seventeen couplets (*dohrā*) in the Deccani language revealing several other vernacular features, composed by Ibrāhīm ᶜĀdil Shāh II, the Sultān of Bijapur from 1580 to 1627 and a great patron of the arts of poetry, music, painting and calligraphy. Most of the ten manuscripts of the *Kitāb-i Nauras* preserved in various libraries in India. have been used for the critical edition published by Nazir Ahmad in 1956, with an English rendering, *op. cit, supra*, Note 19. See Delvoye, "The Verbal Content of Dhrupad Songs: II. The *Kitāb-i Nauras* of Ibrāhīm ᶜĀdil Shāh II...", *op. cit.*, Parts I and II.

cannot be consider as a specific genre. Besides the "Three Prefaces" of Ẓuhūrī, another text which is not well-known as a Indo-Persian source on music, well illustrates a genre of writing belonging to the same literary category, though it provides a different type of information. The Persian preface to the anthology of *dhrupad* song-texts ascribed to Nāyak Ba<u>kh</u>shū - a famous poet-composer of the court of Rājā Mān Singh Tomar, king of Gwalior (r. 1486-1516) - compiled by an anonymous writer, from the oral tradition of court-musicians, under the patronage of Shāh Jahān, expounds how these compositions were collected and selected with a particular care for their authenticity; hence it is a rare document on the circumstances of the noting down of lyrics from the oral tradition to a written form.[72] A critical edition of several manuscripts of the preface in preparation by S.H. Qasemi will throw light on the history of Dhrupad and its main exponents such as Nāyak Ba<u>kh</u>shū and Tānsen.[73]

Memoirs, Personal Writings and Travelogues

Often written by aristocratic personalities, memoirs, personal writings and also travelogues could be considered as a particular literary genre, sometimes close to historical chronicles. Again, the information they provide is of an extremely diverse nature. Hence from the point of view of their contribution to the history of music, these texts cannot represent a separate category, in the attempt to classify Indo-Persian sources on music. Three examples of personal writings will be briefly presented chronologically.

Asad Beg (d. 1631-32) who was born in Qazwin, became a close associate to the Mughal court and was sent by Akbar to the court of Ibrāhīm ᶜĀdil Shāh II, the Sulṭān of Bijapur, in 1603-04, with the mission of getting the Sulṭān's daughter to marry Prince Dāniyāl, the son of Akbar. There he visited Ṭarābābād, the quarter where musicians and dancers used to live in the newly-constructed town of Nauraspur and he also attended musical festivities which he describes vividly in

72. See P.L. Śarmā, *Sahasarasa, Nāyak Bakhśū ke dhrupadoṁ kā saṅgrah*, New Delhi, 1972 and Sharma, "Sahasarasa (A Compilation of Dhrupad Texts Ascribed to Bakshoo), Synopsis of a Treatise", *Indian Music Journal*, 1972-73-74, Vols. VIII-IX-X, N°s 15-20, pp. 41-48; see also Delvoye, "The Verbal Content of Dhrupad Songs from the Earliest Collections: I. The *Hazār Dhurpad* or *Sahasras*, a collection of 1004 *dhrupads* attributed to Nāyak Ba<u>kh</u>sū", *Dhrupad Annual 1990*, pp. 93-109 and Delvoye, "Les chants *dhrupad* en langue braj des poètes-musiciens de l'Inde Moghole", *op. cit.*, pp. 170-4.

73. To be published in *Qand-e-Pārsī*, ed. S.H. Qasemi, New Delhi, Cultural Counsellor, Embassy of the I.R. of Iran.

his *Waqā'iᶜ-i Asad Beg*, also known as *Ḥālāt-i Asad Beg* and *Aḥwāl-i Asad Beg*.[74] His testimony is unique on Deccani music in performance and also for the Mughal court-music to which he refers elsewhere in his memoirs.[75]

In his travelogue *Bahr ul-Asrār*, Maḥmūd b. Amīr Walī Balkhī who came to India in 1624, describes musical scenes in different places which he visited in North India, such as Mathura. A careful study of terms used for different genres of music and dance and for performers would add to the information provided by court-chronicles of the late sixteenth-early seventeenth century.[76]

In another autobiographical account, which is both a memoir and a travelogue, Navāb Dargāh Qulī Khān (b. 1710) describes various aspects of life in Jahānābād (*i.e.* Delhi), where he accompanied Niẓām ul-Mulk Āṣaf Jāh, in 1737. His vivid account of religious Sufi places and of cultural activities and festivities in the Delhi of Muḥammad Shāh, is known as the *Risāla-i Sālār Jang* or more commonly today as the *Muraqqaᶜ-i Dehlī*, and seems to be a portion of a much bigger work.[77] It includes a series of lively notices about the religious leaders, poets, singers, musicians and courtesans, whom he happened to meet during his stay in Delhi. Such a detailed first-hand account reveals a number of features

74. See Storey, *op. cit.*, N° 712, pp. 553-4, for references to manuscripts. See also some excerpts translated into English in H.M. Elliot & J. Dowson, *The History of India as Told by its Own Historians* (1867-77), Delhi, Repr., 1990, Vol. 6, pp. 150-74, especially pp. 162-4. See also P.M. Joshi, "Asad Beg's Mission to Bijapur, 1603-1604", *Mahāmahōpādhyāya Prof. D.V. Potdar Sixty-First Birthday Commemoration Volume. Studies in Historical and Indological Research...*, ed. S.N. Sen, Poona, 1950, pp. 184-96.

75. *Ibid.*

76. See Maḥmūd b. Amīr Walī Balkhī, *The Baḥr ul-Asrār. Travelogue of South Asia*, Intro., ed. & annot. Riazul Islam, Karachi, 1980. See also I. Husain, "Hindu Shrines and Practices as Described by a Central Asian Traveller in the First Half of the 17th Century", *Medieval India 1. Researches in the History of India, 1200-1750*, ed. I. Habib, Delhi, 1992, pp. 141-53, with some illustrative passages translated into English. See also S. Digby, "Some Asian Wanderers in Seventeenth Century India: An Examination of Sources in Persian", *Studies in History*, 1993, Vol. 9, N° 2, pp. 247-64.

77. See Storey, *op. cit.*, N° 1532, pp. 1118-9, for references to manuscripts. See the Persian edition, under the title *Muraqqaᶜ-i Dehlī* az Dargāh Qulī Khān, ed. N.H. Anṣārī, Delhi, 1981; see especially the chapter on musicians and courtesans who were singers and dancers (*arbāb-i ṭarab*), pp. 81-113; English Transl., *Muraqqaᶜ-e-Dehli. The Mughal Capital in Muhammad Shah's Time*, with introduction and notes by Chander Shekhar and S.M. Chenoy, Delhi, 1989, especially pp. 75-125. See also S.P. Blake, *Shahjahanabad. The Sovereign City in Mughal India, 1639-1739*, Cambridge, 1991, pp. 57 ff., *passim*, especially pp. 150-60 concerning what Blake wrongly calls "popular culture". See also M. Trivedi, "An Appraisal of the Musical Arts at Shahjahanabad during the First Half of the Eighteenth Century", *Art and Culture. Felicitation Volume in Honour of Professor S. Nurul Hasan*, eds., A.J. Qaisar and S.P. Verma, Jaipur, 1993, pp. 95-103.

of cultural life not well documented elsewhere.

A systematic exploitation of poetical and prose works produced in India with references to music would certainly constitute a rich corpus complementary to musicological treatises and historical chronicles. Contrary to common belief, their literary bent does not create any hindrance to their contribution to musicological and technical knowledge and to the light they throw on musicians and their aristocratic patrons.

In the Persian or Indo-Persian contexts, numerous miniature paintings depict music and dance scenes attended by a prince, a sultan or an emperor or musicians playing various instruments, independently or as an illustration to a text. They add a visual testimony to the literature suggesting the official status of music and dance in the court-life of Indo-Islamic rulers.[78]

It appears that among the available textual sources on music, some literary genres were fairly well represented at particular times; nevertheless, it cannot be simply inferred that it was due to the direct effect of a specific cultural policy. As a typical example, it was believed that the high number of important Indo-Persian texts on Indian music produced during the reign of the Mughal emperor Aurangzeb (r. 1658-1707), would have been the result of his "hatred" for music, hence the reconversion of court-musicians and practitioners into music theorists ! Mention may be made of the popular account left by K͟hāfī K͟hān in his *Muntak͟hab al-lubāb* (1732) and by the Venetian physician and traveller Niccolao Manucci (d. 1717), about Aurangzeb's orders prohibiting music and dance. The result of the so-called command, which the Mughal chronicler dates to 1078/1668 (the eleventh year of Aurangzeb's reign) is allegedly that court-musicians organised a mock funeral for "music" - which is said to have provoked some cynical comments by the Emperor about how deep "it" should be buried, so "that no sound or cry might afterwards arise from it". This episode

78. See among numerous publications on Mughal painting, some works published in French, which are perhaps not particularly well known in India, such as *A la cour du Grand Moghol*, Catalogue of an Exhibition in the Bibliothèque Nationale, Paris, 1986, in particular the introductory contribution of F. Richard on artistic patronage, pp. 15-21, and also "Des princes bibliophiles", pp. 153-60 and on *Rāga-mālā* paintings, G. Colas, "La guirlande des Rāga-s", pp. 163-83. See also *Miniatures de l'Inde impériale. Les peintres de la cour d'Akbar (1556-1605)*, Catalogue of an Exhibition at the Musée Guimet, Paris, 1989 and M.-C. David & J. Soustiel, *Miniatures orientales de l'Inde - 4*, Catalogue of an Exhibition at the Galerie Jean Soustiel, Paris 1986, pp. 4-22. As an example of an illustrated text, see the *Jawāhir al-Musīkat-i Muḥammadī* of ᶜAbd al-Karīm b. Farīd Anṣārī Qādirī (in Deccani Urdu), preserved at the British Museum, (Or. 12,857) with forty-eight Deccani paintings, dedicated to Muḥammad ᶜAdil Shāh (r. 1627-56), the son of Ibrāhim ᶜĀdil Shāh II, described in Zebrowski, *op. cit.*, pp. 62-3.

became famous later, and the story is endlessly repeated in school-books on music as "history", or more fairly but still disparagingly, as a "musical parable", along with fanciful accounts of Tānsen's extraordinary musical powers.[79]

A more systematic analysis of Indo-Persian texts referring to music - and possibly of vernacular literature - produced in the second half of the seventeenth century and early eighteenth century and a thorough study of the personalities and the motivations of their authors, would certainly lead to a serious questioning of this simplistic vision, still persisting with scholars and teachers of Indian music, in India and elsewhere.

Problems in the Depiction of Indian Music

We may briefly evoke some difficulties faced by Persian writers, more familiar with the Arabo-Persian system of music, while trying to describe Indian music. Some authors adopted a comparative approach, meant for readers who were presumably aware of the Persian tradition and keen to understand the Indian system in a better way.

One basic difference between the two modal systems lies in the concept of "mode" itself; hence the common "translation" of *rāga* by *maqām* is misleading for the listener brought up in the Persian tradition.[80] Concepts of *dastgāh*, *gushe*, *shoᶜbe*, *parde*, *uṣūl*, *naghma*, etc. are foreign to the Indian system, and a term like *āvāz*, with its numerous meanings, such as scale, succession of short melodico-modal sequences (*gushe*), expressive character, seems to be known in the Indian context with a far more restricted meaning. The use of *naghma* and *ṣaut* (plural *aṣwāt*) for notes, modes, songs, voice, etc. is also problematic.

The determination of the height of the tones in the scale according to the fretting of string-instruments is common to both system. Indo-Persian music privileged the *ᶜūd* and Indian music the *vīṇā*, both fretted long-necked string instruments.

The link between music and poetry is also rather different in the

79. See Muḥammad Hāshim, Khāfī Khān, *Muntakhab al-Lubāb*, Persian edn., Calcutta, 1860-74, passage quoted, Vol. II, p. 213; English Transl., *The History of India as Told by its Own Historians*, *op. cit.*, Vol. 7, pp. 207-533; passage quoted, pp. 283-4. See also N. Manucci, *Mogul India or Storia do Mogor*, English Transl. by William Irvine, Four Vols., (1907-08), Repr., Delhi, 1990, Vol. II, pp. 5-6. Among many examples of standard books on Indian music referring to this episode, see for instance F. Tupper, *Musiques de l'Inde du Nord. Guide d'Ecoute & Discographie CD*, Paris, 1993, p. 103. But see also details about singing and dancing women in Aurangzeb's court, in Manucci, *op. cit.*, Vol. II, pp. 312-4.

80. See H.S. Powers, *op. cit.*

two contexts, as is the link between poetry and metrics, or at another level, the link between various modes and seasons, planets, animals, etc. Hence different conceptions and definitions are found in both systems for a poet, a music composer and a poet-composer (operating in India in vernacular languages, and not in Persian) and also a performer. Similarly, some ornamental devices like repetition are appreciated in both systems, though the rules of their actual practice may be different. It would be interesting to study systematically various concepts in both systems.

The idea of "repertoire" could be compared in both traditions to find out if a Persian "repertoire-type" including about hundred melodico-modal sequences (*gushe*) was rather different from the Indian musician's repertoire of about a hundred *rāga* and thousands of poetical compositions meant to be sung in some specific modes, according to a tradition inherited from his teacher (often his father or a close relative).

The classification of instruments according to Indo-Persian authors who describe Persian or Indian music may also be worth examining in a comparative way. Descriptions of Indian instruments in texts using, translating or commenting on Sanskrit treatises, generally employs the Indian traditional classification into four categories, as followed by the anonymous author of *G͟hunyat al-Munya* or Abū'l Faẓl in the *Ā'īn-i Akbarī*.[81]

Sanskrit and vernacular technical terms, with their long and short vocalisation, were difficult to render in the Arabo-Persian script. In a true effort to transcribe Indian words as closely as possible to their original forms, most Indo-Persian authors of treatises on music, from the *G͟hunyat al-Munya* onwards, used diacritical marks and often spelt each technical word of Indian origin.[82]

Musicians Described in a Socio-cultural Perspective

Data provided on the categories of musicians are precious to understand their social importance in courtly life, in spite of their humble origin, often indicated in their "titles" (*e.g. kalāvant* or *mīrāṣī*). Sanskrit texts on music generally classify musicians into various kinds, according to their "virtues" (*guṇa*) and "defects" (*doṣa*). Indo-Persian authors

81. See *Ghunyat al-Munya, op. cit.*, Book I, Chapter II, pp. 51-65 and Abū'l Faẓl, *Ā'īn-i Akbarī*, Persian edn. by H. Blochmann, Calcutta, 1877, Vol. II, pp. 140-42; English Transl. by H.S. Jarrett, Repr. New Delhi, 1978, Vol. III, pp. 268-71.

82. Two remarkable examples of diacritical marks and precise spelling are found in the *Ghunyat al-Munya, op. cit.* and Mīrzā K͟hān's *Tuḥfat al-Hind, op. cit.*

often use the same categories, to which they add information about musicians of the past and present.[83] Most authors give the titles of musicians along with their name, which is of great help for the reconstruction of a sociological history of music performers. Though categories of musicians (*gandharva*, *nāyak*, *kalāvant*, *gunī*, *ḍhāḍhī*, *mīrāṣī*, *qavvāl*, etc.) have changed since the medieval period, a strong hierarchy is very much "felt" today by musicians for whom the family lineage is often more important than their actual personal musical abilities.

The precise and lively observations about the socio-cultural background of musicians and their protectors, makes Indo-Persian texts a source of valuable material, which is not to be found in Sanskrit sources on music and which historians, music-historians and musicologists have not yet well exploited.

The information collected from Indo-Persian texts documents both the Persian and Indian forms of music performed in medieval India by mobile and migrant musicians from diverse cultural backgrounds, interacting and competing with each other, with the basic aim of pleasing rulers with ever-changing tastes. Such information is not to be found in more conventional and traditional musicological literature (in Sanskrit), in which there is hardly any space for artistic creativity and musical experimentation, though, presumably, they had been encouraged by refined patrons, with a more open attitude.

Conclusion

Persian texts devoted or referring to music written in India from the fourteenth century till the late nineteenth century, testify to the double culture of their authors, and indicate the interest of their patrons who encouraged musicians, musicologists and artistic creativity. One may notice the striking didactic concern which dictated the composition in Persian of so many treatises and literary texts on an alien musical tradition. Such practice and performance-oriented texts provide guidelines to familiarize Persianized courtiers and nobility with the theory and aesthetics of Indian music, which was nowhere to be found in more conventional Sanskrit musicological treatises. With their remarkable sociological perception, they attest to the importance of music in Indo-Islamic court-life as shown for example by the inclusion of a chapter on music in works of encyclopaedic nature or the inclusion of lyric-composers and musicians in poetic anthologies, to which may be added a rich iconography.

---

83. See for instance Mīrzā Khān's *Tuḥfat al-Hind*, *op. cit.*, pp. 336-62.

Among sources documenting the history of art-music in India, Indo-Persian texts which have been surveyed widen the research-field of scholars of medieval Indian socio-cultural history, musicologists and literary specialists. Indo-Persian literature highlights the interaction of both the Persian and the Indian traditions of art-music, with precious remarks on folk and regional forms of music. However, it still does leave open the crucial question of the existence of any "Indo-Persian music" in performance.

REFERENCES

I. Catalogues of Manuscripts and Bibliographical Surveys Cited (classified library-wise)

Indian Libraries

Andhra Pradesh Government Oriental Manuscripts Library and Research Institute (A.P.G.O.M.L.& R.I.), Hyderabad. Manuscripts in all languages mixed (Arabic, Persian, Urdū, Hindustānī, Sindhī, etc.) are described in hand-written catalogues, classified subject-wise. "Music" is catalogued under "Falsafa".

Āṣafīyah Collection, Government Oriental Manuscripts Library and Research Institute, Hyderabad. *Catalogue of Arabic, Persian and Urdu Books in the Āṣafiyah Library, Haidarābād*, Hyderabad, 1332-33 AH. (in Persian)

Asiatic Society of Bengal, Calcutta. Ivanow, Wladimir, *Concise Descriptive Catalogue of the Persian Manuscripts in the Collection of the Asiatic Society of Bengal*, in Calcutta, First Supplement, Calcutta: The Asiatic Society of Bengal, 1927. [Bibliotheca Indica, N° 244]

Buhar Collection, National Library, Calcutta. Maulvi ᶜAbd-ul-Muqtadir *et al.*, *Catalogue Raisonné of the Buhar Collection,* Vol. 1, *Catalogue of Persian Manuscripts in Buhar Collection* (1921), Calcutta: National Library, Rev. edn., 1982.

Government Oriental Manuscripts Library (G.O.M.L.), University of Madras, *A Descriptive Catalogue of the Islamic Manuscripts in the Government Oriental Manuscripts Library, Madras*, Four Vols., Madras: Government of Tamil Nadu, 1939, 1950, 1954, 1961.

Gujarāt Vidyā Sabhā Collection and Apārāo Bholānāth Collection, Ahmedabad. Naik, Chhotubhai Ranchhodji, *Descriptive Catalogue of Arabic & Persian Manuscripts,* [Gujarāt Vidyā Sabhā Collection and Apārāo Bholānāth Collection], Part I, Ahmedabad: Gujarat Vidya Sabha, 1964.

Khuda Bakhsh Oriental Public Library, Patna. Maulavi Abdul Muqtadir, *Catalogue of the Arabic and Persian Manuscripts in the Khuda Bakhsh Oriental Public Library at (Bankipur) Patna*, Vol. XXXII, (Persian Manuscripts), Mixed Contents, Patna: Khuda Bakhsh Oriental Public Library, 2nd impr., 1980. First appeared as *Supplement to the Catalogue of the Persian Manuscripts*, Vol. II, 1933; *Supplement to the Catalogue of the Persian Manuscripts in the Oriental Public Library at Bankipore*, Vol. II, Patna: The Superintendent, Government Printing, Bihar and Orissa, 1933.

Rampur Raza Library, Rampur. Subject-wise catalogues of Persian manuscripts, prepared by Imtiāz ᶜAlī ᶜArshī (unpublished).

Salar Jung Museum and Library, Hyderabad. Muhammad Ashraf, *Catalogue of the Persian Manuscripts in the Salar Jung Museum & Library*, Nine Vols. (subject-wise), Hyderabad, Salar Jung, 1965, 1966, 1967, 1969, 1975, 1980, 1983, 1988. Manuscripts specifically "on music" kept in the Oriental Mss Section of the Sālār Jung Museum and Library, are listed in an unpublished hand-written catalogue, n.d. (c. 1965-66 as per Rahmat Ali Khan's estimation), as a part of Vol. XI. The Sciences, Mental, Moral and Physical (Contd.). 9. Arts, Agriculture, Technology, Music, Games, etc. (Forthcoming)

Shri Raghuvir Library, Sitamau. Nizami, A.H., *Catalogue of Persian Manuscripts and Records in the Shri Raghuvir Library, Sitamau*, Delhi, Idarah-i Adabiyat-i Delli, 1993. [IAD Oriental (Original) Series N° 42]

European Libraries

Bibliothèque Nationale, Paris. Blochet, Edgard, *Catalogue des manuscrits persans de la Bibliothèque Nationale*, Tome I, Paris: Leroux, 1905, Tome II, Paris: Leroux, 1912, Tome III, Paris: Réunion des Bibliothèques Nationales, 1928, Tome IV, Paris: Bibliothèque Nationale, 1934.

— Richard, Francis, *Catalogue des Manuscrits Persans de la Bibliothèque Nationale*, Vol. I, Paris, Bibliothèque Nationale, 1989.

Bodleian Library, Oxford. Sachau, E. and H. Ethé, *Catalogue of the Persian, Turkish, Hindustani and Pushtu Manuscripts in the Bodleian Library*, begun by E. Sachau and continued by H. Ethé, Part I, Persian Manuscripts, Oxford, 1889.

Oriental and India Office Collections, British Library, London. Ethé, Hermann, *Catalogue of Persian Manuscripts in the Library of the India Office*, Vol. I, Oxford: Printed for the India Office by Horace Hart, Printer to the University, 1903.

— Rieu, C., *Catalogue of the Persian Manuscripts in the British Museum*, Vols. I-III, London, 1879-83.

Bibliographical Surveys

Marshall, D.N., *Mughals in India. A Bibliographical Survey of Manuscripts* (1967), London/New York, Mansell Publishing Limited, 1985.

Shiloah, Amnon, *The Theory of Music in Arabic Writings (c. 900-1900). Descriptive Catalogue of Manuscripts in Libraries of Europe and the U.S.A.*, Munich: G. Henle Verlag, 1979.

Storey, Charles Ambrose, *Persian Literature. A Bio-Bibliographical Survey*, Vol. II, Part 3, F. Encyclopaedias and Miscellanies, G. Arts and Crafts, H. Science, I. Occult Arts, Leiden: Royal Asiatic Society - E.J. Brill, 1977.

II. Arabic and Indo-Persian Texts Cited (Editions and Translations)

^{c}Abd al-Qādir al-Badā'ūnī, *Muntakhab al-tawārīkh*, Persian edn. in Three Vols. by Kabīr al-dīn Aḥmad, Aḥmad ^{c}Ali and W.N. Lees, Calcutta: Asiatic Society of Bengal (Bibliotheca Indica), 1864-69. See also the English Transl. in Three Vols. by G. Ranking (vol. I), W.H. Lowe (vol. II) and T.W. Haig (vol. III), Calcutta: Asiatic Society of Bengal (Bibliotheca Indica), 1884-1925, Repr., Delhi, Idarah-i Adabiyat-i Delli, 1978.

^{c}Abd al-Qādir b. Gheybī al-Ḥāfiẓ al-Marāghī, *Maqāsid al-alḥān*, ed. Tāqī Binesh, Tehran, 1977-1986.

— *Jāmi^{c} al-alḥān*, ed. and comment. Tāqī Binesh, Tehran: MMTF, 1367.

Amīr Khusrau, *Ijāz-i Khusrawi*, (*Risāla* II, *Khaṭṭ* 9, *ḥarf* iii), Lithograph, Lucknow: Nawal Kishor Press, 1876-77.

Bābur (Zaḥiru'd-dīn Muḥammad Bābur Pādshāh Ghāzī), *Bābur-Nāma, Memoirs of Bābur*, (1921) Tr. Annette Susannah Beveridge, Two Vols., Repr., New Delhi: Atlantic Publishers & Distributors, 1989.

Baranī, Ẓiā ud-dīn, *Tārīkh-i Fīrūzshāhī*, ed. Saiyid Aḥmad Khān, Calcutta: Asiatic Society of Bengal, 1862; Reprint, Osnabrück:

Biblio Verlag, 1981. [Bibliotheca Indica, Vol. 33]

Burhān Khān Hāndī (Munshī), *Tūzuk-i Wālājāhī*, edited with notes by T. Chandrasekharan, Madras, Government Press, 1957. [Madras Government Oriental Manuscripts Series, Nº 38]. English Transl. by S. Muhammad Husayn Nainar, (Two Vols.), Madras, Governement Press, 1934 and 1939.

Dargāh Qulī Khān, *Muraqqa^{c}-i Dehlī*, ed. N.H. Anṣārī, Delhi: Department of Urdū, University of Delhi, 1981; English Transl. *Muraqqa^{c}-e-Dehli. The Mughal Capital in Muhammad Shah's Time*, with introduction and notes by Chander Shekhar and Shama Mitra Chenoy, Delhi: Deputy Publication, 1989.

'Faqīrullāh', Navāb Saïf Khān, *Rāg Darpan*: "Rāga Darpana" and "Ṣaut al Nāqaus" by Muḥammad ^{c}Oṣman Qais, eds. N.H. Anṣārī and Sh. Shukla, *Persian Research Journal Special Number*, Delhi, Department of Persian, University of Delhi, 1981; *Rāg Darpan*, pp. 11-86; '*Ṣaut al-Nāqaus*, 2nd part, pp. 1-24.

Ghunyat-ul-Munya. The Earliest Known Persian Work on Indian Music, ed. Shahab Sarmadee, Bombay: Asia Publishing House, 1978.

Gul-Badan Begam, *The History of Humāyūn, Humāyūn Nāma*, Persian Text and English Transl. with Introduction and Notes by Annette S. Beveridge (1900), Reprint, New Delhi: Atlantic Publishers & Distributors, 1989.

Ibn Baṭṭūṭa, *The Reḥla of Ibn Baṭṭūṭa* (India, Maldive Islands and Ceylon) (1953), Translation and Commentary, ed. Mahdi Husain, Baroda: Oriental Institute, 2nd repr. edn., 1976. [Gaekwad's Oriental Series, Nº 122]

^{c}Ināyat Khān Rāsikh, *Risāla-i zikr-i mughanniyān-i Hindūstān*, edition of the manuscript Nº 1734-35 of the Khuda Bakhsh Library, in Patna, by Sayyid ^{c}Alī Haider, Patna: Arabic & Persian Research Institute, 1961. [Arabic & Persian Research Institute Publication Series, Nº 7]

Kaīkā'ūs, *Kitāb Naṣīhat Nāma ma^{c}arūf be Qābūs Nāma,* tālīf Amīr ^{c}Anṣar Alma^{c}ālī Kaikā'ūs bin Iskandar bin Qābūs bin Washamgīr, ed. Ruben Levy, Hertford: Stephen Austin, 1951; English Transl. by Reuben Levy, *A Mirror for Princes, The Qābūs Nāma by Kai Kā'ūs ibn Iskandar, Prince of Gurgān*, London: The Cresset Press, 1951.

Khāfī Khān, Muḥammad Hāshim, *Muntakhab al-Lubāb*, Persian edn., Calcutta: Asiatic Society of Bengal, 1860-74; English Transl., H.M. Elliot and J. Dowson, *The History of India as Told by its*

Own Historians (1867-77), Repr., Delhi: Low Price Publications, 1990, Vol. 7, pp. 207-533.

Maḥmūd b. Amīr Walī Balkhī, *The Baḥr ul-Asrār. Travelogue of South Asia*, Introduced, edited & annotated by Riazul Islam, Karachi: Institute of Central & West Asian Studies, University of Karachi, 1980.

Masᶜūd Saᶜd Salmān, *Divān*, ed. Rashīd Yāsimī, Tehran, n.d.

Mīrzā Khān, *Tuḥfat al-Hind*, ed. N.H. Anṣārī, Vol. I, Tehran: Intishārāt-i Bunyād Farang-i Irān, AH 1354/1968; Vol. II, 2 Parts, Delhi, *Persian Research Journal*, Delhi: Department of Persian, University of Delhi, 1983.

Niẓām al-dīn Aḥmad (Khwāja), *Ṭabaqāt-i Akbarī*, Persian edn. by B. De, in Three Vols., Calcutta: The Asiatic Society of Bengal, 1913-35; English Transl. by B. De, rev. and ed. by B. Prasad, for the 3rd Vol., Calcutta, 1927-39.

Risāle-ye mūsīqī, Bahjat al-rūh, ed. H.L. Rabino de Borgomalo, Tehran: Buniyād-i Farghang-i Irān, 1346/1967.

Zeyn al-ᶜAbedīn Maḥmūd Ḥuseynī, *Qānūn-i ᶜilmī va ᶜamali-i mūsīqī*, edited with the English title *The Canon of Theory and Practical Music* of Zayn-al-Abidin Husayny, Preparation, research, manuscript's facsimile and notes by Askarali Rajabov; Supplemented with the Russian translation by A.A. Semenov [(1940), in facsimile]; Preparation and preface by K.S. Aini, Dushanbe: Publishing House "Donish", 1987. [with the facsimile of the unique Persian-Tajik manuscript and its transliteration in Cyrillic]

III. Other References

Ahmad, Najma Perveen, *Hindustani Music. A Study of its Development in 17th and 18th Centuries*, New-Delhi: Manohar Publications, 1984.

A la cour du Grand Moghol, Paris: Bibliothèque Nationale, 1986. (Exhibition Catalogue)

Askari, S.H., "Historical value of *Basatin-ul-Uns*, A Rare Literary Work of the Early 14th Century", *The Journal of the Bihar Research Society*, Jan.-Dec. 1962, XLVIII, Parts I-IV, pp. 1-29.

Bayly, Susan, *Saints, Goddesses and Kings. Muslims and Christians in South Indian Society, 1700-1900*, Cambridge: Cambridge University Press, 1989; Indian edn, 1992.

Bhanu, D., "Promotion of Music by the Turco-Afghans Rulers of India", *Islamic Culture*, Jan. 1955, Vol. XIX, N° 1, pp. 9-31.

Blake Stephen P., *Shahjahanabad. The Sovereign City in Mughal India, 1639-1739*, Cambridge: Cambridge University Press, 1991. [South Asian Studies, 49]

Chander Shekhar, "Tauṣīf-i ālāt-i mūsīqī dar āṣār-i Amīr Khusrau Dehlevī", *Persian Research Journal*, Delhi: Department of Persian, University of Delhi, 1988, pp. 148-65. (in Persian)

Chander Shekhar and Shama Mitra Chenoy, *Muraqqa[c]-e-Dehli. The Mughal Capital in Muhammad Shah's Time*, with introduction and notes, Delhi: Deputy Publication, 1989.

Colas, Gérard, "La guirlande des Rāga-s", *A la cour du Grand Moghol*, Paris: Bibliothèque Nationale, 1986, pp. 163-83.

David, M.-C. & J. Soustiel, *Miniatures orientales de l'Inde - 4*, Paris: Galerie Jean Soustiel, 1986. (Exhibition Catalogue)

Delvoye, F., "The Verbal Content of Dhrupad Songs from the Earliest Collections: I. The *Hazār Dhurpad* or *Sahasras*, a Collection of 1004 *dhrupad*s attributed to Nāyak Bakhśū", *Dhrupad Annual 1990*, pp. 93-109.

— *Inventaire des textes indo-persans sur la musique savante de l'Inde*, in collaboration with S. Sarmadee, Project of Institut Français de Recherche en Iran (IFRI), Paris-Tehran, hosted by the Centre for Human Sciences (CSH), New Delhi. (Unpublished)

— "Les chants *dhrupad* en langue braj des poètes-musiciens de l'Inde Moghole", *Littératures médiévales de l'Inde du Nord. Contributions de Charlotte Vaudeville et de ses élèves*, ed. F. Mallison, Paris: Ecole Française d'Extrême-Orient, 1991, pp. 139-85.

— "The Verbal Content of Dhrupad Songs from the Earliest Collections: II. The *Kitāb-i Nauras* of Ibrāhīm [c]Ādil Shāh II, Sulṭān of Bijapur (r. 1580-1627) and its Persian Preface by Mullā Nūr al-Dīn Muḥammad 'Ẓuhūrī' - I", *Dhrupad Annual 1991*, Vol. VI, pp. 38-54; Part II, *Dhrupad Annual 1993*, Vol. VIII, pp. 1-23.

— "Tānsen and the Tradition of Dhrupad Songs in the Braj Language, from the 16th Century to the Present Day", *Dhrupad Annual 1993*, Vol. VIII, pp. 37-44.

— "The Verbal Content of Dhrupad Songs from the Earliest Collections: III. Dhrupad Songs attributed to Tānsen in Court-musicians Repertoires", *Dhrupad Annual 1994*, Vol. IX, pp.1-12.

— "The Image of Akbar as a Patron of Music in Indo-Persian and Vernacular Sources", read at the Seminar on "Akbar and His Age", Aligarh Muslim University, (Oct. 1992), in *Medieval India*, ed. I.

Habib, Vol. II, Delhi: Oxford University Press. (Forthcoming)
— "Indo-Persian Texts on the Artistic Patronage of the Sultans of Gujarat (14th-16th c.)", paper presented at the Indo-French Seminar on "The Evolution of Medieval Indian Culture: The Indo-Persian Context", organised by the Centre for Human Sciences and the Centre for Historical Studies (Jawaharlal Nehru University), New Delhi, 14-16 Feb. 1994. (Forthcoming)

Digby, Simon, "Some Asian Wanderers in Seventeenth Century India: An Examination of Sources in Persian", *Studies in History*, 1993, Vol. 9, N° 2, pp. 247-64.

During, Jean, *Musique et extase. L'audition mystique dans la tradition soufie,* Paris: Albin Michel, 1988.
— *La musique traditionnelle de l'Azerbayjān et la science des muqams*, Baden-Baden & Bouxwiller: Editions Valentin Koerner, 1988.
— Book-review of *Qānūn-i ᶜilmī va ᶜamali-i mūsīqī* of Zeyn al-ᶜAbedīn Maḥmūd Ḥuseynī (Dushanbe, 1987), *Abstracta Iranica*, 1989, Vol. 12, Entry N° 1071, p. 279.

Elliot, H.M. and J. Dowson, *The History of India as Told by its Own Historians* (1867-77), H.M. Elliot & J. Dowson, Eight Vols., Repr., Delhi: Low Price Publications, 1990, Vols. 6 and 7.

Farmer, H.G., "Observations on 'Music in Muslim India'", note by the editor, *Islamic Culture*, 1943, Vol. XVII, N° 4, p. 444.

Fatimi, S. Qudratullah, "Amir Khusrau's Contribution to the Indus-Muslim Music", Islamabad, Publication Cell, Pakistan National Council of the Arts, Oct. 1975 (Published on the Occasion of 700th Anniversary of Amir Khusrau), pp. 3-39.

Habib, Muhammad, *Life and Works of Hazrat Amir Khusrau of Delhi*, Aligarh, 1928.

Halim, A., "Music and the Musicians of the Court of Shāh Jahān", *Islamic Culture*, Oct. 1945, Vol. XIX, N° 4, pp. 354-60.
— "Muslim Contribution to the Development of North Indian Music", *The Muslim Year Book of India*, Bombay, 1948-49, pp. 107-21.
— "History of the Growth and Development of North-Indian Music during Sayyid-Lodi Period", *Journal of the Asiatic Society of Pakistan*, 1956, Vol. I, N° 1, Dacca, pp. 46-64.
— "Muslim Rulers as Great Patrons of Music", *Essays in History of Indo-Pak Music*, Dacca, 1962, pp. 17-9.

Huda, M.Z., "Sultān Sikandar Lūdī - A Poet and Patron of Letters", *Journal of the Asiatic Society of Pakistan* (Dacca), 1969, Vol. XIV, N° 3, pp. 289-304.

Husain, Iqbal, "Hindu Shrines and Practices as Described by a Central Asian Traveller in the First Half of the 17th Century", *Medieval India 1. Researches in the History of India, 1200-1750*, ed. I. Habib, Delhi: Oxford University Press, 1992, pp. 141-53.

Husaini, Syeda Bilqis Fatema, *A Critical Study of Indo-Persian Literature, during Sayyid and Lodi Period (1414-1526)*, New Delhi: Author, CAAL / School of Languages, Jawaharlal Nehru University, 1988.

Jones, William (Sir), "On the Musical Modes of the Hindus" (1784), *Asiatick Researches*, 1792, N° 3, pp. 55-87; Repr. in S.M. Tagore, *Hindu Music from Various Authors*, Calcutta, 1875; 2nd edn. 1882; 3rd edn., Varanasi: The Chowkhamba Sanskrit Series Office, 1965. pp. 125-60.

Joshi, P.M., "Asad Beg's Mission to Bijapur, 1603-1604", *Mahāmahōpādhyāya Prof. D.V. Potdar Sixty-First Birthday Commemoration Volume. Studies in Historical and Indological Research presented to M.M. Prof. Datto Vaman Potdar, by his friends and old pupils in honour of his sixty-first birthday*, ed. Surendra Nath Sen, published by O.K. Sathe, Poona, for Mahāmahōpādhyāya Prof. D.V. Potdar... Celebration Committee, 1950, pp. 184-96.

Khalidi, Omar, "Qawwali and Mahfil-i Sama^c", *Muslim Shrines in India. Their Character, History and Significance*, ed., Ch.W. Troll, Delhi: Oxford University Press, 1989, pp. 257-61.

"Khusrau Nāma", *Persian Research Journal*, Special Number, ed. S.M. Ahmad, Delhi: Department of Persian, University of Delhi, 1988. (in Persian)

Lawrence, Bruce B., "The Early Chishti Approach to Samā^c", *Islamic Society and Culture*, eds. M. Israeli and N.K. Wagle, New Delhi: Manohar, 1983.

Life, Times and Works of Amir Khusrau Dehlavi, ed., Zoe Ansari, published by Hasnuddin Ahmad, New Delhi: National Amir Khusrau Society, 1975.

Miniatures de l'Inde impériale. Les peintres de la cour d'Akbar (1556-1605), Paris: Editions de la Réunion des Musées Nationaux, 1989. (Exhibition Catalogue, Musée Guimet, Paris)

Manucci, Niccolao, *Mogul India or Storia do Mogor*, English Transl. by William Irvine, Four Vols., (1907-08), Repr., Delhi: Low Price Publications, 1990.

Mirza, Mohammad Wahid, *The Life and Works of Amir Khusrau*,

Delhi: Idarah-i Adabiyat-i Delli, 1st edn., 1935, Repr., 1974. [IAD Religio-Philosophy Series, N° 3]

Nazir Ahmad, *Kitab-i-Nauras by Ibrahim Adil Shah II*, Introduction, Notes and Textual Editing, New Delhi: Bharatiya Kala Kendra, 1956.

Nazir Ahmed, "The Lahjat-i-Sikandar Shahi, A unique book on Indian music of the time of Sikandar Lodi (1489-1517)", *Islamic Culture*, Vol. XXVIII, N° 3, July 1954, pp. 410-17.

Neuman, Daniel M., *The Life of Music in North India. The Organization of an Artistic Tradition*, Detroit, 1980, Indian edn., New Delhi: Manohar Publications, 1980, Paperback edn., Chicago and London: The University of Chicago Press, 1990.

— "Patronage and Performance of Indian Music", *The Powers of Art. Patronage in Indian Culture*, ed. Barbara Stoler Miller, Delhi: Oxford University Press, 1992, Chapter 16, pp. 247-58.

Nijenhuis, Emmie te, *Musicological Literature*, Wiesbaden: Otto Harrassowitz, 1977.

Powers, Harold S., "Mode", *The New Grove: Dictionary of Music and Musicians*, London/New York, Macmillan, 1980, Vol. XII, pp. 376-450, Section V, 2, pp. 422-36.

Qureshi, Regula Burckhardt, *Sufi Music of India and Pakistan. Sound, Context and Meaning in Qawwali*, Cambridge: Cambridge University Press, 1986.

Richard, Francis, *A la cour du Grand Moghol*, Catalogue of an Exhibition in the Bibliothèque Nationale, Paris: Bibliothèque Nationale, 1986.

Rizvi, S.N.H., "Music in Muslim India", *Islamic Culture*, Jul. 1931, Vol. XV, N° 3, pp. 331-40.

Roychaudhuri, M.L., "Music in Islām", *Journal of the Asiatic Society*, 1957, Letters Vol. XXIII, N° 2, pp. 44-103.

Śārṅgadeva, *Saṅgīta Ratnākara of Śārṅgadeva*, Sanskrit Text and English Translation with Comments and Notes, Vol. I (Chapter I, Treatment of Svara), English Translation by by R.K. Shringy, Under the Supervision of P.L. Sharma, Delhi/Varanasi: Motilal Banarsidass, 1978; Vol. II (Chapters II-IV), by R.K. Shringy, under the Supervision of P.L. Sharma, New Delhi: Munshiram Manoharlal, 1989.

Śarmā, P.L. *Sahasarasa, Nāyak Bakhśū ke dhrupadoṁ kā saṅgrah*, New Delhi: Sangeet Natak Akademi, 1972.

Sarmadee, Shahab, "About Music and Amir Khusrau's own Writings on Music", *Life, Times and Works of Amir Khusrau Dehlavi*, published by Hasnuddin Ahmad, New Delhi: National Amir Khusrau Society, 1975, pp. 241-64.

— "Ghazal aur Sarud-i Ghazal", *Khusrau Shinasi*, ed., Z. Ansari, New Delhi, 1975.

— "Musical Genius of Amir Khusrau", *Amir Khusrau, Memorial Volume,* New Delhi: Publications Division, Govt. of India, 1975, pp. 33-61.

— *Nūr-Ratnākar, A Bio-Bibliographical Survey,* (*and techno-historical study, of all available important writings in Arabic, Persian, Sanskrit and other allied languages on the subject of song, dance and drama*), Two Vols. Calcutta: Sangeet Research Academy. (Forthcoming)

Schimmel, Annemarie, *Islamic Literatures of India*, Wiesbaden: Otto Harrassowitz, 1973. [*A History of Indian Literature*, ed. Jan Gonda, Vol. VII, Part 1, N° 1]

Sharma, Premlata, "Sahasarasa (A Compilation of Dhrupad Texts Ascribed to Bakshoo), Synopsis of a Treatise", *Indian Music Journal,* 1972-73-74, Vols. VIII-IX-X, N°s 15-20, pp. 41-48.

Siddiqui, Iqtidar Husain, *Perso-Arabic Sources of Information on the Life and Conditions in the Sultanate of Delhi*, New Delhi: Munshiram Manoharlal Publishers Pvt Ltd, 1992.

Trivedi, Madhu, "An Appraisal of the Musical Arts at Shahjahanabad during the First Half of the Eighteenth Century", *Art and Culture. Felicitation Volume in Honour of Professor S. Nurul Hasan*, eds., Ahsan Jan Qaisar and Som Prakash Verma, Jaipur: Publication Scheme, 1993, pp. 95-103.

Tupper, F., *Musiques de l'Inde du Nord. Guide d'Ecoute & Discographie CD*, Paris: Editions du Makkar, 1993.

Wright, O., *The Modal System of Arab and Persian Music, A.D. 1250-1300*, London: Oxford University Press, 1978.

Zebrowski, M. *Deccani Painting*, London: Sotheby Publications, 1983; Indian edn., New Delhi: Roli Books International, 1983.

Ziauddin, *Mirza Khan's Grammar of the Braj Bhakha*, Calcutta: Visva-Bharati Book-Shop, 1935.

Mughal Gardens in Benaras and its Neighbourhood in the Eighteenth and Nineteenth Centuries

KLAUS RÖTZER AND KHANDU DEOKAR

A particular style of garden corresponding to the climate and the life-style common to the Iranian plateau and the steppes of Central Asia, was introduced in northern India by Bābur from 1526. Bābur and his men belonged to the Timurid culture, very different from the culture of the country which they had just conquered. Although they found the climate of India disagreeable, the conquest having been made, it was necessary to stay and govern, and, therefore, to adapt.

Following the model of their native country, these men created gardens which would enable them, to some extent, to bear the Indian climate. These gardens helped them to recreate the surroundings to which they were accustomed, and where they could, from time to time, forget the country which it was now their lot to administer.

The 'Mughal' dynasty, founded by Bābur, dominated India politically until the eighteenth century, and culturally up to 1857. It contributed to the development of a special culture which, though rooted in the Timurid past, managed to adapt itself easily to the Indian milieu, without ever losing its connection with the 'Iranian' world, in the broader sense of the term. The culture of the elite profoundly transformed the civilization of the sub-continent, so much so that the Indians living in the Indo-Gangetic plain in the eighteenth century recognised it as their own.

The gardens belonging to this culture are also qualified as 'Mughal'. The earliest, designed by Bābur and his contemporaries, must have been very similar to their counterparts in Herat and Samarkand, but of these, only some traces now remain. Most of the studies of the Mughal gardens carried out so far, have concentrated on those gardens which were laid out by the Mughal Imperial family, and belong to the end of the sixteenth century and the seventeenth century. However, such gardens represent only a minute portion of the gardens constructed and planted during this period in India. They are, in fact, examples of a type of architecture which is not easy to preserve and in which, moreover, for a long time, British archaeologists of the nineteenth century took little or no interest. Added to this, urban expansion of the twentieth century obliterated or destroyed a majority of the remaining specimens since most of them had been established on the outskirts of large towns.

The aim of this article is to study the Mughal style of gardens as it evolved in a predominantly Hindu region - Benaras and its surroundings - in the second half of the eighteenth century and the nineteenth century, when Mughal power was no more than a memory. Benaras was, at that time, one of the most important centres of pilgrimage and Hindu learning, a premier financial centre, and a place reputed for its commerce and handicrafts (brocade and brassware). While qualified artisans were generally Muslims, the elite was essentially Hindu, comprising of Pandits, Agrawal and Khatri bankers, revenue officials, eminent persons who were attracted by the sacred character of the town, and from 1782 onwards, Indian political figures who had been deprived of power by the Company. As for its cultural life, the dominant figure was the Rājā of Benaras.

Our objective is to study these gardens, which, though based on the Mughal model, were created in a context which was particularly Hindu, and to examine the adaptations and transformations in this style, in a general perspective. In order to provide more descriptive details, however, plans of ten gardens have also been included in this article, along with brief comments.

Prolegomena

Before understanding the transformations which this style underwent in the area selected by us, viz. Benaras and its surroundings, it is necessary to define its origins, its forms and its functions. More important, it is also necessary for us to determine what the new style dislodged, or replaced.

1. The extremely dry climate of the Iranian plateau and the steppes of Central Asia, is conducive to mud architecture. A boundary wall, three to four metres high, made of clay or unbaked bricks holds for many years in these regions. In addition, high walls are also necessary to protect the orchards and vineyards of the settlers, against sandstorms and nomadic droves.

Dryness necessitates irrigation. Water harnessing techniques were, therefore, always vital to these regions. The best source here is the fresh water available from the mountains, in the form of streams and water-falls, or that which is subterranean, coming from the depths of the *kārez**.

The essential principle of the Iranian garden lies in this: irrigation by gravity and a high enclosure wall, which protects the garden from winds and beasts, and which creates a micro-climate.

The climate of the Indo-Gangetic plain is entirely different. Rains and the all-pervading humidity during four months of the monsoon period render mud architecture much less durable, and make a tile or thatch covering necessary. Terraces of mortar made of a special type of lime (*barī*) are to be seen only in houses constructed with baked bricks. It was unlikely that a high uncovered mud wall would hold for a long time. Farmers of this region who wish to protect their gardens and orchards usually construct a boundary wall like a little dyke, about a metre high, on which they plant thorny bushes, elephant grass or cactii. Mango orchards which are most common in these parts are often left unenclosed. Each village has some and it is in their shade that children play.

As for the water, it appears forceful and muddy in the monsoon, and stagnant and green during the rest of the year in the large reservoirs, called *pokharā**, usually located near the villages.

The type of garden which we propose to study was created, to a great extent, by the climate of the Iranian plateau, where all orchards present the features intrinsic to this type, features that they preserved despite the passage of time.

2. The life-style in these two regions was also different. Some examples would suffice to illustrate this remark.

Let us look at the Iranian world first. To a vast, perpetually blue sky, to the limpidity of the air allowing near-infinite visibility, to a geological landscape with its scorching-hot summers and icy winters, corresponds a society which is obliged to protect itself not only from the sun, the wind, and the cold, but also from the view of others. Loose clothes, which completely envelop the body, mud houses with concealed entries, both seclusive and protective, gardens surrounded by high walls, safe from the view of passers-by, covered water-tanks, and *hammāms* for bathing and personal hygiene are typical to this region.

In traditional India, on the contrary, open-air bathing in broad daylight, with cold water, was the rule. Before the prevalence of Islamic and western mores, one dressed mostly in jewelry and fine transparent cloth. Ancient architecture attempted above all to create shade and currents of air - terraced roofs were always the most comfortable part of the house after sunset. Winter being rather mild, one did not seek protection against it. Only the long months of suffocating heat counted when all that mattered was to make the most of the available cool and refreshing breeze and shade. Bathing usually meant immersing the body in cold water, irrespective of the season, after coating it with oil. Bathing in common, in crowds, men and women together, in the rivers, in reservoirs and at public wells - all these are typical to this region.

We have dwelt upon the Indian habit of bathing, which may still be observed, and which we repeatedly encounter in literature and the visual arts, because for an Indian, the bathing place is a *locus amoenus* par excellence, whereas for an Iranian the garden was such a place. In the bare and mineral lanscape of Iran, man dreams of an idyllic place with luxurious vegetation, and his mind turns to designing gardens. In the suffocating plains and jungles of India, where the obsessive fear is one of lack of water, one waits for the rains with anxiety. Here man dreams of deep and cool waters, in which he can bathe.

3. In India, Al-Berūnī was struck by these large reservoirs, with stone steps on the four sides. In our times, the essential beauty of a city like Benaras, marked profoundly by Hinduism, lies in the *ghāṭ*s* of pink sandstone. Pilgrims use them to descend into the Ganges for their ritual baths. The residents of the city, excepting those who possess bathrooms, bathe here every morning. The time passed by an Indian on the *ghāṭ* of a stream, a river, a tank or a reservoir, or the raised sides of a well, or at the bottom of a *bāolī**, has always been a time of leisure, because washing his clothes in the company of friends, consuming *bhang* - an intoxicant -, then going together into the countryside to defecate, returning to bathe, playing about in the water, and finally rendering homage to a divinity - this is the very essence of happiness.

Prior to Muslim invasions, stone masonry around water points is probably the most original feature of Indian architecture. Such architecture, however, did not extent as much to the construction of complex water-harnessing devices like dam or a *kārez*, as to the improvement of the area around the water point, aiming primarily at rendering the access to the water clean, easy and pleasant, and the transformation of the water point into an agreeable place. These improvements could also include the planting of trees and the laying out of gardens, as learnt from contemporary inscriptions. However, the essential focus was the water point, meant for the user.

The Muslims in India, prior to Bābur's conquest, had retained this type of architecture. Two examples would suffice to illustrate this point: the tombs of Sher Shāh and Salīm Shāh Sūrī at Sasaram, which date from the middle of the sixteenth century, and represent the most beautiful specimens of this architecture. It must be remembered that the policy followed by Sher Shāh and his son was to establish harmonious relations between Hindus and Indian Muslims, in order to prevent the return of the Mughals. In architecture they consciously favoured Indian styles and resisted Timurid influences as far as possible. It is therefore not surprising that their tombs have been constructed at such water points.

4. With the return of the Mughals under Humāyūn, the Iranian garden in its adapted version became *à la mode*. This pleasure spot par excellence of the new ruling elite did not, however, replace the traditional pleasure spot built around a water body. In this regard, there was addition rather than substitution during the Mughal period, the two traditions subsisting side by side.

Hiran Mīnār near Lahore or Chashma-i Nūr at Ajmer amply confirm this. They date to the reign of Jahāngīr, whose mother was Rajput. Though built in the Mughal style, the general plan in both the cases is typically Hindu. At Hiran Mīnār we find all the elements which characterise the tombs of the Sūrīs at Sasaram - a building constructed on an island in the middle of a man-made reservoir (*pokharā*) connected by a bridge - except that the building is a hunting pavilion. The Chashma-i Nūr, for its part, borrows liberally from the Nīlkanṭh at Mandu. The latter, a building from Akbar's period in a mixed style (Mughal and Sultanate of Malwa) representative of local Muslim architecture, is also an attempt to embellish and transfigure an artificial source of water. Such examples can be multiplied.

In our view, it would be inaccurate to postulate the existence of two types of gardens - pre-Mughal and Mughal, and to believe that the latter supplanted the former. The issue is different. We prefer to think in terms of two types of pleasure spots, each corresponding to a particular climate and life-style. Let us give some supplementary data to prove our point. If we compare the plans of the palaces of the Sultans of Malwa at Mandu, Nalcha, Sadalpur and Kalyadeh with those of the Imperial Mughals at Agra, Delhi and Lahore, we notice that the residential areas of the former are organised around water points and those of the latter around gardens. The water points at Mandu and at Nalcha vary immensely in size, going from a small artificial pond to a reservoir with a barrage. At Sadalpur and Kalyadeh, on the contrary, it is riverbeds which have been restructured and enclosed with walls and barrage bridges. A building with cupolas stands on one of the banks while a series of ponds and a portico, with a terraced roof, are located on the river-bed itself. Akbar and Jahāngīr stayed at these sites and appreciated the architecture. Its influence on Akbar can be seen at Fatehpur Sikri where the hydraulic works are more important than the gardens.

Let us remind the reader that the end of the fifteenth and the beginning of the sixteenth century was a period of architectural exploration and creativity in North India. New forms were invented, like the near-gothic arch in the "theatre" at Mandu palace. Architectural influences from outside were utilised. The structure of the tomb of Sikandar Lodī with its double vault and a space separating the cupola and the dome clearly testifies to the presence of Timurid influence even before the arrival of Bābur. Generally, however, only some decorative or structural elements were borrowed, while the spirit and general plan remained "Indian", so to speak. This is particularly clear in the building called Malcolm kī Koṭhī at Nalcha, where we have a rectangular building placed on a dyke along with two artificial ponds and accompanying pavilions - the whole arranged in a very picturesque manner. Though the laws of symmetry so dear to the hearts of Timurid and Mughal architects have not been followed here, Iranian influence can be clearly seen in the form of the pavilions and their glazed tile decor.

General Characteristics of Mughal Gardens

The remarkable work of C.M. Villiers-Stuart, *Gardens of the Great Moghals*, published in 1913, still remains the best introduction to these gardens, and the art of living, for which they constituted the ideal setting. The author not only visited a large number of gardens, both those designed for the imperial family and other more modest ones, but was also able to observe how life was lived in the latter. The ideal Mughal garden is, above all, an enclosed space. The walls and the buildings serve the purpose of excluding the exterior and protecting the garden from trespassers and intruding eyes - on no account should the stranger know what happens inside. This trait is not shared by the Hindu world, where the caste system ensures that each one knows his limits and the screen is required only for protecting food from pollution of the sight.

Inside the garden, the space reserved for plants and trees is at a distinctly lower level than the pathways (*khiyābān**) and the platforms. Plants and human beings are thus clearly separated. But once planted, no attempt is made to impose an architectural form or fantasy on the trees and they are allowed to develop as they please, unlike the practice in French-style gardens.

Water is usually drawn from wells outside the enclosure and stored in raised reservoirs. The garden is paradise, and the hard work, the sweat, and the noise involved in the business of drawing water have no place in it. Water arrives in the garden in the form of cascades and fountains, as if by miracle. It flows in rectilinear channels, filling up geometrical cavities cut out in the axis of the *k̲h̲iyābān*s and the platforms. In these raised spaces, reserved for human use, it is constrained to follow a precise course and to recreate, as it flows, the various moods and aspects of the sprightly water of the ancestral mountains. This last point is clearly mentioned in the memoirs of Bābur.

The buildings are constructed on a set of platforms at different levels. Their disposition strictly follows the rules of symmetry. There are nine principal emplacements: the centre of the garden, the four corners and the centre of each side. Of the latter, one serves as the entry. In a funerary garden, the tomb is generally situated in the centre. In others, the centre is kept clear so as not to obstruct the view and only a platform, a pond or sometimes a pavilion is constructed on the point where the *k̲h̲iyābān*s intersect. The imposing buildings have wide openings facing the garden, and they provide shade and protection from rain. Their terraced roof is pleasant after sunset and it is possible to pass a comfortable night here during the hot season. However, rooms fitted with doors are rare.

In the Timurid gardens of Samarkand, as described by Clavijo,[1] the residential portion was located in the centre. In the gardens of Herat, comprising of a succession of terraces on the hillside, the principal pavilion was situated on the highest terrace from where it overlooked the whole landscape.

The terrace in the Mughal gardens at Agra which rises above the Jamuna by several metres, provides a soothing panorama of the garden as well as a distant relationship with the exterior. The same is true for the gardens in the fort of Delhi. The emperor appears before the people every morning, and the begums watch discreetly through the *jālī*s*, without being observed. In the multi-terraced gardens laid out on hillsides, such as those in Kashmir or the Shalimar in Lahore, it is the highest terrace, reserved for the begums, which constitutes the private

1. Cf. G. Lestrange, Transl., *Clavijo Embassy to Tamerlane, 1403-1406*, London, pp. 215-77.

area par excellence.

Let us now try to examine what one did in these gardens. It is important to understand that in the Mughal world 'garden' denotes planted spaces and architectural structures including pathways, platforms, pavilions and fountains which surrounded and defined these spaces. It is thus an entirely 'habitable' space comparable, in this sense, to the English bungalow which can be defined as a habitation in the middle of a garden. Hence one 'lived' in these gardens. As the entire furniture consisted of carpets and curtains, which were easily transportable, the same garden could, if required, accomodate the pomp of a coronation ceremony, or the picnic of a group of begums. We are thinking, in particular, of the Shalimar gardens in Delhi where Aurangzeb was crowned Emperor. In a complex like the Delhi fort, the residential portion has a series of gardens of the *chahār bāgh** type linked by an artificial stream. The long terrace with pavilions overlooking the Jamuna, where this stream flows, also overlooks the planted spaces. The largest gardens are located in the part reserved for men which is semi-public. The royal *hammām* is also situated here. The gardens of the *zanānā** are smaller, and here the planted spaces have also been scaled down. We shall see that in the dwellings of the elite at Benaras a century later, the women were confined to the *havelī*, whereas the *mardānā** was generally situated in the garden.

In Delhi, the residences of important personages also included gardens with large ponds in their centre. But it was mainly outside the walls, in those suburbs where more water was available, that the largest gardens were situated. These gardens were characterized by abundant vegetation. Trees, particularly fruit trees, occupied the major part of the planted space. In fact, most of the fruits served at the tables of the Khāns came from here. These gardens were extremely pleasant places to stay in during the hot season and the monsoons. Completely secluded, they provided a 'paradise' for the begums, to whom public spaces and streets were forbidden. They passed from one garden to another in closed palanquins, safe from the view of passers-by. As a matter of fact, all Mughal towns possessed a suburb comprising principally gardens.

When the Great Mughals started going to Kashmir to escape the dreadful and dusty heat of the Indian summer, they made their residence in the multi-terraced garden on the mountainside overlooking Dal Lake. Each terrace had its specific function. The lowest was public, whereas the highest was reserved for the family — particularly the women. Certain gardens, like the one at Nimla between Kabul and Jalalabad were set up as stop-overs, where it was possible to camp for a short while.

Funerary gardens do not form a clearly distinct category. Bābur had resided in the two gardens at Agra and Kabul which served successively as his last resting place.[2] Wealthy men usually had their tombs constructed in their gardens situated in a suburb. It may be noted that these tombs had the same form and layout as a residential pavilion. And in an architectural project as large as that of the Tāj Mahal in Agra, the white marble tomb is, after all, only one building amongst many others, even if it is the largest and the most beautiful.

Mughal Gardens of Hindu Princes

As stated earlier, the Mughal court provided the cultural model for North India up to 1857, and Mughal gardens were constructed by many Hindu chiefs. Here we will briefly indicate the most important ones, highlighting their originality.

a) The Rāṇās of Rajasthan were the first to extend their support to the Mughals, serving them with loyalty and devotion. Not only were they among the earliest to develop privileged relations with the imperial family, but they also contributed to the elaboration of Mughal culture. Certain architectural innovations of Akbar's period can be attributed to Mān Singh. The buildings that were constructed under his direction at Rajmahal, Amber, Bairat, Benaras and Rohtasgarh allowed architectural elements of diverse origins to unite in a new style and helped in the diffusion of early Mughal art in North India.

In their domestic architecture, the Rajputs admitted little Mughal influence, retaining the traditional lay-out of the *havelī* which corresponded with their own life-style. But the flowing waters, the fountains and the unreal air of the Mughal gardens fascinated them. It is hardly surprising that in this desert region, with its scorching heat and parched sands, men yearned for luxuriant vegetation.

It is this 'unreal' aspect of the Mughal garden that was developed in Rajasthan. We will give only one example - the huge palace (city palace) of the *Rāṇā* by the lakeside in Udaipur. Built in the Rajput style, the interior of this multi-storeyed palace is an intricate maze, full of surprises, the very opposite of the clarity and symmetry of Mughal architecture.

The maze gives way suddenly and unexpectedly to a *chahār bāgh*

2. Bābur was initially buried at Agra; his remains were later trasnferred to Kābul.

(Bāṛī Mahal, 1698-1710) which, as if dropped from the clouds, is situated at the very top of the palace. The reservoir in its centre is disproportionate to the planted spaces and probably served as a bathing tank.

b) The Rajputs of the Bundela dynasty also enjoyed privileged relations with the Mughals. Like the *Rāṇā*s of Rajasthan, they evolved a unique style of their own in domestic and religious architecture. If they borrowed decorative elements and construction styles from the Mughals, their proportions and layouts were typical of the region. Since the region lacks good building stone, their monuments mainly utilise rubble stone and lime mortar for the walls and the vaults.

Two gardens at Orchha merit our attention: the Lāl Bāgh to the north of the Rāmjī temple, and a much larger one, situated to the north of the Jahāngīrī Mahal. Both these gardens have adopted the layout of a *chahār bāg͟h*, but a sort of *jālī* has been constructed above each of the four flower-beds, confining the vegetation in octogonal honeycombs around which one can promenade. In these two gardens one has the impression that the overpowering masonry is likely to strangle the plants. We can discern here the transition from the concept of luxuriance, to that of confinement of the garden.

c) The Jats constructed a great deal in the region of Mathura in the eighteenth century, picking their models from nearby Agra. The most prestigious complex built by these agriculturist-soldiers is undoubtedly the palace of Deeg, around 1760-68. Here also a garden was constructed - a *chahār bāg͟h* placed between two large artificial reservoirs with *ghāṭ*s. The residential pavilions are situated in the south of the garden, on a vast raised platform, and reflect in the waters of the southern reservoir. Though their architectural decor retains the rigid form of the Mughal model, it exhibits a repetitive profusion which deprives it of the sobriety and elegance of this style.

Their hydraulic works exhibit a taste which can be called baroque for its extravagance. Ponds and fountains abound. The latter are even placed in niches under the awning of a pavilion to give the impression of monsoon rains. One has even gone to the extent of reproducing the rumbling of thunder, by placing pebbles in a space provided in the thickness of the ceiling, which create the effect when they are moved around by water. A huge water tower, fed by three wells, was constructed to meet the requirements of this intricate set-up. A week of continuous drawing of water is required to fill this reservoir. Only a few hours suffice to empty it when all the fountains are in operation.

The palace of Deeg, as this garden is called, is indeed the work of

Indian farmers whose dreams centre around abundant monsoons which one welcomes with dances, or vast reservoirs where one can bathe and purify oneself and where fleshy, red lotuses bloom. Although the lay-out of the Mughal garden is maintained at Deeg, the concept of the garden has again undergone a change.

The Iranian garden is the fulfilment of the dream of a roving no-mad in a mineral and desert landscape. Set in the centre of an architec-turally secluded place are trees of all kinds - plane trees, cypresses and jasmine, fruit trees, almond trees in blossom - and along with trees, delicate sprays of water, thin brooks, clear and cascading. At Deeg, the Indian farmer has copied a model conceived elsewhere, which he has instilled with his own dream - a dream of torrential monsoons and calm waters full of lotuses.

The Gardens of Benaras and its Neighbourhood

A. Historical Overview

In the first half of the eighteenth century, Benaras was in the po-litical and cultural orbit of the Nawābs of Awadh whose capital was initially at Faizabad, and later at Lucknow. From 1738 onwards, Balwant Singh, a *Bhūmihār* Rājā of Gangāpur, taking advantage of the difficulties of the Nawābs, and with the help of British protection, succeeded in founding a small kingdom there. His son Chet Singh attempted to free himself from British control but failed, and from 1782 the Rājā of Benaras, remained, politically speaking, no more than a big landowner. However, he continued to dominate the cultural life of the city. In 1857, the British rewarded Ishwarī Nārāin Singh, the then Rājā, for his loyalty by bestowing on him the title of Mahārājā. Having received a sound English education, young Prabhu Nārāin, who was placed on the throne in 1889, strove to modernise the kingdom, particu-larly Rāmnagar, situated slightly upstream from Benaras on the other bank of the Ganges, where he resided.

Balwant Singh's dynasty built a number of Mughal-style gardens, most of which have come down to us in a more or less ruined state. Our principal documentation is based on these gardens. However, in the eighteenth and nineteenth centuries, many other gardens of this type were in existence. As we have already mentioned in the introduction, the city of Benaras was, during this period, one of the largest cities of India. It comprised of several zones: the old (Indian) city situated on the heights overlooking the river, with its narrow alleys and austere, many-storeyed residence, huddled together, followed by a zone of low-roofed houses of mud, and finally a fairly large zone, where some villages, the *sarā'īs*, the big reservoirs of water, and particularly, the gardens were situated.

At the end of the eighteenth century, the Civil Lines of the English constituted another zone located well away from this region, towards the north-west on both sides of the river Varuna. A cantonment was added to this from 1811 onwards.

B. The Gardens: General Characteristics

1. Almost all the gardens that we will be examining are *chahār bāghs*. However, a distinction must be made between those gardens which formed part of the main residence and those which constituted a secondary residence. Let us consider the case of the royal family up to 1750. The main residence was the mud fort of Gangāpur where two gardens have survived till today. A few kilometres west of Gangāpur, on the route of the *Panch Koshī*, at Bhaironāth, was another unit probably dating to the same period. The Rājā or the members of his clan visited it sometimes and could stay there for a few days. This is what we call a secondary garden residence.

Balwant Singh founded the fort of Rāmnagar in 1750. Shīsh Mahal, the garden at Kamachchhā where the coronation ceremony of Chet Singh took place, perhaps belongs to the same period. In times of peace Chet Singh lived at Shivālā, on the banks of the Ganges, in the southern suburb of Benaras. When danger threatened he sought refuge in the nearby fort of Rāmnagar, on the other side of the river. He thus had two principal residences. He also constructed a garden on the outskirts of the town of Rāmnagar, and called it Rāmbāgh.

During the entire nineteenth century, the successors of Chet Singh had two main residences, one in the suburb of Kamachchhā and the other in the fort of Rāmnagar. They created the Rājā Tālāb complex on the Grand Trunk Road with the object of developing a market, and a garden called Ratanbāgh in the south-east of Rāmnagar, outside the town. This was the starting point of the route to Vindhyāchal, a sacred place where they had constructed another garden. They also owned a garden in the sacred city of Allahabad.

These Mahārājās were fond of hunting and tigers abounded in the jungle which covered the massifs of sandstone, about twenty kilometres from Rāmnagar. This region was part of the area which they administered directly. A holiday garden was established at Chakia, the regional centre. Shikārganj, intended specially for hunting, was established nearer the jungle.

Rich families of old stock in Benaras usually possessed a *havelī* residence in the city and one or more gardens in the suburbs. As for the *nouveaux riches*, among whom we can count the royal family of Benaras as well, they either had a residence on the banks of the river in the southern part of the city and a garden in the suburbs (Peshwā Amrit Rāo, Rānī Bhawānī of Natore, the princely family of Delhi) or only one residence in the suburbs consisting of a *havelī*, gardens, a temple and a *ganj** (families of Ausan, of Shiv Lāl Dube and of Devakī Nandan).

2. When a main residence possessed two gardens, they usually served two distinct functions, one being reserved for business transactions and the other serving as the *mardānā*. It is evident that this facility existed only in the very rich residences like the Shivālā of Chet Singh, the Ausan Ganj complex, or the royal residence at Kamachchhā which was transformed into the Hindu College in 1898.

These gardens were of modest proportions and often possessed a water tower to feed the fountains. Some examples are the gardens of Gangāpur, the *tahsīl* garden of Shivālā, *mardānā*-garden of Ausan Ganj, and Shīsh Mahal after it was incorporated into the Kamachchhā complex.

It is to be noted that the system of fountains in these gardens is quite modest and not at all comparable to what existed in the Deeg palace. Perhaps due to financial considerations, the style remained sober and discreet at Benaras, closer to the Mughal rather than the Jat spirit.

The residential building is always situated in the southernmost part of the garden facing the north, thus avoiding the direct rays of the sun. Built on a raised platform with a pond, a panoramic view of the entire garden is possible from here. It comprises generally of a long but narrow rectangular hall in the middle, adjacent lengthwise to the garden and with a series of arches opening on the garden side. This hall is covered with a terraced roof where it is pleasant to sit after sunset. On both ends of this long hall are rooms provided with doors. These are the only rooms which can be closed and locked, if required. Above these rooms, opening out on the terrace, are two *barsātī*s with archways.

A pedestrian gate provides an entrance to the garden. On both sides of this gate, within and without, are stone seats. No guard room was provided in the gate itself, though there was a check while entering.

Adjuncts of the monumental entrance like guard rooms and kiosks on the terrace for musicians (*naubat**) were usually situated in the entrance to the residential complex, opening into the street.

3. The gardens which functioned as secondary residences are usually quite large. Fruit trees were generally planted here, particularly mango and breadfruit trees. The four *k͟hiyābāns*, are only slightly higher than ground level, and are sometimes replaced by flower-beds in French style (as seen in photographs of Rāmbāgh in 1890).

If the location of the main building is still in the south as in the other gardens, it often takes the form of a bungalow (Ratanbāgh) and is never the only building. Other more modest structures are located in the centre of the other sides as well as in the corners. These additional buildings contributed to a better regulation of life in the garden, permitting each one to find his place according to his rank and sex.

The entrance is generally a large habitable structure, high enough to allow a mounted elephant to pass (Chakia, Ratanbāgh, Rāmbāgh). However, the essential feature of these gardens was their relationship with water. The water provided for irrigating the garden was still drawn from wells situated outside the walls - a practice which we have already noted in the Mughal gardens. But the aim was no longer the same. It was not in order to exclude tedious manual labour from this paradise but to make the water point available to the general public that this exteriorisation of the water was resorted to.

In royal gardens, the northern end of the garden was extended to include a large reservoir with *ghāṭs* in stone or brick and lime mortar. This reservoir was a public bathing place and had a lay-out analogous to the *chahār bāg͟h*. It was designed in such a way that the queens could also bathe there. In Bhaironāth, one of the approach ramps was enclosed by high walls to create a bathing area for females. At Rāmbāgh, a special gate allowed one to pass from the garden to the reservoir and a text dated to the eighteenth century informs us that the western part was protected by hedges and reserved for women.[3]

What we have here is a combination of the Mughal garden with a water point set up in the Indian style. To complete this picture a temple, which generally has the form of a Muslim tomb, is inevitably situated near the reservoir. This is the case in Rājā Tālāb, Bhaironāth, Lankā of Rāmnagar and Chakia. At Rāmbāgh, on the contrary, the temple is a highly original structure belonging to a style created around 1770.

Comparable gardens were also created by rich merchants at the end

3. Cf. W. Hunter, *The Oriental Miscellany*, Calcutta, 1798, pp. 114-5.

of the nineteenth century, e.g. at Salarpur. The reservoir here possesses only two ramps facing each other, one for the buffaloes and the other for the people from the garden. We can already see the influence of the English bungalow on the residential building situated at the junction of the reservoir and the garden.

Though it is beyond the scope of this study, it would be interesting to examine the manner in which the Mughal garden in Benaras gradually transformed itself, under English influence, into a bungalow in the middle of a garden, comprising a large house with a central drawing-room. This garden usually had low boundary walls which allowed passers-by in the street to have a view of the interior.

C. Presentation of Ten Gardens

But for two exceptions, all the gardens described hereafter were created for the Mahārājās of Benaras. We have selected them not only because they are the best preserved (without being actually looked after) but also because they best illustrate our main contentions.

The two gardens which are part of the residence at Gangāpur are quite close to the Mughal model with fountains, etc.

The Shīsh Mahal and the garden of the Delhi princes are the best illustrations of a secondary residence outside the town. Of these two, the one which belonged to the descendants of the Mughal Emperors is the more incoherent.

At Shikārganj we leave behind the Mughal tradition and see a later example of the typically Indian *locus amoenus* built around a reservoir.

The six remaining gardens illustrate the union of the Mughal garden with the Hindu reservoir (*pokharā*), which is also to be found among the Jats of the same period, and was already present in the Shalimar gardens at Delhi constructed for one of the wives of Shāh Jahān. With respect to Benaras, it seems that this idea, which was in a nascent form at Bhaironāth, was developed more fully at the Rāmbāgh of Rāmnagar. The addition of a large reservoir results in the disappearance of the water tower and consequently of the fountains. The movement of the crystalline water which recalled the torrents of Afghanistan is replaced by calm waters in which one can immerse and purify oneself. The model which was, for long, restricted to the Mahārājās was also imitated by the rich merchants but only at the end of the nineteenth century.

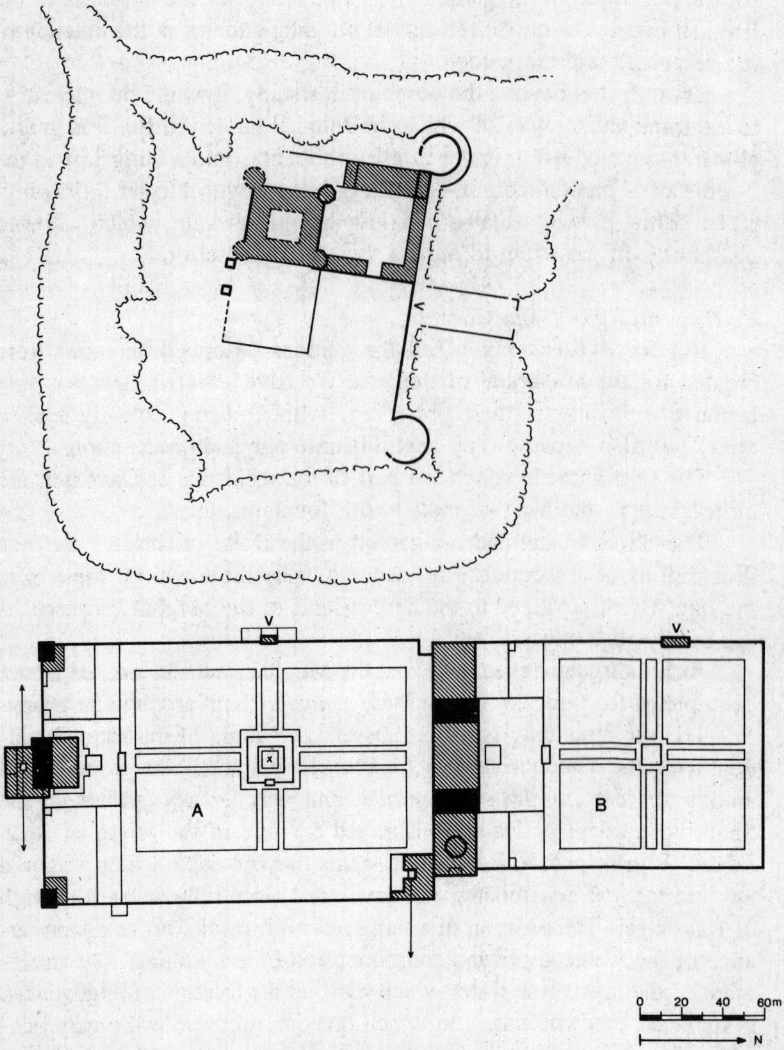

Fig. 1 - GANGĀPUR
A. - Southern garden; B. - Northern garden; x. Pond on platform

1. Gangāpur: The Gardens in the Fort

The royal family of Benaras was originally from Gangāpur, a small market town situated 16 kilometres west of Benaras, where vestiges of the ramparts and the moat of the mud fort built by Mansā Rām, the founder of the dynasty, survive till today. The family lived there until Balwant Singh, who succeeded Mansā Rām in 1738, shifted his residence to the strategically better located fort of Rāmnagar. In the present times, two quite distinct complexes have survived inside the ramparts: a fortified area surrounded by moats where traces of a *havelī* can still be seen in the ruins, and two rectangular gardens, one extending into the other.

The southern garden A is larger and probably older. The height of its boundary wall is only 3.7 metres and its entrance is pedestrian. The residential area, situated in its southern extremity, consists of a rectangular pavilion in each corner, with a *barsātī* on its Bengali roof, and a three-storeyed structure similar to the Panch Mahal at Fatehpur Sikri, in the centre. Each storey of this structure has a terrace in front; the lowest, situated on the large base, is adorned with fountains. Adjoining this structure, on the other side of the wall, is a water tower of the same height, with a well between two reservoirs. Water was drawn from the highest level, while the animals which pulled the goatskin bag moved below, on either side of the tower parallel to the boundary wall. In the north-eastern corner of the garden, another water tower of the same type serviced a *hammām*. The garden itself is a *chahār bāgh* with a raised, square shaped platform in the centre containing an ablution pond. From a small seat (*takht*) in stone, straddling the eastern edge of this platform, it is possible to keep watch on the entrance across the water. The *khiyābān*s, which are no higher than a step, are adorned in the middle with a row of small ponds between two narrow strips of flowers.

The boundary wall of the northern garden is 5.3 metres high. The gate which is off the east-west axis is large enough for a horseman to pass. The square planted space is intersected by the *khiyābāns*. There is a raised platform in the centre but no pond. There are also no pavilions in the corners, which is unusual. The residential portion is concentrated in the north. In the centre, a *darbār* opens on to a large raised platform with a pond. It is covered by a terraced roof which has *barsātī*s on both sides. A high *jāli* parapet secludes the southern side of the terrace from the other garden, which was probably a *mardānā*. In the *hammām*, situated in the east, a corridor separates the hot and cold areas and also provides a passage from one garden to the other. The hall which opens into the garden in the west has a two-tiered platform in its front like the *hammām*.

These two gardens, the *hammām* and the seclusion of women in a *havelī* or behind *jālī*s, bear evidence that, in the middle of the eighteenth century, Gangāpur had followed the Mughal style of Delhi.

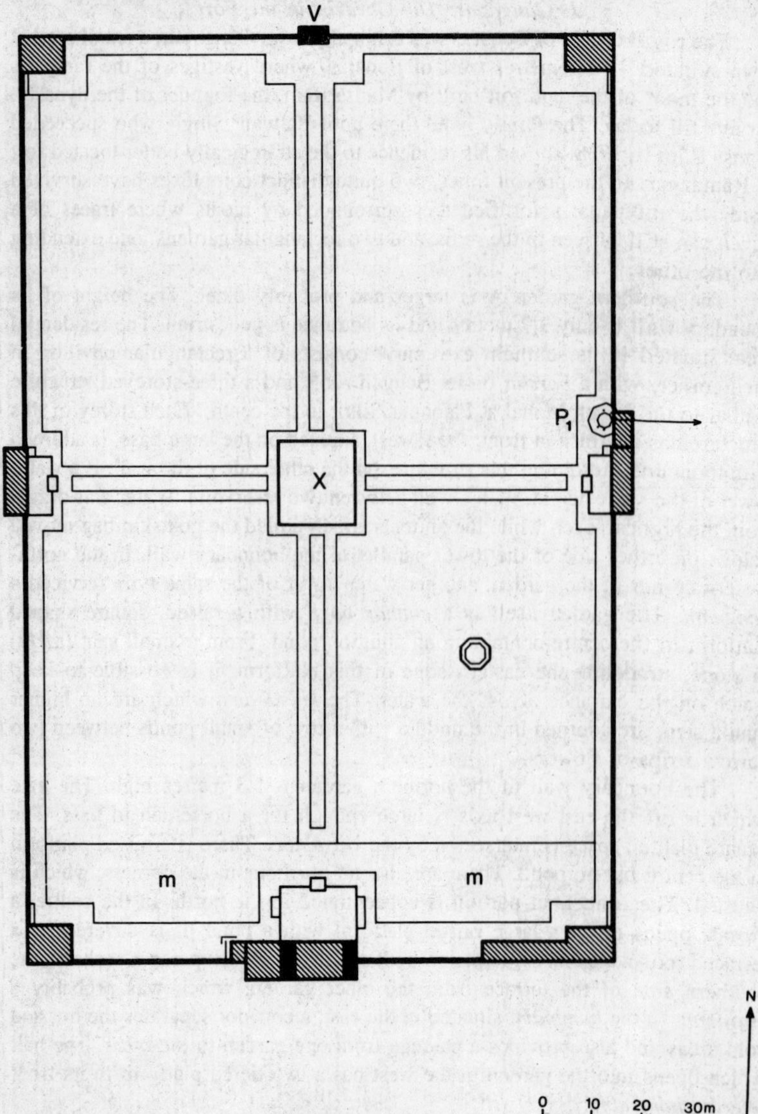

Fig. 2 - BENARAS: Shīsh Mahal

X. - Central pond

P̲1 - Well. The arrow indicates the trajectory followed by the animals used for drawing water meant for the fountains

m. - Platform in masonry for gatherings

V. Entrance with naubatk̲h̲āna

2. *Benaras: Shīsh Mahal*

The suburb of Kamachchhā where this garden is situated is in the south-west of the town, and to the west of the famous garden of Rānī Bhawānī of Natore. Some of the ceremonies associated with the coronation of Chet Singh in 1770 took place at the Shīsh Mahal. The map of James Prinsep, published in 1822, shows that the garden was, at this time, an integral part of the residence of the Rājā of Benaras, constructed as a replacement for Chet Singh's Shivālā, which had been confiscated by the East India Company in 1782. The garden was probably built by Balwant Singh, Rājā from 1738 to 1770.

We are thus dealing with a garden of the eighteenth century, contemporary to those at Gangāpur and situated outside the city, in a zone where the large Mughal caravanserais like the one at Aurangabad were located; a zone where the reservoirs were built, and around which the young male population of the village indulged in wrestling, bathing and consuming *bhang*; a zone also where the gardens of the big merchants and the residence of the *nouveaux riches*, mostly revenue officials honoured with the title of Rājā, were situated, and lastly, where, slightly isolated, lay the villages of the untouchables, *ḍoms* in particular. In the nineteenth century, Kamachchhā was the principal residence of the Rājās Udit Nārāyan Singh (1795-1835) and Ishwarī Prasād Singh (1835-89). The Shīsh Mahal is a rectangular *chahār bāgh* measuring 120 x 187 metres. The enclosure wall in brick is 3.5 metres high, and is built on a stone foundation. There were originally four raised pathways in masonry (*khiyābān*) forming a cross, and a pond X in the centre, which have recently been demolished due to the construction of modern housing. At the foot of the wall inside the garden, a pathway of the same type but without a water channel in the middle, links eight pavilions placed in the corners and in the centre of each side. In the south, it is wider and preceded by an area which is completely in masonry. Like most of the gardens in this period in the region, the principal residential area, with *darbār*, occupies the southern end and opens towards the north, providing protection from the direct heat of the sun while allowing the advantage of a complete view of the garden. The general plan of this garden follows, in the main, the same lines as the one at the Tāj Mahal in Agra.

Water for irrigating the garden and for feeding the water channels of the *khiyābān* and the pond in the centre was drawn from the well (P_1) which is older than the garden. A water tower whose base rested partially against the octogonal border of the well fed a set of fountains. The remaining canalisations that we have been able to observe are in baked earth. Before the inclusion of this garden in the residential complex of Kamachchhā, the draught animals used for drawing water were supposed to remain outside the garden as at Gangāpur and in the gardens of the Great Mughals.

The entrance placed in the centre of the northern side is a modest construction and meant only for pedestrians. It is preceded by a step. There is a pavilion for the *naubat* on the terrace.

The *darbār* which was opposite the entrance rises above the vegetation and a set of fountains from a high base, which becomes a platform in front. It was, in the past, shaded by shimmering curtains. This type is most common in Benaras: the archways of a hall flanked by rooms on both sides opening onto a terrace; a terraced roof containing two laterally placed *barsāṭī*s facing each other.

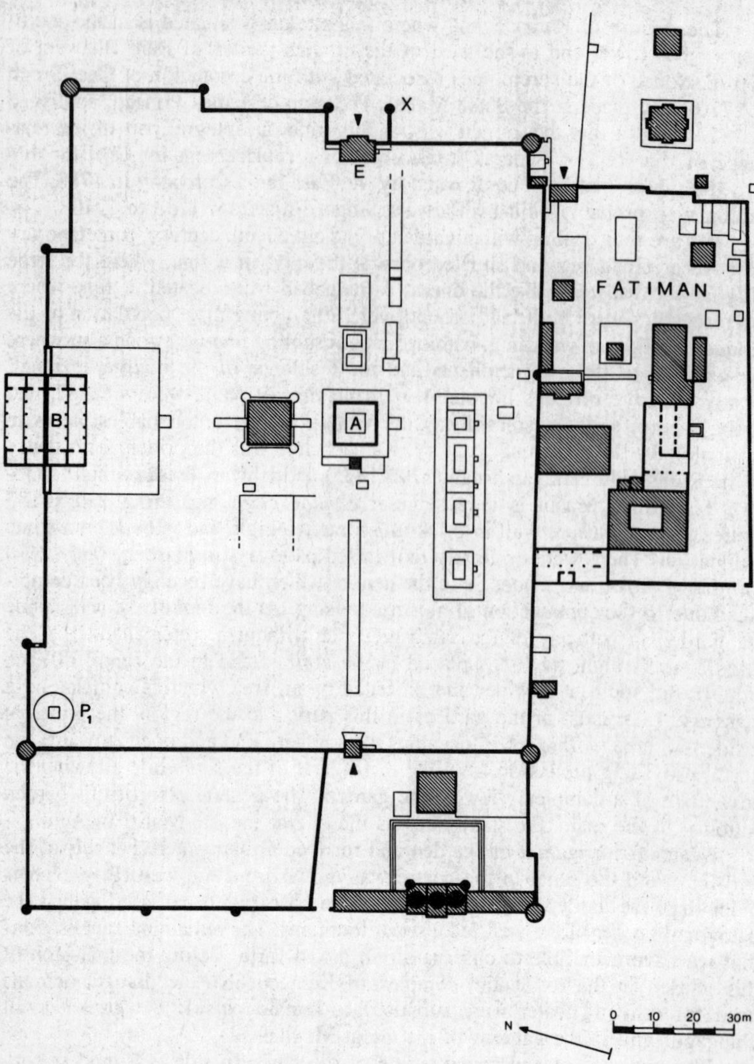

Fig. 3 - BENARAS: The Garden of the Princes of Delhi
A. - Tomb of Jawān Bakht
B. - Pavilion
E. - Entrance in the west
X. - Extension intended to create an effect of symmetry
$\underline{P_1}$ - Well with circular coping

3. *Benaras: The Garden of the Princes of Delhi.*

On May 31 1788, Jawān Bakht (Jahāndār II Nawāb Sāhib), eldest son of the Mughal Emperor Shāh ᶜAlam, died in Benaras, where he had sought asylum from the British. His large family was put up at Shivālā, the palace of Chet Singh. His tomb, now surrounded by those of his descendants, was erected in a garden situated in the north of Fatiman, sacred precinct of Shi'ite Muslims.

One would normally expect this garden to be characterized by a more Mughal style than its counterparts, constructed by the Rājās and Hindu merchants, but this is not so.

Made with briquettes on a base of sandstone rubble, the 3.2 metre high boundary wall follows an extremely irregular course. As a result, the garden has a shape far removed from the square form symbolising paradise. Though pretentious, this family from Delhi had limited means. During a reception at Shivālā, the elderly begum is known to have offered an enormous diamond set in a ring to Fanny Eden, which the interpreter had been instructed to take back at the time of departure !

The garden has two entrances, the more important one being in the east and the other in the west. The tomb of Jawān Bakht is aligned with the gates, although it does not occupy the centre of the garden. In order to create an impression of symmetry at the eastern entrance, a wall X ending in a turret has been constructed parallel to the northern wall.

Water is drawn from a well situated in the most elevated part of the garden which makes irrigation by gravity possible. The circular coping of this well is a rare feature in this region of Benaras, where, in the eighteenth century, wells generally had octagonal copings, and in the nineteenth and twentieth centuries it was the square coping that prevailed. On the contrary, in the region of Agra and Delhi, it was the circular one which was the norm, evidenced also in Mughal miniatures.

A building B on the same axis as the tomb straddles the northern boundary wall. In front of it, on the garden side, is a vast raised platform. This does not figure in the plan of J. Prinsep (1822), but, for that matter, even the tomb is not shown in the plan. On the contrary, it figures clearly in a plan of 1867-68 which also shows a large orchard extending to the north. The building was thus accessible from the garden and overlooked an orchard. It comprises of two halls opening in the south and the north respectively. These halls are flanked by smaller rooms which can be locked. Stairs built in the enclosure wall lead to the terraced roof, from which the view is superb.

The tomb of Jawān Bakht is of the "raised platform" type enclosed by perforated sandstone slabs (*jālī*). The stonework is remarkable in its finesse, and in general the workmanship is of good quality. In the south are situated a row of funerary platforms decorated with *jālī*. These belong to his sons. The other tombstones are much more modest. The financial decline of the family is manifest in this garden-cemetery, which is till today inhabited by Muslims professing to be the descendants of the Great Mughals.

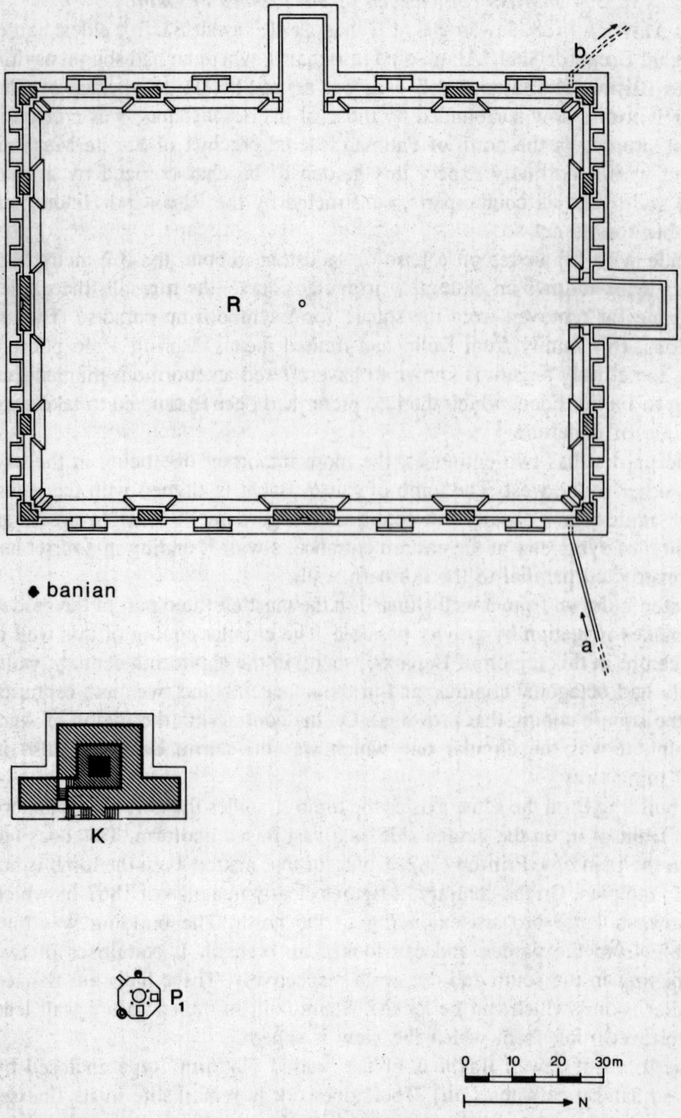

Fig. 4 - SHIKARGANJ

R. - Reservoir with *ghāṭ* in freestone; a. - Arrival point of water; b. - Overflow
Kiosks in hachures
K. - Three-storeyed hunting pavilion-cum-residence
$\underline{P_1}$ - Octogonal well for irrigation of the garden situated between this well and the reservoir

4. *Shikārganj: Reservoir and Hunting Pavilion*

This complex is of particular interest to us because it has none of the features of a Mughal garden. In fact this is a typical Indian pleasure spot, with a well, a pavilion surrounded by trees and a large reservoir. Basically it dates from the second half of the nineteenth century, by which time it was no longer necessary for a Hindu ruler to adopt the Mughal style.

Shikārganj is thirty kilometres south-east of the fort of Rāmnagar, as the crow flies. On an elephant, and going cross-country, the journey takes six hours. After about four hours of such travel, the landscape begins to change, the rich alluvial plains giving way to hills of sandstone and the cultivation yielding gradually to the jungle, which entirely covers the rugged slopes of the tabular massifs. As its name suggest, Shikārganj was a hunting resort of the Mahārājās of Benaras.

The large reservoir R (173 x 173 metres) was dug out in a natural terrace. This terrace overlooks cultivated land in the south and in the west, and during the monsoons, it is furrowed by water from the rivulets coming down from the massifs in the north-east, which abound in vegetation and game. It is in fact a *pokharā*, a man-made reservoir and not a natural lake, in which rain-water collects. Water is brought to this *pokharā* by a canal at a, and its overflow is at b. The banks of the reservoir are of masonry, with paved edges, a set of small pavilions and steps, and *ghāṭ*s. The edges and the terraces of the pavilions permit one to sit or lie down between the water and the greenery particularly in the evening or at night, when it is pleasant to do so. During the day, the pavilions offer shade against the scorching sun. In the centre of the reservoir, a pillar of sandstone symbolizes the axis of the world; this pillar is chiefly used now by the local youth as a diving board when they play around in the green waters of the reservoir. Contrary to the usual practice, ramps were provided only on two sides - the side adjoining the royal gardens, and the side adjoining the route did not have any ramps. The two ramps were used to bathe elephants.

The hunting pavilion K is not on the same axis as the reservoir. It is surrounded by an unenclosed garden, irrigated by the well P_1, which has octagonal parapets. It is clear that the pavilion was constructed in several stages. Nevertheless, it is a harmonious structure of the same type as the Panch Mahal of Fatehpur Sikri. Each storey recedes in relation to the preceding, making a sort of graduated pyramid. The ground floor is reserved for the servants. The next two floors constituted the portion where the Mahārājā lived and received visitors. From the upper terrace one had a commanding view of the whole landscape, the reservoir, the plain and the jungle. The first terrace placed one at level with the foliage of the trees in the garden. A gigantic banyan tree between the pavilion and the reservoir creates a large, cool and shady area.

All that is likely to remain when this complex is no longer maintained, is a dried-up *pokharā*, and a heap of ruins. The garden would have disappeared and its existence would only have the consistency of an hypothesis.

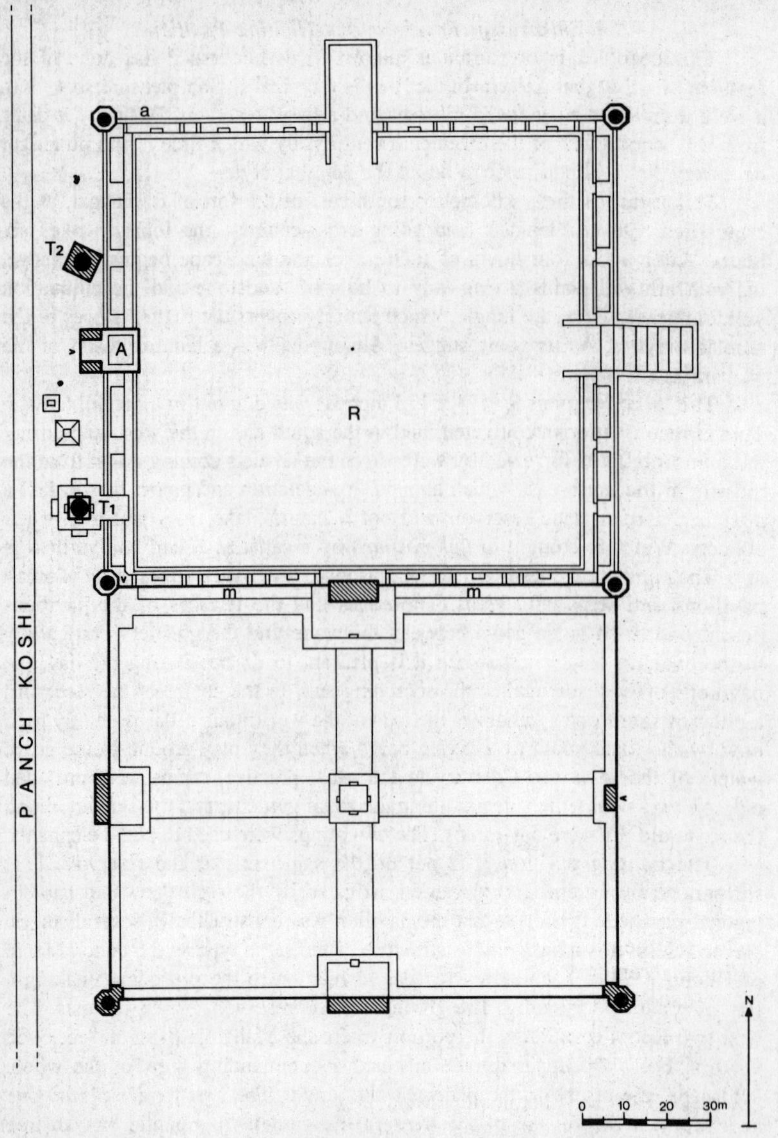

Fig. 5 - BHAIRONĀTH: *Pokharā*, Temples and Garden

R. - Reservoir; a. - arrival point of water

A. - Ramp reserved for the ablutions of women

$\underline{T_1}$ & $\underline{T_2}$ - Temples

m. - Platform from which one could enjoy the view of both the reservoir and the garden complex

5. *Bhaironāth: Pokharā, Temples and Gardens Combined*

Bhaironāth or Zamīn Shivsāgar is a village situated about two kilometres west of Gangāpur, the native place of the royal family of Benaras. It lies on the side of the *Panch Koshī*, a route that Hindu pilgrims are obliged to follow in order to carry out the *pradakshiṇā* of the sacred land of Kāshī. The complex in question is hence situated on sacred territory, towards the right side of this route. In accordance with the custom, temples and reservoirs related to this pilgrimage are invariably towards Kāshī. With the Ganges being about sixteen kilometres, and the Varuna about ten kilometres from it, Bhaironāth is far away from any navigable waterway. Stone construction here in the eighteenth century was therefore an expensive proposition.

The reservoir R called Shivsāgar dug at the behest of Balwant Singh, the first Rājā of Benaras, was completed in 1746. It measures 124 x 110 metres. Its *ghāṭs*, constructed not in stone but in brick and lime mortar, are larger in the east and the west. Each of the corners is occupied by an octagonal pavilion. The western, northern and eastern sides are marked by ramps in the middle. The western one is protected by high walls, and was reserved for women who could perform their ablutions here without being seen by men. The two others were intended for elephants and buffaloes, which had to be washed and brushed every day. As usual, a pillar was erected in the centre of the reservoir. Water arrives through inlet a. The earth excavated at the time of construction of this reservoir was deposited in the area where the garden is situated. Between the western *ghāṭ* and the route of *Panch Koshī*, there are two temples, T_1 and T_2, as well as a recreation area for villagers with a well P, some trees, and a wrestling ground.

The temple T_2 is of little interest to us as it is related purely to pilgrimage. But the plan of the other temple T_1 has a relation with the *pokharā*. Architecturally, it belongs to a style influenced by the Mughal tomb (structure with dome in a square area) but with a tendency towards elongation. This style was quite common in the eighteenth century. At Benaras where it was customary for the Rājās to follow the cultural trends of Lucknow and Delhi, most of the royal buildings are characterized by this style.

The garden is situated behind the reservoir. It is a rectangular *chahār bāgh* (123 x 98 metres) with a platform (*chabutara*) in the centre, from which four *khiyābāns* with water channels and flower-beds emanate. Each side has a pavilion in the centre and each corner an octagonal kiosk. The boundary wall has two small entrances for pedestrians. One links the garden to the temple T_1 and the other, situated in the middle of the eastern side, points towards Gangāpur. The *Panch Koshī* lies at the back of the garden. One dismounted from a horse or an elephant in front of the gate to slip into a garden planted with mango trees. The raised platforms in front of each pavilion place the visitor at the level of the foliage. An overall view of the garden and the neighbouring countryside is available from their terraced roofs. On the side of the *pokharā*, a long platform m, with a parapet replaces the boundary wall. From here one can enjoy a view of the bathers as well as the refreshing coolness and the perfume of the vegetation. Of the octagonal pavilions in the corners, the ones in the south-eastern and south-western corners are part of the garden, while the other two form part of the reservoir.

In the neighbourhood of Benaras, Bhaironāth is perhaps the oldest complex which unites reservoir, garden and temple.

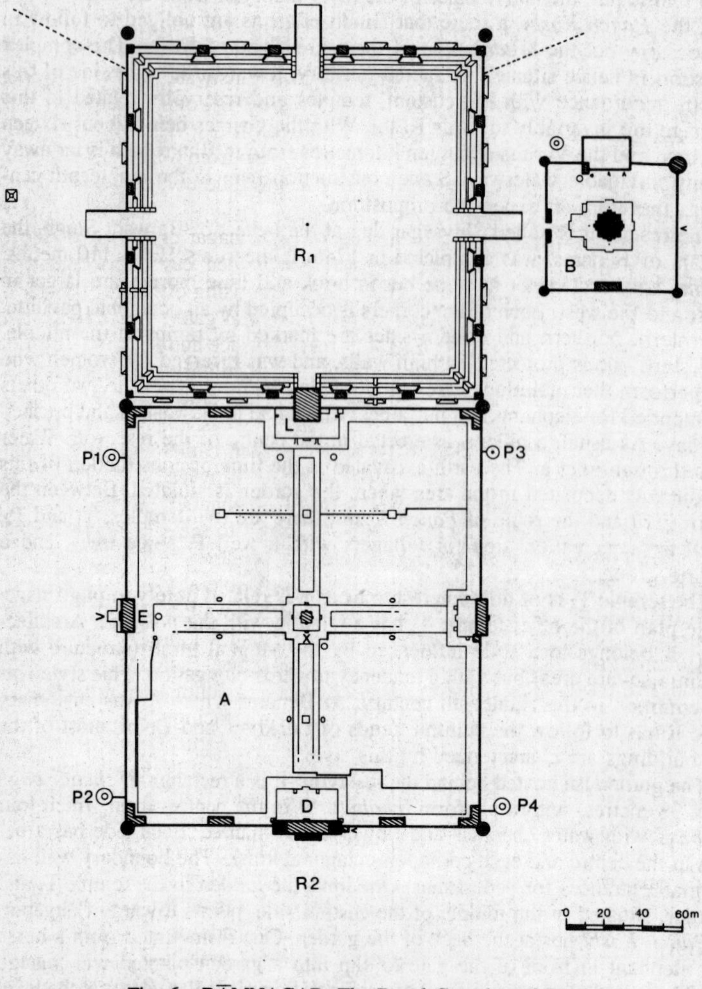

Fig. 6 - RĀMNAGAR: The Royal Complex of Rāmbāgh

R1 - Reservoir in masonry

R2 - Man-made reservoir, without masonry (not shown in this plan)

A. - Central pavilion

B. - Sumeru temple and garden

E. - Entrance

D. - Principal Building (*darbār*)

X. - Residential pavilion

P1, P2, P3 & P4 - Wells for irrigation of the garden

6. *Rāmnagar: The Royal Complex of Rāmbāgh*

Situated in a zone of gardens to the north-east of the town of Rāmnagar, this complex, mentioned from 1798 onwards,[4] is attributed to Chet Singh (1770-81). It is a rectangular *chahār bāgh* A (219 x 187 metres), placed between two reservoirs like the palace garden at Deeg (1760-68). The southern reservoir R_2 is not of masonry; only buffaloes bathe in its water which is always dirty. A village is situated on its banks. The reservoir R_1, on the contrary, is a remarkable piece of work. Known as the "Sea of Milk", it is a square surface (187 x 187 metres) completely covered with sandstone from Chunar. To its east is the Sumeru temple completed only around the middle of the 19th century, when a walled garden B was built around it.

During the time of Chet Singh, the plan of Rāmnagar consisted of a fort on the banks of the river Ganges. A royal avenue led eastwards from the monumental gate to the Chowk, a market-place comprising of four buildings at right angles, forming a cross, and another monumental gate to the east of the crossroads. The town developed around this market-place and the fort. Clusters of villages and gardens lay outside the town. Two military chiefs possessed properties in the south, which was the more vulnerable side of the town. Chet Singh conceived of Rāmbāgh, which lay in the north-east of the town, as the place where his army would be stationed before each campaign. The garden would then serve as the royal residence, while the army camped around the *pokharā* in the north, so that the soldiers and the elephants could bathe under the vigilant eyes of the Rājā. This set-up corresponds to the scheme which we normally find in most capital cities in traditional India.

Rāmbāgh comprises of a pavilion x in white marble at the intersection of the *khiyābāns*, and other structures along the boundary wall; an octagonal room in each corner, with a square portico in its front and a kiosk on the roof; a building in the middle of each side, with the entrance E in the west, large enough for a mounted elephant to pass through; in the south, a large *darbār* D for receptions; in the north, a residential building L facing the *pokharā* (the present construction dates from the beginning of this century, but another was in existence in the eighteenth century). As for the water, it is drawn from four wells situated outside the wall (P_1, P_2, P_3, and P_4). There is no water tower, and consequently neither fountains nor cascades. The *khiyābāns* are unpaved and virtually at the same level as the spaces planted with fruit trees. Obviously, in a prestigious complex like Rāmbāgh, the Mughal model is somewhat blurred. The garden *per se* is no longer a paradise. The accent is on the buildings, with their terraced roofs, from where one can enjoy the shade of the foliage and a view of the countryside and the villages at the same time.

The reservoir is the most important construction. In the centre, where the two principal axes intersect, there is a monolithic pillar. The Sumeru temple, dedicated principally to Durgā, goddess of war, is situated on the east-west axis. The garden which adjoins the reservoir is situated on the north-south axis. On the symbolic level, all the elements are present: a well-positioned square, four corners, four ramps, and a central axis of the world. This *pokharā* served alike queens, soldiers, farmers and elephants.

---

4. Cf. C.M. Villiers-Stuart, *Gardens of the Great Mughals*, London, 1913, p. 104.

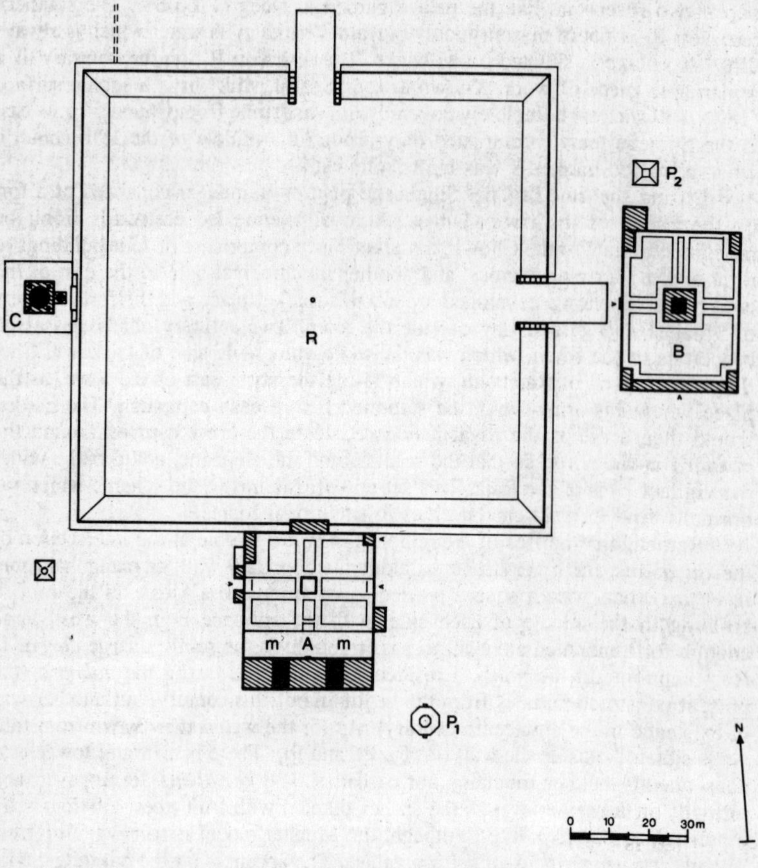

Fig. 7 - RĀJĀ TĀLĀB AND RĀNĪ BĀZĀR: Reservoir, Gardens and Temples

R. - Reservoir

A. - Garden with *darbār*

B. - Garden attached to the temple of Rām

C. - Temple in the form of a Muslim tomb

m. - Raised platform

P_1, P_2, - Wells

7. Rājā Tālāb and Rānī Bāzār: Reservoir, Gardens and Temples

This market town is at the crossing of the *Panch Koshī*, the Grand Trunk Road, and the north-eastern railway. Benaras is 16 kilometres to its west. Bhaironāth is at 2 kilometres distance, and Gangāpur at 4 kilometres. A market developed at this place, under the auspices of the Rājā of Benaras, who possessed in this region a stronghold at Gangāpur, a *locus amoenus* at Bhaironāth, and a commercial centre at Rājā Tālāb.

The principal element of this architectural complex is a large reservoir, about 125 metres square. The *ghāṭs* which enclose this reservoir are in brick and lime mortar. Here, as in Bhaironāth, one is far away from a navigable body of water, making it expensive to transport large quantities of stone. In the centre of this reservoir stands a sculpted monolithic pillar, axis of the world, dwelling-place of the *Nāga*-protector, diving board for the children. As for the ramps, here again there are only two - in the north, and the east. The high walls of the garden residence A in the south, and a temple C in the west are aligned with these two ramps. The temple bears the influence of Mughal funerary architecture, of the type encountered at Bhaironāth and at Chakia, except that it is more squat. In the nineteenth century, another garden B containing a temple dedicated to Rām, was added in the eastern part of this complex by a queen. The garden residence A faces the north to avoid the sun. The boundary walls are very high, protecting the green intimacy of the garden. After the customary check at the entrance, one enters into a *chahār bāgh* which has a *chabutara* in the centre. All adornment in terms of canals, cascades and fountains is, however, completely absent. Water for irrigating this garden is brought from a public well P_1 with an octagonal coping, situated outside the walls. In the north, a gate opens into a portico facing the reservoir; a flight of stairs leads to its terraced roof rising above the green waters and the dusty air of the market. On its left stands the vermilion temple C with its white dome and on the right, the spire of a Rām temple soars above the foliage of the mango trees. The residence itself is in the southern part of the garden. It consists of a high platform m draped with shimmering curtains and onto which open the archways of three halls. These halls are separated from one another by two rooms. An external staircase leads to the first floor where three terraces corresponding to the halls below, and two rooms corresponding to the rooms on the ground floor are to be found. The terraces are sequestered from the outside world by stone *jālīs*. They are at the level of the upper branches of the fruit trees, making it possible to pluck a mango simply by stretching the hand. The garden, platform, halls and terraces - all these are open to the air, except for the two ground floor rooms, which alone can be locked.

The rectangular garden B was also a *chahār bāgh*, but one of the pathways has disappeared. A temple dedicated to Rām is situated on a high platform in the centre of the garden with a tall *shikhar* pointing a bow and arrow towards the sky. The entrance is opposite the eastern ramp of the reservoir. The southern side has a building; in each corner also, there is a construction with a terraced roof, accessible through a staircase parallel to the boundary wall. From this roof we can enjoy both the cloistered shade of the foliage in the garden, and the dusty flat world outside. Water comes from the public well P_2 outside the walls.

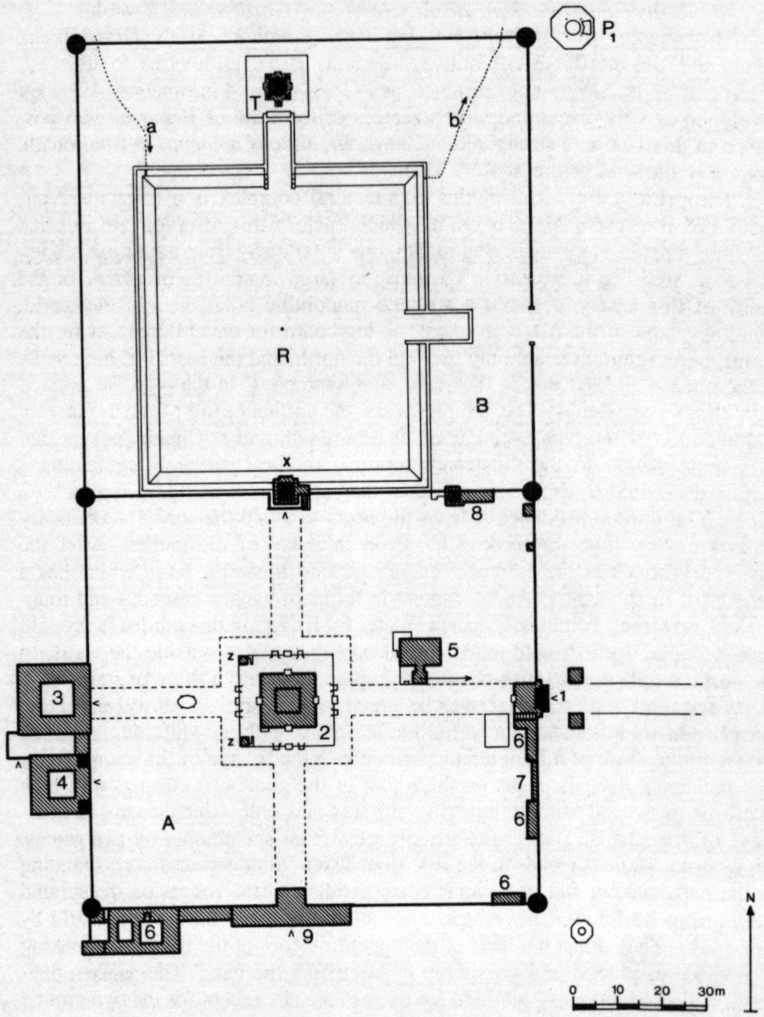

Fig. 8 - CHAKIA: The Royal Complex, Garden and Pokharā and Temple

A. - The garden, 1) Entrance, 2) Royal pavilion, 3) Kitchens, 4) *Havelī* of queens, 5) *Hammām*, 6) Houses meant for Brahmins, 7) Pigeon house, 8) Caretaker's dwelling, 9) Stables

x. - Two storeyed pavilion between the garden and the reservoir

B. - The *pokhāra*, R. - Reservoir, a. - Arrival point of the water, b. - Overflow

T. - Temple with dome in the form of a Muslim tomb

P_1 - Well to provide water to an area of the encampment

8. *Chakia: The Royal Complex, Garden and Pokharā with Temple*

The town of Chakia is located 32 kilometres as the crow flies south-west of Benaras, in a well irrigated valley, surrounded by sandstone hills with forest cover. There are many stone quarries in the area, and the houses are made of stone rather than brick. Till the middle of this century, the neighbouring forests were rich in big game, particularly the tiger.

When the East India Company assumed power in the region of Benaras in 1782, Chakia continued to remain under the authority of the Rājā, as part of the family domains, which the English allowed to be retained by Mahīp Nārāin Singh. It was his son Udit Nārāin Singh, Rājā from 1795 to 1835, who constructed the complex which we are going to describe here. The Rājā who wielded considerable power in the region came to the garden for long stays, both to administer the property, and to hunt. Situated on the southern edge of the town, the complex consists of a garden residence A, and a public zone B, surrounded by a wall, with *pokharā* R and temple T.

This is the only example of a complex having a reservoir constructed inside an enclosed area. The edges, the *ghāṭs* and the two ramps, as well as the boundary walls and the kiosks in the corners are all in sandstone. Water comes through a from the countryside, and the overflow is drained out from outlet b, towards the town. On the side of b, and outside the wall, one can see the high coping of a well P_1, which supplied drinking water to the encampment. The crowds could camp on the vacant lands to the north and the west of zone B. A high platform provides the base for the temple T, which is built on the pattern of the Mughal tomb.

Opposite the temple, on the other side of the reservoir, is a two-storeyed kiosk x. The first storey is accessible from the reservoir, and the second from the garden.

The garden A consists of an entrance (1), a *hammām* (5), the royal bungalow (2), the kitchens (3), the *havelī* of the queens (4), a pigeon house (7), the stables (9), and various types of accomodation for the Brahmins (6). The caretaker, a Brahmin also, still lives in his quarter (8), from where he can keep a watch both on the garden, particularly the royal bungalow (the view between these two buildings is clear and completely unobstructed by trees), and the area around the *pokharā*.

Just before the principal entrance are two sentry boxes (evidence of British influence). Large enough to allow an elephant to pass, this entrance has a terraced roof which has a kiosk for the *naubat*. Inside the *hammām*, which is flanked by a well also meant for irrigating the garden, a corridor separates the part reserved for bathing from the part reserved for rest, where a temple is situated.

The exterior is quite surprising - a kind of rococo-Mughal. The kitchens are outside the garden, with their facade in alignment with the boundary walls. The queens resided here, before the construction of the *havelī* (4). The royal bungalow is an amazing building, firstly because of its location in the centre of the garden, at the point of intersection of the two principal axes, which are architecturally highlighted by a series of balconies at the level of the platform on which the building stands, and at the level of the terrace; secondly, because of the presence of two toilets (z), and, lastly because of murals on the veranda around the drawing room, giving an impression of wall-paper - the English influence is evident.

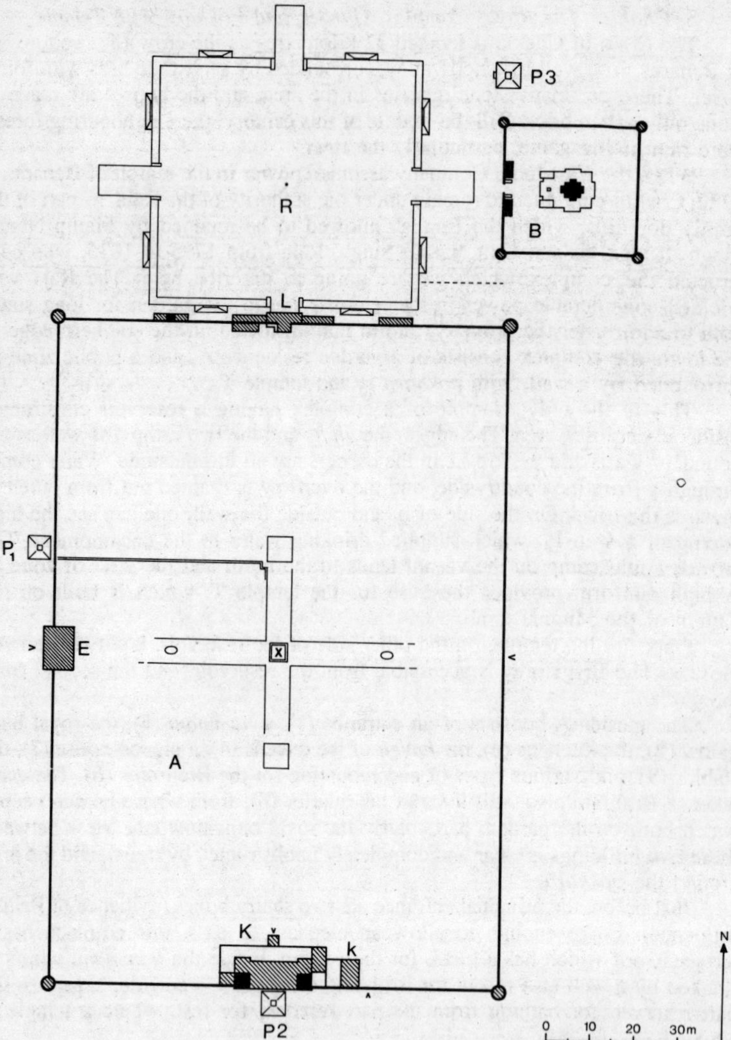

Fig. 9 - RATANBĀGH: *Garden, Pokharā and Temple*

A. - Garden
E. - Entrance; x. - Pond in the centre
K. - Queen's pavilion, k. - Stable
L. - Pavilion situated between garden and reservoir
$\underline{P_1}$, $\underline{P_2}$, $\underline{P_3}$, - Wells
R. - Reservoir (*pokharā*)
B. - Temple in the middle of a garden

9. *Ratanbāgh: Garden, Pokharā and Temple*

This complex is situated in the countryside, 3 kilometres south-east of the fort of Rāmnagar, beyond a small stream called Ghurnā Nalā. It is hence beyond the suburban gardens of Rāmnagar, beside the route to Vindhyāchal, an important Hindu religious centre (in the nineteenth century, this was a principal haunt of the famous Thugs). This is also the route to Latifpur and Bijaigarh forts, belonging to the kingdom of Benaras. It is possible that the preparations necessary for the movement of the Rājā to these places were made here.

As it stands today, the Ratanbāgh is an imitation of the Rāmbāgh of Rāmnagar, which is situated 3 kilometres to its north. Like Rāmbāgh, it also has a rectangular garden A, a reservoir R and a temple in the centre of another garden B, and it even adopts the same layout as Rāmbāgh.

The garden A (104 x 153 metres) has a boundary wall in brick. Each corner of the garden is marked by a simple octagonal structure. The entrance E is the most remarkable building in the complex, high enough for a mounted elephant to pass. It is here that the guards lived. Its terrace could serve as the *naubatkhāna*. It dates probably from the beginning of the nineteenth century. The centre of the garden is marked by a small reservoir x. Water for irrigation is drawn from two particularly striking wells P_1 and P_2, situated, as was the practice, outside the walls. Two buildings served as the residence of the masters, of which one in the north is a sort of elevated kiosk at the edge of the garden and the reservoir. The kiosk is airy, and permits a panoramic view of a varied landscape of water and trees. The other building K constructed at the end of the nineteenth century by a queen who liked to live here, is much more developed. Although situated at a height, it appears to fold back into itself, and is separated from the garden by a high wall. It has a single entry under a porch, and the decor is influenced by both Mughal and English styles. On the ground floor, there is a large drawing room, with a veranda in front. Along with several other rooms, it also has a toilet and a bathroom. On the first floor, there is a terrace with two rooms (a kitchen and a bedroom). A high parapet protects the occupants from public view. A stable k is attached to this building in its east, at level with the garden.

The reservoir R has four ramps but the southern ramp is blocked by the building L. It is always full of water, even during the dry season. The monolithic pillar in its centre is generally immersed in the water. The visible portions in masonry - the edges around the reservoir, the steps and the *ghāṭs*, as well as the walls of the ramps - are entirely covered with sandstone slabs. Four porticos have been constructed between the wall of the garden and the southern edge of the reservoir. These are utilised by ascetics, pilgrims and travellers.

The temple B which dates from the end of the nineteenth century is in the centre of the garden irrigated by well P_3. The entrance of this garden is a Mughal version of the entrance of the Sanskrit University of Benaras, which was designed by Markham Kittoe. As for the temple, it stands on a high base, like the Sumeru of Rāmbāgh, and contains rooms to accomodate the priest and his family. It is built in "Hindu revival" style, characterized by a detailed but rather dry decor, which was typical at the end of the nineteenth and the beginning of the twentieth century.

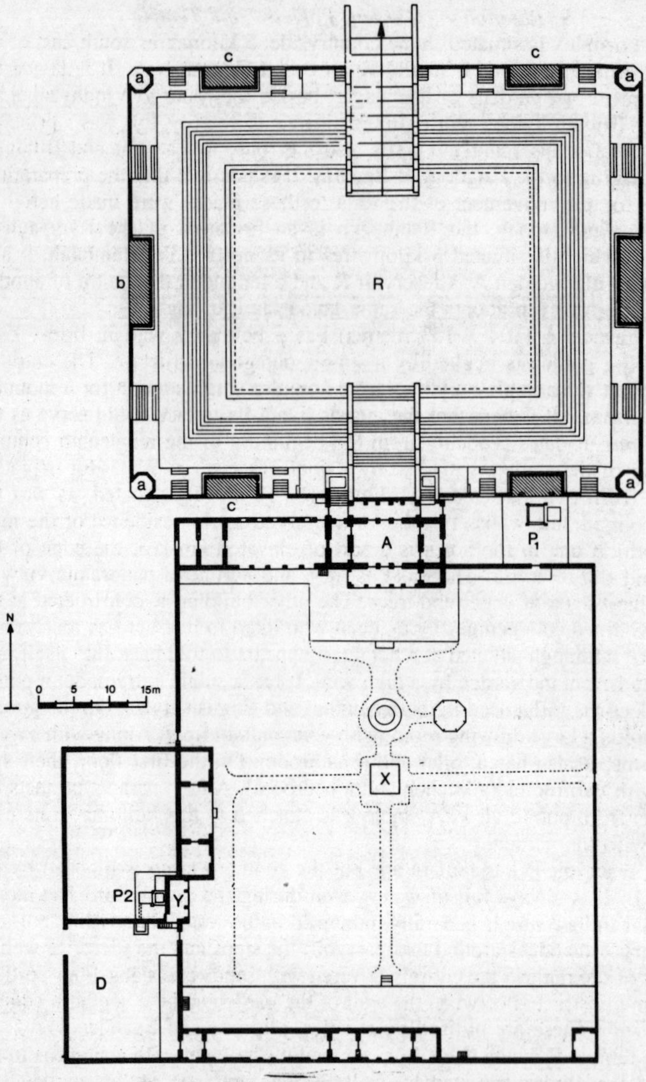

Fig. 10 - SALARPUR: The Garden and Pokharā

R. - Reservoir, b. & c. - Kiosks, a. - Platform in the corners

P_1 - Well with an area meant for *bāhrī alang*

A. - *Koṭhi* (residential pavilion)

X. - Central platform of the garden

D. - Courtyard with stable

P_2 - Well

Y. - Portico through which water can be drawn directly from the garden

10. *Salarpur: The Garden and Pokharā Complex*

Non-existent on a map of Benaras and its neighbouring areas dated 1867-68, this complex is situated to the north of the river Varuna beside the *Panch Koshī*, to the east of the point where it intersects the route to Sarnāth. Unlike the other complexes described in this article, this was not the creation of the royal family, but of a rich merchant of Benaras at the end of the nineteenth century.

A quick look at the plan is enough to reveal that the most important element in this complex is the reservoir intended for public use. Enclosed and private, the garden is primarily lush vegetation, growing in a disorderly and unchecked manner. The boundary wall, the central platform X, the residential buildings located along the edges, and the well situated outside the walls, are the only elements that remind one of the Mughal model. Whereas the reservoir was constructed on a north-south axis strictly according to the rules of symmetry, the regular layout of the buildings in the original conception of the garden, has been completely destroyed by additions. The absence of *khiyābān*s and a central structure were conducive to the revival of a more natural garden, liberated from the constraints of geometric form. This trend, present in Benaras from the second half of the eighteenth century, can be observed in Chet Singh's Rāmbāgh. It represented a Hindu feature, with its emphasis on living in harmony with nature rather than attempting to control it.

The rectangular reservoir R, with octagonal supports in the corners, reminiscent of the kiosks of Bhaironāth and Rāmbāgh, has two ramps, one towards the village for bathing buffaloes, and the other meant for the ladies of the garden. It is entirely covered with sandstone. With the Varuna in the neighbourhood, boats had no difficulty in transporting the stone from Chunar to a zone in proximity of the site in question. It is also true that, by this time, English technology had helped bring about improvements in carts, facilitating the transport of heavy loads. Between the edges of the reservoir and the *ghāṭ*s which permit access to the water, there is a zone of recreation consisting of platforms at different levels, and kiosks with terraced roofs (b and c). In the present times, the primary school of the village is located here, with the kiosks serving as classrooms, and the blackboard consisting of a stone slab covered with black paint. It is here that people meet in the evenings for a chat or to play cards.

We have already pointed out the essential elements of the garden. It is irrigated by a well P_1, situated outside the walls and hence open to the public. Palettes for the preparation of *bhang* suggest that it was expected to serve as a centre for *bāhrī alang**. The upper part of the well P_2 accessible by a staircase is also a recreation spot. It fed a drinking trough, the courtyard D serving as a stable. Discreetly and without creating disturbance, water could be drawn from this well from the garden also, through a window opening at the bottom of portico Y and equipped with a pulley. The building A called *koṭhī* partook of the reservoir, the garden and the zone demarcated for *bāhrī alang* P_1. English influence could clearly be seen in its layout - a drawing room at the centre, porticos in the north and the south and rooms on the sides. But the terraced roof shaded by two gigantic mango trees and protected by a *jālī* parapet, with a commanding view of the water and the greenery of the garden, reflects a typically Indian life-style.

Conclusion

Any place where trees, vegetables and flowers have been planted is not a garden in the sense in which we have used the term in this paper. In the present context, "garden" is a concept that denotes complex artistic creation, such as we find in the Chinese garden, the French garden, or the Irano-Mughal garden. The last mentioned contrasts with a certain type of landscape: arid, mineral and completely devoid of all vegetation. It corresponds to a land of dreams; to paradise as imagined by a people who rarely see even a green sprig. When transplanted in India, it acclimatized itself, to provide a balm to a certain nostalgia.

In the past, for an Indian from the plains of the north and the jungle,[5] a good monsoon and a daily bath were essential to fight the persistent heat of the dusty, long summers. Bath by immersion was considered necessary also because it purified. Here lies the origin of the art of architectural beautification of water points, banks of rivers, reservoirs, *bāolī*s and wells.

But Indians were also attracted to the civilisation of their Muslim conquerors and later, of their English masters. In Benaras, these three civilisations encountered each other in the second half of the eighteenth century. Each one had its own dream of an idyllic place. The Mughal garden first assimilated the *pokharā*, to be later assimilated by the English bungalow with running water. In our times it is usual to bathe at a municipal tap or a well rather than in a reservoir. And the ultimate dream of an Indian today is to have a private bathroom.

Translated from French by Rashmi Patni

Glossary

Bāolī: Stepwell.

Bāhrī alang: A common pastime of the inhabitants of Benaras, particularly the artisans. It consists of leaving one's place of work to go and join friends at a well or a *ghāṭ*. There one prepares *bhang* (hemp) in their company and consumes it before going to defecate in a group in an open area. Subsequently one returns to the well to wash clothes and bathe before finally returning to work, chewing a betel (*pān*).

---

5. As defined by *Robert Méthodique*, Paris, 1990, p. 781, the jungle "in monsoonal countries was a form of tropical grassland covered with tall grass, bushes and trees". Before the industrial revolution this was the natural landscape most frequently encountered in North and Central India.

Chahār bāgh: Iranian style garden divided into four parts by raised pathways.

Ganj: Commercial centre, particularly a rectangular building with a central courtyard reserved for commerce.

Ghāṭ: Steps constructed against the bank of a river or a reservoir which facilitate access to the water, whatever be its level.

Jālī: Transenna (lattice work) in stone, brick or wood.

Kārez: Subterranean tunnel which allows water to flow, by gravitational force, from a space in which it is confined at the base of a hill or mountain towards the irrigated land of a valley. Iranian invention dating back to the beginning of the first millenium BC.

Khiyābān: A paved pathway constructed distinctly above the level of the soil and generally carrying a water channel in its centre.

Mardānā: Part of a palace or a residence reserved for men.

Naubat and *Naubatkhāna*: Part of the entrance of a palace reserved for musicians who play either to announce the arrival or the departure of the sovereign or at certain fixed times of the day and the night.

Pokharā: Large reservoir dug in the earth to collect rain water during the monsoon. It does not refer to a reservoir with barrage. The word is of Sanskrit origin.

Zanānā: Part of a residence reserved for women.

REFERENCES

Aijazuddin, F.A., *Lahore Illustrated Views of the 19th Century*, Ahmedabad: Mapin Publishing Pvt. Ltd., 1991. [The Shalimar Gardens, pp. 162-9]

Andrews, Peter A., "The Architecture and Gardens of Islamic India", in *The Arts of India*, ed. Basil Gray, Oxford, Phaiton Press, 1981, pp. 95-124.

Ansari, M. Azher, "Palaces and Gardens of the Mughals", *Islamic Culture*, 1959, XXXIII, pp. 61-72.

Sackville-West, Victoria, "The Gardens of Mughal India" in *Legacy of Persia*, ed. A.J. Arberry, Oxford: 1952.

Baqir, M. *Lahore Past and Present*, Lahore: Punjab University Press, 1952.

Clavijo, R.G. de, *Narrative of the Embassy of Ruy Gonzales de Clavijo to the Court of Timour at Samarcande*, Transl. C.R. Markham, London: Hakluyt Society, Series I, N° 26, 1870.

Crowe, Sylvia & S. Haywood, *The Gardens of Moghal India. A History and A Guide*, London: Thames & Hudson, 1972; Delhi: Vikas Publishing House, 1973.

Deokar, Khandu, "The Garden as A Residence", in Pierre-Daniel Couté and Jean-Michel Léger, *Bénarès, un voyage d'architecture*, Paris: Ed. Créaphis, 1989, pp. 99-103.

Desai, Z.A., "Inscriptions from the Khusrau Bagh, Allahabad", EIAPS, 1961, pp. 64-8.

Dickie, James, "The Mughal Garden: Gateway to Paradise", *Muqarnas*, 1985, N° 3, pp. 128-37.

Foster, W., ed., *The Embassy of Sir Thomas Roe in India*, London: Oxford University Press, 1926.

Goetz, Hermann, "The Qudsia Bagh at Delhi: Key to Late Mughal Architecture", *Islamic Culture*, 1952, XXVI, 1, pp. 132-51.

Huegel, Baron von, *Travels in Kashmir and the Panjab*, with notes by T.B. Jervis, London, 1845; Repr., Lahore: Qausain, 1976.

Hunter, W., *The Oriental Miscellany*, Calcutta, 1798.

Jairazbhoy, R.A., "Early Garden-Palaces of the Mughals", *Oriental Arts*, 1952, N° 4, pp. 68-75.

Kak, Ram Chandra, *Ancient Monuments of Kashmir*, London: The Indian Society, 1933.

Koch, Ebba, "The Zahara Bagh (Bagh-i-Jahanara) at Agra", *Environmental Design*, 1986, pp. 30-7.

Kumar, Nita, "Open Space and Free Time: Pleasure for the People of Banaras", *Contributions to Indian Sociology*, Jan. 1986, XX, 1, pp. 41-60.

Latif, S.M., *Lahore: its History, Architectural Remains and Antiquities*, 1892.

Lestrange, Guy, Transl., *Clavijo Embassy to Tamerlane, 1403-1405*, London: The Broadway Travellers.

MacDougall, Elisabeth B. & Richard Ettinghausen, eds., *The Islamic Garden*, Dumbarton Oaks Colloquium on the History of Landscape Architecture, Cambridge (Mass.): Harvard University Press, 1976.

Moynihan, Elisabeth B., *Paradise as a Garden in Persia and Mughal India*, New York: G. Braziller, 1979 and London: Scolar Press, 1980.

Muhammad, K.K., "The House of the Nobility in Moghal India", *Islamic Culture*, 1986, LX, 3, pp. 81-104.

Mundy, Peter, *Travels of Peter Mundy in Europe and Asia, 1608-67*, ed. R.C. Temple, Five Vols., London: Hakluyt Society Papers,

Series II, Vol. XXXV, 1907-36.

Osborne, W.G., *The Court and Camp of Runjeet Sing*, Karachi: Oxford University Press, 1973.

Sanderson, Gordon, *A Guide to the Buildings and Gardens, Delhi Fort* (1914), Delhi: Manager of Publications, 4th edn., 1937.

Thévenot, Jean de, *Voyages de Monsieur de Thévenot contenant la relation de l'Indostan, des nouveaux Mogols et des autres peuples et pays des Indes*, Paris, 1684.

Titley, Norah & Frances Wood, *Oriental Gardens*, London: The British Library, 1991.

Vigne, G.T., *A Personal Narrative of a Visit to Ghuznin, Kabul and Afghanistan*, London, 1840.

Villiers-Stuart, C.M., *Gardens of the Great Mughals*, London: A. & C. Black, 1913; Repr., Allahabad: R.S. Publishing House, 1979.

Wali Ulla Khan, M., *Lahore and its Important Monuments*, Islamabad, Ministry of Education, Government of Pakistan, 1964.

Late Persian, Early Urdu: The Case of 'Wahhabi' Literature (1818-1857)

MARC GABORIEAU

It is commonly held that in the 19th century, Urdu replaced Persian as the religious and cultural language of the Indian Muslims. This is, chronologically speaking, only partly true. The transition from one language to the other was a very long process which lasted for centuries and which has continued over the 20th century. Sufis started composing poems in vernacular languages from the Middle Ages; but Iqbal (d. 1938) gained an international reputation for his Persian poems in this century. Secondly, the moment of transition was not the same in the various parts of the Indian sub-continent: Urdu became a literary language in the Deccan earlier than in the North. It varies also according to literary genre: in Northern India, Urdu poetry - inspired by Deccani models - became a noble genre recognized in the Mughal court in the second half of the 18th century; but Urdu prose acquired a religious and scientific "authority" only gradually during the 19th century.[1]

This paper studies the transition from Persian to Urdu prose in a particular case: the religious literature of the so-called 'Wahhabis'. What can we learn from this case about the process of transition and its stages ? Did the Wahhabis just follow a process started by others? Or did they make an original contribution to it ? Such are the questions we will try to answer after describing the context and making an inventory of the literature produced by the Wahhabis.

1. Chronology of the Transition

In order to understand the changes which occured during the period under study (1818-57), we must have an idea of the situation as it obtained before - when only Persian prose was used - and after - when Urdu prose was dominant.

1. D. Lelyveld, "Eloquence and Authority in Urdu: Poetry, Oratory, and Film", in K.P. Ewing, ed., *Shariᶜat and Ambiguity in South Asian Islam*, Berkeley, 1988, pp. 98-113.

1.1 Up to the Beginning of the 19th Century

Although Indian Muslims at that time did speak some form of Urdu (then styled as "Hindī") at home, they would write on religious subjects (as on any other subject in prose) only in Persian. For there was no formal education in Urdu or in any other vernacular language: after a compulsory reading of the Quran (without translation), the basis of traditional education was reading and writing Persian.[2] Except for Islamic exoterical religious sciences like Quranic exegesis or law (for which Arabic books had to be used) all reference books were in Persian, which was the language of administration (replaced by English only in 1835), of literature, of sciences and even of Islamic mysticism.

Two examples will illustrate these statements in the religious domain. The great Delhi scholar, Shāh Walīu'llāh (1703-62) - whom all 19th century reformers claimed as their ancestor - wrote only in Arabic and in Persian; and even when he made an effort to popularize the Holy Quran, he wrote a translation and commentary "for the sons of craftsmen and soldiers" in Persian, not in Urdu.[3]

The most famous of his four sons, Shāh ᶜAbdu'l-ᶜAzīz (1746-1824), who is considered as his successor, also wrote only in Arabic and Persian.[4] It is a remarkable fact that his *fatāwā* are all drafted in Persian,[5] even those which deal with pressing political problems like the British conquest of Delhi in 1803[6] or those which treat of religious reform, a theme which was taken over by the Wahhabis.[7]

To be complete and accurate, we must however note that the use of Urdu for religious purposes was not completely unknown in Shāh Walīu'llāh's lineage: two of his other sons, Shāh Rafīᶜu'd-Dīn (1750-1818) and Shāh ᶜAbdu'l-Qādir (1753-1813), wrote translations and commentaries of the Quran in that language, in the last years of the 18th century.[8] These translations were used and printed by the later

2. Lelyveld, *Aligarh First Generation*, Princeton, 1978, pp. 49-53; G. Minault, *Voices of Silence. English Translation of Khwaja Altaf Hussain Hali's* Majlis un-Nissa *and* Chup ki Dad, Delhi, 1986, pp. 22-30 and 119-26.

3. Walīu'llāh Dihlawī, *Fathu'r-raḥmān bi-tarjamatu'l-Qur'ān* (1743), (Literal transl. and commentary of the Quran); J.M.S. Baljon, *Religion and Thought of Shāh Walī Allāh Dihlawi (1703-1762)*, Leiden, 1986, pp. 11 and 149.

4. S.A.A. Rizvi, *Shāh ᶜAbd al-ᶜAziz and his Time: Puritanism, Sectarianism, Polemics and Jihād*, Canberra, 1982, pp. 98-100, 580, 586-7.

5. ᶜAbdul-ᶜAzīz Dihlawī, *Fatāwā-yi Shāh ᶜAbdu'l-ᶜAzīz* (various dates), Delhi, 1893, *passim.*

6. Rizvi, *op. cit.*, pp. 225-44.

7. *Ibid.*, pp. 188-99

8. Sh. ᶜAbdu'l-Qādir Dihlawī, *Mūẓiḥu'l-Qur'ān* (1790), 1st known edn., Hoogli, 1829; Rafīᶜu'd-Dīn Dihlawī, Literal Urdu Translation of the Quran, 1786; see Rizvi, *op. cit.*, pp. 103-5.

reformers, including the Wahhabis, who considered Shāh Walīu'llāh's sons as forerunners of their movement.

1.2 From the Second Half of the 19th Century

After 1857, the ratio of Persian to Urdu is reversed. The use of Persian, though still a must in the *curriculum studiae* of respectable Muslims, becomes more and more rare. The common medium of expression now is Urdu, with frequent Arabic or Persian quotations, when needed for technical discussions or as a show of conspicuous erudition.

This is of course true of books of vulgarisation on religious subjects. Urdu had now become the medium of religious instruction for Muslims: learning to read and write that language became a must for all Muslims, as it had become a symbol of Muslim identity. Cheap editions of the Quran with an Urdu translation between the lines of the Arabic text became available everywhere. Popular textbooks in the same language multiplied. The two most popular of them, written in the beginning of the 20th century by scholars of the Deoband school have been recently studied and partially translated: a lengthy compendium for the education of women, called *Bihishtī zewar* by Ashraf ᶜAlī Thānawī (1863-1943),[9] and a short catechism entitled *Taᶜlīmu'l-islām* by Kifāyatu'llāh (1875-1952).[10]

Technical discussions and studies of religious matters were also from that time on conducted in Urdu, which had by then replaced Arabic and Persian. In the famous seminary of Deoband, founded in 1867, Urdu was the medium of instruction. The many collections of *fatāwā* which appeared from the second half of the 19th century onwards, were no longer in Persian unlike those of Shāh ᶜAbdu'l-ᶜAzīz, but in Urdu. It is very significant that the manifestos of the various theological schools which divided Sunni Muslims in the second half of the 19th century were in Urdu: for instance Sayyid Aḥmad K͟hān (1817-98) who had conducted controversies in Persian before 1857,[11] chose

---

9. B.D. Metcalf, *Perfecting Women: Maulana Ashraf Ali Thanawi's* Bihishti Zewar. *A Partial Translation with Commentary*, Berkeley, 1990.

10. M. Gaborieau, N. Grandin, P. Labrousse and A. Popovic, eds., *Dictionnaire biographique des savants et grandes figures du monde musulman périphérique*, Fasc. N° 1, Paris, 1992, pp. 14-5; Gaborieau, "The Transmission of Islamic Reformist Teachings to Rural South Asia. The Lessons of a Case Study", in H. Elboudrari, ed., *Modes de transmission de la culture religieuse en Islam*, Le Caire, 1993, pp. 132-41.

11. S.S. Aḥmad K͟hān, *Namīqa dar bayān-i mas'ala-yi taṣawwur-i shaik͟h* (1852), Aligarh, 1883; B. Lawrence, "Introduction" and "Mystical and Rational Elements in the Early Religious Writings of Sayyid Aḥmad Khan", in B. Lawrence, ed., *The Rose and the Rock: Mystical and Rational Elements in the Intellectual History of South Asian Islam*, Durham, 1979, pp. 3-13 and 61-103.

Urdu as the medium of expression for his revolutionary modernist theology;[12] and the debates raised by his doctrine were conducted in Urdu, as for example the *Taṣfiyyatu'l-ᶜaqā'id* written by Muḥammad Qāsim Nānautawī (1833-77) of the Deoband school.[13] It should finally be emphasized that for biographical literature (biographies and biographical dictionaries) concerning *ᶜulamā* and Sufis, Urdu quickly replaced Persian after 1857.[14]

The crucial time to understand the transition from Persian to Urdu is thus in between the two periods mentioned above, in the first half of the 19th century, when Persian progressively lost its importance to Urdu. We now turn to this period: we will first outline the contribution of the Wahhabis, and then we will place this contribution in a wider context to assess its originality.

2. The Contribution of the Wahhabis

2.1 A Historical Sketch of Indian Wahhabism

In 1818, after the British defeated the Marathas and demilitarized India, there appeared among the Indian Muslims two militant missionary movements which made extensive use of vernacular languages at the expense of Persian. They were collectively labelled as 'Wahhabis' by their adversaries and by later British officers such as William Hunter (d. 1900);[15] although their connection with the Arabian Wahhabis has been denied by many contemporary Muslim historians in India and Pakistan, there is little doubt in my mind that they had some link with the reform movements which emerged in the Near East at the turn of the 19th century.[16] The first Indian reform movement was that of the Farā'iẓis, whose influence was limited to Bengal, and who utilized Bengali more than Urdu;[17] they lie beyond the scope of this paper.

We are interested here in the second one, usually called Ṭarīqa-yi

12. Ch.W. Troll, *Sayyid Ahmad Khan: A Reinterpretation of Muslim Theology*, Delhi, 1978.

13. A. Ahmad and G. E. von Grunebaum, *Muslim Self-Statement in India and Pakistan*, Wiesbaden, 1970, pp. 5-6 and 60-76.

14. For a conspectus of this literature see Metcalf, *Islamic Revival in British India: Deoband 1860-1900*, Princeton, 1982, pp. 44, 214 and 338; Gaborieau *et al.*, *op. cit.*, pp. 3-22.

15. W. Hunter, *Our Indian Musulmans. Are they Bound in Conscience to Rebel against the Queen ?*, London, 1871; Repr., Varanasi, 1969.

16. Gaborieau, "A Nineteenth-Century Indian 'Wahhabi' Tract Against the Cult of Muslim Saints: *Al-Balagh al-Mubin*", in Troll, ed., *Muslim Shrines in India. Their Character, History and Significance*, Delhi, 1989, pp. 198-239.

17. M.A. Khan, *History of the Fara'idi Movement in Bengal, 1818-1906*, Karachi, 1965; 2nd edn., Dhaka, 1984.

Muḥammadiyya, or the Mujāhidīn movement.[18] It was founded by Sayyid Aḥmad Barelwī (1786-1831), a mystical and charismatic figure, with the help of his main disciple, the scholar and ideologist Ismāᶜīl Shahīd (1779-1831) who was a most prolific writer. In 1818 they started preaching against the cult of Muslim saints, against rites and customs borrowed from the Hindus, and all kinds of customs they deemed contrary to the pure monotheism of the Holy Prophet and his Companions. In 1822-24 Sayyid Aḥmad Barelwī and about six hundred of his disciples made a pilgrimage to Mecca. In 1826, with thousands of his followers he embarked on a holy war (*jihād*). Leaving British territory, they travelled through Sind and Afghanistan to attack from the rear the Sikhs who were then the masters of the Indus valley. After establishing a short-lived theocratic state in the North West Frontier, Sayyid Aḥmad and Ismāᶜīl Shahīd were defeated and killed by the Sikhs in Balakot in 1831.

By that time, they had produced a corpus of doctrinal and missionary literature and established a network of missionaries all over India, some of whom were also prolific writers. Several of them like Wilāyat ᶜAlī of Patna (1790-1852), continued the armed struggle; others remained content with peaceful missionary activies such as Karāmat ᶜAlī Jaunpūrī (1800-73). Finally, other scholars, without being full members of the movement, participated in the growth of Wahhabi literature. Prominent among the latter is Sayyid Aḥmad K͟hān. Before elaborating his modernist theology, he wrote several tracts between 1841 and 1852, inspired by Wahhabi teachings.[19] Finally the Wahhabis engaged in lively controversies with their opponents: an impressive number of refutations and counter-refutations were written from the beginning of the movement.

All these books constitute an important corpus in Arabic, Persian and Urdu: they can be viewed from the perspective of the topic studied here, that is the transition from Persian to Urdu. What is the relative status of the three languages used in this literature ? How far did the Wahhabis contribute to the promotion of Urdu at the expense of Persian ?

2.2 The Importance of Oral Expression

Before examining written works, we must stress the importance of oral expression for the members of the Wahhabi movement. They were first of all missionaries, and many of their works originated from their

18. Q. Ahmad, *The Wahhabi Movement in India*, Calcutta, 1966.
19. Troll, *Sayyid Ahmad Khan...*, *op. cit*, pp. 28-57.

preaching in the mosques of Delhi and in the towns and the countryside of the Gangetic Valley down to Calcutta from where they embarked for the Meccan pilgrimage. Since Persian was at that time no longer a spoken language in India, and was besides not understood by the common people they wanted to reach, preaching had necessarily to be done in Urdu. Indeed, some of the Urdu tracts attributed to Sayyid Aḥmad Barelwī are just transcriptions of lectures he gave.[20] It has been argued by scholars that it is only from that time, with the popularity of the Wahhabi preachers, that Urdu became an authorized language to discuss and explain religious matters.[21] This phenomenon may be compared to what happened in politics in the second half of the 19th century when speeches in vernacular languages became an acceptable genre for the elite.[22] The form of these preachings can only be tentatively reconstructed from the testimony of the disciples and biographers of Sayyid Aḥmad Barelwī.[23]

2.3 Writing and Printing

Fortunately, the writings of these movements have been better preserved. They were, of course, like the works of preceding generations, kept in princely or scholarly libraries. Many of them, though not all, also had the privilege of being amongst the first Muslim religious books ever to be printed, or rather lithographed. Most Muslim countries refused to use the printing press until late in the 19th century. The only exceptions were the Ottoman Empire, India and Tsarist Russia, where, in the latter two cases, Muslims started printing religious books in the first quarter of the 19th century.[24] The Wahhabis were among the first Muslims in India to avail themselves of this new technology, in the same way as they used steamboats for the pilgrimage and firearms for their *jihād*. On his way back from the *ḥajj* in 1824, Sayyid Aḥmad Barelwī established a printing press in Calcutta with the help of his

20. S. Aḥmad Shahīd Barelwī, *Ḥaqīqatu'ṣ-ṣalāt* (based on a lecture made in 1817-18), n.d. and Exegesis of the Sūra *Fātiḥa* (1822), published in M.ᶜA. Chishtī, "Tafsīr sūra-yi fātiḥa", *Ar-Raḥīm*, Sept. 1965, pp. 263-4; see Rizvi, *op. cit.*, p. 508.

21. H.O. Pearson, "Islamic Reform in the Nineteenth Century: the 'Tariqa-i Muḥammadiyya'", Ph.D. Dissertation, Durham, Duke Univ., 1979, p. 139; Lelyveld, "Eloquence and Authority in Urdu...", *op. cit.*, 105-6.

22. Lelyveld, "Eloquence and Authority in Urdu...", *op. cit.*, pp. 106-8.

23. Chishtī, "Sayyid Aḥmad Shahīd-kī tahrīk-kā aṣar Urdū adab par", *Ar-Raḥīm*, Feb. 1966, pp. 636-58; March 1966, pp. 705-20; April 1966, pp. 798-803; Rizvi, *op. cit.*, pp. 498 and 508.

24. F. Robinson, "Technology and Religious Change: Islam and the Impact of Print", *Modern Asian Studies*, 1993, Vol. XXVII, N° 1, pp. 229-51.

disciple ᶜAbdu'llāh.[25] Eight years later, a British judge, J.R. Colvin, testified to the fact that Wahhabi tracts and books in Persian and Urdu were available in good number in the bazaars.[26] The first Muslim newspapers also appeared in the 1830s.[27] According to British administrators, the market for religious books in India in the 19th century was dominated by Muslims.[28]

How can we classify the Wahhabi texts, both those which were printed and those which were not ? What languages were used for each category of text ?

2.4 *Books of Vulgarization*

A great part of the literature printed in the period under examination was specially written to popularize religious knowledge among people who lacked formal education (i.e. did not know Persian or Arabic). This point is noted by some of the reformers themselves in the preface to their books; they identified these uneducated people not in terms of social class but of age and sex. This literature is intended, they say, not only for men but also for children and women.[29] In 1854, the Austrian orientalist, Aloys Sprenger (1813-93) who was then working in Calcutta, Lucknow and Delhi, also remarked in the preface to his catalogue of the books in the library of the Nawwāb of Awadh that this new literature considerably enlarged the circle of those who had access to religious education:

> "The number of works lithographed at Lucknow and Cawnpore may amount to about seven hundred [...] The books most in request are of course school books and such other dialectical and religious tracts as every Mawlavy reads or pretends to read. But we may observe symptoms that the press is enlarging the narrow circle of learning and - what is more important - that it extends education to all classes and even to ladies [...] After the Musalmans had, several centuries ago, entirely lost

---

25. J.H.S.V, Garcin de Tassy, *Histoire de la littérature hindouie et hindoustanie* (1839-47), Three Vols., 2nd edn., Paris, 1870-71; Repr. New York, n.d., Vol. I, art. 'Abdullah', pp. 81-7, Vol. III, art. 'Saiyid Aḥmad', pp. 32-7; M. Aḥmad, *Saiyid Aḥmad Shahid. His Life and Mission*, Lucknow, 1975, pp. 312-3.

26. J.R.C. [C = Colvin], "Notice on the Peculiar Tenets held by the Followers of Syed Ahmed, taken chiefly from the "Siràt-ul-Mùstaqìm", A Principle Treatise of that Sect, written by Moulavi Mahommed Ismail", *Journal of the Royal Asiatic Society of Bengal*, 1832, Vol. I, Nº 11, p. 494.

27. Robinson, *op. cit.*, p. 240.

28. Metcalf, *op. cit.*, pp. 198-203.

29. Khurram ᶜAlī Bilhaurī, *Naṣīḥātu'l-muslimīn* (1822), 1st known edn., Calcutta, 1848, pp. 28-9; Karāmat ᶜAlī Jaunpūrī, *Miftāḥu'l-jannat* (1827), Lucknow, 1954, pp. 6-7; also see Metcalf, *Islamic Revival in British India...*, *op. cit.*, pp. 199-201.

sight of the original ideas of their religion, they are now beginning to make their sacred books intelligible to all. This must lead to results analogous to those which the translation and study of the Bible produced in Europe".[30]

As far as language is concerned, one finds in these books Arabic, Persian, Urdu and even Hindi in Devanagari script;[31] Bengali also became common in Eastern India.[32] But all these languages did not have the same status. Arabic was limited to the text of the Quran and Traditions. According to Garcin de Tassy, these were the first printed versions of the Arabic text of the Quran in the Muslim world. The first known edition, with ᶜAbdu'l-Qādir's translation, appeared in 1829.[33] Qurans are by far the best represented in the Western collections of manuscripts and prints of this time.[34] While the Arabic texts on their own could be printed for scholars, in popular editions of the Quran and the Traditions, a Persian, and later more commonly, an Urdu translation was inserted between the lines of the Arabic text in a fashion long attested in Iran and still common in India.

Persian was still used for vulgarization among people who did not belong to the circle of the *ᶜulamā*. Persian translations of the Quran and of the Traditions were printed at that time.[35] Popular books in Persian were also composed.[36] They were soon accompanied by Urdu translations which were this time printed, not between the lines, but in the lower half of each page.[37]

But by far the most common books in this category were those written directly in Urdu. The earliest dated one, that we are aware of, is the *Naṣīhātu'l-muslimin* of K͟hurram ᶜAlī Bilhaurī (d. 1855) which was composed in 1822-23, but printed rather late in 1848. In the wake of the *Taqwiyyatu'l-imān* of Ismāᶜīl Shahīd (see § 2.5), which was composed in 1824 and printed soon after, popular books in Urdu

30. A. Sprenger, *A Catalogue of the Arabic, Persian and Hindustani Manuscripts of the Libraries of the King of Oudh*, Vol. I, *Persian and Hindustani Poetry*, Calcutta, 1854; quoted from the repr. edn., Osnabrück, 1979, pp. xii-xiii.

31. K.A. Fārūqī, *Urdu men wahhābī adab*, Delhi, 1969, pp. 24-5, 38, 50; Q. Ahmad, "The Missionary Literature of the Wahhabis: Its Historical Significance", in Troll, ed., *Islam in India. Studies and Commentaries*, Vol. I, Delhi, 1982, p. 15.

32. M.A. Khan, *op. cit.*

33. ᶜAbdu'l-Qādir Dihlawī, *op. cit.*

34. See e.g. J.F. Blumhardt, *Catalogue of the Hindustani Printed Books in the Library of the British Museum*, London, 1889 and *Catalogue of the Hindustani Manuscripts in the Library of the India Office*, London, 1926.

35. Sprenger, *loc. cit.*

36. e.g. M. Wilāyat ᶜAlī, *ᶜAmal bi'l-ḥadīs̤* (c. 1837), (Transl. into Urdu by Ilāhī Bak͟hsh).

37. Q. Aḥmad, "The Missionary Literature of the Wahhabis...", *op. cit.*, p. 56.

flourished and were lithographed in large numbers.[38] The early religious works in Urdu of Sayyid Aḥmad Kh̲ān may also be placed in this category.[39]

2.5 Statements of the Doctrine

A second category of books was constituted by those works which offered a learned statement of the doctrine of the school. Here, Persian comes first. The first manifesto of the Wahhabi movement, the *Ṣirāt̤u'l-mustaqim* which was compiled around 1818, was written in Persian, as was a short account of the mystical doctrine of Sayyid Aḥmad Barelwī, accompanied with his Sufi genealogy.[40] The political doctrine of the movement is also stated in a treatise, the *Manṣab-i imāmat*[41] and in the letters of Sayyid Aḥmad Barelwī;[42] both are in Persian. Several other Persian tracts are also attributed to these two leaders of the Wahhabi movement.

Ismā^cīl Shahīd, a great scholar of his time, was also a prolific writer in Arabic. His *^cAbaqāt* is a learned exposition of his mystical theosophy.[43] The *Radd al-ishrāk*[44] which was never published, is said to be a first version of the *Taqwiyyatu'l-imān.*[45] Several other books in Arabic are also attributed to him. As no proper study has yet been done of their content and of their impact, it is difficult to gauge their importance.

We are fortunately better informed about the content and the impact of the second manifesto of the movement, the *Taqwiyyatu'l-imān* which was written in 1824 and soon published. It expresses with vigour

---

38. A.A. Orainwī, *Bihār men urdū zabān o adab-kā irtiqā*, Patna, 1957; Chishtī, "Sayyid Aḥmad Shahīd-kī tahrīk-kā aṣar...", *op. cit.*; Fārūqī, *op. cit.*; Q. Aḥmad, *The Wahhabi Movement in India, op. cit.* and "The Missionary Literature of the Wahhabis...", *op. cit.*

39. Aḥmad Kh̲ān, *Jilāu'l-qulūb bi-z̤ikri'l-Maḥbūb* (1841), Aligarh, 1883; Aḥmad Kh̲ān, *Kalimatu'l-ḥaqq* (1849), Lahore, 1962 and Aḥmad Kh̲ān, *Rāh-i sunnat dar radd-i bid^ca* (1850), Lahore, 1962.

40. Sh.M. Ismā^cīl Shahīd, *Ṣirāt̤u'l-mustaqīm* (c. 1818), Delhi, 1904; Aḥmad Shahīd Barelwī, *Risāla-yi ashgh̲āl* (1827), Urdu Transl. published by Sayyid Nafīs Ḥusainī, Lahore, 1399/1978.

41. Ismā^cīl Shahīd, *Manṣab-i imāmat* (c. 1827), Delhi, n.d.

42. Aḥmad Shahīd Barelwī, *Makātib* (Various dates), Lahore, 1975 (Reproduction of the Lahore manuscript); for other manuscripts, see Appendix.

43. Ismā^cīl Shahīd, *^cAbaqāt* (n.d.), Arabic Text, Karachi, 1380/1960; Urdu Transl. by M.H. Gilānī, Hyderabad, n.d.

44. Ismā^cīl Shahīd, *Radd al-ishrāk* (c. 1823), Manuscript, Asafiyya Collection, Andhra Pradesh Government Oriental Manuscripts Library & Research Institute, Hyderabad.

45. Rizvi, *op. cit.*, p. 509; Ismā^cīl Shahīd, *Taqwiyyatu'l-imān* (1824), 1st printed in the 1820s, numerous editions.

the Wahhabi conception of pure monotheism and its struggle to eradicate all kinds of *shirk* (i.e. Worship of beings other than Allāh, such as Muslim saints or Hindu gods) and *bidᶜa* (i.e. Innovations, religious practices not in use in the time of the Prophet and His companions). It aroused a well-known controversy (see § 2.6). It is to be emphasized that this is the first book in which a theological doctrine was expressed in Urdu. It must be mentioned too, that the *Ṣirāṭu'l-mustaqīm* was also translated into Urdu in 1824 and printed several times. Thus the two manifestos of the movement were available in Urdu.

Although Persian remained the most important language to express the doctrine of the Wahhabis, the publication of the *Taqwiyyatu'l-imān* and of the translation of the *Ṣirāṭu'l-mustaqīm*, raised Urdu to the level of an authoritative language to express a theological doctrine.

2.6 Controversies

A survey of the controversies raised by these two manifestos lead me to similar conclusions. Arabic texts are attested too, but have not yet been properly studied.[46]

The earliest and most substantial refutations of the Wahhabi doctrine were written in Persian. They consist mainly of three books. The first one was written around 1822 by a Shia, Musharraf ᶜAlī who accused Sayyid Aḥmad Barelwī and his disciples of propagating in India the violence of the Arabian Wahhabis.[47] Two years later, after the *Taqwiyyatu'l-imān* was first circulated, the most well-known series of polemics between the Wahhabis and the Sunni theologians of Delhi erupted. Among several others, two books have remained famous: one is a thick detailed refutation of the Wahhabi refusal to believe in intercession and of their belief in the possibility of God creating other Prophets;[48] and a short pamphlet of Ismāᶜīl Shahīd in defence of his own theories.[49] Similarly a large amount of polemical literature in Persian against the Wahhabis was produced by the Naqshbandi Sufis of

---

46. e.g. Ismāᶜīl Shahīd, *Tanwīr al-ᶜainain fī iṣbāt rafᶜal-yadain* (n.d.), published with the Urdu Transl. and commentary, Lahore, 1882; S.D.Kh. Azurda, *Muntaha'l-maqāl fī sharḥ ḥadīṣ "lā tashudd al-riḥāl..."* (n.d.), (A refutation of the objections of Ibn Taimiyya against the cult of Muslim saints); M. Maḥbūb ᶜAlī, *Tārīkhu'l-ā'imma fī ẕikr khulafāi'l-ummat* (1828-35), Manuscript, Indian Institute of Islamic Studies, Delhi.

47. S.ᶜA. Musharraf ᶜAlī, *Izāhat al-ghayy fī radd-i ᶜAbd al-Ḥayy* (c. 1822), Manuscript, Khuda Bakhsh Oriental Public Library, Patna; Rizvi, *op. cit.*, pp. 498 and 517.

48. Fazl-i Ḥaqq Khairābādī, *Taḥqīq al-fatwā fī ibṭāl at-taghwa* (1825), with an Urdu Transl., Sargodha, 1979; Rizvi, *op. cit.*, pp. 518-22.

49. Ismāᶜīl Shahīd, *Risāla-yi yak rozī* (c. 1825), Manuscript, India Office Library, London; Rizvi, *op. cit.*, p. 518.

Delhi;[50] Sayyid Aḥmad Khān also vindicated the Naqshbandi view on a technical point - the liceity of the meditation on the image of one's Shaikh - by issuing a short tract in Persian.[51]

But it is interesting to note that the controversy did not remain confined to the Persian medium: the first Urdu polemical tracts appeared before 1857. An early refutation of the *Taqwiyyatu'l-imān* was printed in the 1820s.[52] Similarly a book of Karāmat ᶜAlī Jaunpūrī was refuted in the very year it was published.[53] It seems that Urdu was most widely used for controversies from that time on in the Eastern regions of Bihar and Bengal.[54] In the Western provinces, if one reads the catalogues of libraries with important collections of Wahhabi literature like that of Tonk,[55] one realizes that polemical literature written in Urdu before 1857 was still not very abundant and came rather late in the 1850s in the form of original works[56] or as translations of earlier tracts in Persian.[57] But the pro- and anti-Wahhabi polemical literature in Urdu was to grow considerably after 1857; indeed, it is still being produced.[58]

2.7 Letters and Hagiography

In the records left by the Wahhabis before 1857, Persian predominates. The correspondence of both Sayyid Aḥmad Barelwī and Ismāᶜīl Shahīd is written in that language.[59] The hagiography of the move-

---

50. Sh. Aḥmad Saᶜīd, *Risāla al-fawā'id al-ẓabiṭa fi iṣbāt al-rābiṭa* (n.d.), Manuscript; *Saᶜīd al-bayān fi muwallid sayyid al-uns wa'l-jān* (n.d.), Kanpur, n.d.; *Taḥqīq al-ḥaqq al-mubīn fi ajwibat masā'il arbaᶜīn* (n.d.), ed. H. Maḥmud az-Zamān, Hyderabad (Sind), 1966; W. Fusfeld, "The Shaping of Sufi Leadership in Delhi: The Naqshbandiyya Mujaddiyya, 1750-1920", Ph.D. Thesis, Philadelphia, Univ. of Pennsylvania, 1981 (Unpublished) and "The Boundaries of Islam and Infidelity" in K.P. Ewing, ed., *op. cit.*, pp. 205-19.

51. Aḥmad Khān, *Namīqa...*, *op. cit.*; Lawrence, *op. cit.*

52. Anonymous, *Ibṭāl-i taqwiyyatu'l-imān*, n.d.

53. Karāmat ᶜAlī Jaunpūrī, *Quwwatu'l-imān*, Calcutta, 1837; ᶜAbdu'l-Jabbār, *Radd-i quwwatu'l-imān* (1837), Manuscript, Dhaka.

54. M.A. Khan, *op. cit.*, pp. lii-lviii.

55. Sh.ᶜA. Khan, *Qasr-i ᶜilm. A Bibliographical Survey of Arabic and Persian Rare Works of Tonk*, Tonk, 1980 and *Khazinatu'l-makhtutat. A Descriptive Catalogue of the Arabic, Persian and Urdu Manuscripts in the Arabic and Persian Research Institute, Rajasthan, Tonk*, Tonk, 1985.

56. Muḥammad Murtaẓā Khān Ṭonkī, *Dafiᶜu'l'fasād* (1853), Manuscript, Arabic and Persian Research Institute, Tonk.

57. Sirāj Aḥmad al-Sahasawī, *Sirāju'l-imān* (1824), Manuscript, Arabic and Persian Research Institute, Tonk.

58. A.H.Z. Fārūqī, *Maulānā Ismāᶜil Shahid aur Taqwiyyatu'l-imān*, Delhi, 1984; A.H. Qāsimī, *Shāh Ismāᶜīl aur un-ke nāqid* (n.d.), Bhera, District Sargodha, 1984.

59. Aḥmad Shahīd Barelwī, *Makātib*, *op. cit.*; Ismāᶜīl Shahīd, *Makātib-i Maulānā Muḥammad Ismāᶜil* (various dates), Manuscript (compiled in 1828), Arabic and Persian Research Institute, Tonk; Manuscript (compiled in 1879), Bhopal; Manuscript, Nadwatu'l-ᶜulama Library, ᶜAbdu'l-Hayy Collection, Lucknow.

ment[60] was also first written in Persian, as for instance the *Makhzan-i Aḥmadī* and the *Tārīkh-i Aḥmadiyya*, the earliest books on the subject.[61] Even after 1857, the bulk of the hagiography is to be found in Persian. Biographical accounts in Urdu before 1857 are few: the first known ones are the biographies of Sayyid Aḥmad Barelwī and of Ismāᶜīl Shahīd in the description of Delhi published in 1847 by Sayyid Aḥmad Khān.[62] The first full biography of Sayyid Aḥmad Barelwī in Urdu was written after 1884 and published as late as 1891.[63]

2.8 Apocryphal Texts

In the second half of the 19th century, Urdu was increasingly used to express their doctrine by the theological schools which were the heirs of the Wahhabis, particularly Deoband and the Ahl-i ḥadīṣ. But they would still resort to Persian for special purposes. I happen to have studied in detail the case of such a late use of Persian.[64] Two pamphlets explaining very thoroughly the Wahhabi objections to the cult of Muslim saints were widely circulated and often lithographed. They were attributed to the 18th century scholar Shāh Walīu'llāh (1703-62) and respectively called *Al-balāghu'l-mubīn* and *Tuḥfatu'l-muwaḥḥidīn*;[65] the second text, in what may not be a coincidence, bears the same title as an early book in Persian by the Hindu reformer Ram Mohan Roy (1772-1833), who wanted to purify Hinduism from idolatrous cults and to reduce it to a pure monotheism.[66] When carefully analysed, they proved to be, on stylistic and doctrinal grounds, late 19th century fabrications. Their unknown author (or authors) must have belonged to the Ahl-i ḥadīṣ school, since no other group, not even the Deobandis consider them authentic.[67] The use of the Persian language, as well as the attribution to Shāh Walīu'llāh, served as marks of author-

60. See Gh.R. Mehr, *Sayyid Aḥmad Shahīd*, Two Vols. bound together, Lahore, 1952-54, Vol. I, pp. 12-26; Q. Ahmad, *The Wahhabi Movement in India, op. cit*, pp. xi-xx.

61. S. Muḥammad ᶜAli, *Makhzan-i Aḥmadī* (1845), 1st printed, Agra, 1881; S. Jaᶜfar ᶜAlī Naqwī, *Manẓūratu's-suᶜadā fi ahwāli'l-ghazāt wa'sh-shuhadā* (1855), Manuscripts, Lahore, Tonk, Lucknow.

62. Aḥmad Khān, *Aṣāru's-Sanādīd*, Delhi, Maṭbaᶜ-i Aḥmadī, 1847; Reprint by Khalīq Anjum, Delhi, 1990, pp. 35-8 and 86-91.

63. Muḥammad Jaᶜfar Thānesarī, *Sawāniḥi Aḥmadī* (1891), Delhi, 1891; new edn., Karachi, 1968, under the title *ḥayāt-i Sayyid Aḥmad Shahīd*.

64. Gaborieau, "A Nineteenth-Century Indian ᶜWahhabi' Tract Against the Cult of Muslim Saints: *Al-Balagh al-Mubin*", *op. cit*.

65. Pseudo-Walīu'llāh Dihlawī, *Al-Balāghu'l-mubīn fi ittibāᶜi khātamu'l-nabiyin* (n.d.), (1st known edn., Lahore, c. 1890), Lahore, 1962 and *Tuḥfatu'l-muwaḥḥidīn* (n.d.), (1st known edn., Delhi, c. 1912), Lahore, 1962.

66. R.M. Roy, *Tuḥfatu'l-muwaḥḥidīn* (1803), Repr., Calcutta, 1859.

67. Sh.ᶜA. Khan, *Khazinatu'l-makhtutat, op. cit.*, p. 201.

ity and antiquity for a rather recent doctrine. These two texts may be considered as the last doctrinal production of the Wahhabis in Persian.

2.9. Conclusion

Although the Wahhabis did play a part in promoting Urdu, this language was not their main medium of expression before 1857. Learned and lay business was still mainly conducted in Persian, which also remained the most common medium of controversy and hagiography. The use of Urdu was still in most cases confined to vulgarization; but, with the release in 1824 of the *Taqwiyyatu'l-imān* and the controversies which followed, it surfaced as a means of expressing a religious doctrine.

3. Other Promoters of Urdu

The Wahhabis thus played a role in promoting Urdu at the expense of Persian, but they were not the only ones to do so. In order to evaluate their contribution, a word must be said about the other promoters of the new medium. We have already noted (§ 1.1) that the sons of Shāh Walīu'llāh, in the last decades of the 18th century, had already used Urdu for the translation of and commentary on the Quran. It must also be kept in mind that when, in 1835, the British dropped Persian as the official language of the East India Company, they promoted both English and the vernacular languages (including Urdu), in administration and education. Besides them, two other promoters were active in the first part of the 19th century; we may begin however with the Company.

3.1 Early East India Company Texts

If one sets apart the family of Shāh Walīu'llāh and a few pioneering Muslim authors in various Muslim courts, chronologically, the first promoter of Urdu prose was the East India Company after the establishment in Calcutta of Fort William College by Lord Wellesley in 1800. There, John B. Gilchrist (1759-1841), professor of Hindustani and the author of a grammar and a dictionary for that language, encouraged Muslim scholars in his service to write and publish works in simple Urdu prose. The *Bāgh o Bahār*, the story of the four dervishes written in 1801 by Mīr Amman of Delhi has remained famous.[68] This phase also witnessed the publication of the first history of India in Urdu called

68. A. Schimmel, *Classical Urdu Literature from the Beginning to Iqbal*, Wiesbaden, 1975, pp. 210-1.

Arā'ish-i maḥfil, by Afsos (1736-1809).[69] A less well-known activity of Fort William is relevant for our purpose: Gilchrist commissioned a group of Muslim scholars, including Arabicists, to produce an Urdu translation of the Quran. It was completed and fifty-six pages were already printed in 1805, when the Governor-General, probably for fear of orthodox opposition, stopped the project and the work was destroyed.[70] Thus, while the East India Company encouraged the writing and printing of Persian works, it also stood as a promoter and model for the diffusion of simple Urdu prose, even in the religious field.

3.2 Christian Missionaries

In the religious field, however, the greatest challenge came from Christian missionaries. In the Mughal period, Christian missionaries who were called to the court of Akbar (1556-1605) and his successors, had used Persian to translate the Gospel.[71] This continued up to the beginning of the 19th century when, for instance, the Persian apologetic book of Carl Gottlieb Pfander (1803-65), the *Mīzānu'l-Ḥaqq*, known all over the Eastern Muslim world, was widely discussed and refuted.[72]

But in the first two decades of the 19th century, missionaries resorted more and more to Urdu: a translation of the Bible had been made as early as 1741 by German protestant missionaries.[73] An Anglican missionary, Henry Martyn (1781-1812), the author of many missionary tracts, composed another Urdu translation of the Gospel published in 1814.[74] The year 1813 marked yet another important step: the East India Company lifted all restrictions on the proselytism of Christian missionaries and from then, translations of the Bible in vernacular languages were printed from Serampore in Bengal. When Pfander came to India in 1838, he had his Persian book translated into Urdu.[75] Northern India, and especially the Delhi-Agra area, witnessed vivid contests between Christian missionaries and Muslim divines through printed pamphlets and oral debates.[76]

---

69. M.Sh.ᶜA. Afsos, *Ārā'ish-1 maḥfil,* Calcutta, 1808; Garcin de Tassy, *Histoire de la littérature hindouie et hindoustanie*, *op. cit.*, Vol. I, pp. 120-36.

70. Rizvi, *op. cit.*, p. 62.

71. Troll, *Sayyid Ahmad Khan...*, *op. cit.*, pp. 58-9; E.R. Hambye, "The First Jesuit Mission to Emperor Akbar", in Ch.W. Troll, ed. *Islam in India*, *op. cit.*, Vol. I, 1982, pp. 9-10.

72. Troll, *Sayyid Ahmad Khan...*, *op. cit.*, p. 61.

73. Schimmel, *Classical Urdu Literature...*, *op. cit.*, p. 205.

74. *Loc. cit.*

75. Troll, *Sayyid Ahmad Khan...*, *op. cit.*, p. 61.

76. *Ibid.*, pp. 60-70.

The influence of the missionaries on the young Sayyid Aḥmad Khān is attested.[77] Was it also felt earlier by the Wahhabis who started their missionary activity in 1818 ? Did it act as an incentive to write and print Quran translations and popular tracts in Urdu ? This is a matter of controversy: some scholars would argue for such an influence;[78] others would be inclined to deny it.[79] No direct evidence is available, but in this context, seeing how quickly the Wahhabis appropriated the methods and means of the Christian missionaries, such an influence is most plausible (see above § 2.3).

3.3. Early Scientific Texts

Later, another incentive from the British side also contributed to raise the status of Urdu at the expense of Persian. This was the encouragement to translate scientific texts from English, or even to write them directly in Urdu. Till the beginning of the 19th century, Persian had been the usual medium of scientific publications. From about 1825 people gravitating around Delhi College,[80] or belonging to several learned societies started using Urdu.[81] One of the first archaeological and historical works published in Urdu was the *Āṣāru'ṣ-ṣanādid* of Sayyid Aḥmad Khān on the antiquities of Delhi.[82] It contains, as we have seen above (§ 2.7), the first biographies of the Wahhabi leaders.

General Conclusion

From the above survey it is clear that, in the process of the transition from Persian to Urdu, the Wahhabis were no radical innovators: scholars of Shāh Walīu'llāh's family and men of letters in various Muslim courts, the East India Company, Christian missionaries, and learned societies all played their part in progressively substituting Urdu for Persian as an authoritative language.

But as Garcin de Tassy emphasized long ago, the Wahhabis were prompt in joining the movement and using, for proselytization, all the means offered by their epoch.

But, for the Wahhabis before 1857, the transition from Persian to Urdu was not yet complete. Urdu in this period remained mainly con-

---

77. *Loc. cit.*
78. Schimmel, *Classical Urdu Literature...*, *op. cit.*, p. 205.
79. Rizvi, *op. cit.*, p. 104.
80. Metcalf, *Islamic Revival in British India...*, *op. cit.*, pp. 73-4.
81. Troll, *Sayyid Ahmad Khan...*, *op. cit.*, pp. 63-4.
82. Troll, "A Note on the Early Topographical Work of Sayyid Aḥmad Khān: *Āṣār al-ṣanādīd*", *Journal of the Royal Asiatic Society*, 1972, N° 2, pp. 135-46.

fined to vulgarization. The bulk of literature they produced in the period was in Persian, which was still considered as a more authoritative language to discuss technical and religious matters.

If we judge the 1818-57 period in retrospect, we also see that Urdu was not the only heir to Persian. From what we have written above (§ 3.3), it would seem that Urdu was destined to become not only a religious language, but also a scientific language. This did not happen: in this latter field, its place was taken by English. This may be illustrated by an anecdote: Sayyid Aḥmad Khān had been one of the promoters of scientific Urdu prose in his youth; later in his life he advocated the use of English, which was the medium of instruction in the Aligarh College which he founded in 1875. In 1863, he made a speech in Calcutta to encourage Indian Muslims to learn foreign languages and sciences: the speech was however in Persian ![83] Urdu was bypassed: a direct shift was made from Persian to English.

In the religious field, however, the Wahhabi episode had a lasting legacy. Urdu became the medium and symbol of religious education for all South Asian Muslims and not only for the popular classes: it became the medium of instruction in the seminary of Deoband. Early Urdu texts of Ismāᶜīl Shahīd, Karāmat ᶜAlī Jaunpurī, etc. are still recommended, often reprinted, easily available in the bazaars and found even in remote villages.

On the other hand, today, Persian texts are very difficult to find. In the bazaars one finds easily the Urdu translation of the *Ṣirāṭu'l-mustaqīm*, but the Persian original has not been reprinted in India since 1904.[84]

83. Lelyveld, "Eloquence and Authority in Urdu...", *op. cit.*, p. 106.

84. Gaborieau, "Mission en Inde, au Bangladesh et au Népal", *La transmission du savoir dans le monde musulman périphérique, Lettre d'information N° 13*, Paris, 1993, pp. 2 and 6-7.

Appendix

Works in Arabic, Persian and Urdu

In this appendix, the date given before each title is that of composition, not of publication. When the date of composition is not available, the title is preceded by the mention "n.d.". When possible, the location of manuscripts, and/or place and date of the most commonly-known editions have been indicated after the title. Arabic, Persian and Urdu works are listed separately.

ᶜAbdu'l-ᶜAzīz Dihlawī, Shāh (1746-1824)
[Persian]
Various dates: *Fatāwā-yi Shāh ᶜAbdu'l-ᶜAziz*, Delhi: Mujtabā'ī Press, 1893.

ᶜAbdu'l-Jabbār, Maulwī
[Urdu]
1837: *Radd-i quwwatu'l-imān*, Manuscript, Dhaka.
1840: *Taqwiyyatu'l-muslimīn fī ittibāᶜ-i sunnat-i Sayyid al-mursalīn*, Calcutta.

ᶜAbdu'l-Qādir Dihlawī, Shāh (1753-1813)
[Urdu]
1790: *Mūẓihu'l-Qur'ān*, 1st known edn., Hoogli, 1829.

Afsos, Mīr Sher ᶜAlī (1736-1809)
[Urdu]
1805: *Ārā'ish-i Maḥfil*, Calcutta, 1808.

Aḥmad Khān, Sir Sayyid (1817-98)
[Persian]
1852: *Namīqa dar bayān-i mas'ala-yi taṣawwur-i shaikh*, Aligarh, 1883.

[Urdu]
1841: *Jilāu'l-qulūb bi-ẕikri'l-Maḥbūb*, Aligarh, 1883.
1847: *Āṣāru'ṣ-Ṣanādīd*, Delhi: Maṭbaᶜ-i Aḥmadī, 2nd rev. edn., 1854; Repr. of the 1st edn. by Khalīq Anjum, Three Vols.,

Delhi: Urdu Academy, 1990.
1849: *Kalimatu'l-ḥaqq*, Lahore, 1962.
1850: *Rāh-i sunnat dar radd-i bidᶜa*, Lahore, 1962.

Aḥmad Saᶜīd, Shāh (1802-60)
[Persian]
n.d.: *Risāla al-fawā'id al-ẓabiṭa fī iṣbāt al-rābiṭa*, Manuscript.
n.d.: *Saᶜīd al-bayān fī muwallid sayyid al-uns wa'l-jān*, Kanpur: Shams al-Maṭabiᶜ.
n.d.: *Taḥqīq al-ḥaqq al-mubīn fī ajwibat masā'il arbaᶜīn* (n.d.), ed. Ḥakīm Maḥmud az-Zamān, Hyderabad (Sind), 1966.

Aḥmad Shahīd Barelwī, Sayyid (1786-1831)
[Persian]
n.d.: *Risāla dar namāz wa ᶜibādāt.*
n.d.: *Risāla dar nikāḥ-i ᶜaqd-i bīwagān.*
Various dates: *Makātib*, Lahore: Maktaba Rashīdiyya, 1975 (Reproduction of the Lahore manuscript). Other manuscript recensions: Arabic and Persian Research Institute, Tonk, Salar Jung Library, Hyderabad and British Museum, London.
1827: *Risāla-yi ashghāl*, (Urdu Transl. published by Sayyid Nafīs Ḥusainī, Lahore: Maktaba Maḥmūdiyya, 1399/1978).

[Urdu]
n.d.: *Ḥaqīqatu'ṣ-ṣalāt* (based on a lecture made in 1817-18).
1822: Exegesis of the Sūra *Fātiḥa*, published in M.ᶜA. Chishtī, "Tafsīr sūra-yi fātiḥa", *Ar-Raḥīm*, Sept. 1965, pp. 263-4.

Anonymous
[Urdu]
n.d.: *Ibṭāl-i taqwiyyatu'l-imān.*

Āzurda, Ṣadru'd-Dīn Khān (1789-1868)
[Arabic]
n.d.: *Muntaha'l-maqāl fī sharḥ hadīṣ "lā tashudd al-riḥāl..."* (A refutation of the objections of Ibn Taimiyya against the cult of Muslim saints).

Fārūqī, Abu'l-Ḥasan Zaid
[Urdu]
1984: *Maulānā Ismāᶜil Shahīd aur Taqwiyyatu'l-imān*, Delhi: Shāh Abū'l-Khair Academy.

Faẓl-i Ḥaqq Khairābādī (1797-1861)
[Persian]
1825: *Taḥqīq al-fatwā fī ibṭāl at-taghwa*, Sargodha, 1979 (With an Urdu Transl.).

Ismāᶜīl Shahīd, Shāh Muḥammad (1779-1831)
[Arabic]
c.1823: *Radd al-ishrāk*, Manuscript, Asafiyya Collection, Andhra Pradesh Government Oriental Manuscripts Library & Research Institute, Hyderabad.
n.d.: *ᶜAbaqāt*, Arabic Text, Karachi, Al-majlis al-ᶜilmī, 1380/1960. (Urdu Transl. by Manāẓir Ḥasan Gilānī, Hyderabad: Al-Lajnata al-ᶜilmiyya, n.d.)
n.d.: *Tanwīr al-ᶜainain fī iṣbāṭ rafᶜ al-yadain*, published with an Urdu Transl. and Commentary, Lahore, 1882.
n.d.: *Risāla usūl al-fiqh*, Delhi, 1893.
n.d.: *Irshād al-ᶜibād ilā sabīl al-rashād*, Manuscript, British Museum, London.

[Persian]
c.1818: *Ṣirāṭu'l-mustaqīm*, 1st published in 1823, latest Indian edn., Delhi: Mujtabā'ī Press, n.d. (c. 1904), (Urdu Transl. by Maulvī ᶜAbdu'l-Jabbār, often reprinted).
c.1825: *Risāla-yi yak roẓī*, Manuscript, India Office Library, London.
n.d.: *Manṣab-i imāmat*, Delhi, Maṭbaᶜ-i Fārūqī, n.d. (With an Urdu Transl. (c. 1827), Delhi: Maṭbaᶜ-i Fārūqī, n.d.)
n.d.: *Iẓāḥ al-ḥaqq al-ṣarīḥ fī aḥkām al-mayyit wa'l ẓarīh.*
Various dates: *Makātib-i Maulānā Muḥammad Ismāᶜil*, Manuscript (compiled in 1828), Arabic and Persian Research Institute, Tonk; Manuscript (compiled in 1879), Bhopal.

[Urdu]
1824: *Taqwiyyatu'l-imān*, 1st printed in the 1820s; often reprinted (For English Transl., see References under Shahamat Ali).

n.d.: *Silk-i nūr* (Book of mystical poetry), Lucknow, 1852.

Ja[c]far [c]Alī Naqwī, Sayyid (1795-1871)
[Persian]
1855: *Manẕūratu's-su[c]adā fī aḥwāli'l-ghazāt wa'sh-shuhadā*, Manuscripts, Lahore, Tonk, Lucknow (Also called *Tārikh-i Aḥmadiyya*).

Karāmat [c]Alī Jaunpūrī (1800-73)
[Urdu]
1827: *Miftāḥu'l-jannat*, Lucknow, 1954.
1837: *Quwwatu'l-imān*, Calcutta.
n.d. : *Rafīqu's-sālikīn*, Calcutta, 1860.

Khurram [c]Alī Bilhaurī (d. 1855)
[Urdu]
1822: *Naṣīḥātu'l-muslimīn*, 1st known edn., Calcutta, 1848.

Maḥbūb [c]Alī, Mīr
[Arabic]
1818-35: *Tārīkhu'l-ā'imma fī Ẕikr khulafāi'l-ummat*, Manuscript, Indian Institute of Islamic Studies, Delhi.

Muḥammad [c]Alī, Sayyid
[Persian]
1845: *Makhzan-i Aḥmadī*, 1st printed, Agra, 1881.

Muḥammad Isḥāq Diḥlawī, Shāh (1782-1854)
[Persian]
n.d.: *Masā'il arba[c]īn* (Manuscript Urdu Transl. by Aḥmad Allāh b. Dalīl Allāh Ṣiddiqī, 1830, in India Office Library, London).

Muḥammad Ja[c]far Thānesarī (1832-1905)
[Urdu]
1891: *Sawāniḥ-i Aḥmadī*, Delhi: Mujtabā'ī Press, 1891; new edn., Karachi: Nafīs Academy, 1968, under the title *Ḥayāt-i Sayyid Aḥmad Shahīd*.

Muḥammad Murtaẓā Khān Ṭonkī
[Urdu]
1853: *Dafiʿu'l'fasād*, Manuscript, Arabic and Persian Research Institute, Tonk.

Muḥammad Sulṭān
[Urdu]
1834: *Tazkīru'l-ikhwān* (A continuation of the *Taqwiyyatu'l-imān*), numerous lithograph editions.

Musharraf ʿAlī, Sayyid ʿAlī bin Ḥasan al-ʿAskarī
[Persian]
c.1822: *Iẓāhat al-ghayy fi radd-i ʿAbd al-Ḥayy*, Manuscript, Khuda Bakhsh Oriental Public Library, Patna.

Pfander, Carl Gottlieb (1803-65)
[Persian]
n.d.: *Mīzān al-Ḥaqq*.

Pseudo-Walīu'llāh Dihlawī
[Persian]
n.d.: *Al-Balāghu'l-mubīn fi ittibāʿi khātamu'l-nabiyīn* (1st known edn., Lahore, c. 1890), Lahore: Al-Maktabatu'l-salafiyya, 1962.
n.d.: *Tuḥfatu'l-muwaḥḥidīn* (1st known edn., Delhi, c. 1912), Lahore: Al-Maktabatu'l-salafiyya, 1962.

Qāsimī, Akhlāq Ḥusain
[Urdu]
n.d. (1984 ?): *Shāh Ismāʿīl aur un-ke nāqid*, Bhera, District Sargodha: Zū'n-Nūrain Academy.

Rafīʿu'd-Dīn Dihlawī, Shāh (1750-1818)
[Persian]
n.d.: *Tanbīhu'l-ghāfilīn* (Often attributed wrongly to Sayyid Aḥmad Barelwī). Numerous editions.

[Urdu]
1786: Literal Urdu Translation of the Quran.
n.d.: *Tafsīr-i rafīʿī*. Exegesis of the *Sūra al-Baqra*.

Roy, Rām Mohan (1772-1833)
[Persian]
1803: *Tuḥfatu'l-muwaḥḥidīn*, Repr., Calcutta, 1859.

Sirāj Aḥmad al-Sahasawī
[Persian]
1824: *Sirāju'l-imān*, Manuscript, Arabic and Persian Research Institute, Tonk (Urdu Transl. dated 1856).

Walīu'llāh Dihlawī (1703-62)
[Persian]
1743: *Fatḥu'r-raḥmān bi-tarjamatu'l-Qur'ān* (Literal Transl. and Commentary of the Quran).

Wilāyat ᶜAlī, Maulwī (1790-1852)
[Persian]
c. 1837: *ᶜAmal bi'l-ḥadīṣ* (Transl. into Urdu by Ilāhī Bak̲h̲sh).

[Urdu]
n.d.: *Risāla-yi daᶜwat*, Delhi, n.d.
n.d.: *Risāla-yi tibyānu'l-shirk*, Delhi, n.d.

REFERENCES

ᶜAbdu'l-Ḥaqq, Ḍāktar Maulwī, ed., *Qāmūsu'l-kutub urdū*, Vol. I, *Maẕhabiyyat*, Karachi, 1961. [Catalogue of Urdu Books, Vol. I, Religious Books]

Ahmad, Aziz and Gustav E. von Grunebaum, *Muslim Self-Statement in India and Pakistan*, Wiesbaden: Otto Harrassowitz, 1970.

Ahmad, Mohiuddin, *Saiyid Ahmad Shahid. His Life and Mission*, Lucknow: Academy of Islamic Research and Publications, 1975.

Ahmad, Qeyamuddin, *The Wahhabi Movement in India*, Calcutta, K.L. Mukhopadhyay, 1966; 2nd edn., Delhi: Manohar, 1994.

— "The Missionary Literature of the Wahhabis: Its Historical Significance", in Ch.W. Troll, ed., *Islam in India. Studies and Commentaries*, Vol. I, Delhi: Vikas Publishing House, 1982, pp. 52-63.

Baljon, J.M.S., *Religion and Thought of Shāh Walī Allāh Dihlawī (1703-1762)*, Leiden: E.J. Brill, 1986.

Bari, M.A., "A Nineteenth Century Reform Movement in India", in G. Makdisi, ed., *Arabic and Islamic Studies in Honour of Hamilton A.R. Gibb*, Leiden: E.J. Brill, pp. 84-103.

Blumhardt, James Fuller, *Catalogue of the Hindustani Printed Books in the Library of the British Museum*, London: Longman & Co, 1889.

— *Catalogue of the Hindustani Manuscripts in the Library of the India Office*, London: Oxford University Press, 1926.

Brockelmann, C., *Geschichte der arabischen Literatur*, Two Vols., Weimar-Berlin, 1898-1902; 2nd edn., Leiden, 1943-49; *Supplemenbänden*, Three Vols., Leiden, 1937-39.

Chishtī, Muḥammad ᶜAbd al-Ḥalīm, "Tafsīr sūra-yi fātiḥa", *Ar-Raḥīm*, Sept. 1965, pp. 263-4.

— "Sayyid Aḥmad Shahīd-kī taḥrīk-kā aṣar Urdū adab par", *Ar-Raḥīm*, Feb. 1966, pp. 636-58; March 1966, pp. 705-20; April 1966, pp. 798-803.

Encyclopaedia of Islam, Leiden: E.J. Brill, 2nd edn., 1960- (See the following articles: 'Aḥmad Barelwī', 'Āzurda', 'Faḍl-i Ḥaḳḳ', 'Ismāᶜīl Shahīd', 'Karāmat ᶜAlī Djawnpūrī').

Ethé, Hermann, *Catalogue of Persian Manuscripts in the Library of the India Office*, Oxford: Printed for the India Office by Horace Hart, Printer to the University, 1903.

Ewing, Katherine P., ed., *Sharīᶜat and Ambiguity in South Asian Islam*, Berkeley: University of California Press, 1988.

Fārūqī, K.A., *Urdu men wahhābī adab*, Delhi: Delhi University, 1969.

Fusfeld, Warren, "The Shaping of Sufi Leadership in Delhi: The Naqshbandiyya Mujaddiyya, 1750-1920", Ph.D. Thesis, Philadelphia: University of Pennsylvania, 1981 (Unpublished).

— "Naqshbandi Sufism and Reformist Islam", in B. Lawrence, ed., *Ibn Khaldun and Islamic Ideology*, Leiden: E.J. Brill, 1984, pp. 89-110.

— "The Boundaries of Islam and Infidelity", in K.P. Ewing, ed., *Sharīᶜat and Ambiguity in South Asian Islam*, Berkeley: University of California Press, 1988, pp. 205-19.

Gaborieau, Marc, "Les oulémas/soufis dans l'Inde moghole: anthropologie historique de religieux musulmans", *Annales E.S.C.*, 1989, N° 5, pp. 1185-1204.

— "A Nineteenth-Century Indian 'Wahhabi' Tract Against the Cult of Muslim Saints: *Al-Balagh al-Mubin*", in Ch.W. Troll, ed., *Muslim Shrines in India. Their Character, History and Significance*, Delhi: Oxford University Press, 1989, pp. 198-239.

— "Le sous-continent Indo-Pakistanais: bilan des activités (1962-1990)", in *La transmission du savoir dans le monde musulman périphérique, Lettre d'information N° 10*, Paris: Ecole des Hautes Etudes en Sciences Sociales, 1990, pp. 4-17.

— "The Transmission of Islamic Reformist Teachings to Rural South Asia. The Lessons of a Case Study", in H. Elboudrari, ed., *Modes de transmission de la culture religieuse en Islam*, Le Caire: Institut Français d'Archéologie Orientale, 1993, pp. 119-57.

— "Mission en Inde, au Bangladesh et au Népal", *La transmission du savoir dans le monde musulman périphérique, Lettre d'information N° 13*, Paris: Ecole des Hautes Etudes en Sciences Sociales, 1993, pp. 1-17.

— Nicole Grandin, Pierre Labrousse and Alexandre Popovic, eds., *Dictionnaire biographique des savants et grandes figures du monde musulman périphérique*, Fasc. N° 1, Paris: Ecole des Hautes Etudes en Sciences Sociales, 1992.

Garcin de Tassy, Joseph Héliodore Sagesse Vertu, Compte-rendu de: *Mūẓih-i-Qur'ān*, "c'est-à-dire l'exposition du Coran (texte et traduction interlinéaire en hindoustani)", in *Journal des savants*, 1834, pp. 435-42.

— *Histoire de la littérature hindouie et hindoustanie* (1839-47), 2nd edn., Paris: Eugène Labitte, 1870-71; Reprint, New York, Burt Franklin, n.d.

— *Chrestomathie hindoustani* [sic] *(urdu et dakhni) à l'usage des élèves de l'école royale et spéciale des langues orientales vivantes*, Paris, 1847.

— *Catalogue des livres orientaux et autres composant la bibliothèque de feu M. Garcin de Tassy, suivi du catalogue des manuscrits hindoustanis, persans, arabes, turcs, rédigé par M. F. Deloncle, élève de M. Garcin de Tassy*, Paris: Labitte, 1879.

Hardy, Peter, *The Muslims of British India*, Cambridge: Cambridge University Press, 1972.

Hambye, Edward R., "The First Jesuit Mission to Emperor Akbar", in Ch.W. Troll, ed. *Islam in India. Studies and Commentaries*, Vol. I, Delhi: Vikas Publishing House, 1982, pp. 3-13.

Hedayatullah, Muhammad, *Sayyid Ahmad. A Study on the Religious Reform Movement of Sayyid Ahmad of Rae Bareli*, Lahore: Sh. Muhammad Ashraf, 1970.

Hunter, William, *Our Indian Musulmans. Are they Bound in Conscience to Rebel against the Queen ?*, London: Trübner & Co. 1871; Repr., Varanasi, Indological Book House, 1969.

Hussain, Sayida Suraiya, *Garcin de Tassy. Biographie et étude critique de ses oeuvres*, Pondichéry: Institut Français d'Indologie, 1962.

Ikrām, Shaikh Muḥammad, *Mauj-i Kauṣar* (c. 1948), 4th edn., Lahore: Feroz Sons, 1968.

Ishaq, Muḥammad, *India's Contribution to the Study of Hadith Literature*, Dacca: Asiatic Society, 1955.

J.R.C. [C = Colvin], "Notice on the Peculiar Tenets held by the Followers of Syed Ahmed, taken chiefly from the "Siràt-ul-Mùstaqìm", A Principle Treatise of that Sect, written by Moulavi Mahommed Ismail", *Journal of the Royal Asiatic Society of Bengal*, 1832, Vol. I, N° 11, pp. 479-98.

Kaul, H.K., *Urdu Manuscripts. A Descriptive Catalogue of Manuscripts in Delhi Libraries*, Delhi: Heritage, 1977.

Khan, Muin-ud-Din Aḥmad, *A Bibliographical Introduction to Modern Islamic Development in India and Pakistan, 1700-1955*, Appendix to the *Journal of the Asiatic Society of Pakistan*, Dacca, Vol. IV, 1959.

— *History of the Fara'idi Movement in Bengal, 1818-1906*, Karachi: Pakistan Historical Society, 1965; 2nd edn., Dhaka: Islamic Foundation Bangladesh, 1984.

Khan, Shaukat ᶜAli, ed., *Qasr-i ᶜilm. A Bibliographical Survey of Arabic and Persian Rare Works of Tonk*, Tonk: Arabic and Persian Research Institute, 1980.

— ed., *Khazinatu'l-makhtutat. A Descriptive Catalogue of the Arabic, Persian and Urdu Manuscripts in the Arabic and Persian Research Institute, Tonk*, prepared by Maulana Muhammad Imran Khan, Vol. III, Tonk: Arabic and Persian Research Institute, 1985.

Lawrence, Bruce, "Introduction" and "Mystical and Rational Elements in the Early Religious Writings of Sayyid Ahmad Khan", in B. Lawrence, ed., *The Rose and the Rock. Mystical and Rational Elements in the Intellectual History of South Asian Islam*, Durham: Duke University Press, 1979, pp. 3-13 and 61-103.

Lelyveld, David, *Aligarh First Generation*, Princeton: Princeton University Press, 1978.

— "Eloquence and Authority in Urdu: Poetry, Oratory, and Film", in K.P. Ewing, ed., *Sharīᶜat and Ambiguity in South Asian Islam*, Berkeley: University of California Press, 1988, pp. 98-113.

Mehr, Ghulām Rasūl, *Sayyid Ahmad Shahīd*, Two Vols. bound together, Lahore: Kitāb Manzil, 1952-54.

Metcalf, Barbara D., *Islamic Revival in British India. Deoband 1860-1900*, Princeton: Princeton University Press, 1982.

— *Perfecting Women: Maulana Ashraf Ali Thanawi's* Bihishti Zewar. *A Partial Translation with Commentary*, Berkeley: University of California Press, 1990.

Minault, Gail, *Voices of Silence. English Translation of Khwaja Altaf Hussain Hali's* Majlis un-Nissa *and* Chup ki Dad, Delhi: Chanakya Publications, 1986.

Nadwī, Sayyid Abū'l-Ḥasan ᶜAlī, *Sīrat-i Sayyid Aḥmad Shahīd* (1939), 7th edn., Lucknow: Academy of Islamic Research and Publications, 1986.

Nawshahrawī, Abū Yaḥyā Imām Khān, *Tarājim-i ᶜulamā-yi ḥadīṣ-i Hind*, Delhi, 1937.

Orainwī, Aḥmad A., *Bihār men urdū zabān o adab-kā irtiqā*, Patna, 1957.

Pearson, Harlan O., "Islamic Reform in the Nineteenth Century: the 'Tariqa-i Muḥammadiyya'", Ph.D. Dissertation, Durham: Duke University, 1979.

Rizvi, Sayyid Athar Abbas, *Shāh ᶜAbd al-ᶜAzīz and his Time: Puritanism, Sectarianism, Polemics and Jihād*, Canberra: Maᶜrifat Publishing House, 1982.

Robinson, Francis, "Technology and Religious Change: Islam and the Impact of Print", *Modern Asian Studies*, Vol. XXVII, Nº 1, 1993, pp. 229-51.

Schimmel, Annemarie, *Islamic Literatures of India*, Wiesbaden: Harrassowitz, 1973.

— *Classical Urdu Literature from the Beginning to Iqbal*, Wiesbaden: Harrassowitz, 1975.

— *Islam in the Indian Subcontinent*, Leiden: E.J. Brill, 1980.

Shahamat Ali, Mir, "Translation of the *Takwiyat-ul-Imàn*, preceded by a notice of the Author, Maulavi Isma'il Hajji", *Journal of the Royal Asiatic Society of Great Britian and Ireland*, 1852, XIII, N° 1, pp. 310-72. Rev. edn. by M. Ashraf Darr, under the title *Support of the Faith*, Lahore: Sh. Muhammad Ashraf, 1969.

Sprenger, Aloys, *A Catalogue of the Arabic, Persian and Hindustani Manuscripts of the Libraries of the King of Oudh*, Vol. I, *Persian and Hindustani Poetry*, Calcutta: 1854 (quoted from the reprint edn., Osnabrück, Biblio Verlag, 1979).

Storey, H., *Persian Literature. A Bio-bibliographical Survey*, London: Luzac & Co, 1927-58.

Troll, Christian W., "A Note on the Early Topographical Work of Sayyid Aḥmad K͟hān: *ās̤ār al-ṣanādīd*", *Journal of the Royal Asiatic Society*, 1972, N° 2, pp. 135-46.

— *Sayyid Ahmad Khan: A Reinterpretation of Muslim Theology*, Delhi: Vikas Publishing House, 1978.

— ed., *Muslim Shrines in India. Their Character, History and Significance*, Delhi: Oxford University Press, 1989.

The Reform of Islam in Ismaili Shīᶜism from 1885 to 1957

MICHEL BOIVIN

Introduction

The recent history of Ismaili Shīᶜism provides an excellent subject for a scholar of Indo-Persian studies. This article is not aimed at assessing the place of Persian literature and language in the Indian subcontinent, but rather, at evaluating the consequences of the encounter between an Iranian and an Indian religious tradition.[1] This encounter began around 1845 when the 46th Imām, Ḥasan ᶜAlī Shāh, established himself in Bombay following his forced departure from Persia.[2] Here he received an enthusiastic welcome from the Khojās, who constitute the principal Ismaili community of India. A minority amongst the Ismailis however, refused to acknowledge his presence in India which they considered to be undesirable, because of the challenge it posed to the traditional caste system. The matter was brought before the British judiciary which, in the famous 'Aga Khan

1. It is only since 1990 that Farhad Daftary's comprehensive study of the Ismailis (reviewed in *Bulletin Critique des Annales Islamologiques*, 1992, N° 9, pp. 67-9) is available, see Bibliography. (For Ismailian philosophy, see Corbin). Two works indispensable for the study of the Indian Ismaili tradition are A. Nanji, *The Nizārī Ismāᶜīlī Tradition in the Indo-Pakistan Subcontinent*, Delmar (New York), 1978 and Ch. Shackle & Z. Moir, *Ismaili Hymns from South Asia. An Introduction to the Ginans*, London, 1992. On the Iranian tradition, see R. Keshavjee, "The Quest for Gnosis and the Call for History. Modernisation Among the Ismailis of Iran", Ph.D. Thesis, Cambridge (Mass.): Harvard Univ., 1981 (unpublished). See also the treatises of the Aga Khan's stepbrother, Shihāb al-Dīn Shāh al-Ḥusaynī, *Risālat dar Ḥaqīqat-i Dīn or True Meaning of Religion*, Transl. from Persian into English by W. Ivanow, London, 1947; *Khiṭābāt-i ᶜĀliyya. Supreme Admonitions*, ed. by H. Ojaqi, Intr. by W. Ivanow, Tehran, 1963. We still know very little about numerous contemporary Ismaili traditions. For example, there are as yet no monographs on the traditions prevalent in Yemen, Syria, Afghanistan, etc... not to mention the Republics of the ex-USSR especially Uzbekistan and Tajikistan as well as China (Sin-Kiang).

2. On the transfer of the Imāmat to India, See Z. Noorally, "The First Aga Khan and the British, 1838-1868: A Study in British Indian Diplomacy and Legal History", M.A. Dissertation, Univ. of London, 1964 (unpublished); H. Algar, "The Revolt of Aga Khan Mahallati and the Transference of the Ismaili Imamate to India", *Studia Islamica*, 1969, XXIX, pp. 51-81; N. Eboo, "The Revolt of Aga Khan Mahalatti and the Establishment of the Nizari Imamate in India", B.A. Dissertation, Victoria Univ. of Manchester, 1979 (unpublished).

case' (1866), confirmed Ḥasan ᶜAlī Shāh's prerogatives as the spiritual head of the community, and consequently his proprietorship over its communal property.[3] Yet, while the problem appeared to have been settled on the legal plane, it still remained unresolved on the doctrinal level.

His son, ᶜAlī Shāh, could not attend to the problem during his brief Imāmat from 1881 to 1885. The responsibility therefore devolved upon his grand son, Sulṭān Muḥammad Shāh, better known as the 'Aga Khan',[4] who remained Imām from 1885 to 1957. By what means did Sulṭān Muḥammad Shāh attempt to harmonize the Iranian and Indian traditions ? He substituted a third which could be termed 'neo-Ismailism'. Its characteristics were: 1) a partial and extremely gradual elimination of manifestly Hindu notions, 2) a relativisation of notions stemming from Iranian Shīᶜism, and finally, 3) a reshifting of the focus towards Islam by redefining its essential principles. The purpose of this theological reflexion was to enable Islam to provide pertinent responses to contemporary challenges. A study of the reform of Islam is the subject matter of this article.[5]

There are two kinds of sources that have been utilised for this study. The first set consists of the numerous articles and the few books by the Aga Khan, almost all of which have been published in English. The second set comprises of publications of a more confidential nature, addressed by the Aga Khan to the Ismailis in Urdu, since they did not understand Persian, his mother tongue. Known as farmāns and taᶜliqas, these communications were later translated into Gujarati and English.[6]

The Crisis of Islam

The Aga Khan devoted his first important speeches to the theme of the crisis faced by Islam.[7] He did not refer to the problem of the 'back-

---

3. See A.A.A. Fyzee, *Cases in the Muhammadan Law of India and Pakistan*, Oxford, 1965, pp. 504-49.

4. It seems more reasonable to use this nomenclature to designate Sulṭān Muḥammad Shāh since, but for one instance when he signed his name as Muḥammad al-Ḥusaynī in Arabo-Persian script, 'Aga Khan' was the signature used by him. *Idem* for Ameer Ali, Zaki Ali and Aly Khan.

5. The other aspects have been dealt with elsewhere, see for example, M. Boivin, "Islam, Nationalisme et avenir de l'Inde chez Sulṭān Muḥammad Shāh Aga Khan (1877-1957)", *Cahiers D'Histoire* (Lyon), XXXVIII, 1, 1993, pp. 55-73.

6. The farmāns and the taᶜliqas, often transcribed as 'firmans' and 'talikas' by the Khojās are the sayings of the Imam intended for the Ismaili community; the farmāns usually dealt with religious questions. For a general idea, see Bibliography.

7. On the subject of the crisis faced by Islam, see A. Merad, 'Iṣlāḥ', *Encyclopédie de l'Islam* (new edn.), Vol. IV, pp. 146-70.

wardness' of Islam, because of his contention that the Muslims themselves, and not what was contained in their scriptures, should be held responsible for the current state of affairs. His argument in support of this contention was simple: he referred to a Golden Age of which the period varied, fluctuating between the Omayyad and the Ottoman eras, when Muslim civilisation was the most advanced. In his view the power and the influence known by the Muslim civilisation of that time was linked to the authenticity of Islam. The issue therefore was to determine the cause of the inertia which had crept in Islam in the twentieth century. The Aga Khan attributed it to three factors: the rigid adherence of pious Muslims to rites, the system of purdah (*parda*), and fatalism.

During a speech at Delhi in 1902, the Aga Khan denounced the excessive ritualism of religion. Too many pious Muslims felt that the performance of rites - which were merely the external manifestation of religion - constituted the totality of Islam. They had forgotten the true spirit behind the message of the Prophet and the Koran. In addition, some of these rites, for example the pilgrimage to Mecca, were the cause of wasteful expense. Some of these practices were foreign to Islam and led to the division of the community. Finally, the barbarism associated with some of them - the Aga Khan was referring to the celebrations of al-ᶜAshūrā - was contrary to the spirit of the Prophet.

Another practice totally opposed to the Prophet's work was the confinement of women. It should be kept in mind that the Koranic prescriptions relating to women were meant to improve the condition of Arab women in the seventh century. Thus, the purpose of these injunctions was to resolve a specific problem and they had no relevance outside that context. Would it be possible for the Muslim world to uplift itself again, if half its population remained in slavery ?

Aga Khan related the problem of fatalism to free will. He was convinced that free will is affirmed in the Koran thus: how a man would ultimately act is foreknown to God, but the freedom to act or not is his own.

Ultimately, the causes identified by the Aga Khan to explain the crisis faced by Islam were all internal in origin. He attributed this crisis to practices which he described as 'degenerating customs', by which he was evidently referring to the concept of *bidᶜa*, commonly translated as 'blameable innovation'. For him, all that was incompatible with the liberal credo of the nineteenth century amounted to *bidᶜa*.

In his initial pronouncements, he did not hold any particular section responsible for this crisis. But in a small work which he published in English in 1944, he alluded to the closing of the door of *ijtihād*, defined as 'a living and personal research',[8] while maintaining that no reform in Islam was possible without the concurrence of the *ᶜulamā*. Later, towards the end of his life, he denounced them and accused them of converting Islam into a machine which was out of touch with reality. The main function of this 'machine' was to perpetuate the rites, thereby ensuring the perfect reproduction of the past. For this purpose, they had even formulated a theory of knowledge termed as '*allamah*' (*allama*), according to which, adherence to tradition and blind imitation were the only method of attaining knowledge. One may observe in this principle, the theory of *taqlīd* which, a generation after al-Shāfiᶜi, (d. 204/820) marked the end of *ijtihād*.

The Dynamic Qualities of Islam

In the course of its evolution, Islam had assimilated certain practices foreign to it while losing some of its intrinsic qualities. Two such dynamic qualities which characterized Islam in the period, referred to as the Golden Age, were simplicity of faith and openness of spirit. In his memoirs, the Aga Khan emphasized that simplicity of faith signified that faith was essentially expressed by the *shahāda*.[9] This is quite different from the Christian belief in the divine Trinity in which God, the Father is incarnated in his son Jesus. Simplicity of faith also signifies unity of faith. In the period when Islam was still pristine, a period which, for the Aga Khan, extended beyond the early schisms, the Muslim community remained united around the Prophet and, later, around his memory. It is interesting to note that the Aga Khan employs the term *purity* to denote the most significant quality of this period.

But this mythical conception of the foundational Age did not imply that the Aga Khan was in favour of a literal application of all the practices of this period, whether or not they were of Koranic origin. The idea of simplicity ultimately leads to the idea of common sense. It refers to the famous 'practical reason' of the Koran, implying that the doctrine is simple and capable of being grasped by human understanding, that is, by reason.

The second dynamic quality, that is, open mind, refers to a certain number of achievements and practices during the Prophet's lifetime, as evidenced by the progress made by the Muslim world in such widely differing domains as the social, the intellectual and the artistic. It was

8. Aga Khan, *Glimpses of Islam* (1944), Lahore, 1973, p. 73.
9. Aga Khan, *Memoirs. World Through and Time*, London, 1954, p. 177.

this open mind which permitted the Muslims to assimilate a certain amount of Greek knowledge. This quality was also evident in what concerned the status of women. The Aga Khan devoted the 26th chapter of *India in Transition* to this subject, which he introduced with a citation from the *ḥadīth* of the Prophet where it is said that on the path to Paradise men would have to follow the footsteps of their wives.[10] Elsewhere, he referred to this question again while mentioning the intellectual role of Sakīna, daughter of Ḥusayn, and Ayesha - traditionally rejected by the Shīᶜites - for her political role. Islam ensures the economic independence of women by bestowing on them the right of succession, and in this respect it is many centuries ahead of the legislations enacted by the British, the French or the Italians.

The Return to Sources

Like other reformers, the Aga Khan felt that a return to the sources was indispensable to religious renewal. The first source was obviously the Koran. Although he was not oblivious to the fact that certain passages which had designated ᶜAlī as the successor of the Prophet had been expunged from the Koran, the Aga Khan did not question the Othmanian vulgate. Abandoning all casuistry concerning the Sacred Book (inimitability, uncreatedness, etc.), he perceived the Koran as a vast semantic matrix which contains all, but often in a latent form.

The duty of the Muslim is to learn to find in the Koran what he seeks. The Koran is a compendium of signs and indications waiting to be invested with meaning. As such it contains the rudiments of all responses to contemporary challenges. Although sometimes this position led the Aga Khan to accept concordism, he still held that interpretation of the Koran was the fundamental obligation of every Muslim. According to him, the main function of the Sunna, for which he employed terms like 'tradition' or 'teaching', was to supplement the Koran, and he felt that it was necessary to subject it to a critical examination.

In 1869, Sayyid Aḥmad K͟hān published a biography of the Prophet, in response to a work by Muir, employing the same critical approach as the latter. This was the first occasion when a Muslim had authored a critical biography of the Prophet.[11] In 1873, Ameer Ali

10. Aga Khan, *India in Transition. A Study in Political Evolution*, Bombay - Calcutta, 1918, p. 253.

11. W. Muir, *The Life of Mahomet and the History of Islam to the Hegira*, Four Vols., London, 1858-61; This work was reedited and brought out in a single abridged volume under the title *The Life of Mahomet from the Original Sources*, London, 1894; Sayyid Ahmad Khan, *Essays on the Life of Muhammad* (1870), London, 1969.

wrote another biography in the same genre, which later became the basis of his famous work *Spirit of Islam*, which has been re-edited several times, and translated into many languages.[12] For the Aga Khan, the person and the message of the Prophet represented the earliest interpretation of the Koran as lived experience. But his Prophet was markedly endowed with Christ-like qualities, which resulted from the deep imprint on him of the Islamo-Christian polemics, which led him to compare the Prophet point by point with Jesus.

The Prophet is the paradigm of a virtuous man, in whom speech and action are in harmony. Although the Aga Khan recognized that the Prophet's authority was both religious and secular, it was the religious element which was primary to him, the secular being, by the circumstances and accidents of his life, joined to it. Subsequently, the authority was transmitted to the famous *ūlu' l-Amr* of the Koran, understood by the Aga Khan to be the Caliphs and the Imāms. Since the Prophet was the model for Muslims, he had many emulators, beginning with ᶜAlī, to whom strangely, there are very few references in the Aga Khan's writings although the Shīᶜites regard him as their first Imām. In his memoirs, the Aga Khan presented him as he had been characterized in Sunnite hagiography, that is, as a model of valour. In contrast, in his private writings, he presented ᶜAlī as a key symbol of Ismailian esoterism, making him the archetype of a superman or a Man-God.[13]

The Aga Khan made reference to two categories from amongst the Prophet's emulators: the saint, and the hero. Though the two are often indistinguishable from each other, the saint's role is primarily to mediate between man and God. As one who had direct experience of divine reality, the idea of this mediation would imply initiation into esoteric knowledge.

The hero is identified by his heroic deeds contributing to the grandeur of Islam considered as a civilisation, and some Muslims of the contemporary period are also included in this category by the Aga Khan. Thus Atatürk and Jinnah are mentioned in this category alongwith Abū Bakr. The common attribute of contemporary heroes is their having revived or established a Muslim state. The principal notion defining the heroes of the classical period is that of sacrifice. It appears that the categories in this typology are essentially ethical, since, in the

---

12. Ameer Ali, *The Spirit of Islām. A History of Evolution and Ideals of Islam* (1922), London, 1946.

13. See for example the farmān cited by A. Meherally, *Understanding Ismailism. A Unique Tariqa of Islam*, Burnaby (Canada), 1988, p. 33.

final analysis, these heroes and saints are people who, modelling themselves on the Prophet, incarnate Islamic virtues. This conception reveals, finally, the importance which the Aga Khan accorded to mediation.

The Reformation

The Aga Khan's religious conception consisted of two distinct elements: personal beliefs and fundamentals. The first is mainly concerned with the dialectic between the immanent and the transcendent in the Islamic context. According to him, there was an omnipresent and unknowable God, as well as a certain number of hypostases of this divinity, whom it was possible to know.

God in his transcendental form was referred to, by the Aga Khan with such metaphors as the Absolute, the Infinite etc. The closest notion which could characterize him, is contained in the Koranic root Q.Y.M., which signifies 'to support or to uphold', implying thereby that the world would not exist, but for God. Ghazālī also agrees that this notion is the most appropriate to designate one without whom all existence would perish.

While invoking God in the context of one of his creations, or in relation to his direct link with the believer, the Aga Khan employed a series of hypostases, such as Universal Soul, Divine Will, Eternal Reality, Universal Spirit, etc. These expressions, which denote a protean quality, are part of the Sufi as well as the Ismaili vocabulary, and establish a close connection between the Aga Khan and Persian Sufism. There is no evidence of a strict hierarchy amongst these hypostases. However, the Aga Khan attributed a specific function to one of them, the Holy Spirit, as the vector of Divine Grace, on which all spiritual progress was ultimately dependant.

When Nature is considered as an emanation of Divinity, it is often difficult to distinguish from the Universal Soul. This question was extremely important for the Aga Khan, particularly because it was on this issue that the Europeans and the Muslims had parted ways. Neglect of the study of Nature by the Muslims had enabled the Europeans to overtake them in the domain of knowledge. This idea is one of the leitmotifs of Sayyid Aḥmad K͟hān who proclaimed, "The work of God is identical to the Word of God".[14] This axiom had earned him the nickname '*necarī*', an Urdu term derived from the English 'nature'. Al

14. Cited by J.M.S. Baljon, 'Aḥmad K͟hān', *Encyclopédie de l'Islam* (new edn.), Vol. I, p. 297.

Afghani particularly denounced what he regarded as the resurgence of materialism, but actually he felt that the most important fault of the Necarī was to be a blind British loyalist.[15]

As for the Aga Khan, he was convinced that the Koran refers to nature as proof of the existence of God. The importance accorded by the Koran to Nature - in the form of numerous injunctions to understand natural phenomena - makes Islam a naturalistic religion.[16] Nature is here envisaged as order, harmony, regularity, or in other words it reflects divine perfection. Nature is also the model for the causal chain in the form of the law of cause and effect. It was for this reason that whether Islam was termed a naturalistic religion, or a rationalistic religion was a matter of no significance to the Aga Khan. The emphasis laid in Koranic exhortations on understanding makes Reason a pillar of religion. The Ismailis were reminded by the Aga Khan that there could be no religion without Reason (*ᶜaql*), meaning thereby the faculty of understanding.

Whereas no normative function attached to the Aga Khan's personal beliefs, it was otherwise with respect to what he designated as the fundamentals, which comprised of articles of faith, and principles. The term 'fundamentals' refers to *uṣūl al-Dīn*, an expression employed only once in the Aga Khan's writings, where it is transcribed as '*usulat*'.[17] In his memoirs he described them as "those tenets of Islam which are professed and held in common by all Muslims of any and every sects and subsects".[18] The three fundamental tenets are: prophecy, monorealism and interpretation.

Prophecy is an universal principle, and the Prophet - a messenger illumined by Divine Grace. One of his essential functions is to bring civilisation. In fact every great civilisation owes itself to a Prophet who has founded a monotheistic religion: the Buddha in the East, Jesus in the West, etc. The Muslims recognize other Prophets.[19] It was only because other religions had perverted the divine message by practices such as idolatory, polytheism, belief in incarnation, pantheism, etc., that a fresh revelation was made by God to Muḥammad.[20] Besides,

15. See the English translation of the original Persian text by N.R. Keddie and H. Algar in N.R. Keddie, *An Islamic Response to Imperialism* (1968), Berkeley, Los Angeles, 1983, pp. 130-74.

16. See, for example, *A Collectanea of Some Recent Speeches and Writings of His Highness the Aga Khan*, Mombasa, 1955, p. 75.

17. *Ibid.*, p. 83.

18. Aga Khan, *Memoirs*, *op. cit.*, p. 177.

19. This aspect has been particularly developed in the first chapter of *India in Transition*, *op. cit.*, pp. 1-15.

20. Aga Khan, *Memoirs*, *op. cit.*, pp. 175-6.

Muḥammad alone sought to integrate other religious messages: consequently Islam is founded not on the rejection of other religions but on their integration.

With respect to monorealism, the Aga Khan asserted that this term characterized Islam better than monotheism. If the Aga Khan retained the prefix 'mono', while replacing 'theism' by 'realism', it was certainly because he wished to emphasize what, in his eyes, constituted the essence of the conception of divinity in Islam - nothing exists but the Supreme Reality, that is, God. It is a neologism in which one perceives a remanence of the Sufi theory of *waḥdat al-wujūd*.[21] Utilised by Ṣadr al-Dīn Qūnāwī (d. 1272) to describe the thought of Ibn ᶜArābī (d. 1240), this expression is based on certain Koranic verses (e.g. II, 115: "All is perishable but for His Face"). It proclaims that the world is merely a reflection of the one and only Divine Existence (*Wujūd* = *Ḥaqq*), the multiplicity of existents being only illusory, and that God and the world are one.

Monorealism seeks to explain the nature of the relationship which unites God to Creation. God has created man so that He may be known. All that man perceives has its origin in a unique principle. The origin of existence, as much as it can be known, is the Universal Soul. The desire of God to make himself known is the unique basis of the relationship between the Universal Soul and the individual soul. According to the Aga Khan, each molecule and each atom had its own relationship with the Universal Soul. Monorealism thus permitted the Aga Khan to resolve the contradiction between the plurality of existents and the unicity of divinity. It also permits Islam to avoid the extremes as opposed to Judaism (extreme transcendentalism) and Christianity (with its belief in incarnation).

The third principle, namely interpretation, was for the Aga Khan, the most important. In the absence of consensus with regard to the recognition of a supreme authority in Islam, the Aga Khan laid great stress on the need to interpret. Moreover, this principle, which permits Islam to adjust to the changing requirements of each period, constitutes the most important distinction between Islam and other religions and makes it superior to them. Interpretation signifies conferring meaning. Through interpretation, the passage from the Eternal Word to action is accomplished.

---

21. Few scientific works have focussed on this subject. In the Iranian context, the thesis of Djamshid Mortazavi may be indicated. This has, however, been published in the disappointing form: *Le Secret de l'unité dans l'ésotérisme iranien*, Paris, 1988.

To some extent, the Aga Khan's conception of interpretation was similar to the idea of *ijtihād* as conceived by the reformers of the *Iṣlāḥ*, who saw it as an operational and multifunctional concept which made it possible to take account of contemporaneity.[22] Likewise, with respect to the classical approach to interpretation in Ismailism (*ta*ᶜ*wīl*), the Aga Khan enlarged its scope. However, as distinct from reform-oriented *ijtihād*, which was simply an attempt to comprehend the real through a more rational approach, the Aga Khan adopted an hermeneutic approach based on the elaboration of analogies. But, for him, the interpretation should necessarily take place within the normative framework provided by the Koran. Besides, the dialogue had to be carried out within an *épistémè* which shared the cognitive base of Islam. And, finally, it had to be guided by two considerations: 1) to ameliorate certain Islamic predispositions and 2) not to distort or force the meaning of the scriptural sources.

A Spiritual Pan-Islamism

For the Aga Khan faith (*imān*) was given and not acquired. In sum, it is the adhesion to two articles: 1) Muḥammad is the last and the greatest Prophet and 2) it is only through him that salvation is possible in this world and the other. But faith is primarily an ensemble of qualities and virtues. The idea of Pan-Islamism epitomised for the Aga Khan a certain number of these qualities. It represented a spiritual fraternity which shared a common faith. The two substantives 'moral' and 'spiritual' were synonymous in the vocabulary of the Aga Khan. Thus when he spoke of the 'spiritual union' or the 'moral union' of the Muslim community, he was referring to the common ethics shared by the community. For him the ethical aspect of Islam constituted a strong stabilising factor in the contemporary world.

Virtues represent 'the eternal truths of faith'. However, his definition of these 'truths' evolved between 1902 (Delhi speech) and 1954 (Memoirs). Their common feature was their emphasis on action, whatever be the circumstances. In 1902, devotion and self sacrifice were recognized as 'the eternal truths', but later two other virtues became important: tolerance and charity. The idea of tolerance was inferred from the Koran (IV, 48). The Aga Khan cited this verse on one occasion asserting that where religious was concerned, there could be no question of constraint. Besides, he pointed out that though the Muslims

22. On this subject, See B.(ensalem) Himmich, *De la formation idéologique en Islam. Ijtihadat et Histoire*, Paris, 1980.

had allowed Christian communities to survive in the Middle East, there were no longer any Muslims in Spain.

With regard to charity, a quality which was also essential in the thought of Ameer Ali, another Koranic citation of the Aga Khan indicates that he related it to the notion of *birr*, pious gentleness (II, 72). In an article published in the *Times* on 6th November 1951, he wrote that there was an 'eternal truth' which was the sum total of all the other truths: the *ḥilm*. In fact he regarded it as the supreme form of tolerance particularly because *ḥilm*, in its strict sense, signified the control that an individual exercised on himself. It is interesting to note that the Aga Khan's conception of *ḥilm* was quite close to the definition of charity as enunciated by Saint Paul (1st Epistle to the Corinthians). But *ḥilm* also refers to an action motivated by divine commandment with the objective of bringing about welfare.

The Question of Authority in Islam

How did the Aga Khan's political activity relate to this ethical ideal ? Like Sayyid Aḥmad K͟hān, the Aga Khan also believed that political action was possible only after the problem of education was settled. In India, the Aga Khan restricted his work to safeguarding the interests of the Muslim minority within the framework of the British Empire, which he regarded as the best guarantee of religious freedom. He was in fact one of the first to conceive the theory of 'a nation within a nation'. It is for this reason that he submitted his resignation as the President of the All India Muslim League in 1913 when the League joined the Congress in its demand for self determination (Lucknow Pact).

At the international level, his aim was to safeguard the interests of Muslims all over the world in the face of the hegemonist designs of the West. The question of the Caliphate saw the culmination of both these endeavours. The Aga Khan recognized the legitimacy of the Caliphate, in accordance with the view of the Shīᶜite Imāms, with the exception of Ḥusayn. In contrast to Sayyid Aḥmad K͟hān who rejected the pretensions of the Ottomans to supreme authority, the Aga Khan merely contested the excessive politicisation of the Caliphate under Sultan Abdül Ḥamid II. In a secret note written for the India Office he stated that in the absence of temporal power, the credibility of the Ottoman Caliph as the spiritual head of Islam would be severely undermined in the eyes of the Muslims.[23] He did not give up the cause despite the

23. India Office, L/P & S/18/C 146, p. 9.

Treaty of Sèvres (10th August 1920) which led to the dismemberment of Turkey. In fact, along with Ameer Ali, he stepped up the publication of manifestos in the *Times* and elsewhere, an activity which continued until his participation as a non-official negotiator in the discussions leading to the Treaty of Lausanne (23rd July 1923), which invalidated the Treaty of Sèvres.[24]

On 24th November 1923 the Aga Khan and Ameer Ali wrote a letter to the leaders of the new Turkish state requesting them to maintain the Caliphate which represented in their eyes the symbol of Muslim unity.[25] The Turkish press published this letter before it could reach Ismet Inönü, the head of government, to whom it was addressed. A veritable storm was raised in the Grand National Assembly over the issue. Finally Atatürk abolished the Caliphate on 3rd March, 1924 on the pretext that it was redundant given that a government was already in existence. In 1944 the Aga Khan proposed the establishment of a sort of 'Muslim Society of Nations' which would have the *ᶜulamā* and other savants in Islamic Sciences as representatives.[26] Their mandate would make it possible to promote welfare by reactivating the principle of *ijmāᶜ*.

The Sanctification of Activities

The Aga Khan generally used the term *happiness* to denote spiritual happiness, preferring to employ the term *welfare* for material happiness or well being. In 1905, he wrote: "I feel that I owe a duty to both India and England, countries that seem, by Providence, to be so designed that their welfare and happiness can only be complete when they are thoroughly united".[27] He spoke frequently of economic welfare, social welfare or worldly welfare, and in all these cases, the term welfare could be replaced by well-being, uplift, upliftment, which he translated in French as 'prospérité', 'développement' or 'progrès'. This type of welfare which the Aga Khan termed 'common' concerned sectors such as education, hygiene, health, economic development, etc. It related to the country or nation, or to the people, and envisaged measures of a permanent nature.

But the Aga Khan was of the view that the institution of welfare could also be based on religious criteria. He demanded, alongwith Zaki

24. It is difficult to determine the exact role of the Aga Khan in this affair. He describes himself as 'a watching brief', *Memoirs*, *op. cit.*, p. 162.
25. Published in the *Times* of 14th December 1923.
26. Aga Khan, *Glimpses of Islam*, *op. cit.*, p. 71.
27. Aga Khan, "The Defence of India", *The Nineteenth Century*, 1905, LVIII, p. 375.

Ali, that an assembly of Muslim scholars should "discuss the religious problems affecting the welfare of Muslim people around the world".[28] It is interesting to note, however, that in the writings addressed to the Ismailis, he willingly employed the term *welfare* in connection with the spiritual domain. On the occasion of the visit of his son Aly Khan to Africa, he recommended to his disciples, in a *talika* dated 26th November 1950, that only such receptions should be organised as would include members of all communities including Africans and, in particular "our Moslem bretheren permanently domiciles (sic) in Africa; it is necessary once and for all that this should be understood for the Welfare of Iman and Ismaili Faith".[29] In another *talika*, he proclaimed to the Ismailis "Hence your welfare in both worlds, this and next is my constant thought and I must always warn you of evils and dangers".

In a speech at Delhi in 1902, the Aga Khan mentioned *self-sacrifice* - which he equated with 'supreme service' - as an "eternal verity of the Faith". In fact, referring to the Companions of the Prophet, he affirmed that "Islam made heroes of such men, not only on the battlefield, but in the more difficult daily sacrifices of healthy and patriotic society".[30] Two years later, *self-sacrifice* was defined as sacrifice for the national cause.[31] It may be noted that the definition of 'sacrifice' had undergone a transformation, or, more precisely, the Aga Khan had adapted it to the 'demands of his times'. The fact that he referred to sacrifice in the context of the motherland or the Islamic nation, for India and the *umma*, did not in any way negate the importance of the sacrifice of an Ismaili for the Imām who, in fact, represents the community, protects it and symbolises it on the spiritual plane. and in sum, is its guide.

In 1939, the Aga Khan advocated the inculcation of two ideas amongst the Ismailis - service and self-sacrifice.[32] This shift from one to the other - which put both these ideals at par - occurs in this period. In a collection of articles published in 1935, the Aga Khan still considered *self-sacrifice* as the factor which would enable the Muslims to attain equality with the Christians.[33] In the *talikas* of this period, it is

28. Aga Khan, *Glimpses of Islam, op. cit.*, p. 71.

29. Aga Khan, *Mubarak Talika and Messages. Mowlana Hazir Imam's Guidance & Advice in Spiritual and Worldly Matters to Ismailis of Africa*, Mombasa, 1955, p. 16.

30. Cited by Ikbal Ali Shah, *The Prince Aga Khan. An Authentic Life Story*, London, 1933, p. 69.

31. N.M. Dumasia, *The Aga Khan and his Ancestors*, Bombay, 1938, p. 87.

32. *Ibid.*, p. 93.

33. Aga Khan, *Message. Six Articles on Religion and Politics*, Bombay, 1935, p. 7.

service which is emphasised, and in one of them, which is unfortunately not dated, he asserted that all Ismailis were equal, regardless of their status and their responsibilities in the community. The important thing was that each should do his utmost to serve the Ismaili faith: "I therefore expect that every Ismaili to consider the work allotted to his sacred duty to perform to the best of his abilities, as a great responsibility and not to his utmost. He that serves me most becomes nearer me".[34]

In *India in Transition* the Aga Khan established a link between service rendered to the nation and its *welfare*. In 1939, he maintained that loyalty towards the King-Emperor was the best way to serve Islam.[35] But in his article "Le libéralisme musulman" published in 1943, he declared that in Islam, free and honest agriculture and commerce "are encouraged as being divine services, because the happiness of men depended on the intensification of these legitimate activities".[36] In 1944, the Aga Khan reverted to the same idea in *Glimpses of Islam*, but here he translated the French expression 'bonheur des hommes' as *welfare of mankind*. The same expression is used again in his memoirs in 1954.[37]

But how did the Aga Khan justify that 'service to man' was the key to welfare ? In a radio broadcast in February 1950, he asserted that according to the Koran and the Sunna, Nature is the book of God and its secrets must be unravelled for the well being of humanity. All the natural phenomena described in the Koran should be utilised in the service of man.[38] This assertion was undoubtedly based on the Koran that all creation was subordinate to man. In *Glimpses of Islam*, many verses are cited from the version translated by Yusuf Ali: "Seest thou not that God has lade subject to you (men) all that is on earth" (XXII, 65); "It is God who has subjected the sea to you, that ships may sail through by His command, that ye may seek His bounty, and that ye may be grateful. And He has subjected to you, as from Him, all that is in the Heavens and on Earth: behold, in that signs indeed for those who reflect" (XIV, 12-13).[39]

On the lines of the economic thinkers of the 19th century, like J.S.

---

34. Aga Khan, *Mubarak Talika*, *op. cit.*, p. 48.
35. *Ibid.*, p. 5.
36. Aga Khan, "Le libéralisme musulman", *Le Monde religieux* (Lausanne), Oct. 1943, Vol. IV, p. 32. This is the only article in French by the Aga Khan.
37. Aga Khan, *Memoirs*, *op. cit.*, pp. 9 and 177.
38. Aga Khan, *Collectanea*, *op. cit.*, p. 58.
39. Aga Khan, *Glimpses of Islam*, *op. cit.*, p. 76.

Mill, Ricardo or Marx, the Aga Khan tried to locate his concept of work in his general world view. In his article on modernity in Islam, Ameer Ali had explained that the Prophet himself had valued work.[40] Although he did not go so far back in time to explain the importance of work, and, in fact, made no reference whatsoever to any specific source, the Aga Khan added an important dimension to the notion of work by defining it as divine service.

The Aga Khan also went a step beyond other reformers, who sought only to legitimize the liberal notion of work by finding support for it in the Islamic scriptures.[41] He sacralized the notion of work, and in the process, sacralized also its objective, which was the *welfare* of humanity. His implicit reasoning was simple: *welfare* is the realization of the good of humanity; it is known that this is one of the pillars of Koranic ethics; consequently work aimed at *welfare* is equivalent to the service of God. Addressing the Ismaili community, the Aga Khan asserted: "Labour for the welfare of others is the way of improving ourselves because results are sure and certain. If you work for yourselves, you are never happy".[42] Thus the Aga Khan converted general welfare into a sacred duty.

Another association of ideas is found at the end of the Aga Khan's memoirs. He reaffirmed what he had earlier set out, namely, the idea that those who have not been blessed with a direct communion with the *Divine Presence* "may yet attain blessed and pure felicity if they achieve the heights of human love and companionship - something not won lightly or easily, but the crown of lifelong attachment, in which one human being devotes all that he has, and feels to love and service of another".[43] Ultimately *service of another* is a form of neighbourly love and the Aga Khan was convinced that this love allowed one to attain a higher form of happiness.

On the subject of the faith and of deeds, and over and above the adherence to prescriptions regarding rituals, the Aga Khan attached particular importance to action resulting from the practice of the 'Eternal Truths of the Faith'. It has already been noted that in his first speeches at Delhi and at Bombay, the Aga Khan mentioned *self-sacrifice* as an eternal truth. He explained that in the earlier days of Islam,

40. Ameer Ali, "The Modernity of Islam", *Islamic Culture*, 1927, I, p. 5.

41. On the notions of work and service in the Muslim milieu, see J.C. Vadet, "La *Futuwwa*, morale professionnelle ou morale mystique", *Revue des Etudes Islamiques*, 1978, XLVI, 1, specially pp. 74-6 and S. Sohrab, "Die Arbeits wertheorie in schiitischen Islam", *Orient*, June 1969, XXV, 2, pp. 270-9.

42. Aga Khan, *Precious Pearls: Farman Mubarak, op. cit.*, p. 45.

43. Aga Khan, *Memoirs*, *op. cit*, p. 249.

the real hero was not one who gave proof of bravery on the battlefield, but one who had sacrificed himself for the well-being of his nation.[44] He repeated this in a different form by stating that the supreme eternal truth was self-sacrifice for "the well being of the people". If he mentioned this quality only in his earlier speeches, it must be noted that the new values by which it was 'replaced' expressed the same idea in a less accentuated form (*gentleness, kindness*, etc.). But in his memoirs, the Aga Khan, writing on the subject of economic activities, that is work, states that "they manifest a Divine service, and the welfare of mankind depends upon the continuation and the intensification of these legitimate labours".[45]

The Aga Khan established a new connection between 'divine service' and the 'well-being of humanity'. The scope of the idea of service was no longer restricted to the motherland or the nation but was singularly enlarged to cover humanity as a whole.

Conclusion

The elaboration of that aspect of Islam which the Aga Khan called its 'Fundamentals' was meant to achieve several objectives:

1. To establish a common platform within the Ismaili tradition.
2. To construct a bridge between the Ismaili community as a whole and the rest of the Muslim community.
3. To promote the foundation of a new Muslim ethics which could help in finding solutions to contemporary challenges.

This interpretation of Islam constituted a profession of faith for the Ismailis which did not in any way negate the specific rites inherent in their various traditions. The Arabisation of their prayers, with which this elaboration was to culminate did not begin until 1950 and it has not been fully achieved till today.[46] The prayers of the Khojās are drawn from their centuries old sacred texts, the *gināns* composed in Gujarati.[47]

---

44. Cited by I.A. Shah, *op. cit.*, p. 69 and Dumasia, *op. cit.*, p. 184.

45. Aga Khan, *Memoirs, op. cit.*, p. 177.

46. See D. Rattansi, "Islamization and the Khojah Ismā'īlī Community in Pakistan", Ph.D. Thesis, Montreal, McGill Univ., 1987 (unpublished) and A.S. Asani, "The Khojahs of Indo-Pakistan: the Quest for an Islamic Identity", *Journal of the Institute of Muslim Minority Affairs*, 1987, VIII, 1, pp. 31-34.

47. See Shackle & Moir, *Ismaili Hymns from South Asia, op. cit.*; A.S. Asani, "The Ismaili *Gināns* as Devotional Literature", in R.S. McGregor, ed., *Devotional Literature in South Asia. Current Research, 1985-1988*, Cambridge, 1992, pp. 101-12 and A.S. Asani, "The Ginān Literature of the Ismailis of Indo-Pakistan: Its Origins, Characteristics and Themes", in D.L. Eck and F. Mallison, eds., *Devotion Divine. Bhakti Traditions from the Regions of India (Studies in Honour of Charlotte Vaudeville)*, Groningen - Paris, 1991, pp. 1-18.

Although the Aga Khan's reform of Islam bears the mark of the Shīᶜite Ismaili heritage, its most innovative aspect resides in the sanctification of activities which contribute, by means of divine service in the form of work, to the *welfare* of humanity. This mutation of beliefs and practices, which in a way corroborates certain theses of Max Weber, permits the Aga Khan to propose pertinent responses to contemporary challenges for which he has generally been recognized by the Shīᶜite Ismailis despite some voices of dissent and protest.[48]

An important question which arises concerns the position of the present Imām, Shāh Karīm: has he continued the work of his predecessor since 1957 ? How has he dealt with the recent exile of Indian communities from East Africa and their movement towards Western Europe and North America ? The compilation and analysis of the Imām's *firmāns* which are to be published from Canada would provide the necessary elements to answer these and other questions.

Translated from French by Rashmi Patni

REFERENCES

Aga Khan, "The Defence of India", *The Nineteenth Century*, 1905, LVIII, pp. 367-75.

— *Memorandum on Relations with Turkey*, 1916, India Office, L/P & S/18/C 146.

— *India in Transition. A Study in Political Evolution*, Bombay - Calcutta: Bennett, Coleman and Co. Ltd., 1918.

— *Message. Six Articles on Religion and Politics*, compiled and published by Ismail M. Jaffer, Bombay: Karnatak Press, 1935.

— "Le libéralisme musulman", *Le Monde religieux* (Lausanne), October 1943, IV, pp. 69-74.

— (with Zaki Ali), *Glimpses of Islam* (1944), Lahore: Ashraf Press, 1973.

— (with Zaki Ali), *L'Europe et l'Islam*, Genève - Anemasse: Ed. du Mont-Blanc, 1945.

— *Memoirs. World Through and Time*, London: Cassel & Co., 1954.

— *Precious Pearls. Farman Mubarak of Hazrat Imam Mowlana Sultan Mohammad Shah* (1954), compiled and translated by Sherali

48. See Boivin, "Contestation et identité chez les Shīᶜites ismaéliens (1851-1908)", in Th. Bianquis, ed., *Désordres ruraux et troubles urbains dans la Méditerranée traditionnelle*, Damascus (Forthcoming).

Alidina and Kassim Ali M.J., Karachi: Ismailia Association Pakistan, 1961.

— A Collectanea of Some Recent Speeches and Writings of His Highness the Aga Khan, compiled by Sultan Nazerali El-Africi, Mombasa: Platinum Printers, 1955.

— *Mubarak Talika and Messages. Mowlana Hazir Imam's Guidance & Advice in Spiritual and Worldly Matters to Ismailis of Africa*, Mombasa: Shia Imami Ismailia Associations for Africa, 1955.

Aḥmad, Aziz, *Islamic Modernism in India and Pakistan. 1857-1964*, London: Oxford University Press, 1967.

Algar, Hamid, "The Revolt of Aga Khan Mahallati and the Transference of the Ismaili Imamate to India", *Studia Islamica*, 1969, XXIX, pp. 51-81.

Ameer Ali, *The Spirit of Islām. A History of Evolution and Ideals of Islām* (1922), London: Christophers, 1946.

— "The Modernity of Islam", *Islamic Culture*, 1927, I, pp. 1-7.

Asani, Ali Sultan, "The Khojahs of Indo-Pakistan: the Quest for an Islamic Identity", *Journal of the Institute of Muslim Minority Affairs*, 1987, VIII, 1, pp. 31-41.

— "The Ginān Literature of the Ismailis of Indo-Pakistan: Its Origins, Characteristics and Themes", in D.L. Eck and F. Mallison, eds., *Devotion Divine. Bhakti Traditions from the Regions of India* (*Studies in Honour of Charlotte Vaudeville*), Groningen, Egbert Forsten - Paris: Ecole Française d'Extrême-Orient, 1991, pp. 1-18.

— "The Ismaili *Ginān*s as Devotional Literature", in R.S. McGregor, ed., *Devotional Literature in South Asia. Current Research, 1985-1988*, Cambridge: Cambridge University Press, 1992, pp. 101-12.

Baljon, J.M.S., 'Aḥmad Khān', *Encyclopédie de l'Islam* (new edn.), Leiden: E.J. Brill, 1975, Vol. I, p. 297.

Boivin, Michel, "Shīʿisme ismaélien et modernité chez Sulṭān Muḥammad Shāh Aga Khan (1877-1957)", Ph.D. Thesis in History, Paris: Université de la Sorbonne Nouvelle, Paris III, 1993 (unpublished).

— "Islam, Nationalisme et avenir de l'Inde chez Sulṭān Muḥammad Shāh Aga Khan (1877-1957)", *Cahiers D'Histoire* (Lyon), 1993, T. XXXVIII, N° 1, pp. 55-73.

— "Contestation et identité chez les Shīʿites ismaéliens (1851-1908)", in Th. Bianquis, ed., *Désordres ruraux et troubles urbains dans la Méditerranée traditionnelle*, Damascus: Publications de l'Institut Français de Damas (Forthcoming).

Corbin, Henry, *Histoire de la philosophie islamique*, Paris: Gallimard, 2nd edn., 1986 (especially pp. 115-54, presentation of Ismaili philosophy and pp. 444-8).

Daftary, Farhad, *The Ismā'īlīs. Their History and their Doctrines*, Cambridge: Cambridge University Press, 1990.

Dumasia, N., *The Aga Khan and his Ancestors*, Bombay: Times of India Press, 1938.

Eboo, Nadia, "The Revolt of Aga Khan Mahalatti and the Establishment of the Nizari Imamate in India", B.A. Dissertation, Manchester: Victoria University of Manchester, 1979 (unpublished).

Fyzee, Asaf A.A., *Cases in the Muḥammadan Law of India and Pakistan*, Oxford: Oxford University Press, 1965.

Guimbretière, André, "Le réformisme musulman en Inde", *Orient*, 1960, 16, pp. 15-41.

Himmich, Bensalem, *De la formation idéologique en Islam. Ijtihadat et Histoire*, Paris: Anthropos, 1980.

Ikbal Ali Shah, *The Prince Aga Khan. An Authentic Life Story*, London: John Long Ltd., 1933.

Keddie, Nikki R., *An Islamic Response to Imperialism* (1968), Berkeley, Los Angeles: University of California Press, 1983.

Keshavjee, Rafique, "The Quest for Gnosis and the Call for History. Modernization Among the Ismailis of Iran", Ph.D. Thesis, Cambridge (Mass.): Harvard University, 1981 (unpublished).

Meherally, Akbarally, *Understanding Ismailism. A Unique Tariqa of Islam*, Burnaby (Canada): A.M. Trust, 1988.

Merad, Ali, 'Iṣlāḥ', *Encyclopédie de l'Islam*, (new edn.), Leiden: E.J. Brill, 1973, Vol. IV, pp. 146-70.

Merad, Ali, *L'Islam contemporain* (1984), Paris: Presses Universitaires de France (Que sais-je N° 2195), 1992.

Mortazavi, Djamshid, *Le secret de l'unité dans l'ésotérisme iranien*, Paris: Dervy-Livres, 1988.

Muir, William, *The Life of Mahomet and the History of Islam to the Hegira*, Four Vols., London: Smith, Elder & Co., 1858-61; new abridged edn. in One Vol., *The Life of Mahomet from the Original Sources*, London: Smith & Elder, 1894.

Nanji, Azim, *The Nizārī Ismā'īlī Tradition in the Indo-Pakistan Subcontinent*, Delmar (New York): Caravan Books, 1978.

Noorally, Zawahir, "The First Aga Khan and the British, 1838-1868. A Study in British Indian Diplomacy and Legal History", M.A. Dissertation, University of London, 1964 (unpublished).

Rattansi, Diamond, "Islamization and the Khojah Ismā'īlī Community in Pakistan", Ph.D. Thesis, Montreal: McGill University, 1987 (unpublished).

Sayyid Ahmad Khan, *Essays on the Life of Muhammad* (1870), London: Premier Book House, 1969.

Shackle, Christopher & Zawahir Moir, *Ismaili Hymns from South Asia. An Introduction to the Ginans*, London: School of Oriental and African Studies, University of London, 1992.

Shihāb al-Dīn Shāh al-Ḥusaynī, *Risālāt dar Ḥaqīqat-i Dīn or True Meaning of Religion*, Transl. from Persian into English by W. Ivanow, London: Thacker & Co., 1947.

— *Khiṭābāt-i ᶜĀliyya. Supreme Admonitions*, ed. by Hushang Ojaqi, Intr. by W. Ivanow, Tehran: Ismaili Society Series, A N° 14, 1963.

Sohrab, Siawash, "Die Arbeits wertheorie im schiitischen Islam", *Orient*, June 1969, XXV, 2, pp. 270-9.

Vadet, Jean-Claude, "La *Futuwwa*, morale professionnelle ou morale mystique", *Revue des Etudes Islamiques*, 1978, XLVI, 1, pp. 57-90.

10

The Influence of the Indo-Persian Medical Tradition on Muslim Cookery in Hyderabad, India

DELPHINE ROGER

Hyderabad: A Crossroads of Influences

The present case-study bears on the food habits of the Muslims of Hyderabad city in the Deccan, an urban area historically defined as the past twin cities of Golconda-Hyderabad and the present twin cities of Hyderabad-Secunderabad. Hyderabad proper was founded 400 years ago by Muḥammad Qulī (1580-1612), the fifth king of the Quṭb Shāhī dynasty, reigning over the kingdom of Golconda. It initially comprised a few thousand people[1] and now accomodates with the utmost difficulty more than 4.2 millions inhabitants. This population is about 40% Muslim, and the city is regarded, alongside Delhi and Lucknow, as one of the major centres of Islamic culture in India.

The Muslim population of Hyderabad, however, holds a special position in that it grew as an isolated entity in a culturally alien environment. Though they were never really cut off from the North Indian Muslim groundswell and its Central Asian and Middle Eastern hinterlands, the Muslim rulers of the Deccan rose to power in defiance of their North Indian overlords. As subjects of the Deccan kings, and because of their relative geographical remoteness, the Muslims of Hyderabad worked at first towards greater integration with the numerically dominant Hindu population. In addition, with a view to maintaining a firm political alliance, the Muslim population of the Deccan - which was mainly urban and most numerous in Hyderabad - also cul-

1. The size of the population can be estimated in comparison with the size of the Friday mosque built by Muḥammad Qulī Quṭb Shāh (it accomodates a congregation of around 800). Muḥammad Qulī Quṭb Shāh however estimated that the growth of the city would be rather quick: he had 14,000 shops built along the roads radiating from the Charminar, the center of his town. See H.K. Sherwani, *History of the Quṭb Shāhī Dynasty*, Chapt. IV, Delhi, 1974, pp. 300 *et seq.*

tivated strong links of friendship with Persia.[2] This gave a specific shade to their culture, which imbibed a noteworthy Shi'a influence, and nurtured a rich tradition of cultural exchange with Persia, in which scholars, poets and religious leaders figured prominently, as also in recent times the owners of the *Irani* "hotels" which are seen everywhere in the city nowadays !

The Persian Heritage

The Persian heritage is illustrated in many aspects of Hyderabadi culture, including food. The Muslim community of Hyderabad has always been noted for its cookery. From the seventeenth century onwards, that is from the birth itself of the town, foreign travellers have drawn attention to its numerous tastefully used quality food products.[3] Local poets have praised the glitter of the festive tables at the court.[4] Hyderabadi gastronomy is even now celebrated all through India. It is a cookery which is rich in fat, meat and sugar, typical therefore of a Muslim community that claims the inheritance of the Mughal empire. A traditional menu includes *biryānī*, *halīm*[5]... and many more delicacies of Persian origin.

The Persian influence is even more noticeable in a specific aspect of the Muslim cookery in Hyderabad: its links with an old medical tradition, that travelled from Greece to India, through Persia. As will be seen, the culinary wealth of Hyderabad is in fact a screen for deeper

---

2. From the reign of Muḥammmad Qulī onwards, envoys were regularly exchanged between the kingdom of Golconda and Persia. The first mission that of the Persian Aghuzlū Sulṭān, was sent by Shāh ᶜAbbās Safavī in 1603 with rich presents. In return, the Quṭb Shāhī king sent Qamhar ᶜAlī and Mehdī Qulī, but not what the Persian was asking for: a daughter of the king for his master. See Sherwani, *op. cit.*, p. 291.

3. See for example F. Bernier, *Travels in the Mogul Empire* (A.D. 1656-1668), eds. V.A. Smith and A. Constable, Oxford, 2nd edn., 1934 or J.B. Tavernier, *Travels in India* (1889), Transl. from French by V. Ball, rev. edn. by W. Crooke, Two Vols., London, 1925, Repr., New Delhi, 1977 and J. de Thévenot, *Indian Travels of Thévenot and Careri*, ed. S.N. Sen, New Delhi, 1949. Tavernier describes the country as abounding in wheat, rice, cattle, a fish of delicate taste... Bernier remarks that in Golconda are found the best mangoes and that the bread is quite good. See also Ferishta, *Gulshan-i Ibrahimi* (*Tārīkh-i Ferishta*), Mss. N° 111, Salar Jung Museum Library, Hyderabad; (Abridged) English Transl. by J. Briggs, *History of the Rise of the Mahommedan Power in India* (1829), Calcutta, 1908-10; Repr., Delhi, 1989, Vol. III. Ferishta sums up the feelings by saying that he has never found a country richer in agricultural products in India.

4. See for example the *maṣnawī Gulshan-i ᶜIshq*, a 17th century poem in Urdu, edited by S.M. Ahmed, Hyderabad, 1986. It describes with an abundance of details a very sophisticated wedding banquet.

5. *Biryānī*: a dish of rice and spiced meat cooked together, the summit of Hyderabadi cookery. Similar to the *pilavi* of Greece, and the *pilaf* type of cooking typical of the Iranians. *Ḥalīm*: a spiced, pasty mixture of wheat and meat.

motivations. The Muslim cooks insist that their specialities are good for the health too: if they flatter the tastebuds, they also take care of the body. This is why a number of Hyderabadi recipes are explained as prescriptions. This paper is not concerned with the efficacy of this tasty medicine,[6] but with its logic and its functioning. In other words, it aims to show how this medico-culinary discourse is organised, on what scholarly basis it is built and what part it allocates to the doctor and the cook.

Drawing from the daily attitudes of a sample of individuals,[7] we can try to trace back the making of a tradition that goes back a long way in time, to the roots of the Muslim civilization in its Indo-Persian variant.

The Folk Science of Dietetics

Food: A Serious Matter

It is hard not to talk about cookery with the Hyderabadi Muslims. From the bottom to the top of the society, there is a common dream of *biryānī* full of flavour or very hot *kabābs*,[8] a dream which is materialized as often as possible but at the cost sometimes of dangerous financial acrobatics. Taking the bus on Monday mornings is as good as reading a culinary magazine: women exchange the recipes tried at the week-end, the chutney of a sister-in-law or a new sweet... The city at present abounds in "hotels" - very simple restaurants in fact -, in bakeries, sweet-shops and other tongue-ticklers. It can boast of being considered a temple of gastronomy, of a style rather loosely called Mughlai,[9] throughout India and even beyond.

Food represents however more than art or pleasure in Hyderabad.

---

6. One can even doubt the Hyderabadi people's interest in the efficiency of their theories and practices. They just do not question them. They preserve an heritage, believe in acts and thoughts closer to magical experience than to scientifical knowledge and thus not prone to validation.

7. The individuals who have been observed and questioned during the year 1990 mainly come from different parts of the city - the old and the new -, are of different origin - they claim an Iranian, Arabic or Turkish ancestry -, and profess different forms of Islam. They thus quite well represent the diversity of the Muslim population in Hyderabad. In spite of their differences, they all had a similar discourse on food and cookery. As far as cookery proper - and not food only - is concerned, only the wealthiest of these people are really relevant to this study: the lowest part of the Muslim population, as well as the Hindu, survives - and has always survived - on a very simple diet and can only imagine or try to imitate what Hyderabadi cookery is all about.

8. *Kabābs*: roasted spiced meat (in cubes or balls).

9. Mughlai cookery is to India what *Grande Cuisine* is to France. Although the Mughals never directly ruled the Deccan for long, it gives an ancient and sophisticated tradition a legitimacy to call it Mughlai - that is to say: Central Asian and perhaps implicitly "from the emperors".

It is also - and this is not incompatible - a serious matter. If the Muslims of Hyderabad are in the habit of always offering more to eat, it is with a sure discrimination. One does not give anyone anything to eat. It is presupposed, as it is elsewhere in India, that food has an effect on the physical and moral state of the eater. Therefore, one is careful about what is cooked and ingested: quality takes precedence over quantity. What is now specific to the Muslim cookery in Hyderabad is that it aims at the highest quality in both dimensions: gastronomic and dietetic.

Classification of Food: The Hot and the Cold

For the Muslims of Hyderabad, the quality of food defines itself of course through a number of hedonist parameters - smell, look, taste, satisfaction gained - but also through "medical" factors. Food products are indeed classified in two distinct groups, marked as hot or cold, qualities referring to inner properties and influencing the health of the eater. This is a classification found in more or less every society but seldom so clearly expressed - it is for example perverted in a male/female antinomy in western societies[10] or overshadowed by the opposition of the pure and impure in Hinduism[11]... The Muslims of Hyderabad consider in this way that curd is cold - even served boiling hot - and ginger hot - even in ice-cream form. These designations have been joined to their objects on the basis of tradition or according to an

10. As the latest sociological studies of food habits show, salad and all greens, fish and all sea products (that would be held to be cold by Hyderabadis) are commonly considered as suitable for and preferred by women when men would choose red meat and carbohydrates (hot food for Hyderabadis). This seems to be especially true for men from the middle class, who have to assert their power, often confused with their potency. It has to do of course with the modern concern for the feminine figure and the diet the women are likely to prefer is the less caloric one. It is however backed by deeper mental structures like Dumezil's tripartite division of society: blood and therefore red meat is the attribute of the man/warrior and sexually potent, while the vegetarian-oriented diet is the mark of a lower being (because it is still very much attached to the soil and its products) or a peaceful, even fragile being (needing therefore to be protected by the warrior) be it the woman or the priest. Also, something of the original murder still remains attached to the piece of steak, as well as something indecent, it seems, for the "naturally" shy woman to devour it. When this type of hot/violent versus cold/peaceful classification is used by Hyderabadi Muslims, they never point out a possible link with the division of the sexes.

11. Even though L. Dumont's formulation (*Homo Hierarchicus. Essai sur le système des castes*, Paris, 1966) has been severely questioned (see M. Marriott, ed., *India through Hindu Categories*, New Delhi, 1990, Introduction, p. XIII, for example) the pure/impure logic is nonetheless basic in Hindu thought and practices. Traditional Hindus would be in the first place concerned with the purity status of food, not with its taste or medical properties. A suitable meal for them is a meal cooked by the appropriate cook for a particular eater, according to his rank on the scale of ritual purity.

analytical logic. If this ancient knowledge sometimes fails to fulfil its role, when a new food product is introduced for example, the classification resorts to analogy: watery fruit and vegetables are likely to be cold like cucumber, food products heavy with blood - hence with energy - are likely to be hot - or energetic. Something appears here which will be specified later on: a concordance between these categories and the primary elements, here water - cucumber - and fire - red meat - of the classical Greek or Indian cosmogony.

Mixing and Matching Food Products

To this essential couple are, as is often the case, attached other systems of classification: the one that opposes, for example, the spicy to the bland or in Hyderabad the sweet - *mīṭhā*, bland in reality - to the sour - *khaṭṭā*. The *mīṭhī dāl* - split peas or lentils - is thus distinguished from the *khāṭṭī dāl*. But what is typical of Hyderabad is the association in every meal of a sour dish and a "sweet" one, in order "not to fall ill". In the same way, fresh cream, "cold", has to be added to the mango puree, "hot", in summer for health purposes. Or so it is said.

In fact, these antagonisms are worth nothing, for their combinations, with each other and with numerous outer elements. A person subject to cold had better avoid eating cucumbers, a pregnant woman must not eat papaya - its heat causes premature delivery. According to the Muslims of Hyderabad, it is necessary to harmonize all the constituents of the meal, inner and outer: food products, cooking utensils, season, place, the individual it is meant for. Tamarind-flavoured dishes were formerly cooked in earthenware pots only and other cooking was conducted in copper or silver. If skin diseases are nowadays so common in Hyderabad, the reason must be found according to the people, in the use of other metals to make cooking vessels - cheap aluminium, for instance. Menus are designed according to seasons: curds and watermelon in the hot season, and dry fruits and red meat in the cold season. They are more generally adapted to the climate of the Deccan: it is essential, in dry and hot Hyderabad, to consume a lot of sour food - from sweet lime to mutton stewed in tamarind juice or chutney of local sorrel[12] -, or so it is said. It should be noted that this high consumption of sour things is the cause of many acidity problems in the Muslim population of Hyderabad, a fact not acknowledged of course. It is also said that in Hyderabad it is dangerous to eat sweets in the morning, a luxury that should be reserved for North Indians. The old

12. *Ambada: Hibiscus cannabinus,* ambari hemp.

nobility of Hyderabad however indulged in the eating of sweets at any time of the day.

The Meal: A Cosmogonic View

The point is then, to keep in good health, to find the balance between all the constituents of the meal, as numerous as they are defined. One can also play on the opposed values of the products to restore a disturbed balance: give "cold" food to a man suffering from fever or heartburns, give *ajwāyan* seeds (*Trachyspermum ammi*) in the middle of the winter to warm up someone lacking proper clothes. It goes even further: Hyderabadi Muslims know by heart lists of harmful associations - such as fish with milk, considered to induce leprosy - or good combinations of a dangerous substance and its antidote - *badrara*. One might cite the combination of *ghī* (clarified butter) and chillies, or the one of radish and honey. Food itself is then not questioned but its use is. This is why popular wisdom stresses hygiene and the prevention of ailments through the rational choice of food combinations.

The Muslims of Hyderabad think and act therefore in terms of causes to be controlled in order to circumscribe perverse effects. They look for the good combinations because, for them, not only cucumber or mango, but man, earth, metals, and hence the universe itself, are made out of elements that are hot or cold, dry or moist, hard or soft - secondary food classifications but more appropriately applied to other substances than the sweet/sour one. It also means that every sickness is for them fundamentally a food poisoning, because for every disorder a cause is found in a meal wrongly conceived. Every family has stories to tell of sudden death caused by "food allergy". Everyone seems to know also the food that is harmful to him/her: bananas for a woman with a tendency to swelling, guavas for an asthmatic, sugar for a family to which it causes headaches and vomiting. The proper personality of the eater must be therefore taken into account before conceiving a meal.

Using Traditional Knowledge: A Contradiction

Food represents, indeed, to a varying extent, a potential danger for the Muslims of Hyderabad, a danger the more present since gastronomy is one of their chief concerns. Once identified, they circumscribe this danger by the rationalization of their culinary practices, with the help of a pseudo-medical discourse. This however does not give way to a theorization on the human body or its image. It does not involve thoughts on the form and functions of the universe either. Hyderabadis have fully integrated modern scientific knowledge, and their concepts on diet stand on their own, apart from the scientific "truth". It seems that the people observed are trying to preserve the objects and discourse that former generations have transmitted, without questioning their basis. It could be called a process of tradition-making. If we asssume, after C. Levi-Strauss, that cookery is a language which expresses a certain world-view, it is then a contradiction that is expressed here. There is indeed a gap between the culinary discourse - leading to a practice - of the Muslims of Hyderabad and the world-view it refers to, on the one hand, and the world-view they really have integrated, on the other hand. This gap is obviously a way to express the crisis of a society in transition, carelessly uprooted from its past.[13]

The Scholarly Discourse and Practice

The Ayurvedic Foundations

These popular discourse and practices on nutritional hygiene do not permit much improvisation. They are endlessly repeated with the legitimacy time gives to "folk sciences". They can also be linked to scholarly discourse and practices marked, like the history of Hyderabad, by the interference of a millenia-long Hindu heritage, the contribution of Islam and a strong regional identity.

Behind the clouds of seemingly empirical assertions, in common use around Hyderabadi tables, one recognizes first of all a good deal of what might be termed Ayurvedic knowledge.

Ayurveda, a branch of Indian traditional medicine, was, according to tradition, revealed by the god Brahma; it forms a part of the historical oral tradition, passed down from disciple to disciple. It is sometimes claimed as the fifth *Veda* or sacred and legendary book of the Aryans.

It is based on a classification of the universe around five elements[14] - ether, air, fire, water and earth - that are combined to make any animate or inanimate being. From the balance of this combination ensues the quality of the constituted object. Man must therefore pay attention to seasons, his circumstances of life, his own con-

13. Since the creation of the state of Andhra Pradesh, the Muslims have lost their political and financial pre-eminence in Hyderabad. The Hindu majority has confiscated most of the power and seems to be trying to blot the Muslim heritage out of the memories, allowing many important monuments to decay, for example.

14. The *panca mahābhūta* or five elements are: *ākāśa* (ether), *vāyu* (air), *agni* (fire), *jala* (water) and *prithivī* (earth). Each element is itself a combination of the five, with a dominant component. See V.B. Dash, *Fundamentals of Ayurvedic Medicine*, New Delhi, 1982, p. 17.

stitution[15] - Ayurveda counts seven types of constitutions - before conducting any action. But the primary combinations come from the nourishment. This is why Ayurvedic science is based upon careful choice and circulation of the substances ingested. According to it, in fact, ailments are caused by defective circulation and the storage of ill-assimilated materials - a fact rendered in Hyderabad by the terms "indigestion", "food poisoning". These are components of the dietetic discourse of the Muslims of Hyderabad.

Ayurvedic Theories on the Balance of Elements

From Ayurveda also certainly comes the claim to determine the nature of a substance by its external qualities: if it is heavy and hard, say the old Ayurvedic treatises, then it is dominated by the element "earth" and encourages tendencies to heaviness, roundness, stability; if it is liquid, cold and soft, it is dominated by water and will generate humidity, softness and happiness... The taste (*rasa*) of the substance also indicates its nature. A sweet substance is dominated by earth and water, a sour one by wind and ether. Considering the fact that to any excess or lack of one of the elements corresponds a number of ailments, because the internal balance is altered, the link between choice of food and the noted disorder appears to be obvious. Excess of wind, for example, causes deafness, cataract, torticollis... and these ailments will be cured by the taking of sour, salted or sweet food - in other words, the food that announces by its taste another dominant element.

Digestion is essential to this alchemy because it will convert the elements from exogenic bodies into easily assimilated substances. It is all a matter of appropriate "cooking" then: harmful storage in the body is caused by food products that are raw or "ill-cooked". This happens when food is not in accordance with the power of fire of the eater, its *agni*, also flatly translated by enzymes.[16] Food can be too hot or the eater too cold for this central function to be conveyed properly. If to cook in Hyderabad is to have a concern for medicine, medicine can be seen here as a cookery.

---

15. See for example C. Chakrabarty, *An Interpretation of Ancient Hindu Medicine*, Delhi, 1983.

16. Ayurveda distinguishes between four types of *agni*: *viṣamāgni* (erratic state of digestion), *tīkṣṇāgni* (easy digestion of everything), *mandāgni* (unability to digest anything), *samāgni* (easy digestion of a balanced diet). See Dash, *op. cit.*, pp. 36-42. For the metaphors around the sacred fire and the digestion in Hinduism see also C. Malamoud, *Cuire le monde: rite et pensée dans l'Inde ancienne*, Paris, 1989, Chapt. 2, "Cuire le monde", pp. 35-70.

The Other Source: Yūnānī Medicine

Merely by referring to Ayurveda, one already feels the deep link that joins these two functions, of feeding and treating the body. The conceptions of the Hyderabadi Muslims are however backed by another medico-philosophical system. It is another traditional medicine: the *Yūnānī* medicine. *Yūnānī* means Greek (Ionian) in Urdu and this accounts well for the origin of these theories: they are the concepts of Hippocrates (460-377) and Galen (131-210), translated under the Abbassids, into Arabic, for the Muslim world of the 8th and 9th centuries - at the instigation of Caliph Hārūn al-Rashīd and his son Maḥ'mun mainly. They were carried into India in their Persian translation during the 10th and 11th centuries. They are the concepts that the famous Avicenna (Ibn Sinā, 980-1037) amongst others, had popularized. When the Mongols attacked Central Asia, doctors and scholars fled from the region for neighbouring countries, including India. They were carrying in their luggage *Yūnānī* treatises. They were welcomed by the Sultans of Delhi, on good terms with Baghdad, and their medicine soon became popular in the whole sub-continent. Between the 15th and the 17th centuries mostly, a number of *Yūnānī* hospitals and research centers developed. The Quṭb Shāhī dynasty, tightly linked with Persia and at its zenith from the end of the 16th century to the end of the 17th century, sponsored in Hyderabad the blossoming of *Yūnānī* medicine. The founder of the town himself, Muḥammad Qulī (1580-1612) had a "health house" - *Dāru'sh-Shifā* - established, which was at the same time a hospital with a capacity of 400 "beds" and a teaching center.[17] The kings of Hyderabad also are known to have enjoyed discussions with their *ḥakīms* or *Yūnānī* doctors,[18] and encouraged them to write treatises, some manuscripts of which have been preserved.[19]

17. The *Dāru'sh-Shifā* was established in 1595. Treatment and diet were provided to the patients free of cost. The enterprise was planned by Mīr Mu'min Astarābādī, a celebrity of the time. Of Persian origin, he was a talented poet, an architect and doctor of *Yūnānī* medicine. He became *peshwa* of the kingdom of Golconda. Remains of this hospital are still to be seen in Hyderabad. See A. Momin and S.A. Hussain, "Medical Manuscripts of Qutub Shahi Period in the Libraries of Hyderabad", *Bulletin of the Indian Institute on the History of Medicine*, Hyderabad, 1990, Vol. XIX, pp. 129-35. See also the Persian text *Ikhtiyārāt-i Quṭb Shāhi* of Mīr Mu'min Yazdī, Manuscript (451 folios), Salar Jung Museum Library, Hyderabad.

18. To give the names of a few medical personalities of repute during the Quṭb Shāhī period: Mīr Mu'min, Shamsu'd-dīn ᶜAlī al-Ḥusainī al-Juranī, Safīu'd-dīn Gīlānī, and Niẓāmu'd-dīn Aḥmad Gīlānī.

19. See for example the *Ikhtiyārāt-i Quṭb Shāhī*, written by Mīr Mu'min Yazdī for Muḥammad Qulī Quṭb Shāh. Also the *Mīzānu'ṭ-Ṭabā'iᶜ-i Quṭb Shāhī*, written in Persian by Taqiyyu'd-dīn Muḥammad bin Ṣadri'd-dīn ᶜAlī; this manuscript (Salar Jung Museum Library) was written for Muḥammad Quṭb Shāh, the 6th king of Golconda (1612-26) to

Thanks to these manuscripts, it is possible to realize the weight of the *Yūnānī* theories on the culinary activities of Hyderabad.

Basis of Yūnānī Medicine: Combinations, Compensations

Yūnānī medicine is, like Ayurvedic medicine, based on elements, humours, temperaments and their combinations[20]. The *ḥakīm* acknowledges the four common elements of the Greek cosmogony: air, fire, water and earth.[21] They are combined, in his view, to form the spirit and the organs, themselves associated to produce energy. Like Ayurveda, this medicine rests on a causality principle: each individual is the product of heritage, of a temperament and of the effects of external factors - whether natural or not. Neither water nor fire are however primary elements for the *ḥakīm*: they are themselves composed of the four elements or fundamental energies, that is heat/cold and dryness/moisture. Here are found the antagonistic pairings of the popular discourse in Hyderabad. To understand the stress put on the hot/cold opposition, one need only know that, according to Avicenna, who took it from Aristotle, these two principles alone are active, the other two being passive.

According to *Yūnānī* medicine, human beings are themselves more or less hot or cold, and each part of the body has its own warmth. That is why certain foods are more appropriate for certain ailments. Ailments can be cured either by their opposite principle - something cold for an excess of heat[22] - or by their like - something hot for a sick organ classified as hot.[23]

---

remedy the deficiencies of the medical works of the time. The author, Taqiyyu'd-dīn Muḥammad, exerted himself to write the perfect medical treatise. The manuscript deals mainly with the description of drugs and compounds but also includes four prefaces which provide a theoretical framework for the understanding of the principles of *Yūnānī* medicine. The author actually distances himself quite perceptibly from the recognized authorities, occasionally indulging in overt criticism of their conclusions.

20. The *Yūnānī* terms are *arkān* (elements), *mizāj* (temperaments), *akhlāṭ* (humours). See *Fundamentals of Ayurvedic medicine*, *op. cit.*, p. 198.

21. They are *miṭṭī* (earth), *āg* (fire), *pānī* (water) and *hawā* (air). *Ibid.*, p. 199.

22. It can be explained as the relationship of sympathy linking minerals, organs, plants and planets described by M. Mauss (*Sociologie et Anthropologie*, Paris, 1950, p. 70) and that most societies recognize. The sympathy creates classes of things and it is within such classes that the doctor, the magician, and the poet operate. In a universe in which every part is related to the whole and to the other parts, being of the same nature, all things can influence one another. By sympathy they attract their like or by antipathy repel their contrary.

23. See Shamsu'd-dīn bin Nūru'd-dīn Ṭabīb, *Zubdatu'l-Hikam*, Persian Mss. in the Salar Jung Museum and Library, Tibb. 277, from folio 81. Especially 1st discourse, Chapt. 2: organs classified as hot for example: heart, liver, and muscles. On the other hand, hair and bones are cold.

Linking Popular and Scholarly Discourse: A Mixed Tradition

More examples could be given to show how the discourse on nutritional hygiene of the Muslims of Hyderabad is rooted in systems of thought well established in India.[24] Hyderabadis themselves make the link between popular and scholarly discourse, they sometimes resort to the specialist to perfect their imprecise knowledge - the *ḥakīm* in priority for Muslims because he represents an "Arabic" science. However popular and apparently accessible they have become, these medicines have retained an esoteric nature - the magical aura necessary to any cure - and their entire knowledge is not accessible to the common man. This also comes from their strong links with astrology and alchemy and implies the secrecy of most preparations or combinations.[25]

Ayurveda and *Yūnānī* medicine have been distinguished here for the purposes of the discussion. Hyderabadis distinguish between them, as Ayurveda, especially nowadays, is closely connected with Hinduism. Yet it must be noted that many Ayurvedic works were lost or destroyed during the medieval period and that the knowledge they could have transmitted was altered.

In the same way, if Avicenna's *Canon*[26] of medicine is still used by the *ḥakīms* of Hyderabad as a *vade mecum* of *Yūnānī* medicine, the knowledge of the Greeks was largely altered while entering India.[27] It was adapted to the country's conditions. As a matter of fact, this is a necessary factor for the success of the cure. The doctors from Gilan or Shiraz therefore translated, as soon as they arrived in India, the local

24. It is important to note, however, that the theoreticians themselves used a great deal of empirical, traditional knowledge while compiling their works. They were using experiments to confirm their scientifical discourse, not to build it. The author of the *Mīzānu'ṭ-Ṭabā'iᶜ-i Quṭb Shāhī* says (4th preface) that the *ḥakīm* knows the temperament of food by experience or by guessing. Experiments, he notes, are hard to conduct: the doctor never knows if a change in the state of the patient is due to his action or to an external cause. Experiments on animals can however prove useful, he remarks.

25. In this way, it is close to magic, as defined by Mauss, *op. cit.*, p. 95 for example.

26. *Al-Qānūn-fi'ṭ Ṭibb* in Arabic. It was written using Hippocrates's theory (460-377), as modified by Aristotle and Galen. See H. Shah Mazhar, *The General Principles of Avicenna's Canon of Medicine*, Karachi, 1966.

27. Doctors used to write new treatises from works already compiled from the ancient texts, by adding and altering. Mīr Mu'min Yazdī wrote his *Ikhtiyārāt-i Quṭb Shāhī* from different sources, the main authority being the *Ikhtiyārāt-i Badīᶜī* from ᶜAlī bin Ḥusain 'al-Anṣārī (1330-1403). It was already a compilation of the *Qānūn-i Minhaj*, Jamai Ibn Baittar... The practice was then to elaborate on a very famous work. But Mīr Mu'min used both ancient texts and contemporary experts, he even confronted passages of the originals with the results of those whom he consulted. See A. Momin, *A Study of Ikhtiyarat-e-Qutb Shahi* (not published).

medical treatises. To quote Mīān Bhūwa, outstanding courtier in the reign of Sikandar Lodī (1489-1517), composing a book of *Yūnānī* medicine:[28] "*Yūnānī* medicine does not suit the temperament of the people living in the changing climatic conditions of India". Moreover, "the names of the drugs are in Persian or *Yūnānī* language and unknown to the people of India" and "the *Yūnānī* doctors cannot obtain what they want". And hence "there is no other alternative than the translation of the books of the Indian physicians".[29] These two systems of thought have never entered into competition, they have borrowed from each other - without even mentioning their common origin in beliefs originating from Central and West Asia. What the Muslims of Hyderabad elaborated on are the theories and practices of the *ḥakīm* essentially but with their tint of Ayurveda. It is a medicine resembling the community which uses it: Muslim to the point of pretending to be Arabic, but deeply rooted in an India shaped by Hinduism. The oldest known book on *Yūnānī* medicine in India, the *Ṭibb-i Shifā Maḥmud Shāhī*, which founded the conjunction between the Indian and the Persian tradition, belongs to the region of Hyderabad. The Āṣaf Jāhī kings of Hyderabad (1724-1947) were the first Indian rulers to recognize *Yūnānī* medicine officially.[30] Today, *Yūnānī* medicine is still very active in Hyderabad and it very successfully opposes the progress of allopathy.

Cooks and Ḥakīms in Hyderabad: A Common Destiny ?

Ḥakīm*s as Food Consultants*

Ayurveda and *Yūnānī* medicine not only provided a theoretical framework to the thinking of the Muslims of Hyderabad on their cookery. On a very material level, they contributed, it could be said, to the development of the culinary art in Hyderabad.

These two medicines offer indeed simple therapeutics: proper hygiene of life and treatments that are based on vegetable or animal products - even minerals or metals during the medieval period. These are bought on the market or collected in the open air. Both of them imply an effort to classify and circulate the products. This must have

---

28. The book is the *Maᶜdanu'sh-Shifā-i Sikandar Shāhī*. See *Bulletin of the Departement of History of Medicine*, Hyderabad, Osmania Medical College, July, 1964, Vol. II, Nº 3.

29. See Note 27. The article gives the example of a translation of the *Madanavinoda* of Rājā Madana, in Persian, by a certain K͟hān Zamān, in 1663, under the title *Dastūru'l Hunūd*.

30. The 6th Niẓām, 1869-1911.

helped to diversify food ressources. A good Ayurvedic doctor knows 35 types of roots and fruit, 4 types of grain, 5 of salts, 8 of wines and milk.[31] Food stuffs are classified in 14 charts in some *Yūnānī* treatises, 12 in the Ayurvedic books. Their properties are explained.[32] The *Zubdatu'l-Hikam* gives for example those of the fruits, vegetables, cereals, oils, and meats used in India - from mutton to peacock, to fresh or salted fish. This *Yūnānī* treatise gives lists of dangerous nutritional combinations and the antidote to each food: mutton for lentils, old wine for duck, honey sweetmeat - *ḥalwā* - for mutton *kabāb*s. This will all be very useful to the cooks, if they want to avoid major mistakes: creating deafness in the eater for example, by mixing black gram and radish in a meal. This allows them also to combine the ideal menu for everyone. For a tuberculosis patient it reads as follows: beef fried in *ghī* and rice bread, violet sherbet and *fālūdā* - a semi-liquid sweet favoured in Hyderabad.

These treatises even provide the properties of ready-made dishes: one is advised to take *ḥalwā* against the bad effects of quail soup, old wine against those of *samosa*s - that is meat-filled puffs. They teach that *harīs* - cooked wheat and mutton mashed in a paste - strengthens the back or that *qalyā* - a dish of meat or fish in a sauce with a special mixture of spices or *masālā* - makes one a genius. They offer lists of heavy or light, rich or poor dishes. It means that the *ḥakīm* addresses himself to an audience of connoisseurs and practitioners of cookery and that he himself knows these typical Hyderabadi delicacies.

Ḥakīm*s as Cooks*

Ayurvedic and *Yūnānī* treatises even provide their own recipes. Ayurvedic cures are, in order of preference: drinks, diet, drugs, operations.[33] When one must resort to drugs, Ayurvedic treatises often stress their palatability. The 5th section of the *Unani Pharmacopoeia* is, for example, entitled "*Ḥalwā*" (sweets or sweetmeats), i.e. soft preparations of drugs which are pounded with sugar and honey "in order to give them a pleasant taste". Section 13 is about *mājūn*, pastes which are based on sugar or honey "so that they may be taken with pleasure".

31. See *Fundamentals of Ayurvedic Medicine*, *op. cit.*, for example (Chapt. VI, "Diet").

32. See P. Sharma (ed. and transl.) *Caraka Samhita, Agnivesa's Treatise refined and annotated by Caraka and redacted by Dridhabala*, Delhi, 1981 (p. 197 for example).

33. *Fundamentals of Ayurvedic Medicine*, *op. cit.* gives a list of best drugs, diet and regimens (pp. 134-5), starting with food, water, wine, milk, meat, meat soup, salt, sour things, meat of cock and honey. It comes to medicinal plants only under section 30.

This is why the "drugs" often consist in spiced gruels, fruit or meat juices, medicated *ghīs*,[34] syrups or preserves. There are different processes to make the drugs assimilable and tasty. These tasty treatments are indeed considered more like food than drugs by the doctors, although taken in limited quantities.

Yūnānī medicine is even more precise on these links between food and remedy. It distinguishes between four degrees of substances, more or less effective on the body. The grade I substances have a little effect. The grade II substances are active if they are repeatedly administered. The grade III substances produce a noticeable change and the grade IV ones harm or destroy the organism. It is a scale from food to poison, through medicine, that the Hyderabadi Muslim have integrated. There does not exist for them any gap between these three categories. In fact, grade I substances include food as well as well-balanced drugs, grade II comprise food and medicines. The *Mīzānu'ṭ-Ṭabā'iᶜ-i Quṭb Shāhī* mentions in its preface that every thing going into the body is of one of these four types: pure drug, pure food or a combination of both with a predominance of one or the other element. For example, egg yolk and meat juices are considered close to the nature of blood and thus purely nutritive, meat or bread are in between, medicated food is seen as closer to drugs.

As far as the *Yūnānī* medicated foods are concerned, they are tempting:[35] preserves - *murabbā* - of apple or quince, syrups - *sharbat* - of pomegranate or rose.[36] The *ḥakīms* know how to make drugs palatable and assimilable. They even know, if the patient feels reluctant to take a pure drug, how to treat food to give it curative virtues. They can provide, for example, preparations to be given to chickens and pigeons before consuming them and it is told in Hyderabad that a king, under the Abbassids, was cured from constipation by grapes coming from medically-treated vines.

The Ḥakīm *and his Patient: A Contemporary Perspective*

These medical treatises stimulate then the culinary creation process

34. See E. Sharpe (Transl. from Hindi), *An 800 Year Old Book of Indian Medicine and Formulas*, New Delhi, 1979.

35. See *The Unani Pharmacopoeia (Formulary of Unani Medicine)* published by the Indian Medical Practitioner's Cooperative Pharmacy and Stores, Madras, 1982. It describes a *ḥalwā* of egg yolk (with nutmeg, zafran, musk and sugar) to improve the patient's complexion, another of carrot (with milk, *ghī*, sugar, walnuts, hazelnuts, almonds, coconut and pistachios) reputed as an aphrodisiac (Section V, "*Halwā*").

36. *Sharbat* or syrup of rose is a sedative, *sharbat* of pomegranate is good for the heart, and *sharbat* of violet heals cough (See *Unani Pharmacopoeia, op. cit.*).

or the gourmet's appetite. Even nowadays, in Hyderabad, the Muslims order from the *ḥakīms* favourite *sharbats* and preserves. For they can be consumed without any danger even if there is nothing to cure: the nature of these remedies is said to be such that they suit a healthy as well as a sick body. They can be used also in a preventive manner, as tonics. The *ḥakīms* are indeed often recognized as good cooks. Heirs of their family traditions,[37] they know where and how to purchase the best products, they prepare them cautiously and like to try new recipes.

It can be added that the medical treatises even provide advice for the composition of diets according to seasons,[38] individuals and ages,[39] as well as advice to set the order of the meal.[40] The task of the cook is underpinned in this way by the thought and practice of the doctor. The *ḥakīm* can even make up for the mistakes of the cook: once a careless cook had used bad *ghī* in a festive *biryānī* and the desperate host called the *ḥakīm* for help; he put white and red sandal sachets in the rice thus saving the dinner. Because sandal keeps its good smell while absorbing the bad ones, the wedding meal went off well.

The image of the doctor is then far from being unprepossessing for a Hyderabadi Muslim. The *ḥakīm* reassures because what he knows as a professional is what every one practises as an amateur.[41] The principles of the medicine he uses have long been forgotten by the common man but its sweetness still seduces. A relationship is established between the doctor and the patient, the sick man and the remedy, that might have existed but has been long lost in western societies: a relationship of pleasure. The *ḥakīm* does not promote asceticism, he helps enjoy all food, by the use of appropriate combinations.[42] Moreover, he develops them. So doing, he proves to be the faithful servant of a certain spirit of the *Qurān*, which encourages the disciples to eat what-

37. As Marcel Mauss points out (*op. cit.*, p. 36), "magical powers" are attributed to corporations, not to individuals. It is a quality transmitted from father to son. One can also call it a *savoir-faire*, a talent, as the common man would say.

38. To each season corresponds the intensification of a certain element, says Ayurveda. *Vāyu* gets aggravated during June-August for example (*Fundamentals of Ayurvedic Medicine*, *op. cit.*, p. 22).

39. The ages themselves are classified as hot, cold, moist and so on. Adults are supposed to be dry and hot. Children are moist and of a temperate heat (See *The General Principles of Avicenna's Canon of Medicine*, *op. cit.*).

40. The *Zubdatu'l-Hikam*, *op. cit.*, suggests meat, wheat bread, a sweet dish and a pure sweet-scented drink as the perfect diet for a normal adult (1st discourse, Chapt. 2). Sweet dishes are supposed to help the digestion of salty and spicy preparations.

41. The *ḥakīm* masters all things through their classification and description.

42. According to the *Mīzānu'ṭ-Ṭabā'iᶜ-i Quṭb Shāhī*, *op. cit.*, all food can be mixed if the right combinations are found (3rd preface).

ever is best, as a reward.[43] He also proves to be the faithful ally of a culinary tradition developed early in Baghdad but probably brought to perfection under the Mughals in India.

A Well-being Oriented Cookery in Hyderabad

For the Muslims of Hyderabad, to eat well and be healthy has since long been considered compatible. The cookery of well-being has always formed part of their mode of thinking - on principles that are not those of modern dietetics. This ambivalence seems even deeper: all the recipes of the Hyderabadi Muslim cookery seem to have been influenced by the *ḥakīm* and the cook does not seem to exist there apart from as a dietician.[44] Hyderabadi Muslims claim that many recipes have been invented by the *ḥakīms*. To be a *ḥakīm*, one must be a perfect cook: know ingredients and master the stages of cooking.[45] *Ḥakīms* are fine sweetmakers in particular because many of their drugs involve the use of sugar or honey in their various stages. They are thought to have perfected the recipes of the *sharbat*, *ḥalwā* and *murabbā*, probably at the court of the Muslim rulers in Delhi and later of the Deccan. They were attached to princely personages and when they did not have to cure them, they spent their time making life sweeter for them in laboratories both medical and culinary. When a new substance was presented at the court, it was their task to test its harmfulness and to find the ideal combination to make it assimilable. It was for them to establish good recipes rather than good prescriptions - as a matter of fact, the same word conveys both meanings in Hyderabad. In the descriptions of meals in old poems, there are clues about the influence of the medical theories: food is often presented in a definite order, food combinations

43. See *Qurān*, II-167, III-26, V-6,7,89 for example in Kasimirski's translation of the *Qurān*, Paris.

44. A view shared by Melitta Weiss-Amer, in an article entitled "The Role of Medieval Physicians in the Diffusion of Culinary Recipes and Cooking Practices", in C. Lambert, ed., *Du manuscrit à la table, essais sur la cuisine au Moyen-Age et répertoire de manuscrits médiévaux contenant des recettes culinaires*, Montréal, 1992, pp. 69-80. She is exploring "the relationship between cooking and preventive medicine in Medieval Europe" and notes that "culinary recipes are found in the specific lists of foodstuffs" of medical works (*Ibid.*, p. 74). She too comes to the conclusion that "physicians... also contributed to the spread of culinary recipes and cooking practices (*Ibid.*, p. 78).

45. As Zimmermann points out (*Le discours des remèdes au pays des épices: enquête sur la médecine hindoue*, Paris, 1989, p. 51), Ayurvedic preparations are elaborated in an ordinary kitchen. In the same way, the *hakīms* of Hyderabad use ordinary vessels mostly to prepare their drugs, in the same kitchen in which they cook food. Their "cookery" can be compared to the highly efficient use of the magical cauldron by the witch (see Mauss, *op. cit.*, p.46). It is the central utensil of an art of mixing, kneading and boiling to create drugs that look like food.

are suggested by the association in a verse of two dishes, to be taken together.[46] In the same way, if *biryānī* is nowadays served along with *būrānī* - curd spiked with onions and herbs - in Hyderabad, it is possibly because the *ḥakīms* have declared their combination healthy - it is supposed to fight the constipation usually caused by rice and to be helpful for the brain. *Yūnānī* medicine should also probably be thanked for the classical association of *khichrī* - rice and lentils or split peas cooked together -, *ghī* and *achār* - hot and oily pickles. According to the specialists, it is good for blood circulation.

Culinary Extravaganzas: Medicine or Alchemy in the Kitchen

The doctors should also be thanked for these strange recipes found in 19th century Hyderabadi cookbooks:[47] mutton stewed with pomegranate or moon flowers - *Ipomoea bona nox* - or a mercury *biryānī*. The latter is a very complicated recipe because the metal must first be introduced into eggs, to be hard-boiled and placed in the rice and then discarded, the mercury "filling" only being kept. The incense flavoured *sharbats*, so popular in Hyderabad in the old days, may have been served also for their antiseptic properties.

The final touch of many a dish in Hyderabad is the *baghār*. To prepare a *baghār*, garlic cloves, caraway seeds, dry whole red peppers and fresh curry leaves - *Murraya koenigi* - are deep fried in boiling oil, separately, until they blacken and their aroma comes out. This crackling and this smell are typical of the Muslim cookery in Hyderabad. The *baghār* is poured over *dāls*, on *qūt* - a thick tomato soup; through this process, the essential oils of the spices and condiments are extracted. This only could speak of an influence of the naturopathic doctor. But it seems that the *baghār* was in the past done in a more complex manner. The spices were blackened separately, then the oil set to cool. It was filtered then poured in a vessel containing a red-hot horse-shoe. The whole thing was covered and left to stand for half an hour before this strong scented oil was used. The Muslims of Hyderabad also speak of gold, silver or *ashrafi* - the gold coin of the Niẓām - *baghār*. It seems that the coin was thrown in the oil before the end of the frying process. It is also said that a lady of the town used to have her food cooked in a silver pan with a lid to which a chain was

---

46. See for example the *Gulshan-i ᶜIshq*, *op. cit.*, p. 254: vinegar, *kabābs* and *panīr* (cheese) are presented together. These are typical good combinations from the medical point of view.

47. See for example M. G͟hulām, *Tuḥfatu'l-lazzat Maḥbūbia* or *K͟hwān-i niᶜmat Āṣafiya*, in Urdu, Hyderabad, 1883.

attached, holding a piece of gold. When the dishes were covered, the gold scraped the sides of the silver pan and was cooked with the food. The motivation for such a strange practice was without doubt to mix particles of metal to the food, small though these particles might be. Doctors often mix gold or silver leaves to their drugs in Hyderabad. Ayurvedic medicine too uses metal ashes. The medical properties of metal are widely recognized by the Hyderabadis. It could be that the essential qualities of the metals, like those of garlic or caraway, get released with a high temperature.[48] This could explain these interesting culinary practices, from which gastronomy has nothing to gain. The doctor here has taken over the cook.

Conclusion: An Endangered Tradition

The relationship between cookery and medicine is indeed complex in Hyderabad. The knowledge of cookery is necessary to the doctor, who cooks, preserves, and invents new recipes for the patient's pleasure. The knowledge of medicine is essential to the cook: he must know how to combine food stuffs with a view to a really pleasant meal, that is to say digestible and not harmful to health. They have both exchanged recipes and techniques. This association might have been so close that the doctors were once the cooks *par excellence*. There are many testimonies nowadays of this union. It is really related to a royal notion of food, where everything is clearly luxury and ostentation but with a concern for the health of an irreplaceable person. It developed in the sophisticated Baghdad of the Abbassids and was well acclimatised in Delhi and Hyderabad. It calls for a cookery which is time-consuming and delicate, an alchemy where gold or pearls are transformed into food for the princes. What is the future of such a cookery now ? It has already been said that it is based on a vision of the body and of the universe which is not current any more among the Muslims of Hyderabad. But it is based also on a certain economic and political order which itself has disappeared since the birth of the state of Andhra Pradesh. The time of the Muslim nobility is gone in Hyderabad and its members do not have the financial means or the time any more to realize these highly individualized recipes. The political wane of the nobility is nowadays expressed also in a decline of the gastronomy it patronized. It is accompanied, for its members, by the

48. The temperature can be obtain through dry heat, oil or water. Pregnant women in Hyderabad were in bygone days given a water to drink in which a red-hot horse-shoe had been dipped.

loss of what it seemed to ensure to the privileged few: pleasure and health.

REFERENCES

I. Persian and Urdu Texts (Manuscripts, Editions and Translations)

Dastūru'l Hunūd, Translation of the *Madanavinoda* of Rājā Madana in Persian, by a certain Khān Zamān (1663).

Ferishta Abul Qasim, *Gulshan-i Ibrahimi* (*Tārīkh-i Ferishta*), Mss. N° 111, Salar Jung Museum Library, Hyderabad; (Abridged) English Transl. by J. Briggs, *History of the Rise of the Mahommedan Power in India* (1829), Four Vols., Calcutta, 1908-10; repr., Delhi: Atlantic Publishers & Distributors, 1989.

Gulshan-i ᶜIshq, a 17th century *mathnawī* in Urdu, edited by S.M. Ahmed, Hyderabad: Qadīm Urdu, 1986.

Maḥbūb Ghulām, *Tuḥfatu'l-lazzat Maḥbūbia* or *Khwān-i niᶜmaṭ Āṣafiya*, Hyderabad, 1883. (in Urdu)

Mīān Bhūwa, *Maᶜdanu'sh-Shifā-i Sikandar Shāhī*. See *Bulletin of the Departement of History of Medicine*, Hyderabad, Osmania Medical College, July, 1964, Vol. II, N° 3.

Mīr Mu'min Yazdī, *Ikhtiyārāt-i Quṭb Shāhī*, Persian Manuscript (451 folios), Salar Jung Museum and Library, Hyderabad.

Muḥammad ᶜAbdullāh Sāḥab, *Nauratan ᶜAbbasī*, Hyderabad, 1889.

Shamsu'd-dīn bin Nūru'd-dīn Ṭabīb, *Zubdatu'l-Hikam*, Persian Manuscript, Salar Jung Museum and Library, Hyderabad, Tibb. 277, from folio 81.

Taqiyyu'd-dīn Muḥammad bin Ṣadri'd-dīn ᶜAlī, *Mīzānu'ṭ-Ṭabā'iᶜ-i Quṭb Shāhī*, Persian Manuscript, Salar Jung Museum and Library, Hyderabad.

II. Secondary References

Bernier, François, *Travels in the Mogul Empire* (A.D. 1656-1668), eds. V.A. Smith and A. Constable, Oxford, 2nd edn., 1934; 1st Indian edn, 1983; 2nd. rev. edn., New Delhi: Oriental Books Reprint, n.d.

Chakrabarty, C., *An Interpretation of Ancient Hindu Medicine*, Delhi, 1983.

Dash, Vaidya Bhagwan, *Fundamentals of Ayurvedic Medicine*, New Delhi, 1982.

Dumont, Louis, *Homo Hierarchicus. Essai sur le système des castes*, Paris: Gallimard, 1966.

Lambert, C., ed., *Du manuscrit à la table, essais sur la cuisine au Moyen-Age et répertoire de manuscrits médiévaux contenant des recettes culinaires*, Montréal, 1992.

Malamoud, Charles, *Cuire le monde: rite et pensée dans l'Inde ancienne*, Paris: Editions La Découverte, 1989.

Marriott, M., ed., *India through Hindu Categories*, New Delhi: Sage Publications, 1990.

Mauss, Marcel, *Sociologie et Anthropologie*, Paris: Presses Universitaires de France, 1950.

Momin, A., *A Study of Ikhtiyarat-e-Qutb Shahi* (not published).

Momin, A. and S.A. Hussain, "Medical Manuscripts of Qutub Shahi Period in the Libraries of Hyderabad", *Bulletin of the Indian Institute on the History of Medicine*, Hyderabad, 1990, Vol. XIX, pp. 129-35.

Shah Mazhar, H., *The General Principles of Avicenna's Canon of Medicine*, Karachi: Naveed Clinic, 1966.

Sharma, P. (ed. and transl.) *Caraka Samhita, Agniveṣa's Treatise refined and annotated by Caraka and redacted by Dridhabala*, Delhi, 1981.

Sharpe, E. (Transl. from Hindi), *An 800 Year Old Book of Indian Medicine and Formulas*, New Delhi, 1979.

Sherwani, H.K., *History of the Quṭb Shāhī Dynasty*, Delhi: Munshiram Manoharlal, 1974.

Tavernier, J.B., *Travels in India* (1889), Transl. from French by V. Ball, rev. edn. by W. Crooke, Two Vols., London, 1925; Repr., New Delhi: Oriental Books Reprint Corporation, 1977.

The Unani Pharmacopoeia (Formulary of Unani Medicine) published by the Indian Medical Practitioner's Cooperative Pharmacy and Stores (IMPCOPS), Madras, 1982.

Thévenot, J. de, *Indian Travels of Thévenot and Careri*, ed. S.N. Sen, New Delhi, 1949.

Weiss-Amer, Melitta, "The Role of Medieval Physicians in the Diffusion of Culinary Recipes and Cooking Practices", *Du manuscrit à la table, essais sur la cuisine au Moyen-Age et répertoire de manuscrits médiévaux contenant des recettes culinaires*, ed. C. Lambert, Montréal: Champion-Slatkine, 1992, pp. 69-80.

Zimmermann, F., *Le discours des remèdes au pays des épices: enquête sur la médecine hindoue*, Paris: Payot, 1989.

Index